Educational Foundations: Ideas and Issues

Edited by

Allan C. Ornstein
Chicago State College

W. Eugene Hedley
*State University of New York
at Stony Brook*

Educational Foundations:
Ideas and Issues

Charles E. Merrill Publishing Company
A Bell & Howell Company
Columbus, Ohio

The Coordinated Teacher Preparation Series
under the editorship of
Donald E. Orlosky
University of South Florida

370.8
074e

Published by
Charles E. Merrill Publishing Company
A Bell & Howell Company
Columbus, Ohio 43216

International Standard Book Number: 0-675-09077-6

Library of Congress Catalog Card Number: 72-75799

1 2 3 4 5 6 7 8 — 78 77 76 75 74 73
74-3327

INTRODUCTION

JUST AS ONE SURREPTITIOUSLY SCANS THE CONTENTS OF A MAN'S BOOK-shelves and formulates a judgment regarding his intellectual stature and appetite, so, in examining a book of readings, one cannot help drawing conclusions with respect to the breadth of knowledge and experience evidenced by those who have selected those readings. This impressive collection of material, carefully selected, with perceptive introductions by the editors, is certain to stimulate active student participation in the classroom.

It is often difficult for the student of education to find relevancy in the area of professional preparation included under the "foundations" umbrella. An impatience to engage in the practical arena of the classroom generates an even greater impatience with the struggle to understand the theories upon which effective practice must be based; techniques and strategies become much more immediately important than philosophical concepts. Yet, foundations are literally that — the bases upon which the teaching/learning process is structured.

Of particular worth is the broad-based interpretation of the term *foundations* as used by the authors. Teachers are concerned with the "who," "what," "how," and "why" of education. In addition, if we realize that ours is not a static society, and that our schools ought not merely reflect that which presently exists, but should rather stimulate and facilitate intelligent and purposeful growth, then we must, as the editors imply, consider the teacher as a future-oriented agent of change.

In treating so capably the who — the child, the what — the curriculum, the how — the teacher and his techniques, and the why — the philosophical and cultural rationale for what happens in the classroom, it would seem obvious that Ornstein and Hedley have achieved their objective most effectively, and made the task of those of us who deal with educational ideas and issues potentially far more rewarding.

William E. Salesses

Assistant Dean, School of Education
Indiana University of Pennsylvania

From Allan and Eugene
To Our Respective Parents

PREFACE

STUDENTS ENTERING ANY PROFESSION SHOULD BE EXPECTED TO BE familiar with, and understand, the fundamental ideas and issues of their chosen field. In the field of education, the ideas and issues tend to cover a wide range of disciplines and time. Accordingly, this book is structured around an interdisciplinary approach and around the continuing concerns and current problems that challenge the field.

The book is divided into six parts, beginning with a focus on the teaching profession, then including background selections in philosophy, history, psychology, sociology, and curriculum. In choosing the specific articles the editors relied mainly on the informed judgments of prominent investigators within each field. The editors also attempted to include articles that would raise significant questions and perhaps induce students to explore ideas and issues on their own. They did not hesitate to include controversial material, for this should help stimulate discussion and, in turn, bring forth new data and insights into the field. To some degree the specific selections reflect the editors' biases, but this is a problem with all anthologies.

The editors wish to thank the authors and publishers who granted permission to include their material in this text. Specific thanks are extended to *Phi Delta Kappan* for permitting the use of several of their articles. The editors would also like to acknowledge Steve Branch, of Charles E. Merrill Publishing Company, for encouraging this venture.

Finally, the editors would feel remiss if they did not express gratitude to many professional friends who have provided necessary encouragement and intellectual nourishment on many occasions: John Beck, of the Chicago Consortium of Colleges and Universities; Barney Berlin, of Loyola University; Virgil A. Clift and Hulda Grobman, of New York University; Russell Roll and Daniel U. Levine, of the University of Missouri at Kansas City; Sheldon Marcus, of Fordham University; Harriet Talmage, of the University of Illinois at Chicago; and Philip D. Vairo, of the University of Tennessee at Chattanooga.

Allan C. Ornstein
W. Eugene Hedley

vii

CONTENTS

PART II: HISTORICAL FOUNDATIONS   69

PART III: PHILOSOPHICAL
FOUNDATIONS   137

PART I

The Teaching Profession

The teaching profession should attract the keenest minds, the finest personalities, and the most humane people. This, of course, is not always what happens. In general, the people who enter the profession are "average" people with "average" abilities, who often come from working-class and low-income backgrounds and envision teaching as a means for upward mobility. Women tend to decide earlier than men to go into teaching. One reason, perhaps, is the wider range of professional choices for men. Another reason is that there seems to be more status for women than for men in teaching. Parents often encourage their daughters to become teachers but rarely express similar feelings with their sons. Of course, there are many other motives, both positive and negative, for choosing a career in teaching.

You might ask yourselves why you are thinking of entering the teaching profession. On the positive side, your motives may include (1) love of children, (2) a desire to impart knowledge, (3) an interest and excitement in teaching, and (4) a desire to perform a valuable service to society. On the negative side, such factors may be (1) job security and a pension, (2) relatively short working days and long vacations, (3) the difficulty of preparation in another field, causing you to switch to education, and (4) need for income while you prepare for another profession.[1] Also, at this point you may be undecided on what to do, and teaching may seem at least a viable possibility.

As prospective teachers, you should be aware of the importance of the decision to enter the teaching field. There are many positive and negative reasons, both conscious and unconscious, for choosing teaching as a career. The best you can do is be aware of your reasons, for they will undoubtedly affect your attitude and behavior with your students if you eventually become a teacher. Proper analysis of your feelings could be validated through objective tests and with the help of others. It might be beneficial to discuss your feelings in class, so long as the atmosphere is conducive for it. Ignoring what may appear to be negative motives, denying that they exist, or feeling guilty about them is not the best procedure. Indeed, pure dedication and love of teaching and children seem to be fables from a past when the profession was imbued with the image of the schoolmarm and Mr. Chips.

Whatever your reason for enrolling in this educational course, you have not yet committed yourself to teaching as your life work, but you should be aware of the importance of your eventual decision. The preservice preparation of teachers consists of three components: (1) liberal education, (2) specialized subject field, and (3) professional education. This course is part of the third component. It should introduce you to some aspects of the field of education and teaching. As you evaluate the field of education and the profession, also try to assess your own potential as a teacher.

Although there is no absolute agreement upon the qualities important to a successful teacher, a number of traits appear repeatedly in the literature. Without trying to rank them in order, they are: (1) warmth, (2) friendliness, (3) sense of humor, (4) democratic outlook, (5) responsibility, (6) steadiness, (7) adaptability, (10) maturity, (11) knowledge of subject, and (12) attractiveness. The list overlaps and is not conclusive, but it can serve as a reference point for you to assess your own potential weaknesses and strengths as a teacher. To obtain a relatively valid index of your qualities, some objective testing will probably be required; nevertheless, an honest discussion about your own qualities will be helpful.

In a lighter view, Fred H. Stocking has presented an interesting commentary on a successful teacher.

A good teacher can tell his students a lot of answers to a lot of questions. But the best teacher can play dumb while helping his students think out the answers for themselves.

A good teacher is an eager and enthusiastic talker. But the best teacher knows how to be quiet and patient while his students struggle to formulate their own thoughts in their own words.

A good teacher is humble: he naturally feels that the accumulated wisdom of his subject is far more important than himself. But the best teacher is even humbler: for he respects the feeling of young people that they are naturally far more important than a silly old subject.

A good teacher knows that his students ought to be responsible, honest, and good citizens. But the best teacher knows that responsibility, honesty, and good citizenship cannot be "taught" in a course because such qualities are communicated through daily actions, not daily lectures.

A good teacher strives to keep his class under control. But the best teacher knows that he must first be able to control himself.

A good teacher earns his salary many times over. But the best teacher also earns a deep and secret satisfaction which would be ruined if he tried to talk about it in public or convert it into cash.

The students of a good teacher pass their course, graduate, and settle down with good jobs. But the students of the best teacher go on receiving rewards every day of their lives: for they have discovered that the life of the inquiring mind is exciting.[2]

Focusing on the status of the teaching profession, you should become aware that the field of education lacks a separate and definite body of knowledge. There is also a lack of control over entering teachers, *e.g.,* a professional licensing board, as with the legal and medical professions.

In judging the profession, you should examine the rewards, both monetary and honorary. As for the monetary situation, the pay scales of teachers have increased considerably since the 1960s (approximately 50 percent), with the greatest increase coming from 1967 to 1970 (approximately 30 percent). However, these pay increases have been halved by the rising consumer index. In the 1967–68 school year, the average public school teacher made $7296. Three years later, the average teacher was making $9265. The percentage of teachers paid $9500 or more during 1967–68 was 37 percent; by the 1970–71 period it was 41 percent. It is not uncommon now for some teachers to have salary ranges between $15,000 and $20,000, and there are opportunities to advance to administrative positions with salary ranges from $18,000 to $35,000. On the whole, however, there is still a salary gap (but one which has been diminishing since the late 1960s) between education and business and between teachers and other professionals with the same amount of education.

With regard to honorary rewards, we are referring to achievement on the job, satisfaction in the work, and interest in the clientele (students) and community rather than individual self-interest. Here we are directing our attention to the satisfaction teaching has for the individual and the importance it has to society; we are also including the gratification teachers have in knowing they are successful in reaching and teaching their students.

In our first article, Herbert Kohl seems to have unusual success in working with ghetto children from Harlem. The students' deprivation does not stand in his way. In his discussion of the actual work and progress of his students, he shows that ghetto students *are* educable, given a teacher who is competent and concerned. Although the importance of Mr. Kohl's personality is a key factor for his success, he illustrates that there are ghetto teachers (critics contend there are few in number) who do give a damn and who are good at their work.

In the next article, however, Bel Kaufman, with extraordinary humor, focuses on some of the teaching obstacles — including her students, fellow teachers, and supervisors. She refers to administrative forms and details, nonteaching assignments, educational jargon, and student behavior. It is this type of problems that most beginning teachers are not prepared to face — problems which often perplex and overwhelm them, thus masking the rewards of teaching and transforming it into a difficult, if not unrewarding, job.

Another factor to consider about the teaching profession is the existence of an active professional organization. Of the more than 2.1 million teachers in 1970, approximately 85 percent were members of state teachers' associations affiliated with the National Education Association (NEA), and approximately 50 percent also were members of the national organization. The American Federation of Teachers (AFT) has recently become the bargaining organization of teachers, mainly those located in large cities. Milwaukee is the only large city which is still represented by the NEA. The AFT membership numbers approximately 250,000, and it is considered more militant than the NEA.

The NEA resents the idea that the AFT is affiliated with the labor union (AFL-CIO) and prefers that teacher organizations remain independent and not associate with a nonprofessional organization. In the past the AFT has dismissed this criticism, for it feels that it is through the union that teachers have improved their economic and professional status; the union also criticizes the NEA as a "company organization" because it welcomes principals and superintendents.

Rivalry between the NEA and AFT must eventually cease. Too much money, energy, and time are wasted that could be better directed toward common goals. Myron Lieberman, an expert on teacher organizations, discusses the possibilities of a merger of the two major teacher organizations. He examines the issues that divide them, as well as the consequences of a merger. He predicts a forthcoming merger that will end the NEA's enrollment of administrators and the AFT's affiliation with the labor union. According to Lieberman, the major problem of the merger is not philosophical or ideological but practical, *e.g.*, who gets what job or position in the combined organization.

A new trend that is affecting the profession is the concept of accountability. In the past the students were held accountable for their school performance. Now the finger is beginning to point in other directions, and the concept of accountability is taking on different forms and gaining in popularity. Teacher accountability is one such form, whereby the professional staff is held responsible for specific agreed-upon objectives, mainly in terms of student changes in achievement and behavior. This trend is in part generated by the harsh fact that many teachers seem to be failing to educate their clientele, and with the recent over-supply of teachers it is now possible to stress teacher quality.

In New York City, for example, the Board of Education and teacher union decided in 1971 to take action; they contacted the Educational Testing Service (ETS), a highly respectable nonprofit testing organization, to work out an accountability model by 1972. In the next chapter Henry S. Dyer, the vice president of ETS and an expert on test construction, discusses such a model in terms of the entire staff — teachers, specialists, and principal. His model of staff accountability includes four major variables: (1) input (characteristics of the students), (2) educational process (activities in the school organized to bring about desirable changes), (3) surrounding conditions (home, community, and school), and (4) output (characteristics of students as they emerge from a particular phase of their schooling). All the variables and their respective subvariables are interrelated and measured to form indices by which the staff can judge its effectiveness. According to Dyer, the areas and goals incorporated into the accountability model should be derived from a cooperative effort of teachers, administrators, school board members, parents, and students. Specific objectives should vary among schools and reflect local needs and problems.

In quite a different context, there are a growing number of performance contracts, whereby a private business company or commercial organization contracts to teach reading, mathematics, or other subjects under the provision that the company will be paid a specified amount for each student who gains a specified grade level within a given time period. For example, a contract might stipulate that the school system will pay the company $100 for each student who makes a one-year gain in reading within six months, and $150 for each student who makes the same reading gain in four months. This accountability scheme is presently being tried out in several schools across the country.

In the final article of this part of the book, Robert E. Stake points out several of the problems and limitations related to testing students for performance contracting purposes. In particular, he focuses on the technical errors and misinterpretations in evaluating test scores, the temptation of teaching the test, and the unreliability and validity of tests. Also, he explains why the profession should be apprehensive about appraising the teaching-learning process on the basis of performance tests alone.

---

[1]For a detailed analysis of the reasons for entering the teaching profession, see Allan C. Ornstein, *Urban Education: Student Unrest, Teacher Behaviors, and Black Power*. Columbus, Ohio: Charles E. Merrill Publishing Co., 1972.

[2]Fred H. Stocking, "Who is the Best Teacher?," *Bennington Banner,* Bennington, Vermont, November 14, 1963, p. 4.

HERBERT KOHL

36
Children

I REMEMBERED MY BARREN CLASSROOM, NO BOOKS, A BATTERED PIANO, broken windows and desks, falling plaster, and an oppressive darkness.

I was handed a roll book with thirty-six names and thirty-six cumulative record cards, years of judgments already passed upon the children, their official personalities. I read through the names, twenty girls and sixteen boys, the 6-1 class. . . .

. . . The weight of Harlem and my whiteness and strangeness hung in the air as I droned on, lost in my righteous monologue. The uproar turned into sullen silence. A slow nervous drumming began at several desks; the atmosphere closed as intelligent faces lost their animation. Yet I didn't understand my mistake, the children's rejection of me and my ideas. Nothing worked, I tried to joke, command, play — the children remained joyless until the bell, then quietly left for lunch.

There was an hour to summon energy and prepare for the afternoon, yet it seemed futile. What good are plans, clever new methods and materials, when the children didn't — wouldn't — care or listen? Perhaps the best solution was to prepare for hostility and silence, become the cynical teacher, untaught by his pupils, ungiving himself, yet protected.

I tried for the next six weeks to use the books assigned and teach the official curriculum. It was hopeless. The class went through the readers perfunctorily, refused to hear about modern America, and were relieved to do arithmetic — mechanical, uncharged — as long as nothing new was introduced. For most of the day the atmosphere in the room was stifling. The children were bored and restless, and I felt burdened by the inappropriateness of what I tried to teach. It was so dull that I thought as little as the children and began to despair. Listening to myself on the growth of urban society, realizing that no one else was listening, that though words were pronounced the book was going unread, I found myself vaguely wondering about the children.

One day Ralph cursed at Michael and unexpectedly things came together for me. Michael was reading and stumbled several times. Ralph scornfully called out, "What's the matter, psyches, going to pieces again?" The class broke up and I jumped on that word "psyches."

"Ralph, what does *psyches* mean?"

An embarrassed silence.

"Do you know how to spell it?"

Alvin volunteered. "S-i-k-e-s."

"Where do you think the word came from? Why did everybody laugh when you said it, Ralph?"

"You know, Mr. Kohl, it means, like crazy or something."

"Why? How do words get to mean what they do?"

Samuel looked up at me and said: "Mr. Kohl, now you're asking questions like Alvin. There aren't any answers, you know that."

"But there are. Sometimes by asking Alvin's kind of questions you discover the most unexpected thing. Look."

I wrote *Psyche,* then *Cupid,* on the blackboard.

"That's how *psyche* is spelled. It looks strange in English, but the word doesn't come from English. It's Greek. There's a letter in the Greek alphabet that comes out *psi* in English. This is the way *psyche* looks in Greek."

Some of the children spontaneously took out their notebooks and copied the Greek.

"The word *psyche* has a long history. Psyche means mind or soul for the Greeks, but it was also the name of a lovely woman who had the misfortune to fall in love with Cupid, the son of Venus, the jealous Greek goddess of love. . . ."

The children listened, enchanted by the myth, fascinated by the weaving of the meaning of *psyche* into the fabric of the story, and the character. Mind, playing tricks on itself, almost destroying its most valuable possessions through its perverse curiosity. Grace said in amazement:

"Mr. Kohl, they told the story and said things about the mind at the same time. What do you call that?"

"Myth is what the Greeks called it."

Sam was roused.

"Then what happened? What about the history of the word?"

"I don't know too much, but look at the words in English that come from *Cupid* and *Psyche."*

I cited *psychological, psychic, psychotic, psychodrama, psychosomatic, cupidity* — the children copied them unasked, demanded the meanings. They were obviously excited.

Leaping ahead, Alvin shouted: "You mean words change? People didn't always speak this way? Then how come the reader says there's a right way to talk and a wrong way?"

"There's a right way now, and that only means that's how most people would like to talk now, and how people write now."

Charles jumped out of his desk and spoke for the first time during the year.

"You mean one day the way we talk — you know, with words like *cool* and *dig* and *sound* — may be all right?"

"Uh huh. Language is alive, it's always changing, only sometimes it changes so slowly that we can't tell."

Neomia caught on.

"Mr. Kohl, is that why our reader sounds so old-fashioned?"

And Ralph.

"Mr. Kohl, when I called Michael *psyches,* was I creating something new?"

Someone spoke for the class.

"Mr. Kohl, can't we study the language we're talking about instead of spelling and grammar? They won't be any good when language changes anyway."

We could and did. That day we began what had to be called for my conservative plan book "vocabulary," and "an enrichment activity." Actually it was the study of language and myth, of the origins and history of words, of their changing uses and functions in human life. We began simply with the words *language* and *alphabet,* the former from the Latin for tongue and the latter from the first two letters of the Greek alphabet. Seeing the origin of *alphabet* and the relationship of *cupidity* to Cupid and *psychological* to Psyche had a particularly magical effect upon the children. They found it easy to master and acquire words that would have seemed senseless and tedious to memorize. Words like *psychic* and *psychosomatic* didn't seem arbitrary and impenetrable, capable of being learned only painfully by rote. Rather they existed in a context, through a striking tale that easily accrued associations and depth. After a week the children learned the new words, asked to be tested on them, and demanded more.

"Vocabulary" became a fixed point in each week's work as we went from Cupid and Psyche to Tantalus, the Sirens, and the Odyssey and the linguistic riches that it contains. We talked of Venus and Adonis and spent a week on first *Pan* and *panic, pan-American,* then *pandemonium,* and finally on *demonic* and *demons* and *devils.* We studied *logos, philos, anthropos, pathos,* and their derivatives. I spun the web of *mythos* about language and its origins. I went to German (*kindergarten*), Polynesian (*taboo*), or Arabic (*assassin*), showing what a motley open-ended fabric English (and for that matter any living language) is. The range of times and peoples that contributed to the growth of today's American English impressed me no less than it did the class. It drove me to research language and its origins; to re-explore myth and the dim origins of man's culture; and to invent ways of sharing my discoveries with the children.

The children took my words seriously and went a step further. Not content to be fed solely words that grew from sources that I, the teacher, presented, they asked for words that fitted unnamed and partially articulated concepts they had, or situations they couldn't adequately describe.

"Mr. Kohl, what do you call it when a person repeats the same thing over and over again and can't stop?"

"What is it called when something is funny and serious at the same time?"

"What do you call a person who brags and thinks he's big but is really weak inside?"

"Mr. Kohl, is there a word that says that something has more than one meaning?"

The class became word-hungry and concept-hungry, concerned with discovering the "right" word to use at a given time to express a specific thought. I was struck by the difference of this notion of rightness and "the right way" to speak and write from the way children are supposed to be taught in school. They are supposed to acquire correct usage, right grammar and spelling, the right meaning of a word, and the right way to write a sentence. Achievement and IQ tests give incomplete sentences and the child is instructed to fill in the "right" word. Many teachers correct children's writing on the basis of a canon of formal rightness without bothering to ask what the children's words mean. I did the same thing myself.

·   ·   ·   ·

Later in the semester I taught the class a lesson on naming, a topic that seems deceptively simple yet minimally encompasses history, psychology, sociology, and anthropology. I put everybody's full name on the blackboard, including my own, and asked the class how people got names. The answer was, naturally, from their parents who made the choice — but not the full choice, it emerged, when Michael remembered that his parents' surnames came from their parents. Then how far back can you go? The children thought and Grace raised a delicate question. If the names go back through the generations how come her name wasn't African since her ancestors must have been? In answer I told the class about my own name — Kohl, changed from Cohen, changed from Okun, changed from something lost in the darkness of history; one change to identify the family as Jewish, one change to deny it. Then I returned to the question of slave names and the destruction of part of the children's African heritage that the withholding of African names implied.

Neomia said she knew of someone who changed his name because he wanted to start a new life, and Sam told the class that his brother called himself John X because X meant unknown and his original African name was unknown. We talked of people who named their children after famous men and of others who gave exotic names. From there the discussion went on to the naming of animals — pets, wild animals, racehorses; things — boats, houses, dolls, and places. The class knew by that time in the school year that one doesn't talk of words in isolation from human lives and history, and by then I had begun to know what to teach.

The emphasis on language and words opened the children to the whole process of verbal communication. Things that they had been struggling to express, or worse, had felt only they in their isolation thought about, became social, shareable. Speaking of things, of inferiority and ambiguity, or irony and obsession, brought relief, and perhaps for the first time gave the children a sense that there were meaningful human creations that one could discover in a classroom.

Yet not all concepts have been verbalized, and the children frequently talked of having feelings and desires that no words I gave them expressed adequately. They had to create new words, or develop new forms of expression to communicate, and that can neither be taught nor done upon command. We could go to the frontier, however, and speak about the blues, about being bad or hip or cool—about how certain ways of living or historical times created the need for new words. We talked about the nuclear age, the smallness of the modern world, the jargon of democracy and communism, integration and segregation. The children looked in awe at *Finnegans Wake* and Joyce's monumental attempt to forge a new language; they listened to Bob Dylan, recorded the words of soul songs and classical blues, read poetry. We started out talking about words and ended up with life itself. The children opened up and began to display a fearless curiosity about the world.

I sense that I've jumped ahead too quickly, for the whole thing happened slowly, almost imperceptibly. There were days of despair throughout the whole year, and I never learned how to line the class up at three o'clock. There were days when Alvin was a brilliant inspiring pupil at ten and the most unbearable, uncontrollable nuisance at eleven thirty; when after a good lesson some children would turn angry and hostile, or lose interest in everything. There were small fights and hostilities, adjustments and readjustments in the children's relationships to each other and to me. I had to enlarge my vision as a human being, learn that if the complex and contradictory nature of life is allowed to come forth in the classroom there are times when it will do so with a vengeance.

·   ·   ·   ·

I brought part of my library to school and temporarily substituted it for social studies. The children were curious about those Greeks and Latins who contributed so many words and concepts to our language. I brought in books on Greek and Roman architecture and art, as well as Robert Graves' version of the *Iliad*, a paperback translation of Apuleius' *Cupid and Psyche*, the *Larousse Encyclopedia of Mythology*, and anything else that seemed relevant or interesting. I showed the books to the children and let them disappear into their desks. It was made clear that the books were to be read, the pages to be turned. If someone reads a book so intensely that the book is bruised it is flattering to the book.

For three-quarters of an hour a day the Pantheon circulated along with Floyd Patterson and J. D. Salinger, Partridge's dictionary of word origins made its way through the class with Langston Hughes and the Bobbsey twins. Anything I could get my hands on was brought to class— a great deal remained unread, and some books I hadn't read myself shocked and surprised the class. They were sexy and popular. Later that year my supervisor told me I was running a very effective individualized reading program. That may have been it, but the truth seemed simpler and less structured. I overwhelmed the class with books, many of which I loved, and let them discover for themselves what they liked. There were no reports to be written, no requirements about numbers of pages to be read. Some children hardly read at all, others devoured whatever was in the room. The same is true of my friends.

Robert Jackson grabbed a book on Greek architecture, copied floor plans and perspective drawings, and finally, leaping out of the book, created a reasonably accurate scale model of the Parthenon. Alvin and Michael built a clay volcano, asked for and got a chemistry book which showed them how to simulate an eruption. Sam, Thomas, and Dennis fought their way through war books; through the Navy, the Seabees, the Marines, and the Paratroops. The girls started with the Bobbsey twins and worked through to romantic novels and, in the case of a few, Thurber and O. Henry. I learned that there were no books to fear, and having been divested of my fear of idleness, I also wasn't worried if some children went through periods of being unable to do anything at all.

People entering my classroom during those forty-five minutes of "social" studies usually experienced an initial sense of disorder followed by surprise at the relative calm of the room. If they bothered to look more closely or ask, they would find that most of the children were working.

.   .   .   .

Music became an integral part of the classroom. The children brought in their records; I responded with my own. One morning I put twenty-five records ranging from blues and Fats Waller through Thelonious Monk and Coltrane to Mozart and Beethoven on top of the phonograph. During the morning breaks the kids explored freely, and when the music began to interest some individuals enough, I brought in biographies of the composers, pictures of the musicians. We talked in small groups during social studies of chain gangs, field music, modern jazz, rock and roll, child prodigies, anything that came up. A dialogue between the children and myself was developing.

. . . One day I brought an orange cardboard binder filled with loose-leaf paper to school. It was for my observations on the vocabulary lessons. During free time that morning I became exasperated by the ease with which Robert yielded a book to Margie, who merely glanced at it and stuffed it in her desk. I wanted to say something to him, yet words were useless, would only cause further withdrawal. *Maybe I could give him something that he wouldn't surrender so easily* . . . the only thing on my desk was the notebook. An idea cautiously formed; I took the notebook to Robert and said that his interest in myths and history was so obvious, and his grasp of the discussions in class so full that I felt he might want to go beyond reading books and write and illustrate one himself.

He looked at me as if I were mad.

"Me?"

"Why not you? Somebody writes books; anyone can try. That's the only way to discover how well you can do. Why don't you take this notebook and try. You don't have to show me or anybody else what you do if you don't want."

A sly triumphant look came over Robert's face as he snatched the notebook out of my hand. I retreated to my desk, afraid of spoiling the whole thing with unnecessary words.

It wasn't until a week later that I discovered that my attempt had worked. Maurice came up to my desk before class and asked me if Robert was the only one in class who could write a book. I said no and then Maurice asked me what Robert was writing about anyway. Robert, it seems, refused to tell him or even show him one page.

I explained that I didn't know either, and that Robert could be writing about anything, that the book was private unless he chose to show it to anybody, and that included me.

"What about me? Could I write a book? — even about myself, the truth, you know . . ."

"It's been done before. There's no reason why you can't do it."

I promised to bring Maurice a binder (having the symbol of being sanctioned to write privately and as one pleased was very important) and the next morning brought a dozen to school. I explained to the entire class that some children wanted to write their own books and that the binders were available for anybody who cared to write. I also explained that though I was available to help or to read their work for pleasure, still the books were their private property — the author's control over his work would be respected completely. There was no mention of grading or grammar as it never occurred to me then even to bother with a disclaimer.

The children were suspicious of my talk about privacy and wanted to know what kinds of things people write books about. Though they had seen some of the scope of literature in the books I brought to class, I think the children still believed there were only two kinds of books — the "good" books they read in school which were nice, boring, and unreal, and the "bad" books they sneaked to each other which were filthy, exciting, and unreal. It was hard to explain what people wrote about. Instead of trying, I spent the next week selecting from my library and reading to the children, asking them to attend to the subject and to the writer's voice as well. I read about love, hate, jealousy, fear; of war and religion, quest and loss. I read in voices that were ironic, cynical, joyous, and indifferent. The class and I talked of the writer's selection of his subject and the development of his voice; of the excitement of not knowing entirely where the book you set out to write will take you.

A few children dared at first, then more, until finally most of the children in the class attempted some written exploration. I put an assignment on the board before the children arrived in the morning and gave the class the choice of reading, writing, or doing what was on the board. At no time did any child have to write, and whenever possible I let the children write for as long as their momentum carried them. Time increasingly became the servant of substance in the classroom. At the beginning of the semester I had tried to use blocks of time in a predetermined, preplanned way — first reading, then social studies, arithmetic, and so forth. Then I broke the blocks by allowing free periods. This became confining and so I allowed the length of periods to vary according to the children's and my interest and concentration. Finally we reached a point where the class could pursue things without the burden of a required amount of work that had to be passed through every day. This meant that there were many things that the class didn't "cover"; that there were days without arithmetic and weeks without spelling or my dear "vocabulary." Many exciting and important things were missed as well as many dull things. But the children learned to explore and invent, to become obsessed by things that interested them and follow them through libraries and books back into life; they learned to believe in their own curiosity and value the intellectual and literary, perhaps even in a small way the human, quest without being overly burdened with a premature concern for results.

Not that some of the children in 6-1 weren't initially distressed by the freedom of the room and the increasingly experimental curriculum. They were and told me, and at times I almost wavered and returned to the crutches of standard preplanned material. But I believed in what was happening in class and bore the uncertainty and days of chaos until together we saw work emerge that none of us expected or believed possible.

Maurice was the first to show me his book.

As the year developed the class did a lot of writing. I discovered that if the children were allowed to write without being marked, and if they were challenged and tempted by the subject, they wrote with great pleasure. At first it was just a question of writing sentences using the vocabulary and spelling words. The children tested me to see how far they could go, but they really never went very far.

.   .   .   .

Over the year the creation of myths was one of the children's favorite challenges. Initially we only spoke of Greek mythology, and the children's stores were peopled by their own versions of Cyclops, Psyche, Hades, and Zeus. Maurice and Michael changed that by introducing members of the League of Justice — Superman and Wonder Woman — and movie characters such as Dracula and the Frankenstein monster into their stories. I remember Michael's *Cyclops Meets Frankenstein* in which Cyclops and the Frankenstein monster battled over the lovely Psyche, whom Michael saved at the last minute from both of them. Maurice contributed adventures of the League of Justice in which the members of the League did not always triumph.

We talked about comic books in class, and about heroes and monsters. I brought in pictures of ancient monsters and told the class of the Minotaur and the Sphinx. From the children I learned about Gorgo and Godzilla. For a while some of the children would come up to the room before nine o'clock, and we would swap tales.

I asked the children if there were any neighborhood myths or legends, and though they were reluctant to talk about them at first they began to speak of heroic villains who were "upstate" in prison but unbroken by the police, of stories they heard about beautiful women and strong, bad men who lived down south and got away with fooling and defying the white man. I encouraged the children to talk and blend past and present, to let their imaginations create mythical worlds. I also encouraged them to write and share their fantasies. In the case of a few children, and most notably Robert Jackson, the creation of myths and heroic tales became almost an obsession.

As the writing accumulated in the class and the walls of the room flowered with the children's work, the uneasy pride and generous greed characteristic of many writers developed. The children wanted a larger audience; they wanted to share their work and at the same time receive the praise they felt it deserved and confront the criticism they feared it would evoke. Several children suggested independently that the class create a newspaper or magazine. I think it was in late November that I gathered all the journals and magazines in my apartment and brought them to class. For the first time the children saw *Time, Life, Dissent, i.e., etc.*, and after a while the class fell to discussing titles for their own magazines. There was no need to bother with a discussion on whether or not there would be one.

As I remember, the children were fascinated with the simplicity of magazine titles, something I hadn't thought of myself until the children pointed it out. The idea that abbreviations such as *i.e.* and *etc.* could be used made the process of finding titles easy. If *Life* could be used so could *Death*; *Look* led to *See, Find, Search*; *Time* easily led the children to suggest *Night, Work,* and *Second*.

Robert Jackson suggested *et al, Children,* and *Why*.

Alvin countered with *Because, Often,* and *Maybe*.

Barbara offered *And*, and the class dropped their other words and rhapsodized on its advantages.

"*And* could be used on posters, Robert could draw people and have them say '*And*.' "

The children created *And*. They chose an editorial board, chose the selections to be published, and put them on rexograph paper — going through at least a dozen master sheets for every page that passed their own scrutiny. Robert drew posters, enticing pictures of famous men declaiming . . . *And*. Dennis and Thomas commandeered the rexograph machine while Alvin and Leverne managed to slip copies of Robert's posters into teachers' mailboxes, under doors, even onto the principal's desk.

. . . . .

It was in April . . . that I talked to the class about my limitations within the educational system. Before that, however, I found myself telling them about the demands that the system made upon them. There were compulsory achievement, and at that time, IQ tests given halfway through the year, and it was on the results of those tests that the children's placement in junior high school would be based. Nothing else really counted; classes were formed on the basis of reading grades and my pupils *had* to do well. It was a matter of their whole future since in junior high school all but those few students put in the "top" classes (three out of fourteen in each grade) were considered "not college material" and treated with the scorn that they merited in their teachers' eyes.

The easiest way to bring this up in class was to tell the children exactly where they stood. I braced myself, and defying all precedent as well as my own misgivings, I performed the unforgivable act of showing the children what their reading and IQ scores were according to the record cards. I also taught a lesson on the definition of IQ and of achievement scores. The children were angry and shocked; no one had ever come right out and told them they were failing. It was always put so nicely and evasively that the children never knew where they stood. After seeing the IQ scores — only two of which were above 100, the majority being in the 80 to 90 range — and the reading scores, which with few exceptions were below grade level, the children were furious.

There were no sample tests available, to prepare the children beforehand. The assistant principal told me that if old tests were made available the children would have an unfair advantage over other children. I reminded him that keeping files of old tests was frequently standard procedure at middle-class schools, and that P.S. 6, a predominantly white school located less than a mile down Madison Avenue, even gave after-school voluntary classes in test preparation. He shrugged and told me that a rule was a rule. So I went to friends who taught in white schools and got copies of the old tests and sample questions that they used and went ahead with my plans. No one checked on what I was doing, and no one really cared as long as my class wasn't disruptive.

The first thing I had to do was familiarize the children with test instructions. I spent several weeks on practicing following directions as they were worded on the standard tests. The class asked me why such practice was necessary, and I explained that with all the fine writing they could produce, with all the words of praise and recommendation I could write, they would go nowhere in junior high school unless those grades on paper were up to the standards the Board of Education set. The kids didn't like that idea, I don't like it; but we had to get tough and face the fact that like it or not they *had* to do well. When I put it that way they were willing to try.

After going through the reading of directions, I broke down the types of questions that were asked on the various reading tests and tried to explain something of the psychology of the people who created the test. I frequently found that some of the children were deliberately choosing wrong answers because they had clever explanations for their choices. They had to be convinced that the people who created objective tests believed as an article of faith that all the questions they made up had one and only one correct answer. Over and over, it is striking how rigid teachers tend to be and how difficult it is for children who haven't been clued in on this rigidity to figure out what the teacher expects in the way of suppression of original and clever responses. The children agreed to be dull for the sake of their future.

After these exercises we simulated testing situations, and the children gradually learned to cease dreading and avoiding the testing situation. Their anxiety decreased to a manageable level, and therefore they were able to apply things they had discovered in their own thinking, reading, and writing to situations that arose in the test.

Unfortunately I had no say in determining when the tests were given. Both the reading and IQ tests had to be given before February for administrative reasons, and so the full benefit of the year's work did not show in those tests. The IQ test was close to a disaster. True, there were about ten children who came up over 100 and one — Grace — who scored 135, but the children were not yet able to cope with the test and didn't show themselves as well as they could. With the reading test it was different. The children were almost ready and in a few short months performed the seemingly impossible task of jumping from one to three years in reading. There were a few children on fifth-grade level, about twelve on sixth-grade level, another twelve on seventh-grade level, and eight who ranged from the eighth to the twelfth grades. I couldn't believe it myself. When I told the results to the children, they for once showed their pride in themselves unashamedly.

The children learned that they could do unpleasant but necessary work; they also knew that the test preparation was not all there was to education, that the substance of their work, the novels and stories, the poems and projects they created, were the essential thing no matter how the external world chose to judge them. They were proud of their work and themselves. I felt thrilled and privileged to teach them and witness them create. I offered what I could to them; they offered much in return. I am grateful that over the course of the year I could cease to be afraid and therefore respond to what the children had to teach me of myself, of themselves and the world they lived in and which we shared as human beings.

Not all of the children made it through the year; two moved, and one, John, was too much for me to control. He was tough and shook my confidence. It would take me another year before I could reach children like him. We never fought, he didn't disrupt the class; he just disappeared into the halls and then the streets. I have to admit that I made a very feeble and false effort to stop him; the rest of the class occupied me. The next year I had a class of Johns, and seeing how easily they responded to adult confidence and trust, I have always regretted my lack of effort with John. Yet I have to admit that I did not have the necessary confidence as a teacher and as a human being the year I taught the thirty-six children. It took the thirty-six children to give me that.

BEL KAUFMAN

Up the
Down Staircase

INTRASCHOOL COMMUNICATION
FROM: Mrs. Beatrice Schachter, Room 508
TO: Miss Sylvia Barrett, Room 304
Dear Syl–
Welcome to the fold! I hope it goes well with you on this, your first day.
If you need help, just holler; I'm in 508.
What's your program? Can we synchronize our lunch periods?
Fondly,
Bea

. . . .

INTRASCHOOL COMMUNICATION
FROM: Miss Sylvia Barrett, Room 304
TO: Mrs. Beatrice Schachter, Room 508
Dear Bea–
Help!
I'm buried beneath an avalanche of papers, I don't understand the language of the country, and what do I do about a kid who calls me "Hi, teach!"?
Syl

From the book *Up the Down Staircase* by Bel Kaufman. © 1964 by Bel Kaufman.
Published by Prentice-Hall, Inc., Englewood Cliffs, New Jersey.

INTRASCHOOL COMMUNICATION
FROM: Room 508
TO: Room 304

Nothing. Maybe he calls you *Hi, teach!* because he likes you. Why not answer *Hi, pupe?*

The clerical work is par for the course. "Keep on file in numerical order" means throw in wastebasket. You'll soon learn the language. "Let it be a challenge to you" means you're stuck with it; "interpersonal relationships" is a fight between kids; "ancillary civic agencies for supportive discipline" means call the cops; "Language Arts Dept." is the English office; "literature based on child's reading level and experiential background" means that's all they've got in the Book Room; "non-academic-minded" is a delinquent; and "It has come to my attention" means you're in trouble.

Did you get anything done in homeroom today?

Bea

. . . .

INTRASCHOOL COMMUNICATION
FROM: 304
TO: 508

Dear Bea—

I checked off 2½ items from some 20 on the list of things to be done. A boy fell off his chair.

Nothing in my courses on Anglo-Saxon literature, or in Pedagogy, or in my Master's thesis on Chaucer had prepared me for this. I had planned to establish rapport, a climate of warmth and mutual respect. I would begin, I thought, with First Impressions: importance of appearance, manners, speech, on which I'd build an eloquent case for good diction, correct usage, fluent self-expression. From there it would be just a step to the limitless realms of creativity.

That's what I thought.

What happened was that I didn't get beyond the B's in taking attendance. And I forgot to have them salute the flag, and I have an uneasy feeling that it's illegal.

Syl

. . . .

INTRASCHOOL COMMUNICATION
FROM: 508
TO: 304

You're in the clear. On assembly days they salute in the auditorium. What's illegal now is the Bible reading.

Bea

INTRASCHOOL COMMUNICATION
FROM: 304
TO: 508
Dea Bea–
   What does the SS stand for in Eng. SS? Secret Service? Social Security?
Sesame Seeds? Super-Slows?

Syl

.   .   .   .

INTRASCHOOL COMMUNICATION
FROM: 508
TO: 304
   You're warm: special slow classes. The new teachers are stuck with
the toughest assignments. Don't despair — by the time you get to be my
age, you'll earn the choicest seniors.
   I see by your program you're a "floater" — that means you travel from
room to room. Insist on a desk drawer of your own in each room where
you teach; if not, get a strong-armed boy to lug your things.
   You have Hall Patrol — that's a cinch now that we have Aides to help
with the non-teaching assignments. It means walking up and down the
corridors and stopping kids without passes. It's a higher-class job than
Cafeteria Duty, but carries less prestige than the Book Room or Staircase
Patrol. All of us have one such "building assignment" a day, besides five
teaching classes, a homeroom, and one "unassigned" (don't ever dare to
call it "free") period. Those who play their cards right are relieved of
homeroom, or even a teaching class, by becoming Lateness Coordinators
or Program Integrators or Vocational Counselors or some such thing. We
also have a lunch period. Yours, I see, is at the end of the third period,
which means we can eat together on Wednesdays. Your gastric juices
must start to flow at 10:17 A.M. It's a challenge.

Bea

.   .   .   .

PROGRAM FOR TODAY'S HOMEROOM PERIOD:
(CHECK OFF EACH ITEM BEFORE LEAVING BUILDING TODAY)
MAKE OUT DELANEY CARDS AND SEATING PLAN
TAKE ATTENDANCE
FILL OUT ATTENDANCE SHEETS
SEND OUT ABSENTEE CARDS
MAKE OUT TRANSCRIPTS FOR TRANSFERS
MAKE OUT 3 TESTS OF STUDENTS' PROGRAM CARDS (YELLOW) FROM
     MASTER PROGRAM CARD (BLUE), ALPHABETIZE AND SEND TO 201
MAKE OUT 5 COPIES OF TEACHER'S PROGRAM CARD (WHITE) AND
     SEND TO 211

SIGN TRANSPORTATION CARDS
REQUISITION SUPPLIES
ASSIGN LOCKERS AND SEND NAMES AND NUMBERS TO 201
FILL OUT AGE-LEVEL REPORTS
ANNOUNCE AND POST ASSEMBLY SCHEDULE AND ASSIGN ROWS IN
   AUDITORIUM
ANNOUNCE AND POST FIRE, SHELTER AND DISPERSAL DRILLS REG-
   ULATIONS
CHECK LAST TERM BOOK AND DENTAL BLACKLISTS
CHECK LIBRARY BLACKLIST
FILL OUT CONDITION OF ROOM REPORT
ELECT CLASS OFFICERS
URGE JOINING G.O. AND BEGIN COLLECTING MONEY
APPOINT ROOM DECORATIONS MONITOR AND BEGIN DECORATING
   ROOM
SALUTE FLAG (ONLY FOR NON-ASSEMBLY OR Y2 SECTIONS)
POINT OUT THE NATURE AND FUNCTION OF HOMEROOM: LITER-
   ALLY, A ROOM THAT IS A HOME, WHERE STUDENTS WILL FIND A
   FRIENDLY ATMOSPHERE AND GUIDANCE
TEACHERS WITH EXTRA TIME ARE TO REPORT TO THE OFFICE TO
   ASSIST WITH ACTIVITIES WHICH DEMAND ATTENTION.

·   ·   ·   ·

CALVIN COOLIDGE HIGH SCHOOL
MAXWELL E. CLARKE, PRINCIPAL
JAMES J. MCHABE, ADMINISTRATIVE ASSISTANT
CIRCULAR # 1A
TOPIC: ORGANIZATION
PLEASE KEEP ALL CIRCULARS ON FILE, IN THEIR ORDER
DILIGENCE, ACCURACY AND PROMPTNESS ARE ESSENTIAL IN CARRY-
ING OUT ALL INSTRUCTIONS AS TO PROCEDURES.
PROGRAM FOR MONDAY, SEPTEMBER 7
LONG HOMEROOM PERIOD (SEE CIRCULAR #H16)
SHORT SUBJECT CLASS PERIODS (SEE CIRCULAR # 7C, SECTION 4)
ASSEMBLY BELL SCHEDULE (SEE ASSEMBLY CIRCULAR # 3D, PAR.
   5 & 6)
PUPILS ARE TO REPORT BACK TO THEIR HOMEROOMS TO BE CHECKED
OFF AT 2:56. DISMISSAL BELL WILL RING AT 3:05 SHARP. THIS, HOW-
EVER, IS UNCERTAIN.

·   ·   ·   ·

TO: ALL ENGLISH TEACHERS
PLEASE SEND TO THE ENGLISH OFFICE BEFORE 3 TODAY YOUR
REGISTERS IN ALL SUBJECT CLASSES IN ORDER TO ENABLE US TO
EQUALIZE THE TEACHER-LOAD AND ACHIEVE A GOAL OF 33 STU-
DENTS PER CLASS.
SAMUEL BESTER
CHAIRMAN, LANGUAGE ARTS DEPT.

FROM: JAMES J. MCHABE, ADM. ASST.

TO: ALL TEACHERS

RE: REQUISITION OF SUPPLIES

PLEASE ANTICIPATE YOUR NEEDS AND REQUEST SUPPLIES BEFORE THEY ARE NEEDED. PLEASE DO NOT MAKE EXCESSIVE DEMANDS. TO PREVENT NON-AUTHENTICITY OF SIGNATURES, PLEASE SIGN YOUR FULL NAME IN INK ON YOUR REQUISITION SLIP.

IF YOU WISH TO DECORATE YOUR ROOM WITH POSTERS, WE HAVE A FEW LEFT:

BLOCK LETTERS, BLUE ON WHITE:

"KNOWLEDGE IS POWER"

YELLOW, ON GREEN BACKGROUND:

"TRUTH IS BEAUTY"

ALSO SOME TRAVEL POSTERS IN BROWN AND TAN OF SWISS ALPS, SLIGHTLY TORN BUT STILL USABLE.

JJ MCH

•   •   •   •

TO: ALL TEACHERS

LATENT MALADJUSTMENTS MAY EXHIBIT THEMSELVES IN SOCIALLY UNACCEPTABLE BEHAVIOR IN THE CLASSROOM. THIS IS A CRUCIAL PERIOD IN THE DEVELOPMENT OF THE ADOLESCENT IN THE SCHOOL ATMOSPHERE WHICH CONSUMES A LARGE SEGMENT OF HIS TIME. IN ORDER TO PROVIDE PROPER ORIENTATION TO ADULT RESPON- SIBILITIES IN A DEMOCRACY, PLEASE SEND ALL NEW PUPILS TO ME ON ALTERNATE TUESDAYS FOR DEPTH-COVERAGE ON PERSONAL INTERVIEW SHEETS. THEY WILL BE EXCUSED FROM CLASSES ON THOSE DAYS. IN THE MEANTIME, TEACHERS ARE TO ACQUAINT THEMSELVES WITH THE PPP OF EACH STUDENT AND SEND THE DISRUPTIVE ELEMENTS TO MR. MCHABE.

ELLA FRIEDENBERG
GUIDANCE COUNSELOR

•   •   •   •

TO: ALL TEACHERS

THERE HAS BEEN AN EPIDEMIC OF THEFTS FROM LOCKERS AND WARDROBES. IMPRESS UPON YOUR STUDENTS THE NECESSITY OF KEEPING THEM LOCKED UP AT ALL TIMES, EXCEPT WHEN IN DIRECT USE.

JJ MCHABE
ADM. ASST.

•   •   •   •

FROM: JAMES J. MCHABE, ADM. ASST.

TO: ALL TEACHERS

THE FIRST FACULTY CONFERENCE OF THE TERM IS SCHEDULED FOR MONDAY, SEPTEMBER 28, IN THE SCHOOL LIBRARY, PROMPTLY AT 3:05.

ATTENDANCE IS MANDATORY. NO TEACHER IS TO BE EXCUSED FROM THE CONFERENCE EXCEPT ON WRITTEN REQUEST SIGNED BY THE CHAIRMAN OF THE DEPARTMENT AND COUNTERSIGNED BY THE

PRINCIPAL OR ADMINISTRATIVE ASSISTANT AT LEAST TWO DAYS
PRIOR TO THE DATE SCHEDULED.
THE TOPIC FOR DISCUSSION WILL BE "EDUCATION AS GROWTH IN
A DEMOCRACY." BE PREPARED WITH SUGGESTIONS ON: SHOULD
MARKS BE ENTERED ON THE RIGHT OR LEFT OF THE BLUE LINE
ON THE PRC?

JJ McH

• • • •

TO: ALL TEACHERS
STUDENTS DELINQUENT IN OBTAINING GYM SUITS ARE TO BE AL-
PHABETIZED AND SENT TO ME.
GIRLS WHO WISH TO BE EXCUSED FROM GYM ON "CERTAIN DAYS"
ARE TO BE SENT TO ME WITH ALL THE PERTINENT DATA.
PLEASE DISCOURAGE EXCESSIVE DIETING IN YOUR HOMEROOM.

FRANCIS EGAN
SCHOOL NURSE

• • • •

CIRCULAR # 5B
TOPIC: TEACHERS' WELFARE
PLEASE KEEP ALL CIRCULARS ON FILE, IN THEIR ORDER
TEACHERS SHALL BE REQUIRED TO REPORT TO PRINCIPALS AND
PRINCIPALS SHALL BE REQUIRED TO REPORT TO THE ASSOCIATE
SUPERINTENDENT FOR PERSONNEL AND TO THE LAW SECRETARY
ALL CASES OF ASSAULT SUFFERED BY TEACHERS IN CONNECTION
WITH THEIR EMPLOYMENT.

• • • •

TO: ALL TEACHERS
CALVIN COOLIDGE IS WAGING AN ALL-OUT CAMPAIGN AGAINST
LATENESS AND SMOKING IN LAVATORIES. SEND LEGITIMATE LATE-
NESSES TO LATENESS COORDINATOR, ROOM 201. IF EXCUSE IS IN-
VALID OR SUSPECT, SEND OFFENDERS TO ME, ROOM 211. PLEASE
READ TO YOUR STUDENTS THE ENCLOSED LIST OF INFRACTIONS
AND PENALTIES TO INSTILL IN THEM A SENSE OF CIVIC RESPONSI-
BILITY AND PUNCTUALITY.
POST IN PROMINENT PLACE IN HOMEROOM:

A STUDENT WHO IS LATE
MAY FAIL TO GRAD-U-ATE

JAMES J. McHABE
ADM. ASST.

• • • •

TO: ALL TEACHERS
STUDENTS ARE NOT TO BE SENT TO THE SCHOOL LIBRARY FOR ANY
REASON WHATSOEVER WHILE TEACHERS ARE USING IT FOR THEIR
RECORDS.
NO BOOKS ARE TO BE REMOVED FROM LIBRARY SHELVES BY STU-
DENTS OR TEACHERS UNTIL CARD CATALOGUE IS BROUGHT UP TO
DATE.

CHARLOTTE WOLF
LIBRARIAN

TO: ALL ENGLISH TEACHERS
PLEASE SEND TO THE BOOK ROOM FOR THE FOLLOWING BOOKS
SELECTED FOR YOUR CLASSES BY THE COMMITTEE ON CURRICULUM
INTEGRATION:
   ENGLISH 3—ESSAYS OLD AND NEW
                        or
            MYTHS AND THEIR MEANING
   ENGLISH 5—THE MILL ON THE FLOSS
                        or
            A TALE OF TWO CITIES
DO NOT ALLOW STUDENTS TO PURCHASE PAPERBACK EDITIONS OF
SHAKESPEARE AND OTHER AUTHORS: BECAUSE OF OUTSIDE PRES-
SURES, WE SHOULD NOT EXPOSE THEM TO INSUFFICIENTLY EDITED
OR UNEXPURGATED TEXTS.
                              SAMUEL BESTER
                              CHAIRMAN LANGUAGE ARTS DEPT.

                    •   •   •   •

FROM: JAMES J. MCHABE, ADM. ASST.
TO: ALL TEACHERS
RE: DISTRIBUTION OF BOOKS
BOOKS ARE THE MAGIC DOORS TO ADVENTURE AND KNOWLEDGE;
THEY SHOULD BE TREASURED. KEEP ON FILE A BOOK RECEIPT FOR
EVERY BOOK DISTRIBUTED. ALL BOOKS SHOULD BE COVERED AND
STUDENTS SHOULD BE WARNED NOT TO DEFACE OR MUTILATE
BOOKS. SIGN THE BOOK LABEL, INDICATING THAT YOU AGREE THAT
THE LABEL HAS BEEN PROPERLY FILLED OUT, AND MAKE SURE THAT
EACH BOOK HAS A NUMBER WHICH APPEARS ON THE INSIDE FRONT
COVER AND AGAIN ON PAGE 43, IF THE BOOK HAS THAT MANY
PAGES.
DISREGARD THE NUMBER ON THE FLY-LEAF.
LOVE OF READING LASTS A LIFETIME.
                                              JJ McH

                    •   •   •   •

DEAR COLLEAGUE:
   LOOKING FORWARD TO A NEW SCHOOL YEAR?
EEZYTERM CONFIDENTIAL LOAN COMPANY, WHICH I REPRESENT,
CAN SOLVE YOUR FINANCIAL PROBLEMS:
BROCHURE ENCLOSED.
                    •   •   •   •

Dear Miss Barette,
    I need a dropout slip to work because I'm of age and my income is
needed at home. Most of school is a waste anyhow, every period another
subject Algebra French Eco English one after the other what good is it,
it's all a Jumble and in each class the teacher tells you something different
until you don't know who to believe.

I'm better off out.

Your pupil
Vince Arbuzzi

(I wasn't in Home Room due to the office unable to find my records this morning)

● ● ● ●

FROM: JAMES J. McHABE, ADM. ASST.

TO: ALL TEACHERS

SINCE WE HAVE A LARGE PERCENTAGE OF DROPOUTS, PLEASE MAKE EVERY EFFORT TO ENCOURAGE YOUR STUDENTS TO REMAIN IN SCHOOL BY POINTING OUT THE VALUES OF EDUCATION.

JJ McH

● ● ● ●

CIRCULAR # 4

TOPIC: ETHICAL STANDARDS

PLEASE KEEP ALL CIRCULARS ON FILE, IN THEIR ORDER

TO PROTECT OUR STUDENTS FROM THE TEMPTATION OF FRADU-LENT PRACTICES AND TO ASSURE TEACHERS OF THE AUTHENTICITY OF ALL DATA, THE FOLLOWING PRECAUTIONS MUST BE TAKEN:

1. SUBJECT TEACHERS ARE TO SIGN STUDENT PROGRAM CARDS IN INK, WITH THEIR FULL NAME, AS PROOF THAT STUDENT HAS AP-PEARED IN CLASS. NO INITIALS, PENCIL OR NAME-STAMPERS ARE ACCEPTABLE.
2. THE ABOVE IS ALSO TRUE OF ALL PASSES SIGNED BY THE TEACHER.
3. CHECK THE ROLL BOOK FOR NON-EXISTENT ADDRESSES AND NON-AUTHENTIC PARENT OR GUARDIAN, TO FACILITATE WORK OF TRUANT OFFICER.
4. IN MAKING ENTRIES ON RECORDS, DO NOT ERASE, SCRATCH OUT, OR USE INK ERADICATOR. CORRECTIONS ARE TO BE MADE ONLY WITH THE SIGNATURE OF THE PRINCIPAL OR ADMINISTRATIVE ASSISTANT WHO WILL APPROVE THE CORRECTION.
5. DURING FIRE, SHELTER AREA OR OTHER EMERGENCY DRILLS, INFORM STUDENTS TO BE PARTICULARLY CAREFUL ABOUT THEIR VALUABLES. BOOKS AND NOTE BOOKS ARE TO BE LEFT BEHIND, BUT POCKETBOOKS AND WALLETS ARE TO BE HELD ON TO. WE HAVE HAD AN EPIDEMIC OF UNFORTUNATE INCIDENTS.

WITH THESE PRECAUTIONS IN MIND, WE CAN HELP OUR STUDENTS ACHIEVE THE HIGH ETHICAL STANDARDS WE EXPECT OF THEM.

JAMES J. McHABE
ADM. ASST.

` ● ● ●

I WISH TO TAKE THIS OPPORTUNITY TO EXTEND A WARM WELCOME TO ALL FACULTY AND STAFF, AND THE SINCERE HOPE THAT YOU HAVE RETURNED FROM A HEALTHFUL AND FRUITFUL SUMMER VACATION WITH RENEWED VIM AND VIGOR, READY TO GIRD YOUR

LOINS AND TACKLE THE MANY IMPORTANT AND VITAL TASKS THAT
LIE AHEAD UNDAUNTED. THANK YOU FOR YOUR HELP AND CO-
OPERATION IN THE PAST AND FUTURE.

MAXWELL E. CLARKE
PRINCIPAL

MYRON LIEBERMAN

Implications
of the Coming
NEA-AFT Merger

A MERGER OF THE NATIONAL EDUCATION ASSOCIATION AND AMERICAN
Federation of Teachers will probably be negotiated in the near future.
Such a move will have far-reaching national implications for teacher
militancy. Perhaps because very few educators realize how imminent
merger is, our professional literature is virtually devoid of any consideration of the likely conditions and consequences of merger. Inasmuch as
organizational rivalry plays such an important role in teacher militancy,
it would be unrealistic to consider the dynamics of teacher militancy without serious attention to the effects of merger upon it.

In the following comments, I am going to assume that merger will take
place within a few years. This assumption is based largely upon what
appears to me to be the practical logic of the situation. My purpose here,
however, is not to demonstrate what appears obvious to me, i.e., that the
merger will take place in the next few years at most, but to call attention
and scholarly inquiry into what is problematical, the conditions and consequences of merger. These are the crucial problems, not whether or when
the merger will occur.

Without question, the organizational rivalry between the NEA and
AFT has been an important stimulus to teacher militancy. At all levels,
the two organizations and their state and local affiliates have come under

Myron Lieberman, "Implications of the Coming NEA-AFT Merger." *Phi Delta
Kappan, 50*, 1968, 139–44. Reprinted by permission of the author and publisher.

much more pressure to achieve benefits than would be the case if there were only one organization. A representation election almost invariably causes the competing organizations to adopt a more militant stance in order to demonstrate their effectiveness in achieving teacher goals. For the same reason, any failure to press vigorously for teacher objectives becomes a threat to organizational survival. State and national support are poured into local elections and negotiation sessions in order to protect the interests of the state and national affiliates. Thus at the local level organizational rivalry has led to a vastly greater organiztional effort to advance teacher objectives. This development is consistent with the experience of competing organizations in other fields.

The crucial importance of the NEA-AFT rivalry in stimulating teacher militancy raises the question of whether the merger of the two organizations will reduce such militancy. Probably, the merger will simultaneously encourage some tendencies toward greater teacher militancy and some toward less militancy; the overall outcome is likely to vary widely from district to district and time to time. To see why, it will be helpful to review the issues involved in merger.

Historically, two major organizational issues have divided the NEA and AFT. One was the fact that local, state, and national education associations typically permitted all-inclusive membership, i.e., these associations enrolled administrators and supervisors (hereafter referred to as "administrators" or "administrative personnel") as well as teachers. The other issue was the AFT's affiliation with the AFL-CIO. It is becoming evident, however, that these issues no longer divide the organizations as they did in the past.

In the first place, a number of teacher negotiation laws and/or state administrative agencies have settled the issue of administrator membership substantially along the lines advocated by the AFT. True, in a few other states, such as Connecticut, Washington, and Maryland, state negotiations legislation permits or even mandates the inclusion of administrative personnel in a teacher bargaining unit; but this aspect of the statutes is either ignored in practice or is creating too many practical difficulties for all parties. In any event, the Michigan experience is likely to be the predominant pattern. In that state, many superintendents withdrew from, or did not join, local associations after passage of the Michigan negotiations statute in 1965. In 1966, the Michigan Association of School Administrators withdrew from the Michigan Education Association and joined with the Michigan School Boards Association and Michigan School Business Officials to form a new organization. In 1967, the state organizations of elementary and secondary school principals pulled out of the Michigan Education Association.

It should be noted that in the collective negotiations context, administrator membership in the teacher organization (which is not the same thing as membership in the same negotiating unit as teachers) is dangerous for the school board as well as for the teacher organization. Such membership, especially if the administrative personnel are active in the teacher organization, could lead to charges of employer support or domination of the employee (teacher) organization or to other unfair labor practices. In other words, administrator membership may jeopardize both the organization's right to represent teachers and the legitimacy of the board's approach to teacher bargaining.

The Michigan pattern concerning administrative membership in teacher organization is still a minority one in the country as a whole. Nevertheless, it is likely to prevail eventually because of the difficulties inherent in maintaining all-inclusive membership in a negotiating organization. School boards will increasingly resist situations in which personnel assigned to administrative duties are represented by an organization controlled by the teachers they administer.

At the present time the issue of administrative membership is being debated at all organizational levels. In some districts the issue is seen as pertaining only to local organizations; it is assumed that administrative personnel can and should retain membership in state and national teacher organizations. In other places it is already accepted that administrative personnel cannot continue as regular members of local and state teacher organizations, but it is thought they should continue as members of NEA. Nevertheless, it is clear that even at the national level all-inclusive membership poses many sticky problems; the American Association of School Administrators, National Association of Secondary-School Principals, Department of Elementary School Principals, and Association for Supervision and Curriculum Development are some of the NEA departments already considering the need for modifying their relationships with the NEA in the near future.

The existence of these different approaches is understandable only in terms of intra-organizational perspectives. A state association leader might reluctantly accept the demise of all-inclusive membership at the local level but seek desperately to retain it at the state level. For one thing, he will naturally be unhappy at the prospect of losing dues revenue from administrators and supervisors. And if, as is often the case, such personnel play important roles in recruiting teachers to state membership, the loss of administrative personnel involves much more than the numbers of such personnel. In this situation the state association leader easily convinces himself that all-inclusive membership in the state association is still desirable. After all, he tells himself and others, the local association, not the state, is the negotiating organization. Furthermore, both teachers and administrators have a common interest in more state aid, an improved retirement system, and so on.

As plausible as these arguments are, they ignore the pressures toward separation at the state as well as at the local level. How will administrators be represented in the state association, if not through local associations? What will happen to administrators in districts too small to establish local organizations of administrators? Since the state organization will invariably support teachers in showdowns at the local level — to do otherwise would be organizational hara-kiri — how will administrators be able to work vigorously for their objectives inside the organization? How will school boards react to administrative membership in organizations supporting teachers' strikes or other militant action against the board and its representatives? Will administrators be willing to pay dues to state organizations that support teachers in militant anti-administration activities?

In their frantic efforts to maintain the status quo, some state association leaders have overlooked these hard questions relating to administrative membership in state teacher organizations. Nevertheless, administrators are taking the initiative in withdrawing from the state associations as often or more often than they are being excluded from them by militant teachers.

The same kind of wishful thinking characterized the outlook of NEA leaders until the recent past. For several reasons, NEA leaders did not want to adopt a position on administrative membership at local and state levels. There was concern that the exclusion of administrators from NEA would be damaging in terms of NEA membership, and again, the fear was related to administrative help in recruiting teacher members as well as to the loss of administrators per se. There was an emphasis upon the common interests of teachers and administrators at the national level, e.g., in getting more federal aid. There was also a failure to grasp the interdependence of local, state, and national organizations in a negotiating context.

An even more difficult problem was the tremendous regional, state, and local differences relating to negotiations. Association experience in Michigan or Massachusetts meant nothing to association leaders in Alabama or Mississippi. A membership policy vis-à-vis administrators that would have seemed sensible in Michigan would have horrified association members in Alabama.

The resolution of this difficult organizational problem was deceptively simple. The NEA's *Guidelines to Professional Negotiation* (1965) proposed that the inclusion of administrators in the negotiating unit and the negotiating organization be left to local option. This was not very helpful to local associations who wanted guidance on what their policy should be, but it was probably the only feasible way to avoid the issue until the pro-negotiation forces were stronger and there was a wider understanding of the problem throughout the association structure. Certainly, some NEA leaders realized from the outset of the negotiations movement that local option on administrator membership, without limits or guidelines, was a hopeless long-range policy; but a realistic policy had no chance of acceptance in the early 1960's.

A merger between the NEA and AFT will unquestionably accelerate the flight of administrative personnel from the merged organizations at all levels. First, the very fact that merger talks are taking place will confirm the feelings of many administrators that the associations are becoming "just like the union" — if not worse — and hence that administrators have no business in the association, with or without a merger. A more important point is that the AFT will demand some type of administrative exclusion as a condition of merger. Such a demand would actually make more sense from a propaganda than from a substantive point of view. The reason is that the inclusion of AFT membership in a new organization would tip the organizational balance in favor of administrative exclusion. Thus even if the exclusion of administrators were not a condition of merger, such exclusion would be organizational policy anyway within a year or two after merger. I suggest this independently of any conclusion about the desirability of excluding administrators from teacher organizations; the point is that a sincere belief in the importance of such exclusion does not necessarily justify setting it as a condition of merger.

Note that the issue here is not whether administrators have or should have the right to join teacher organizations. Most assuredly, they do have the right and will continue to have it, insofar as teachers permit it. The real issue is whether a teacher organization which includes administrators should have the legal right to represent teachers on terms and conditions of employment. Teachers and administrators have a constitutionally protected right to join the same organizations, but organizations enrolling both teachers and administrators do not have a constitutionally protected right to represent teachers in negotiations with their employers. Organizational rights to represent teachers are conditioned by law upon a number of public policy considerations. One such consideration is whether the organization can represent employees effectively. In private employment, this consideration has led to the mandatory exclusion of managerial personnel if the organization is to retain negotiating rights. The alleged differences between public and private employment, professional and nonprofessional employment, and between education and other fields are not likely to weaken the public policy arguments for exclusion of administrators from organizations seeking to represent teachers.

Experience in other fields strongly suggests that administrative membership in state and national teacher organizations will probably not survive collective negotiations by teachers. If such membership is to survive, which is doubtful in any case, it is essential for the NEA and its affiliates to examine the issue by some sort of high-level task force in which teachers and administrators alike could have confidence. Such a task force would have to include experts in collective negotiations and public administration who clearly had no vested interest in the outcome and who could propose a feasible structure for all-inclusive membership. Otherwise, the forced exclusion or voluntary withdrawal of administrators from state associations and the NEA will increase rapidly, and the makeshift arrangements to hold everyone together will continue to ignore important practical considerations. One comprehensive study of the problem, adequately staffed and financed, would have served better than the hasty and improvised studies that have been made thus far. In any event, no task force of the kind envisaged has been or is in prospect; since such a group might well conclude that the separation is desirable and inevitable, perhaps little has been or will be lost by the absence of such an effort.

We should recognize, however, that many of the arguments for or against separation are oversimplifications of a complex problem. Teachers and administrators do not have to be in the same organization in order to communicate and cooperate with each other. Likewise, the fact that they are in the same organization would not necessarily reduce tensions or disagreements or conflicts between them. In other words, equating all-inclusive membership with cooperation, or separate organizations with conflict, is an oversimplification. In any case, the most probable outcome is a sort of confederation of educational organizations, in which each controls its own membership, budget, and policies. There could be joint financing and support of activities commanding the support of all organizations while the organizations go their own way in areas where their views or interests clash. Obviously, we can expect such clashes in the areas of collective negotiations and teacher militancy.

The upshot seems to me to be this: Regardless of the formal membership structure of the merged organization, teachers will control the state and national organizations that merge. The emerging organizations will put great pressure on teachers to join, and we can expect a dramatic increase in teacher organizational membership at all levels. With greatly increased membership and resources—none of which are needed to fight a rival teacher organization—and without the internal constraints inherent in administrator membership or control, the new organization will probably pursue more militant policies in behalf of teacher interests and views than anything we have experienced thus far in either NEA or AFT.

I say "probably" because some aspects of merger will tend to reduce teacher militancy. Thus it is often thought that merger will reduce teacher militancy by eliminating competition between the two organizations. So long as two organizations are competing for members, there is great pressure on each to achieve significant results. With merger, this pressure, and the militancy it generates, will disappear. Interestingly enough, many leaders in both organizations, as well as experienced observers familiar with experience in other fields, share this expectation.

Undoubtedly, organizational rivalry typically results in greater organizational militancy. Even if this were not the case in other fields, it is clear that the recent sweeping changes in the NEA and its state and local affiliates would not have occurred (at least not so soon) except for the challenge of the AFT. This conclusion is not questioned, privately at least, by many NEA leaders.

Nevertheless, although organizational rivalry increases teacher militancy, it does not necessarily follow that merger will reduce such militancy, or that every aspect of merger will have this effect. For example, in many school districts, neither the local association nor the federation can afford full-time local leadership. With merger, the teachers may be able to support full-time local leadership with adequate facilities; much of the time and resources that were devoted to fighting the other teacher organization may now be directed at the school board. One of the certain consequences of merger, will be a substantial increase in full-time representation of teachers and in their organizational resources, facilities, and support at all levels.

The increase in organizational capability may not fully offset the loss of dynamism inherent in two competing organizations. The crucial point, however, is that merger will not necessarily end the kind of competition and rivalry that has undergirded so much recent teacher militancy. In short, we must consider the possibility that competition *within* the merged organization will result in as much teacher militancy as competition between the present separate organizations.

I have noted that enrolling everyone in the same organization does not automatically eliminate differences or conflicts of interest among the members. In negotiations where there are rival organizations, the minority organization may criticize the results in order to persuade teachers to vote for and join the minority organization and give it a chance to become the bargaining agent. With one organization, the objective is to persuade teachers to change the leadership of the organization instead of to change their organizational affiliation. However, from the standpoint of teacher militancy, the dynamics of the situation can be much the same. In both situations, there is pressure on organizational leadership to achieve results, and there is also a leadership need to arouse teacher militancy for the same purpose.

The crucial difference between competition between two organizations and competition within a single organization relates to the capacity of those not in control of the organizational machinery to wage an effective campaign against the incumbents. To be specific, NEA publications are controlled by persons independent of AFT control, and vice versa. Thus, regardless of which organization is the bargaining agent in a given school district, there is a rival organizational apparatus not controlled by the bargaining agent. This rival apparatus constitutes a source of information, criticism, and opinion whose very existence places greater pressure on the bargaining agent to achieve every possible gain.

If, however, there is a merger and therefore only one organization, how will critics and opponents of the incumbent leadership get their views publicized? They will no longer have an official organizational publication for this purpose. They will no longer control organizational conventions, conferences, news releases, and other means of disseminating their views. As a result, the incumbent leadership comes under less pressure to achieve results, with a consequent diminution of teacher militancy.

Merger per se will tend to weaken effective capacity to oppose incumbent leadership, and such weakening will inevitably lessen teacher militancy. However, appropriate action could be taken to insure that this does not happen. The appropriate action would be the introduction of the caucus system in the merged organization. Because the long-range effects of the merger will depend on how soon and how effectively caucuses are established in the new organization, and because the existence and effectiveness of caucuses will be the major influence on teacher militancy in the merged organization, it is necessary to analyze their role in some detail.

A caucus system is essentially a system of political parties within the organization. Organization members may join a caucus, pay dues to it, attend its meetings, participate in its deliberations, and perhaps represent it in official organization proceedings. It is essential that caucuses be financed and operated independently of the organizational machinery; otherwise there is the danger that the caucus will lose its ability to function as an independent source of information, criticism, and leadership. The crucial point is that in the absence of a caucus, individual members or convention delegates are helpless before the organizational machinery. To change organizational policy or to launch a campaign to change organizational leadership, collective action is needed. First, there must be a forum not controlled by incumbent leadership in which the opposition has full opportunity to state its case and generate support. Floor fights (hopefully, only verbal ones) must be organized, fall-back positions established, and strategy coordinated. Signs, posters, and other literature may have to be printed and disseminated, and so on. These and other essentials of effective organizational leadership or influence cannot be initiated effectively by ad hoc committees or organizations, which are formed—usually over one issue—at a particular convention and then wither away. At all times there must be an organizational mechanism which can serve all the constructive purposes served by a rival organization. Such a mechanism, however, must be as independent of control by incumbent leadership as is a rival organization.

The incumbent leadership will also need a political mechanism independent of the organizational machinery. The elected officers of the organization should not be able to use organizational funds to finance their election campaign. As in most such situations, the incumbents will have certain political advantages accruing from their incumbency, but they too will have political needs which cannot legitimately be met by using official organizational machinery. It would, therefore, be erroneous to regard caucuses solely as a means for helping the "out's" clobber the "in's." Neither democracy nor militancy will flourish in the merged organization unless there exists practical means of exerting organizational influence and leadership which are not dependent upon the official organizational structure. Policies and leaders must be forged in the caucuses, and thence into the official organizational structure. If this is done, and I believe it can and must be done, we can be optimistic about the level of internal democracy in the merged organization. We can also expect a continuing high level of teacher militancy under the conditions.

AFFILIATION AS A MERGER ISSUE

For all practical purposes, the forthcoming merger will end teacher affiliation with the AFL-CIO. The AFT will need some face-saving concession on this issue, such as a national referendum on the question within the merged organization or local option to affiliate with the AFL-CIO; but the issue is already a dead horse for all practical reasons. The fact that AFT leaders are already proposing a referendum, knowing full well that it would be overwhelmingly defeated in the merged organization, ought to be signal enough for anyone to see. There is even reason to doubt whether such a referendum confined to the present AFT membership would support affiliation. Certainly there is very little sentiment in the AFT to insist upon affiliation at the cost of preventing merger.

Allowing local option to affiliate with the AFL-CIO might be a viable solution, since it would ease the transition problem, support the principle of local autonomy, and quickly lead to disaffiliation anyway. Affiliation with the AFL-CIO is not important to most AFT members, but it is important to some AFT leaders in some large urban centers. If local option is permitted, only a few locals will affiliate with the AFL-CIO, and the impracticalities of such a relationship will lead to their disaffiliation soon afterward. Furthermore, it is doubtful whether the AFL-CIO would find it advantageous to enroll a few teacher locals, even a few relatively large ones.

Since the teacher organizations choosing to be affiliated with the AFL-CIO would not be a rival to the merged teacher organizations, affiliation would not constitute an organizational issue as it does now. Actually, there is no constitutional reason now why an NEA local affiliate cannot affiliate with the AFL-CIO. Such affiliation would probably lead to expulsion by the NEA Executive Committee under present circumstances, but such a reaction would be overkill if there were only one teacher organization. At any rate, despite the enormous importance of the issue in the propaganda war between NEA and AFT, it is not a very important substantive issue, and it will not hold up merger as long as it takes to read this paper.

What will be the impact of disaffiliation on teacher militancy? A popular view is that AFT militancy is due to its affiliation with the AFL-CIO. This seems very questionable. Affiliation has contributed to AFT militancy, in specific communities under specific circumstances; likewise, affiliation has often been a conservative influence in many situations. The teacher stereotype of labor bosses inciting teachers to strike is far removed from the facts, as is the notion that the AFT depends largely upon the AFL-CIO or the IUD [Industrial Union Department, whose main function is recruitment] for support. The AFL-CIO did play an important role in the early stages of the AFT's drive for collective bargaining, but it is not a decisive factor now. Surely, there have been enough teacher strikes, boycotts, sanctions, and other pressures by associations in recent years to end the fallacy that affiliation with the AFL-CIO underlies or is an essential ingredient of teacher militancy. In fact, nonteacher members of the AFL-CIO at any level may view teachers' strikes more critically as parents and taxpayers than favorably as the justified efforts of fellow wage earners. Realistically, there is no strong reason to believe that disaffiliation will reduce teacher militancy in any significant way.

The major problems of merger are not philosophical or ideological; they are practical, such as who gets what job in the merged organization. The practical problems will be complicated more by the political implications of any settlement than by the equities from a strictly organizational or employment point of view. To be candid, there are enough resources to take care of everybody reasonably well. The more difficult problems will arise over the inevitable efforts by the negotiators on both sides to place their political supporters in as many of the key positions as possible. These efforts will create internal problems on each side which may be more difficult to resolve than the issues dividing the negotiators along organizational lines.

It would be naive to underestimate the importance of this problem. Beyond the broad social factors affecting teacher militancy, the quality of teacher leadership is necessarily a crucial factor in the dynamics and future of teacher militancy. For this reason, my concluding comments will relate to this matter.

The most immediate effects of merger upon leadership will be at the state level. In a number of states, federation locals dominate the large urban districts, whereas other districts are largely association-dominated. Especially where the AFT-dominated districts include greater proportions of all the teachers in the state, the impact of merger may be truly traumatic at the state level. In fact, there are states where federation members have no significant reservations about affiliation at the national level but object strenuously to state association leadership. This is especially true in states like California and Minnesota, where state association leadership—to the obvious chagrin of many NEA leaders—has vigorously opposed effective negotiation legislation.

Another point here is that the NEA's national staff is much more oriented to collective negotiations and teacher militancy than is the leadership of many state associations. Many state associations are oriented more to lobbying in the state legislature than to effective support of locals at the bargaining table. It appears that the NEA has had to establish regional field offices to assist local associations in negotiations partly because of state association slowness in responding to the negotiations movement. The state associations in Massachusetts, Michigan, New Jersey, and Rhode Island were the quickest to adapt effectively to negotiations, but in many states the local associations must still look to the NEA rather than the state association for significant help in negotiations. Indeed, this is still necessary occasionally in the states mentioned as having made the most rapid adjustment. The point is, however, that merger will sometimes change the constituency of the state organization more than it will the national; hence changes in leadership and policy in some of the state organizations may emerge rather quickly.

At the national level, full-time leadership in the merged organization will be largely as it is now in the NEA, at least for the near future. This is not only due to the arithmetic of the situation, i.e., the NEA's much greater membership and national staff. It will also be due to the fact that most of the NEA's present leadership is negotiation-oriented. Merger, therefore, will not be seen as a threat but as a step forward toward a more militant organization. On this score, it must be conceded that changes in the NEA within the past few years, and especially since its top leadership changed in 1967, have been truly remarkable.

In the early 1960's, one New York City law firm (Kaye, Scholer, Fierman, Hays, and Handler) provided the national leadership and the expertise which saved the NEA and its affiliates from organizational catastrophe in its competition with the AFT. It is a little known but singular fact that a New York City law firm, which ordinarily represents management in its labor practice, negotiated the first association agreements, trained the association staff, and guided the NEA to an acceptance of, and commitment to, collective negotiations. Ironically, corporation lawyers succeeded in convincing NEA leadership (correctly, it appears) that the NEA had to cease rejecting collective negotiations and demonstrate its determination to negotiate better agreements for teachers than those negotiated by the AFT. As this view prevailed, those who supported it became more influential in the NEA; today, NEA leadership is clearly committed to collective negotiations and includes a capability in this area which is not inferior to the federation's.

Without getting into personalities, therefore, it seems to me that one of the most encouraging aspects of the present situation is the tremendous improvement in the quality of teacher leadership and in the likelihood that merger will strengthen the tendencies in this direction. If this is the case, teacher militancy will continue to increase and will be increasingly devoted to constructive public policy as well as teacher objectives.

HENRY S. DYER

Toward Objective Criteria
of Professional Accountability
in the Schools

I. THE CONCEPT OF
PROFESSIONAL ACCOUNTABILITY

THE CONCEPT OF ACCOUNTABILITY CAN HAVE MANY LEVELS OF MEANING, depending upon where one focuses attention in the structure of the school system. Throughout this paper, I shall be using the term in a restricted sense as it applies to the individual school as a unit. At this level I think of the concept as embracing three general principles:

1. The professional staff of a school is to be held collectively responsible for *knowing* as much as it can (a) about the intellectual and personal-social development of the pupils in its charge and (b) about the conditions and educational services that may be facilitating or impeding the pupils' development.

2. The professional staff of a school is to be held collectively responsible for *using* this knowledge as best it can to maximize the development of its pupils toward certain clearly defined and agreed-upon pupil performance objectives.

3. The board of education has a corresponding responsibility to provide the means and technical assistance whereby the staff of each school

Henry S. Dyer, "Toward Objective Criteria of Professional Accountability in the Schools." *Phi Delta Kappan, 52,* 1970, 206–11. Reprinted by permission of the author and publisher.

can acquire, interpret, and use the information necessary for carrying out the two foregoing functions.

I emphasize the notion of *joint accountability* of the entire school staff in the aggregate — principal, teachers, specialists — because it seems obvious that what happens to any child in a school is determined by the multitude of transactions he has with many different people on the staff who perform differing roles and presumably have differing impacts on his learning, which cannot readily, if ever, be disentangled. I emphasize the notion that staff members are to be held accountable for keeping themselves informed about the diverse needs of their pupils and for doing the best they can to meet those needs. In light of what we still don't know about the teaching-learning process, this is the most one may reasonably expect. To hold teachers, or anybody else, accountable for delivering some sort of "guaranteed pupil performance" is likely to do more harm than good in the lives of the children. Finally, I emphasize that professional accountability should be seen as a two-way street, wherein a school staff is to be held accountable to higher authority for its own operations while the higher authorities in turn are to be held accountable for supplying the appropriate information and facilities each school staff requires to operate effectively.

An important implication in the three principles set forth above is that there shall be developed a district-wide educational accounting system optimally adaptable to the information needs of each school in the district. Later in this paper I shall describe the salient features of such a system and shall suggest the procedures by which it might be developed and put to use. In this connection it should be noted that the type of *educational* accounting system here contemplated is to be distinguished from a *fiscal* accounting system. The kind of information provided by the former should not be confused with the kind provided by the latter. At all levels, the two types should complement each other in an overall management information system capable of relating benefits to costs. At the individual school level, however, educational accounting per se is of prime importance and is not usefully related to fiscal accounting, since the staff in a single school does not have and, in ordinary circumstances, cannot have much if any latitude in the raising and expending of funds for its local operations.

The next section of this paper outlines what a fully functioning educational accounting system might be like and how it could operate as a means for holding a school staff accountable, within certain constraints, for continually improving the effectiveness of its work. The last section briefly sketches plans by which the system might be brought into being and contains some cautions that should be heeded along the way.

II. CHARACTERISTICS OF AN
EDUCATIONAL ACCOUNTING SYSTEM

A. Pupil-Change Model of a School

The theory behind the first of the three principles stated in the preceding section is that if a school staff is to fulfill its professional obligations it must have extensive knowledge of the pupils it is expected to serve. This theory is based on the notion of a school as a social system that effects changes of various kinds in both the children who pass through it and in the professional personnel responsible for maintaining the school. The school as a social system becomes an educational system when its constituents are trying to ensure that all such changes shall be for the better. That is, the school as a *social* system becomes an *educational* system when its constituents — pupils, teachers, principal — are working toward some clearly defined pupil performance objectives.

There are four groups of variables in the school as a social system that must be recognized and measured if one is to develop acceptable criteria of staff accountability. These four groups of variables I call *input, educational process, surrounding conditions,* and *output.* Taken together, they form the pupil-change model of a school.

The *input* to any school at any given level consists of the characteristics of the pupils as they enter that level of their schooling: their health and physical condition, their skill in the three R's, their feelings about themselves and others, their aspirations, and so on.[1] The *output* of any school consists of the same characteristics of the pupils as they emerge from that particular phase of their schooling some years later.

According to this conception, the input to any school consists of the output from the next lower level. Thus, the output of an elementary school becomes the input for junior high, and the output of junior high becomes the input for senior high. It is important to note that the staff of an individual school which is not in a position to select the pupils who come to it has no control over the level or quality of its input. In such a case, the pupil input represents a *fixed condition* with which the school staff must cope. The pupil output, however, is a variable that depends to some extent on the quality of service the school provides.

The third group of variables in the pupil-change model consists of the *surrounding conditions* within which the school operates. These are the factors in the school environment that may influence for better or for worse how teachers teach and pupils learn. The surrounding conditions fall into three categories: home conditions, community conditions, and school conditions. Home conditions include such matters as the level of education of the pupils' parents, the level of family income, the family pressures, and the physical condition of the home. Community conditions include the density of population in the enrollment area, the ethnic character of the population, the number and quality of available social agencies, the degree of industrialization, and so on. School conditions include plant, pupil-teacher ratio, classroom and playground footage per pupil, the esprit de corps of the staff, and the like.

In respect to all three types of surrounding conditions, one can distinguish those that the staff of a school finds easy to change from those that it finds hard to change. For example, in respect to home conditions, the school staff is hardly in a position to change the socioeconomic level of pupils' parents, but it may well be in a position to change the parents' attitudes toward education through programs that involve them in the work of the school. Similarly, in respect to school conditions, it might not be able to effect much change in the classroom footage per pupil, but it could probably develop programs that might influence the esprit de corps of the staff through in-service training. The identification of hard-to-change as contrasted with easy-to-change surrounding conditions is of the utmost impotance in working toward objective criteria of professional accountability, since the staff of a school can hardly be held accountable for changing those factors in its situation over which it has little or no control.

The final set of variables in the pupil-change model are those that make up the *educational process*; that is, all the activities in the school expressly designed to bring about changes for the better in pupils: lessons in arithmetic, recreational activities, consultation with parents, vocational counseling, etc. Three principal questions are to be asked about the educational processes in any school: 1) Are they adapted to the individual needs of the children in the school? 2) Do they work, that is, do they tend to change pupils in *desirable* ways? and 3) What, if any, negative side effects may they be having on the growth of the children?

The four sets of variables just described — input, output, surrounding conditions, and educational process — interact with one another in complex ways. That is, the pupil output variables are affected by all the other variables. Similarly, the educational process variables are influenced by both the pupil input and the surrounding conditions. And certain of the surrounding conditions may be influenced by certain of the educational processes. This last could happen, for instance, if a school embarked on a cooperative work-study program with businesses in its enrollment area.

From the foregoing considerations, it is clear that if a school staff is to maximize pupil output in any particular way, it must be aware of the nature of the interactions among the variables in the system and be given sufficient information to cope with them in its work. This in turn means that, insofar as possible, all variables in the system must be measured and appropriately interrelated and combined to produce readily interpretable indices by which the staff can know how much its own efforts are producing hoped-for changes in pupils, after making due allowance for those variables over which it has little or no control. I call such indices *school effectiveness indices* (SEI's). They are the means whereby a school staff may be held responsible for *knowing* how well it is doing.

B. Nature of the SEI

The functioning of a school can be described by a profile of school effectiveness indices, so that each school staff can readily locate the points at which its educational program is strong or weak. Such a profile is fundamentally different from the traditional test-score profile, which is ordinarily generated from the grade equivalencies attached to the general run of standardized achievement tests. The underlying rationale of an SEI profile rejects grade equivalencies as essentially meaningless numbers that tend to be grossly misleading as indicators of a school's effectiveness. Appropriate indices in the SEI profile of any given school at any given level can be derived only through a procedure involving *all* the schools at the same level in the district. The procedure consists of a series of regression analyses which I shall touch upon presently.

Two features of an SEI profile differentiate it from the usual test-score profile. First, each index summarizes how effective the school has been in promoting one type of pupil development over a definite span of years; for example, the three years from the beginning of grade four to the end of grade six. Second, the profile has two dimensions: a pupil development dimension comprehending different areas of pupil growth (e.g., growth in self-esteem, growth in the basic skills, growth in social behavior) and a level-of-pupil-input dimension which might encompass three categories of children in accordance with their varying levels of development in any area at the time they entered grade four.

With this sort of profile it should be possible to discern in which areas of pupil development a school is more or less effective with different groups of pupils. Thus, an SEI profile for a grade four to six school should be capable of answering questions like the following: In its teaching of reading over the three-year period, has the school done a better or worse job with pupils who entered grade four with a low level of reading performance as compared with those who entered with a high level of reading performance? During the three-year period, has the school been more or less effective in developing children's number skills than in developing their sense of self-esteem, or their social behavior, or their health habits?

The areas of pupil development to be incorporated in the educational accounting system for any district must grow out of an earnest effort to reach agreement among all the parties involved (teachers, administrators, board members, parents, pupils) concerning the pupil performance objectives that are to be sought. Such objectives will vary for schools encompassing different grade levels, and they will also vary, in accordance with local needs, among schools serving any given grade levels.

Securing agreement on the objectives is no mean enterprise, but it is obviously fundamental to a meaningful approach to the establishment of any basis for holding professional educators accountable for their own performance in the schools.

C. Derivation of the SEI

One important point to keep in mind about any school effectiveness index is that it is a measure that must be *derived* from a large number of more fundamental measures. These more fundamental measures consist of three of the sets of variables suggested earlier in the discussion of the pupil-change model of a school as a social system, namely, 1) the pupil input variables, 2) the *hard-to-change* surrounding conditions, and 3) the pupil output variable. Measures of *easy-to-change* surrounding condition variables and of the educational process variables do not enter into the derivation of SEI's. They become of central importance subsequently in identifying the specific actions a school staff should take to improve the effectiveness of its operations.

The fundamental measures from which the indices are to be derived can take many different forms: academic achievement tests; questionnaires to get at matters like pupil self-esteem; physical examinations to assess health and health habits; a wide range of sociological measures to assess community conditions; and measures of various aspects of the school plant, equipment, and personnel. Techniques for securing many of these measures are already available, but new and more refined ones will be required before a reasonably equitable educational accounting system can be fully operable.

Given the total array of measures required for the derivation of the SEI's, the first step in the derivation will be to apply such measures in all schools in the system at any given level — e.g., all the elementary schools, all the senior high schools — to secure the necessary information on pupil input and on the hard-to-change surrounding conditions.

The second step, to be taken perhaps two or three years later, will be to obtain output measures on the same pupils, i.e., those pupils who have remained in the same schools during the period in question.[2]

The third step will be to distribute the pupils within each school into three groups — high, middle, and low — on each of the input measures. Two points are to be especially noted about this step. First, the distribution of input measures must be "within school" distributions, with the consequence that the pupils constituting the "high" group in one school could conceivably be in the "low" group at another school where the input levels run higher with respect to any particular "area of development." Secondly, within any school, a pupil's input level could be high in one area of development (e.g., basic skills) and middle or low in another area of development (e.g., health).

The fourth step in deriving the SEI's is to compute, for each school, the averages of the hard-to-change condition variables that characterize the environment within which the school has had to operate.

FIGURE 1 *Illustration of Method of Deriving School Effectiveness Indices in the Teaching of Reading*

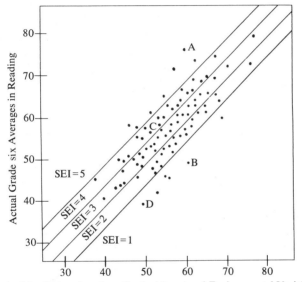

Grade 6 Predictions based on Grade 4 Input and Environmental Variables

The fifth step is to get, again for each school, the average of all the output measures for each of the three groups of pupils as identified by the input measures.

When all these data are in hand it becomes possible, by means of a series of regression analyses, to compute the SEI's that form the profile of each school.

A rough impression of how this process works may be obtained from an examination of the chart in Figure 1, which was developed from reading test scores obtained on pupils in 91 schools.[3] The measures of input in reading were taken at the beginning of grade four, and the measures of output at the end of grade six. The numbers along the horizontal axis of the chart summarize the level of grade four reading input and hard-to-change conditions with which each school has had to contend. This summarization is expressed in terms of the grade six predicted average reading levels as determined by the regression analysis.

The numbers along the vertical axis show the *actual* average reading levels for each school at the end of grade six. For each school, the discrepancy between its *predicted* grade six reading level and its *actual* grade six average reading level is used as the measure of the effectiveness with which it has been teaching reading over the three-year period. It is the discrepancy between predicted and actual level of performance that is used to determine the SEI in reading for any school. In this case the SEI's have been assigned arbitrary values ranging from a low of one to a high of five.

Consider the two schools A and B. They both have predicted grade six reading averages of about 60. This indicates that they can be deemed to have been operating in situations that are equivalent in respect to their levels of input at grade four and the hard-to-change conditions that have obtained over the three-year period during which their pupils have gone from grades four through six.

The actual reading output levels at grade six for schools A and B are considerably different. A's actual level is about 73; B's actual level is about 48. As a consequence, school A gets an effectiveness index for the teaching of reading of five, while school B gets an effectiveness index of only one.

Schools C and D present a similar picture, but at a lower level of pupil input and hard-to-change conditions. Both have predicted averages of about 50, but C's actual average is about 56, while D's is only 38. Therefore C gets an SEI of four, and D gets an SEI of only one.

From these two pairs of illustrations, it should be noted that the proposed method of computing school effectiveness indices *automatically* adjusts for the differing circumstances in which schools must operate. This feature of the index is a sine qua non of any system by which school staffs are to be held professionally accountable.

D. Uses of the SEI

It was suggested at the beginning of this paper that one of the general principles underlying the concept of professional accountability is that the staff of a school is to be held responsible for *using* its knowledge of where the school stands with respect to the intellectual and personal-social development of its pupils. This is to say that it is not sufficient for a school to "render an accounting" of its educational effectiveness. If the accounting is to have any educational payoff for the pupils whom the school is supposed to serve, the indices should point to some specific corrective actions designed to increase the school's effectiveness.

Many of such actions will perforce be outside the scope of the school itself, and responsibility for taking them must rest with the central administration. In most cases, however, a considerable number of such corrective actions should be well within the competence of the professional staff of the individual school. Responsibility for carrying them out can and should rest with that staff.

The function of school effectiveness indices in this connection is to indicate where a school staff might turn to find ways of improving its performance.

To illustrate how the SEI's might serve this purpose, let us speculate further about the relative positions of schools A and B in Figure 1. Since both schools show the same *predicted* output in reading for such pupils, it can be presumed that both schools are operating under equivalent advantages and handicaps in respect to the conditions that affect the reading ability of those pupils. Therefore, it is entirely legitimate to raise the questions: Why is school A doing so much better than school B in the teaching of reading? and What specifically is school A doing for its pupils that school B is not now doing, but presumably *could* be doing and *ought* to be doing to close the gap?

The reasons for the discrepancy between the two schools on this particular SEI are to be sought among the two sets of variables that did not enter into the derivation of the SEI's: namely, those variables that were designated "educational process" and those designated "easy-to-change surrounding conditions." A systematic comparison of how the two schools stand with respect to these variables should provide the professional staff of school B with useful clues for actions that might be taken to increase its effectiveness in the teaching of reading.

The outcome of this exercise might turn up something like this:

1. School A conducts an intensive summer program in reading; school B does not.
2. School A has a tutorial program conducted by high school students for any pupil who wishes to improve his reading; school B has no such program.
3. School A conducts parent-teacher study groups to stimulate more reading in the home; school B has little contact of any kind with the parents of its pupils.

There is, of course, no absolute guarantee that if school B were to initiate such programs it would automatically raise its SEI in reading from one to five. The factors involved in the life and workings of a school are not all that certain and clear-cut. Nevertheless, there should be a plain obligation on the staff of school B to at least *try* the procedures that appear to be working for school A and to monitor such efforts over a sufficient period to see whether they are having the desired effects. This particularization of staff effort contains the essence of what must be involved in any attempt to guarantee the professional accountability of a school staff.

The approach to accountability through a system of SEI's, if it is well understood and accepted throughout the schools of the district, should provide a mechanism for stimulating directed professional efforts toward the continuous improvement of educational practice on many fronts in all the schools.

III. PLANS AND CAUTIONS

A. Short-Range and Long-Range Plans

Clearly a full-scale educational accounting system of the sort here envisaged is hardly one that can be designed and installed full-blown in a year or two. It is one that would have to be worked out, piece by piece, over a considerable period of years. It contains technical problems many of which cannot be forseen in advance and can only be tackled as the accounting system comes into actual operation. More importantly, it would require a massive effort to secure the necessary understanding and cooperation from all the professional and community groups to be affected by it.

Nevertheless, because of the urgency of the situation in urban education and because no adequate and equitable educational accounting system can ever eventuate until some practical action is taken to get it under way, it is strongly suggested that a beginning should be made forthwith by means of a two-pronged approach. One approach would look to the carrying out of a *partial* short-range plan over the next two years; the other to the laying out of a long-range plan for the full-scale operation of the system to be achieved in, say, six years.

The *short-range plan* could begin with the reasonable assumption that there are two areas of pupil development that are of universal concern, especially as they touch the lives of minority group children in the early years of their schooling. These areas are reading and health. Acting on this assumption, one might, from currently available data, obtain input measures of these two variables on all children entering grades one and three with a view to getting output measures on the same children two years later. During the two intervening years a number of the more readily available measures of the hard-to-change conditions affecting each of the elementary schools in the system could conceivably be obtained — e.g., socioeconomic status of pupils' parents, population density and ethnicity of each enrollment area, pupil-teacher ratio, classroom and playground footage per pupil, rate of pupil mobility, and the like. Thus, by the end of the second year, one would be in a position to compute tentative school effectiveness indices and prepare two SEI profiles for each elementary school in the system — one covering grades one and two, the other covering grades three and four. These profiles could then be used as bases for local discussion concerning their meaning and utility as measures of professional accountability.[4]

The purpose of a short-range program of this sort would be twofold: 1) to provide a first approximation of two important and practically useful objective criteria of professional accountability, and 2) to provide a concrete basis for bringing about a genuine understanding of what an educational accounting system is and how it can work for the benefit of the schools and the children who attend them.

Concurrently with the foregoing short-range effort, the development of a *long-range* plan should get under way. The first step in this planning process would be to initiate parent-teacher discussion to try 1) to reach a consensus on educational objectives in terms of the areas of pupil development that should be involved in an overall annual system for professional accounting, and 2) to agree on the priorities among such objectives as they might most appropriately apply to the educational needs of the pupils in each school. The second step in the long-range plan would be to assemble instruments for measuring input and output which would be appropriate and compatible with the objectives for each level of schooling. The third step would be to work out the means for collecting and analyzing the necessary data for measuring the conditions within which each school is operating and the specific processes that characterize its operations.

B. Avoiding False Starts

One reason for initiating long-range planning concurrently with working through a partial short-range program is to try to ensure that the ultimate goal of the full-scale system will not be lost from sight while major attention is necessarily focused on the detailed problems of getting a partial operating system under way quickly. In the search for ways around the short-range problems, it is altogether probable that a number of compromises will have to be made. The danger is that, unless the final end is kept in full view, some of these compromises will be such as to preclude attainment of a viable total system.

One mistake, for instance, that could be made at the outset of the short-range program would be to yield to demands to use the input or output measures as if they were themselves measures of school effectiveness. The whole point of this paper is that a meaningful and equitable accounting of school effectiveness is possible *only* under two stringent conditions: 1) it must rest on at least two measures of pupil performance with a sufficient interval between them — probably not less than two years — to permit the school to have an effect on pupil learning which is large enough to be observable; and 2) any output measure of pupil performance must be read in light of the level of pupil input and also in light of the conditions in which the school has been forced to operate during the period for which its effectiveness in the several areas of pupil development is being indexed. This point cannot be too strongly stressed. To compromise with this basic principle would wreck the entire enterprise.

A second mistake that could seriously damage the development of the system would be to introduce into it measures of I.Q. as though they were measures of pupil input available simultaneously with measures of pupil output. This type of misuse of test scores has had a disastrous effect on the interpretation of educational measurements for at least 50 years. It should not be prolonged.

A third type of mistake to be avoided is that of concentrating the effort to develop SEI's on a certain *selected* group of schools (e.g., those in poverty areas) but not on others. If this is done the SEI's simply will not mean anything. A basic requirement in their derivation and use is that the essential measures must be obtained on *all* schools in the system so as to determine which schools are indeed comparable.

One other type of mistake that could be made in embarking on the short-range project would be to concentrate all the effort on a single area of pupil development, namely, the "basic skills." The danger here — and it is one by which schools have all too frequently been trapped — is three-fold. First, it encourages the notion that, as far as the school is concerned, training in the basic skills is all that matters in a society where so many other human characteristics also matter. Secondly, it tends toward neglect of the fact that if a school gives exclusive attention to this one area of pupil development, it may purchase success in this area at the expense of failure in other areas — social behavior, for instance. Thirdly, it tends to blind people to the interrelatedness of educational objectives, that is, to the fact that pupil development in one area may be heavily dependent on development in other areas. Learning to read, for example, may be dependent on the pupil's maintaining good health. And the pupil's sense of his worth as a human being may be dependent on his ability to read. It is for these reasons that the short-range program suggested above includes at a minimum two widely different areas of pupil development.

C. Avoiding False Analogies

The term educational accountability, as used most recently by certain economists, systems analysts, and the like, has frequently been based on a conceptualization that tends, by analogy, to equate the educational process with the type of engineering process that applies to industrial production. It is this sort of analogy, for instance, that appears to underlie proposals for "guaranteed performance contracting" as exemplified in the much-publicized Texarkana project. The analogy is useful to a point. But there is also a point beyond which it can be so seriously misleading as to undermine any sensible efforts to develop objective criteria of professional accountability.

It must be constantly kept in mind that the educational process is *not* on all fours with an industrial process; it is a social process in which human beings are continually interacting with other human beings in ways that are imperfectly measurable or predictable. Education does not deal with inert raw materials, but with living minds that are instinctively concerned first with preserving their own integrity and second with reaching a meaningful accommodation with the world around them. The output of the educational process is never a "finished product" whose characteristics can be rigorously specified in advance; it is an individual who is sufficiently aware of his own incompleteness to make him want to keep on growing and learning and trying to solve the riddle of his own existence in a world that neither he nor anyone else can fully understand or predict.

It is for this reason that the problems involved in developing objective criteria of professional accountability will always be hard problems. They are problems, however, that must be tackled with all the human insight and goodwill that can be mustered if the schools of this urban society are to meet the large challenges that now confront them.

---

[1]Note the restriction of meaning of the term *input* as used here. It does *not* include such variables as per pupil expenditure, institutional effort, facilities, and the like.

[2]The problem presented by the movement of pupils from school to school is one that can be handled in various ways at the district level, but not at the level of the individual school. Therefore, it will not be discussed here. Under the present conception of staff accountability, it appears reasonable to assume that the only *fair* index of school effectiveness is one that rests on input output data obtained only on those pupils with whom the school staff has been in *continuous* contact over a specified period of months or years.

[3]It should be noted that this example does not include the important refinement that calls for assessing the schools' effectiveness for each of three levels of pupil input in reading.

[4]As rapidly as community acceptance was achieved, the system could be put on an annual basis and enlarged year by year to include more grades and more areas of pupil development.

ROBERT E. STAKE

Testing Hazards in
Performance Contracting

IN THE FIRST FEDERALLY SPONSORED EXAMPLE OF PERFORMANCE
contracting for the public schools, Dorsett Educational Systems of Nor-
man, Oklahoma, contracted to teach reading, mathematics, and study
skills to over 200 poor-performance junior and senior high school students
in Texarkana. Commercially available, standardized, general-achievement
tests were used to measure performance gains.

Are such tests suitable for measuring specific learnings? To the person
little acquainted with educational testing, it appears that performance testing is what educational tests are for. The testing specialist knows better.
General achievement tests have been developed to measure correlates of
learning, not learning itself.

Such tests are indirect measures of educational gains. They provide
correlates of achievement rather than direct evidence of achievement.
Correlation of these test scores with general learning is often high, but
such scores correlate only moderately with performance on many specific
educational tasks. Tests can be built to measure specific competence, but
there is relatively little demand for them. Many of those tests (often called
criterion-referenced tests) do a poor job of predicting later performance
of either a specific or a general nature. General achievement tests predict
better. The test developer's basis for improving tests has been to work

Robert E. Stake, "Testing Hazards in Performance Contracting." *Phi Delta
Kappan, 52*, 1971, 583–89. Reprinted by permission of the author and publisher.

toward better prediction of later performance rather than better measurement of present performance. Assessment of what a student is now capable of doing is not the purpose of most standardized tests. Errors and hazards abound, especially when these general achievement tests are used for performance contracting. Many of the hazards remain even with the use of criterion-referenced tests or any other performance observation procedures.

One of the hazards in performance contracting is that many high-priority educational objectives — for various reasons and in various ways — will be cast aside while massive attention is given to other high-priority objectives. This hazard is not unrelated to testing but will not be discussed here. This article will identify the major obstacles to gathering direct evidence of performance gain on targeted objectives.

ERRORS OF TESTING

Answering a *National School Board Journal* (November, 1970) questionnaire on performance contracting, a New Jersey board member said:

> Objectives must be stated in simple, understandable terms. No jargon will do and no subjective goals can be tolerated. Neither can the nonsense about there being some mystique that prohibits objective measurement of the educational endeavor.

Would that our problems withered before stern resolve. But neither wishing nor blustering rids educational testing of its errors.

Just as the population census and the bathroom scales have their errors, educational tests have theirs. The technology and theory of testing are highly sophisticated; the sources of error are well known.[1] Looking into the psychometrist's meaning of a theory of testing, one finds a consideration of ways to analyze and label the inaccuracies in test scores. There is a mystique, but there is also simple fact: No one can eliminate test errors. Unfortunately, some errors are large enough to cause wrong decisions about individual children or school district policy.

Some educators and social critics consider the whole idea of educational testing to be a mistake.[2] Unfortunate social consequences of testing, such as the perpetuation of racial discrimination[3] and pressures to cheat,[4] continue to be discussed. But, as expected, most test specialists believe that the promise in testing outweighs these perils. They refuse responsibility for gross misuse of their instruments and findings and concentrate on reducing the errors in tests and test programs.

Some technical errors in test scores are small and tolerable. But some testing errors are intolerably large. Today's tests can, for example, measure vocabulary word-recognition skills with sufficient accuracy. They cannot, however, adequately measure listening comprehension or the ability to analyze the opposing sides of an argument.

Contemporary test technology is not refined enough to meet all the demands. In performance contracting the first demand is for assessment of performance. Tests do their job well when the performance is highly specific — when, for example, the student is to add two numbers, recognize a misspelled word, or identify the parts of a hydraulic lift. When a teacher wants to measure performances that require more demanding mental processes, such as conceptualizing a writing principle or synthesizing a political argument, performance tests give us less dependable scores.[5]

Unreached potentials. Many educators believe that the most human of human gifts — the emotions, the higher thought processes, interpersonal sensitivity, moral sense — are beyond the reach of psychometric testing. Most test specialists disagree. While recognizing an ever-present error component, they believe that anything can be measured. The credo was framed by E. L. Thorndike in 1918: "Whatever exists at all exists in some amount." Testing men believe it still. They are not so naive as to think that any human gift will manifest itself in a 45-minute paper-and-pencil test. They do believe that, given ample opportunity to activate and observe the examinee, any trait, talent, or learning that manifests itself in behavior can be measured with reasonable accuracy. The total cost of measuring may be 100 times that of administering the usual tests, but they believe it can be done. The final observations may rely on professional judgment, but this could be reliable and validated judgment. A question for most test specialists, then, is not "Can complex educational outcomes be measured?" but "Can complex educational outcomes be measured with the time and personnel and facilities available?"

When it is most important to know whether or not a child is reading at age-level, we call in a reading specialist, who observes his reading habits. She might test him with word recognition, syntactic decoding, and paragraph-comprehension exercises. She would retest where evidence was inconclusive. She would talk to his teachers and his parents. She would arrive at a clinical description — which might be reducible to a statement such as "Yes, Johnny is reading at or above age-level."

The scores we get from group reading tests can be considered estimates of such an expert judgment. These objective test scores correlate positively with the more valid expert judgments. Such estimates are not direct measurements of what teachers or laymen mean by "ability to read," nor are they suitably accurate for diagnostic purposes. Achievement gains for a sizable number of students will be poorly estimated. It is possible that the errors in group testing are so extensive that — when fully known — businessmen and educators will refuse to accept them as bases for contract reimbursement.

Professional awareness. Classroom teachers and school principals have tolerated standardized test errors because they have not been obligated to make crucial decisions on the basis of test scores. Actually, in day-to-day practice they seldom use test scores.[6] When they do, they combine them with other knowledge to estimate a child's progress in school and to guide him into an appropriate learning experience. They do not use tests as a basis for assessing the quality of their own teaching.

In performance contracting, the situation is drastically changed; tests are honored as the sole basis for contract reimbursement. The district will pay the contractor for performance improvement. An error in testing means money misspent. Course completion and reimbursement decisions are to be made without reliance on the knowledge and judgment of a professional observer, without asking persons who are closest to the learning (the teacher, the contractor, and the student) whether or not they *see* evidence of learning. Decisions are to be made entirely by objective and independent testing. Numerous human errors and technical misrepresentations will occur.

WHICH TEST ITEMS?

It is often unrealistic to expect a project director to either find or create paper-and-pencil test items, administrable in an hour to large numbers of students by persons untrained in psychometric observation and standardized diagnostics, objectively scorable, valid for purposes of the performance contract, and readily interpretable. The more complex the training, the more unrealistic the expectation. One compromise is to substitute criterion test items measuring simple behaviors for those measuring the complex behaviors targeted by the training. For example, the director may substitute vocabulary-recognition test items for reading-comprehension items or knowledge of components for the actual dismantling of an engine. The substitution may be reasonable, but the criterion test should be validated against performances directly indicated by the objectives. It almost never has been. Without the validation the educator should be skeptical about what the test measures.

It always is unrealistic to expect that the payoff from instruction will be apparent in the performances of learners at test-taking time.[7] Most tests evoke relatively simple behavior. Ebel wrote:

> . . . most achievements tests . . . consist primarily of items testing specific elements of knowledge, facts, ideas, explanations, meanings, processes, relations, consequences, and so on.[8]

He went on to point out that more than simple recall is involved in answering even the simplest vocabulary item.

Much more complex behavior is needed for answering a reading-comprehension item. These items clearly call for more than the literal meanings of the words read. The student must paraphrase and interpret — what we expect readers to be able to do.

These items and ones for problem solving and the higher mental processes do measure high-priority school goals — but growth in such areas is relatively slow. Most contractors will not risk basing reimbursement on the small chance that evidence of growth will be revealed by *these* criterion tests. Some of the complex objectives of instruction will be underemphasized in the typical performance-contract testing plan.

The success of Texarkana's first performance-contract year is still being debated. Late winter (1969-70) test results looked good, but spring test results were disappointing.[9] Relatively simple performance items had been used. But the "debate" did not get into that. It started when the project's "outside evaluator" ruled that there had been direct coaching on most, if not all, of the criterion test items, which were known by the contractor during the school year. Critics claimed unethical "teaching for the test." The contractor claimed that both teaching and testing had been directed toward the same specific goals, as should be the case in a good performance contract. The issue is not only test choice and ethics; it includes the ultimate purpose of teaching.

Teaching for the test. Educators recognize an important difference between preparation for testing and direct coaching for a test. To prepare an examinee, the teacher teaches within the designated knowledge-skill domain and has the examinee practice good test-taking behavior (for example, don't spend too much time on overly difficult items; guess when you have an inkling though not full knowledge; organize your answer before writing an essay) so that relevant knowledge-skill is not obscured. Direct coaching teaches the examinees how to make correct responses to specific items on the criterion test.

This is an important difference when test items cover only a small sample of the universe of what has been taught or when test scores are correlates, rather than direct measurements, of criterion behavior. It ceases to be important when the test is set up to measure directly and thoroughly that which has been taught. In this case, teaching for the test is exactly what is wanted.

Joselyn pointed out that the performance contractor and the school should agree in advance on the criterion procedure, though not necessarily on the specific items.[10] To be fair to the contractor, the testing needs to be reasonably close to the teaching. To be fair to parents, the testing needs to be representative of the domain of abilities *they* are concerned about. A contract to develop reading skills would not be satisfied adequately by gains on a vocabulary test, according to the expectations of most teachers. All parties need to know how similar the testing will be to the actual teaching.

A dissimilarity scale. Unfortunately, as Anderson observed,[11] the test specialist has not developed scales for describing the similarity between teaching and testing. This is a grievous failing. Educators have no good way to indicate how closely the tests match the instruction.

There are many ways for criterion questions to be dissimilar. They can depart from the information taught by: 1) syntactic transformation; 2) semantic transformation; 3) change in content or medium; 4) application, considering the particular instance; 5) inference, generalizing from learned instances; and 6) implication, adding last-taught information to generally known information. For examples of some of these transformations, see Table I. Hively, Patterson, and Page,[12] Bormuth,[13] and Jackson[14] discussed procedures for using some of these tranformations to generate test items.

For any student the appropriateness of these items depends on prior and subsequent learning as well as on the thoroughness of teaching. Which items are appropriate will have to be decided at the scene. The least and most dissimilar item might be quite different in their appropriateness. The reading-comprehension items of any standardized achievement battery are likely to be more dissimilar to the teaching of reading than any of the "dissimilarities" shown in Table I. Immediate instruction is not properly evaluated by highly dissimilar items, nor is scholarship properly evaluated by highly similar items. Even within the confines of performance contracting, both evaluations are needed.

TABLE I. *An example of transformations of information taught into test questions.*

Information taught:	Pt. Barrow is the northernmost town in Alaska.
Minimum transformation question:	What is the northernmost town in Alaska?
Semantic-syntactic transformation question:	What distinction does Pt. Barrow have among Alaskan villages?
Context-medium transformation question:	The dots on the adjacent map represent Alaskan cities and towns. One represents Pt. Barrow. Which one?
Implication questions:	What would be unusual about summer sunsets in Pt. Barrow, Alaska?

For the evaluation of instruction, a large number of test items are needed for each objective that — in the opinion of the teachers — directly measure increase in skill or understanding. Items from standardized tests, if used, would be included item by item. For each objective, the item pool would cover all aspects of the objective. A separate sample of items would be drawn for the pretest and posttest for each student, and instructional success would be based on the collective gain of all students.

Creating such a pool of relevant, psychometrically sound test items is a major — but necessary — undertaking.[15] It is a partial safeguard against the use of inappropriate criteria to evaluate the success of instruction.

WHAT THE SCORES MEAN

At first, performance contracting seemed almost a haven for the misinterpretation of scores. Contracts have ignored 1) the practice effect of pretesting,[16] 2) the origins of grade equivalents, 3) the "learning calendar," 4) the unreliability of gain scores, and 5) regression effects. Achievement may be spurious. Ignoring any one of these five is an invitation to misjudge the worth of the instruction.

Grade-equivalent scores. Standardized achievement tests have the appealing feature of yielding grade-equivalent scores. Each raw score, usually the number of items right, has been translated into a score indicating (for a student population forming a national reference group) the average grade placement of all students who got this raw score. These new scores are called "grade equivalents." Raw scores are not very meaningful to people unacquainted with the particular test; the grade equivalents are widely accepted by teachers and parents. Grade equivalents are common terminology in performance contracts.

Unfortunately, grade equivalents are available from most publishers only for tests, not for test items. Thus the whole test needs to be used, in the way prescribed in its manual, if the grade equivalents are to mean what they are supposed to mean. One problem of using whole tests was discussed in the previous section. Another problem is that the average annual "growth" on most standardized tests is only a few raw-score points. Consider in Table II the difference between a grade equivalent of 5.0 and 6.0 within four of the most popular test batteries.

Most teachers do not like to have their year's work summarized by so little change in performance. Schools writing performance contracts perhaps should be reluctant to sign contracts for which the distinction between success and failure is so small. But to do so requires the abandonment of grade equivalents.

TABLE II. *Gain in items right needed to advance one grade equivalent on four typical achievement tests.*

	Grade equivalent 5.0	6.0	Needed for an improvement of one grade equivalent
Comprehensive Test of Basic Skills, Level 3: Reading Comprehension	20	23	3 items
Metropolitan Achievement Test, Intermediate Form B: Spelling	24	31	7 items
Iowa Test of Basic Skills, Test A1: Arithmetic Concepts	10	14	4 items
Stanford Achievement Test, Form W, Intermediate II: Word Meaning	18	26	8 items

The learning calendar. For most special instructional programs, criterion tests will be administered at the beginning of and immediately following instruction, often in the first and last weeks of school. A great deal of distraction occurs during those weeks, but other times for pretesting and posttesting have their hazards, too. Recording progress every few weeks during the year is psychometrically preferred, but most teachers are opposed to "all that testing."

Children learn year-round, but the evidence of learning that gets inked on pupil records comes in irregular increments from season to season. Winter is the time of most rapid advancement, summer the least. Summer, in fact, is a period of setback for many youngsters. Beggs and Hieronymus found punctuation scores to spurt more than a year between October and April but to drop almost half a year between May and September.[17] Discussing their reading test, Gates and MacGinitie wrote:

> ... in most cases, scores will be higher at the end of one grade than at the beginning of the next. That is, there is typically some loss of reading skill during the summer, especially in the lower grades.[18]

The first month or two after students return to school in the fall is the time for getting things organized and restoring scholastic abilities lost during the summer. According to some records, spring instruction competes poorly with other attractions. Thus, the learning year is a lopsided year, a basis sometimes for miscalculation. Consider the results of testing shown in Table III.

TABLE III. *Learning calendar for a typical fifth-grade class.*

	S	O	N	D	J	F	M	A	M
Mean achievement score	5.0		5.3		5.6		5.9	6.2	6.3

The six-week averages in Table III are fictitious, but they represent test performance in many classrooms. The mean growth for the year appears to be 1.3 grade equivalents. No acknowledgement is made that standardized test results in early September were poorer than those for the previous spring. For this example, the previous May mean (not shown) was 5.2. The real gain, then, for the year is 1.1 grade equivalents rather than the apparent 1.3. It would be inappropriate to pay the contractor for a mean gain of 1.3.

Another possible overpayment on the contract can result by holding final testing early and extrapolating the previous per-week growth to the weeks or months that follow. In Texarkana, as in most schools, spring progress was not as good as winter. If an accurate evaluation of contract instructional services is to be made, repeated testing, perhaps a month-by-month record of learning performances, needs to be considered.[19]

Unreliable gain scores. Most performance contracts pay off on an individual student basis. The contractor may be paid for each student who gains more than an otherwise expected amount. This practice is commendable in that it emphasizes the importance of each individual learner and makes the contract easier to understand, but it bases payment on a precarious mark: the gain score.

Just how unreliable is the performance-test gain score? For a typical standardized achievement test with two parallel forms, A and B, we might find the following characteristics reported in the test's technical manual:

Reliability of Test A $= +.84$.
Reliability of Test B $= +.84$.
Correlation of Test A with Test B $= +.81$.

Almost all standardized tests have reliability coefficients at this level. Using the standard formula,[20] one finds a disappointing level of reliability for the measurement of improvement:

Reliability of gain scores (A-B or B-A) $= +.16$.

The test manual indicates the raw score and grade-equivalent standard deviations. For one widely used test, they are 9.5 items and 2.7 years, respectively. Using these values we can calculate the errors to be expected. *On the average,* a student's raw score would be in error by 2.5 items, grade equivalent would be in error by 0.72 years, and grade-equivalent *gain score* would be in error by 1.01 years. The error is indeed large.

Consider what this means for the not unusual contract whereby the student is graduated from the program, and the contractor is paid for his instruction, on any occasion that his performance score rises above a set value. Suppose — with the figures above — the student exits when his improvement is one grade equivalent or more. Suppose also, to make this situation simpler, that there is *no* intervening training and that the student is not influenced by previous testing. Here are three ways of looking at the same situation:

> Suppose that a contract student takes a different parallel form of the criterion test on three successive days immediately following the pretest. The chances are better than 50-50 that on *one* of these tests the student will gain a year or more in performance and appear to be ready to graduate from the program.
>
> Suppose that three students are tested with a parallel form immediately after the pretest. The chances are better than 50-50 that one of the three students — entirely due to errors of measurement — will gain a year or more and appear ready to graduate.
>
> Suppose that 100 students are admitted to contract instruction and pretested. After a period of time involving no training, they are tested again, and the students gaining a year are graduated. After another period of time, another test and another graduation. After the fourth terminal testing, even though no instruction has occured, the chances are better than 50-50 that two-thirds of the students will be graduated.

In other words, owing to unreliability, gain scores can appear to reflect learning that actually does not occur.

The unreliability will give an equal number of false impressions of deteriorating performance. These errors (false gains and false losses) will balance out for a large group of students. If penalties for losses are paid by the contractor at the rate bonuses are paid for gains, the contractor will not be overpaid. But according to the way contracts are being written, typified in the examples above, the error in the gain scores does not balance out; it works in favor of the contractor. Measurement errors could be capitalized upon by unscrupulous promoters. Appropriate checks against these errors are built into the better contracts.

Errors in individual gain scores can be reduced by using longer tests. A better way to indicate true gain is to calculate the discrepancy between actual and expected final performances.[21] Expectations can be based on the group as a whole or on an outside control group. Another way is to write the contract on the basis of mean scores for the group of students.[22] Corrections for the unreliability of gain scores are possible, but they are not likely to be considered if the educators and contractors are statistically naive.

Regression effects. Probably the source of the greatest misinterpretation of the effects of remedial instruction is regression effects. Regression effects are easily overlooked but need not be; they are correctable. For any pretest score, the expected regression effect can be calculated. Regression effects make the poorest scorers look better the next time tested. Whether measurements are error-laden or error-free, meaningful or meaningless, when there is differential change between one measurement occasion and another (when there is less-than-perfect correlation), the lowest original scorers will make the greatest gains and the highest scorers will make the least. On the average, posttest scores will, relative to their corresponding pretest scores, lie in the direction of the mean. This is the regression effect. Lord discussed this universal phenomenon and various ways to correct for it.[23]

The demand for performance contracts has occurred where conventional instructional programs fail to develop — for a sizable number of students — minimum competence in basic skills. Given a distribution of skill test scores, the lowest-scoring students — the ones most needing assistance — are identified. It is reasonable to suppose that under unchanged instructional programs they would drop even farther behind the high-scoring students. If a retest is given, however, after any period of instruction (conventional or special) or of no instruction, these students will no longer be the poorest performers. Some of them will be replaced by others who appear to be most in need of special instruction. Instruction is not the obvious influence here — regression is. The regression effect is not due to test unreliability, but it causes some of the same misinterpretations. The contract should read that instruction will be reimbursed when gain exceeds that attributable to regression effects. The preferred evaluation design would call for control group(s) of similar students to provide a good estimate of the progress the contract students would have made in the absence of the special instruction.

THE SOCIAL PROGRESS

The hazards of specific performance testing and performance contracting are more than curricular and psychometric. Social and humanistic challenges should be raised, too. The teacher has a special opportunity and obligation to observe the influence of testing on social behavior.

Performance contracting has the unique ability to put the student in a position of administrative influence. He can make the instruction appear better or worse than it actually is by his performance on tests. Even if he is quite young, the student will know that his good work will benefit the contractor. Sooner or later he is going to know that, if he tests poorly at the beginning, he can benefit himself and the contractor through his later achievement. Bad performances are in his repertoire, and he may be more anxious to make the contractor look bad than to make himself look good. Or he may be under undue pressure to do well on the posttests. These are pupil-teacher interactions that should be watched carefully. More responsibility for school control possibly should accrue to students, but performance contracts seem a devious way to give it.

To motivate the student to learn and to make him want more contract instruction, many contractors use material or opportunity-to-play rewards. (Dorsett used such merchandise as transistor radios.) Other behavior modification strategies are common. The proponents of such strategies argue that, once behavior has been oriented to appropriate tasks, the students can gradually be shifted from extrinsic rewards to intrinsic. That they *can* be shifted is probably true; that it will happen without careful, deliberate work by the instructional staff is unlikely. It is not difficult to imagine a performance-contract situation in which the students become even less responsive to the rewards of conventional instruction.

In mid-1971, performance contracting appears to be popular with the current administration in Washington because it encourages private businesses to participate in a traditionally public responsibility. It is popular among some school administrators because it affords new access to federal funds, because it is a way to get new talent working on old problems, and because the administrator can easily blame the outside agency and the government if the contract instruction is unsuccessful. It is unpopular with the American Federation of Teachers because it reduces the control the union has over school operations, and it reduces the teacher's role as a chooser of what learning students need most. Performance contracting is popular among most instructional technologists because it is based on well-researched principles of teaching and because it enhances their role in school operations.

The accountability movement as a whole is likely to be a success or failure on such sociopolitical items. The measurement of the performance of performance contracting is an even more hazardous procedure than the measurement of student performances.

SUMMARY

Without yielding to the temptation to undercut new efforts to provide instruction, educators should continue to be apprehensive about evaluating teaching on the basis of performance testing alone. They should know how difficult it is to represent educational goals with statements of

66 *The Teaching Profession*

objectives and how costly it is to provide suitable criterion testing. They should know that the common-sense interpretation of these results is frequently wrong. Still, many members of the profession think that evaluation controls are extravagant and mystical.

Performance contracting has emerged because people inside and outside the schools are dissatisfied with the instruction some children are getting. Implicit in the contracts is the expectation that available tests can measure the newly promised learning. The standardized test alone cannot measure the specific outcomes of an individual student with sufficient precision.

NOTES AND REFERENCES

[1]Frederick M. Lord and Melvin R. Novick, *Statistical Theories of Mental Test Scores*. Reading, Mass.: Addison-Wesley, 1968.

[2]Banesh Hoffman, *The Tyranny of Testing*. New York: Collier Books, 1962; and Theodore R. Sizer, "Social Change and the Uses of Educational Testing: An Historical View," paper presented at the Invitational Conference on Testing Problems, New York, October, 1970.

[3]David A. Goslin, "Ethical and Legal Aspects of the Collection and Use of Educational Information," paper presented at the Invitational Conference on Testing Problems. New York, October, 1970.

[4]Barry R. McGhan, "Accountability as a Negative Reinforcer," *American Teacher*, November, 1970, p. 13.

[5]Benjamin S. Bloom *et al.*, *A Taxonomy of Educational Objectives: Handbook I, the Cognitive Domain*. New York: McKay, 1956.

[6]J. Thomas Hastings, Philip J. Runkel, and Dora E. Damrin, *Effects on Use of Tests by Teachers Trained in a Summer Institute*, Cooperative Research Project No. 702. Urbana, Ill.: Bureau of Educational Research, College of Education, University of Illinois, 1961.

[7]Harry S. Broudy, "Can Research Escape the Dogma of Behavioral Objectives?," *School Review*, November, 1970, pp. 43-56.

[8]Robert L. Ebel, "When Information Becomes Knowledge," *Science*, January, 1971, pp. 130-31.

[9]Dean C. Andrew and Lawrence H. Roberts, "Final Evaluation Report on the Texarkana Dropout Prevention Program." Magnolia, Arkansas: Region VIII, Education Service Center, July 20, 1970 (mimeo). Commentaries on this report include Henry S. Dyer, "Performance Contracting: Too Simple a Solution for Difficult Problems," *The United Teacher*, November 29, 1970, pp. 19-22; and Roger T. Lennon, "Accountability and Performance Contracting," paper presented at the annual meeting of the American Educational Research Association, New York, February, 1971 .

[10]E. Gary Joselyn, "Performance Contracting: What It's All About," paper presented at the Truth and Soul in Teaching Conference of the American Federation of Teachers, Chicago, January, 1971.

[11]Richard C. Anderson, "Comments on Professor Gagne's Paper," in *The Evaluation of Instruction*, ed. M. C. Wittrock and David E. Wiley. New York: Holt, Rinehart and Winston, 1970, pp. 126-33.

[12]Wells Hively II, Harry L. Patterson, and Sara H. Page, "A 'Universe-Defined' System of Arithmetic Achievement Tests," *Journal of Educational Measurement*, Winter, 1968, pp. 275-90.

[13]John Bormuth, *On the Theory of Achievement Test Items.* Chicago: University of Chicago Press, 1970.

[14]Rex Jackson, *Developing Criterion-Referenced Tests.* Princeton, N.J.: ERIC Clearing House on Tests, Measurement, and Evaluation, Educational Testing Service, June, 1970.

[15]Dorsett indicated the desirability of such an item pool in the original Texarkana proposal.

[16]Not discussed here because of space limitations.

[17]Donald L. Beggs and Albert N. Hieronymus, "Uniformity of Growth in the Basic Skills Throughout the School Year and During the Summer," *Journal of Educational Measurement,* Summer, 1968, pp. 91-97.

[18]Arthur I. Gates and Walter H. MacGinitie, *Technical Manual for the Gates-MacGinitie Reading Tests.* New York: Teachers College Press, Columbia University, 1965, p. 5.

[19]L. Wrightman and W. P. Gorth, "CAM: The New Look in Classroom Testing," *Trend,* Spring, 1969, pp. 56-57. Project CAM is described as a model for a continuous (perhaps biweekly) monitoring and recording of classroom performance.

[20]Robert L. Thorndike and Elizabeth Hagen, *Measurement and Evaluation in Psychology and Education,* 3rd ed. New York: Wiley, 1969, p. 197.

[21]Ledyard R. Tucker, Fred Damarin, and Samuel Messick, *A Base-Free Measure of Change,* Research Bulletin RB-65-16. Princeton, N.J.: Educational Testing Service, 1965. This is a discussion of change scores that are independent of and dependent on the initial standing of the learning. A learning curve fitted to test scores could be used to counter the unreliability of individual scores.

[22]This would have the increased advantage of discouraging the contractor from giving preferential treatment within the project to students who are in a position to make high payoff gains.

[23]Frederic M. Lord, "Elementary Models for Measuring Change," in *Problems in Measuring Change,* ed. Chester W. Harris. Madison, Wis.: University of Wisconsin Press, 1963, pp. 21-38.

PART II

Historical
Foundations

Where are we going, where *should* we be going, in education?
By what means should we arrive at our destination? These
frequently asked questions are clear evidence of the current
concern over the future of American education. But before
the full import of these questions can be ascertained—
much less their answers—there are antecedent questions to
be considered: Where has American education been?
What forces shaped this country's modern educational
system? The study of the historical foundations of education
is an important means of orienting the teacher to the
traditions of the past and the possibilities of the future of
American education. To determine what the role of education
should be in a democratic society, we must first discover
what it has been; only then will our answers to the above

questions be complete enough to permit meaningful educational change. The following selections point up some of the purposes of educational history.

R. Freeman Butts' article offers "The Story of American Education." He sees educational history unfolding in terms of man's search for freedom, taking a distinctive form in each of the eras in American history: the colonial period (1600–1770's); the republican period (1770's–1870's); and the democratic period (1870's–1960's). From Butts' historical perspective, we see American education as it struggled through almost four centuries in quest of freedom, both for itself and for free men in a free society. But the most significant observation of Butts' work is that the search for freedom, and its role in American education, is an ongoing process, and as we see it at work in the past we may appreciate its role in the present and future structure of our schools.

An historical account of one very important educational movement is given by Lawrence A. Cremin in his article on the relation of John Dewey to the progressive education movement. Here Cremin provides some insights into the ebb and flow of educational movements in general, and the rise and fall of the progressive education movement in particular. The critics of this phenomenon in the history of American education have been quite emotional, creating in the minds of many Americans a caricature of this educational theory. To put progressivism into its proper historical perspective, to show it to be the complex social phenomenon that it was, is the essential contribution of Cremin's work. In addition, Professor Cremin takes a hard look at John Dewey's contribution to the progressive education movement — and his opposition to it, a circumstance generally ignored by his critics. The implication is clear: before educators can learn from past successes and failures, they must first see them in proper historical perspective.

James S. Coleman then offers an analysis of educational opportunity in the United States and of the attendant theory of equality that the reality of opportunity represents. He notes a radical shift in the concept of equality of educational opportunity in the United States over the past one hundred and fifty years. With the perspective of history to aid us, we may come to an understanding of one of the most pressing social and educational issues of our day, to a realization of the uses to which we have put our educational institutions in the past, and perhaps to an illumination of the kind of society our schools will be helping to make in the future.

Finally, Henry Steele Commager takes a look at the association between the international community and education in the United States. He expresses deep concern over recent trends in education. These trends are characterized by a shift in curriculum contents toward problems and issues which are specific in nature, of immediate concern, and whose relevance is local. This fails to develop in the individual those outlooks and experiences which prepare him to relate in an empathetic and intelligent way to problems and issues of the international community. In short, the present educational trends seem to be producing an increased parochialism rather than the broader range of understandings we so desperately need today. We must prepare the youth in the style of the founding fathers of our country. This means that education should emphasize the universal, permanent, and philosophical aspects of problems and issues. The alternative approach to education, the one now dominant, has already distinguished itself by its glaring failures.

R. FREEMAN BUTTS

Search for Freedom:
The Story of
American Education

THE STORY OF AMERICAN EDUCATION NEEDS CONSTANT RETELLING. IT is a story that few of us know well enough. Yet, education directly involves more than one-half of all Americans and indirectly affects the lives, welfare, security, and freedom of everyone. Students, teachers, and other citizens cannot afford to ignore it.

Fortunately, most Americans have faith in education and believe that educated young people are better equipped to "get ahead" in the world than uneducated ones are. However, the really important reason for believing in the value of education is that it can be the foundation of freedom. In the first place, a truly democratic society must rest upon the knowledge, intelligence, and wisdom of all the people. Without the proper kind of education available to everyone, a free society cannot long endure. Therefore, all people must have the kind of education that will fit them for freedom as responsible citizens.

In the second place, without the proper kind of education, the individual will not be able to develop his own powers as a person. He will not be able to give direction to his own action and thought as he may wish. He will not be able to decide wisely for himself what he should do or think.

Freedom from arbitrary restraint, from compulsion, or from tyranny is essential for the free man, but that alone is not enough. If each person

R. Freeman Butts, "Search for Freedom: The Story of American Education." *NEA Journal, 50*, 1960, 33–48. Reprinted by permission of the author and publisher.

is to achieve the genuine freedom of self-direction and self-fulfillment, he must have an education befitting a free man.

Now, what kind of education will best develop the free citizen and the free person? This is the persistent question that runs through the story of American education. It has been answered in different ways at different times in our history. It is still being debated vigorously, and sometimes angrily, today.

This question is so important that every American — and above all, every student and teacher — should make it his business to learn all he can about it. The first requirement is a knowledge of the history of American education. Here are some of the fundamental questions that mark the highlights of the story:

1. What kind of schools and colleges will promote maximum freedom in society? To what extent should a free society encourage public schools in contrast to private schools? Is freedom better served by religious schools or by secular schools? Is a free society better served by local control or by central control of schools? Should a free society maintain common schools and colleges open equally to all, or should it divide students into separate schools and colleges according to their race, religion, social class, prospective vocation, or intellectual ability?

2. What kind of educational program will promote maximum freedom for all individuals? Should schools and colleges stress practical training or purely intellectual studies? Should schools and colleges offer students preparation for many vocations or for just a few? Should educational methods stress learning by direct experience or by reading books? Should a liberal education be designed for the few or for the many?

If we can understand some of the major answers given to these questions during our history, we shall be on the way to understanding the central idea of American education.

I. EDUCATION UNDER COLONIAL RULE
(1600 to 1770's)

For nearly 175 years, the source of governmental authority for the American colonies was the crown and parliament of England. The colonists were, however, ruled locally by legislative assemblies or by individual proprietors or by royal governors who received their authority from the English government in London.

This authority included jurisdiction over education. From the very beginning of American history, education was a function of government. It continued to be so after the states were independent.

The various colonies, however, handled educational matters differently. In the New England colonies, the governing bodies not only exerted general authority over education but also established, supported, and directly administered their own schools.

For example, the colonial legislature of Massachusetts passed a law founding Harvard College in 1636; in the following years it took hundreds of actions concerning the college. In the 1630's, the governments of several towns in New England established schools under their direct jurisdiction and supervision.

In 1642 the colonial legislature of Massachusetts passed a general educational law applying to all parts of the colony. It required all parents to see that their children were taught to read, learn the major laws, know the catechism, and learn a trade. It authorized and required the town officials to see that parents obeyed the law and to levy fines upon those parents who disobeyed.

In 1647 the Massachusetts legislature passed a second law, this time requiring all towns of fifty or more families to appoint a teacher and permitting the towns to pay him out of public taxes if the people so voted. Such a teacher was to teach reading and writing. (We would call him an elementary-school teacher.) Furthermore, the law of 1647 required towns of one hundred or more families to appoint a teacher of Latin grammar. (We would call him a secondary-school teacher.)

The New England version of state authority in education came to this: The colonial government could require parents to have their children educated; the central government of the colony could require local towns to appoint teachers (establish schools); public funds could be raised by taxation to pay the teachers; and public teachers were subject to direct supervision and control by governmental authorities (either the town meeting as a whole or the selectmen or the education committee).

In the Southern colonies the colonial governments had the same legal authority to legislate on educational matters, but they did not pass laws requiring *all* children to be educated. They rather assumed, as in England, that any parent who could afford to educate his own children should do so by making individual arrangements with a private tutor or by sending them to a private school.

The Southern legislatures, however, did pass laws requiring that poor children and orphaned children be apprenticed to a trade and taught the rudiments of reading and religion by their masters.

The governmental attention in the South was directed mainly at lower-class underprivileged children who had no parents or whose parents could not care for them. Even so, the parish or county governments sometimes legislated on educational matters through their boards of vestrymen or magistrates.

Some efforts were even made in the colonial legislatures of Maryland, South Carolina, and Virginia to establish colony-wide systems of public schools. These were unsuccessful, not because there was no governmental authority for education, but because the people at that time did not believe they were necessary.

In the Middle Colonies the same governmental authority was used by the Dutch to establish public schools in New Netherland and by the Quakers in Pennsylvania. But a more tolerant policy toward religion had attracted several different religious denominations to these colonies.

Each group wanted its own religious principles taught in its own school. It was consequently more difficult to teach a single religious outlook in a public school open to children of different faiths than it had been in New England where most people were Congregationalists or in the South where most people were Anglicans.

In the eighteenth century the colonial governments began to permit the different religious groups to establish their own schools in which they could teach their own religious doctrines and their own languages (whether German, Dutch, French, or Swedish). In this way the state gave to religious and charitable bodies the right to conduct schools.

In like manner the colonial governments began to grant charters to small groups of businessmen or landowners. An educational charter gave these groups the right to incorporate as a board of trustees. They could then buy land, build buildings, appoint teachers, and generally manage a school.

Some of these corporate schools came to be known as "academies." One of the most famous was the Philadelphia Academy founded in 1751 by Benjamin Franklin. Others were the Newark Academy in Delaware, the Washington Academy in New Jersey, and the Dummer Academy and Phillips Academy in Massachusetts.

These incorporated academies made education attractive and available to children of middle-class merchants who could afford the tuition. At first it was unclear whether these denominational schools and incorporated academies were public or private schools, but eventually they came to be known as "private" schools in American terminology.

Other private schools were run by individual teachers as profit-making, business enterprises. In the seacoast cities of the eighteenth century these private teachers began to give young people direct preparation for jobs in commerce and trade. In general, the private-school teacher accepted or rejected students as he pleased. He charged what fees he could get, and he managed his affairs as he saw fit — so long as he had enough students to stay in business.

By contrast, the "public" school in the eighteenth century was a non-profit school under the supervision of a governmental agency or a corporate board of control. The parents had the right to send their children to it; the governing body set the fees and employed the teacher. Hence a "public" school was not run for the teacher's private profit.

The standards of curriculum were established and the achievement of pupils evaluated by the board of control, whether governmental or corporate. Later on, the corporate school came to be known as a "private" school, because it was not operated directly by a governmental board.

In the seventeenth century the "public" or town schools of Massachusetts, Connecticut, and New Hampshire taught the doctrines of a specific religion, that is, Congregational Calvinism. This was so because the Congregational church was established by the law of the legislature in those colonies.

This practice, known as "an establishment of religion," was common throughout Europe in the sixteenth and seventeenth centuries. The laws of the state required all people to accept the doctrines and rituals of the established church and authorized punishment for those who objected. The law levied taxes on everyone to support the ministers of the established church or churches. The Church of England, for example, was the established church in several of the Southern colonies; therefore, orthodox Anglicanism was taught in their schools.

But in the course of the eighteenth century, the idea of religious freedom gained great headway in the American colonies. This meant that such minority religious groups as Quakers, Presbyterians, Baptists, Dutch Reformed, Lutherans, Methodists, Mennonites, and others gained freedom to worship as they pleased. As a result, such groups did not wish to send their children to town schools where their children would be obliged to accept a religion in which they did not believe. The established churches would not at first consent to the removal of their religion from the public schools.

The solution in the eighteenth century was to permit the minority religious groups to establish their own schools. This meant that private religious schools could operate alongside the public schools. Although the public schools were weakened, this arrangement contributed to freedom at a time when the majority religious groups insisted that the public schools teach *their* religion and *only* their religion.

A few voices began to argue that if public schools did *not* teach a sectarian religion then all children could attend them freely. This was argued by William Smith in Pennsylvania, by William Livingston in New York, and by Thomas Jefferson in Virginia.

But the time was not yet ripe for such a solution. Although it was a gain for freedom to permit people to pursue their own way in religion and education, most people were not yet convinced that *others* should have the same freedoms *they* had. Nor were they convinced that an education separated from specific religious doctrines was desirable. The search for freedom continued.

Meanwhile, as people moved out of the New England towns and cities into the unsettled lands of the country, they could no longer send their children long distances back to the town schools. They therefore began to set up their own local schools. This was the origin of the "district" school.

Representing the ultimate in local control, the district system reflected a decline in central state control of schools as the eighteenth century came to a close. This system had the advantage that it kept the schools close to the people, but it had the disadvantage that some districts ran low-quality schools or none at all. Local control was no guarantee that the quality of schools would be uniformly high.

At the end of colonial rule, common schools in which children of different religions or races learned together were still the exception. It was generally felt that schools should perpetuate the religious or cultural beliefs of the sponsoring agency. Some groups did go so far as to try to set up schools for Indians. Few but Quakers tried to do so for Negroes.

Seldom was it argued in colonial times that the aim of education was to empower every individual to make the most of himself as a person. The first system of education set up in America served to maintain the class distinctions imported from Europe.

Children of poor, lower-class parents had no education at all or were bound out as apprentices to learn a trade. Children of upper-class parents (public officials, clergymen, wealthy landowners) were expected to have an education appropriate to their station in life. The New England colonies broke this pattern somewhat when they required the towns to provide a minimum amount of education for *all* children.

Not all children actually received an education, but the principle was established that a commonwealth must rest upon an educated citizenry even if the education amounted only to bare literacy. Added to this was the Protestant belief that all adherents to the true faith should be able to read the Bible for themselves so that they could know the grounds and reasons for their faith. In any case, the New England town schools went a long way in seeing that a large number of their children received some education. This was the first step toward an education for freedom.

Learning to read, write, recite the catechism, and possibly do some arithmetic was the essence of a beginning or elementary education. In the earliest days, school books were rare and materials were scarce. A common device for teaching reading was a hornbook, a piece of wood with the alphabet and Lord's Prayer on it. The child could carry this around with him until he had learned everything on it.

Somewhat later in the seventeenth century, books began to be used; the most famous was *The New England Primer*. This consisted of the alphabet, simple syllables, words, sentences, and stories, all of a religious and moral character. A child may have spent two or three years obtaining this kind of elementary education. Taking the thirteen colonies as a whole, probably only one child in ten went to school at all.

What we would call secondary education was offered in Latin grammar schools. The immediate reason for stress on Latin was that Harvard College required it for admission because the main bodies of knowledge throughout Europe since the days of the Roman Republic and the Roman Empire had been written in Latin.

Even though the common languages of the people (vernaculars) were being used more widely by the sixteenth and seventeenth centuries, it was still the custom for an educated person to know Latin — and some Greek, if possible.

So the Latin grammar school was designed to prepare sons of the privileged classes for college in order that they might eventually enter one of the "higher" professions, such as the ministry, law, medicine, teaching, or simply that of "gentleman." Relatively few in the total population were expected to attain these callings in life. Most were expected to be tradesmen, farmers, workers, mechanics, or servants. For these an elementary education was considered sufficient — or even more than necessary.

In the course of the eighteenth century, however, cities and towns grew rapidly in size, trade and commerce increased, immigration rose, and goods and services were much more in demand than in the seventeenth century.

The cry was heard that the old classical Latin education was no longer appropriate for preparing young people to engage in these new important occupations of making goods, distributing them, and selling them. Education, some said, should become more practical, not solely intellectual or literary.

Two types of intermediate or secondary schools tried to meet this need. Some were "English" schools, so called because they were taught in English rather than in Latin. The instructors tried to offer whatever studies the young people desired, for example, English language; French, German, Spanish, Italian (languages useful for trade); mathematics (useful for navigation and surveying); commercial arithmetic and bookkeeping (useful in business); geography, history, and drawing (useful for leisure).

In the early decades of the eighteenth century these private-venture schools responded to the needs of the growing middle classes (merchants and tradesmen). They gave an education directly aimed at occupations other than the learned professions, and they catered to girls as well as to boys.

A second type of practical school was the academy, which was usually residential and often under the auspices of a religious denomination or a nonsectarian board of control. The curriculum of these schools, at least as proposed by Benjamin Franklin, was likely to be much broader than that of the Latin grammar school. It might include geography, history, science, modern languages, and the arts and music, as well as the classical languages and mathematics.

Both of these types of schools contributed to freedom by increasing the range of occupations for which they gave preparation. In this way an increasing number of young people from all social classes could gain a larger measure of self-direction and improve their position in society. Both types of schools were frowned upon by the classicists, but the academy survived the opposition because it met the needs of the middle classes. It eventually drove the Latin grammar school out of existence.

Meanwhile, the opportunities for college education were expanding. Eight colleges besides Harvard were founded prior to the Revolutionary War. Most of them reflected specific denominational outlooks, and their courses of study were largely linguistic, mathematical and bookish.

Some outstanding leaders tried to change the character of college studies by stressing the new sciences and social sciences. Among these were William Smith at the College of Philadelphia, William Livingston and Samuel Johnson at the founding of Kings College (Columbia), and Thomas Jefferson at the College of William and Mary.

But the tradition of classical studies supported by religious discipline was too strong for these reformers. Harvard (1636), Yale (1701), and Dartmouth (1769) remained Congregational in outlook; William and Mary (1693) and Columbia (1754), Anglican; Princeton (1746), Presbyterian; Brown (1764), Baptist; and Rutgers (1766), Dutch Reformed. The College at Philadelphia, the only college to be nondenominational at the outset (1755), was a forecast of the future, but it soon came under Anglican domination.

In general, then, the colonial period saw gains for freedom in the growth of representative government, the spread of religious freedom, and the rise of energetic middle classes of free men in town and country alike. Education tried to respond to these social movements as well as to a growing liberalism in thought and belief.

At the beginning of the colonial period, orthodoxies in theology, philosophy, and politics dominated the schools. Children were looked upon as sinful creatures who could be ruled only by harsh discipline, fear, and unrelenting obedience. By the end of the period, a growing liberalism meant that, here and there, children and adults alike were treated more humanely and less brutally. Human dignity and respect for persons were safer than they had been.

During most of the colonial period, education for developing a free person moved slowly and haltingly. For the most part, education at all levels was concerned as much with moral training as with intellectual training. If anything, the moral was considered more important and closely bound up with orthodox religion. Teachers were expected to conform in their beliefs to the dictates of whatever group controlled the schools. It was seldom argued that the teacher had a claim to freedom of teaching as an essential characteristic of a free society, a claim to deal freely with ideas even though they might be distasteful to the immediate managers of the school.

The founding of nine colleges of liberal arts in the thirteen colonies was a remarkable achievement by men who would be free, but the dominant view was definitely that a liberal education (and thus the educational basis for freedom) was for the few, not for the many. There was reluctance to expand the range of liberal studies beyond the traditional classics, mathematics, and philosophy, even though the explosion of knowledge was already beginning to crackle and pop in the seventeenth and eighteenth centuries.

The notion that education had a clear responsibility for enabling each individual to develop himself to the utmost was beginning to be stated but was not yet widely accepted. Building schools for a colonial society prior to the Revolutionary War was a dress rehearsal for freedom, not the main performance.

II. A CENTURY OF REPUBLICAN EDUCATION
(1770's to 1870's)

From the 1770's to the 1870's, Americans planned, built, changed, argued, and fought over the kinds of free institutions that should replace colonial rule. One of these institutions was education. As they set up and operated a republican form of government dedicated to equality, democracy, and freedom, they found that they needed an educational system appropriate to such a government.

In many different ways they said that if a republican government — or society — were to prosper and endure, then the people who elected the government, held office, made laws, enforced laws, and consented to be ruled must be educated as responsible citizens.

James Madison, father of the Constitution and author of the Bill of Rights, put it this way:

"A popular Government, without popular information, or the means of acquiring it, is but a Prologue to a Farce or Tragedy; or, perhaps both. Knowledge will forever govern ignorance; and a people who mean to be their own Governors must arm themselves with the power which knowledge gives."

But this was not easy to do. The people who had won the Revolutionary War — these so-called Americans — were not really Americans, at least *not yet*. They were English, Scottish, French, German, Dutch, Swedish, and a good many more. And they were soon to be Irish, Italian, Hungarian, Polish, and Russian as well. They spoke different languages and they had different customs. Some had no tradition of self-government and others were fiercely proud or jealous of rule by others.

When it was finally decided that they should all learn the same language and the same principles of republican government, how was this to be done?

The answer was that it could best be done by a common school, taught in English, to which all the children of all the people could go together and learn how to live together and govern themselves.

But some people were poorer and some richer; some had good manners and others were coarse and rude. Should *all* these people really be educated?

Yes, they must be — if free government is to endure.

Well, but who is to pay for the poor ones?

Everyone must pay for all. If there are weak spots anywhere, the whole community of freedom is weakened. So the common schools must be supported by taxes paid by all.

All right, but who is to control these schools?

The only institution of a free society which serves everyone equally and is controlled by everyone is the government. So the government should control the common schools. And to keep the schools close to the people, the state and local governments, rather than the national government, should control the schools.

But won't the schools be subject to political and partisan prejudice?

Well, they might be, so we must create something genuinely new, something that will give all the people their say but keep the schools free of narrow, partisan politics. This can be done by a series of local boards of education subject to but separate from the executive, legislative, and judicial branches of government.

These school boards, often elected directly by the people, could constitute a kind of "fourth branch of government." They would exert direct control over local education under the general authority set up by the state governments and subject to the guarantees of equality and freedom laid down in the United States Constitution and applying to all Americans.

So far so good, but what about religious education? Don't all these Americans with different religions have freedom to run their own schools under the First Amendment of the Constitution and under their state constitutions?

Yes, indeed, they do. But each American will have to decide for himself whether the education that supports a free society should be conducted in separate schools in which religion provides the fundamental framework for all studies or in common schools devoted primarily to the whole range of free institutions in America. If they decide the first way, the children will be divided into separate schools for their entire education and this division will be along religious lines. If the second way, the children will attend the same public school together for their common education and only be separated for their religious education, which can be conducted as may be desired by the home or by the church or by the synagogue.

In the century of republican education, most Americans chose the common school, controlled and supported in common, and embracing a nonsectarian religious outlook.

Their primary concern was to design a universal, free, public school that would promote free institutions and free citizenship. For the first one hundred years of the Republic, the need for creating the common bonds and loyalties of a free community was paramount.

Less attention was given to the claims of diversity and difference as the essence of freedom for individuals. This came later when the Union had been established, made secure against internal opposition, defended against outside invaders, and preserved despite a war between the states themselves.

The republican ideal of the first century of nationhood gave the following answers regarding the control of education:

A free society required public elementary schools to provide the basic information, literacy, and moral teachings required by every free man. For most Americans the term "free man" was limited to white men, until the Civil War legally introduced Negroes to citizenship. Private elementary schools continued to exist but they were declining in numbers and in importance by the 1870's.

Under the effective and determined leadership of an extraordinary galaxy of "public-school men," the idea of universal common schooling was widely accepted in the new United States during the first half of the nineteenth century. Outstanding among these were Horace Mann and James G. Carter in Massachusetts, Henry Barnard in Connecticut, Calvin Stowe in Ohio, Caleb Mills in Indiana, John D. Pierce in Michigan,

Ninian Edwards in Illinois, Calvin Wiley in North Carolina, and Charles F. Mercer in Virginia. These men and others made speeches before thousands of people; wrote hundreds of pamphlets, articles, and reports; organized scores of groups and societies to agitate for common schools; and held dozens of positions in state governments or school systems.

They argued that the payment of tuition for schooling was unfair to children of poor parents, who could not pay for an education. They argued that the older forms of public support, like land grants from the federal Land Ordinances of 1785 and 1787, would not support schools on the vast scale now necessary.

They argued that the term *free school* should no longer mean a school in which only the poor children were given free education and all others paid tuition.

They argued that class distinctions could be lessened only when a *free school* meant that *all* children were given a free education together and when the entire school system was supported by taxes levied upon everyone.

Aiding their efforts were the newly formed labor unions, which demanded that the public schools provide universal education.

The states gradually accepted this idea of a free public school. The state legislatures passed laws *permitting* local school districts to tax themselves for such schools; they sometimes gave state funds to *encourage* local districts to tax themselves; and they finally *required* all local districts to tax themselves and establish public schools.

By these means, the local freedom of districts to ignore schooling for their children gave way to the larger freedom to be gained by a total population enlightened by education of all. Local control by districts was gradually limited by requirements set by state constitutions, state legislatures, state boards of education, and state superintendents of schools. It was decided that a free society would be better served if education were planned by the central authority of the states rather than left wholly to the completely decentralized control of local school boards. This was not done without bitter conflict, for many believed that state, as opposed to local, control would be undemocratic and destroy freedom.

But in the 1820's, 1830's, and 1840's it was decided that a state government, responsive to public control, could serve freedom as well as, if not better than, the hundreds of local school districts could do. If a local district were left free to provide a poor education or no education at all for its children, those children would be deprived of their birthright to an education that would prepare them for free citizenship. Thereby, the state's own freedom would be endangered.

A smaller freedom must be limited in the interests of a greater freedom. And to guarantee the larger freedom, the state must exert its authority to see to it not only that schools were available to all but that all children actually attended school. Massachusetts led the way by passing its compulsory attendance law in 1852.

The solution was a genuinely creative one. Authority for providing education was defined in state constitutions and in state laws. State authority for education was carried out by state superintendents of schools responsible to a state board of education, elected by the people or appointed by the governor. New York State created the office of state superintendent of schools in 1812. Massachusetts established a state board of education in 1837 with Horace Mann as secretary, and Connecticut did likewise in 1839 with Henry Barnard as secretary. Other states followed.

These state agencies could then set minimum standards for all the schools of the state. Meanwhile, the direct management of schools would be left in the hands of locally elected school boards, local superintendents, and locally appointed teachers. Local management served the cause of flexibility, diversity, and freedom.

This arrangement was designed to assure that schools would serve the whole *public* and would be controlled by the *public* through special boards of education, not through the regular agencies of the state or local governments. This is why in America we use the term *public schools*, not simply *state schools* or *government schools*, as they are often called in those countries that have centralized systems of education.

Since the United States Constitution had not mentioned education as a function of the federal government, the free states after the Revolution reclaimed the authority over education that had been the prerogative of the colonial legislatures.

But the United States Constitution and the state constitutions *did* proclaim freedom of religion and separation of church and state as one of the essentials of republican government. That is, neither the federal government nor state governments could interfere in the affairs of churches or use public funds to support them. Therefore, the states could not give public money to schools under the control of churches.

But what about religious instruction in the common public schools? It was soon evident that if common schools taught the doctrines of a particular church they would violate the freedom of conscience of all those who did not agree.

Could the common schools find a common religious outlook and teach that? Many Protestants thought so. They tried to find the common religious doctrines of Christianity and they found them in the Bible. If the schools would teach only the nonsectarian principles of Christianity as contained in the Bible, they argued, all sects would be satisfied. This might have been the case if America had remained exclusively Protestant.

But immigration had brought increased numbers of Roman Catholics and Jews. Besides, many Americans had never officially belonged to any church. Catholics charged that the so-called "nonsectarian" schools were really Protestant in character and that they were therefore sectarian. So Catholics established their own schools and many demanded a share in the public tax funds to support them. Most Protestants and Jews opposed the giving of public money to parochial schools.

Most states finally decided to prohibit any sectarian control over common schools and to prohibit use of public money for private schools under sectarian control. Especially bitter struggles between Protestants and Catholics were decided for the time being by legislation in New York in 1842 and by constitutional amendment in Massachusetts in 1855. Nearly every state had a similar struggle and enacted similar laws.

By the end of the first century of republican education, the general decision was that a free society was better served if the majority of children went to common, nonsectarian schools than if they went to separate, sectarian religious schools. This made it possible for the United States to build a universal system of free elementary schools sooner than any other country in the world.

The line of argument went like this: Nonsectarianism would provide a greater measure of national unity than could be achieved when each sectarian group shepherded its own children into its own schools. The range of communication among children would be restricted if each group continued to run its own schools differently in religion and language from others. Separate schools would create and perpetuate divisions among the people — thus narrowing their outlooks and reducing free interchange of ideas. Free common schools would more certainly serve the cause of free institutions.

At the end of the first century of the Republic, secondary schools, however, were still largely in private and religious hands. This fact did not seem undesirable to most Americans of that particular period.

The private academies provided considerable opportunity to those who could afford some education beyond the essentials. Likewise, most of the 200 colleges were under private and religious control. This, too, seemed reasonable to the majority of Americans at that time: Elementary education for all at public expense would be sufficient to guarantee the basic security of a republican government; advanced education for *leadership* in the state and in the professions could then be obtained privately by those who could afford it.

A few spokesmen, however, began to argue that a free society needed "free" secondary and higher institutions as well as free elementary schools. The public high school, for example, appeared as early as 1821 in Boston. The idea spread rapidly, but the public high schools did not dominate the secondary-school field till the late nineteenth century.

Advocates of free higher education tried to transform some of the private colleges into state institutions. This happened at the College of

William and Mary in Virginia, at Columbia in New York, and at the College of Philadelphia.

The most notable attempt, however, occurred when the New Hampshire legislature tried to transform Dartmouth College into a state university. But the United States Supreme Court in 1819 (*Trustees of Dartmouth College v. Woodward*) decided that the college was a private corporation and that its charter was a contract which the state could not change unless "the funds of the college be public property."

Following the Dartmouth College decision, private colleges increased in numbers, most of them sponsored by religious denominations. Especially active were Presbyterians, Congregationalists, Episcopalians, Methodists, and Roman Catholics. But the advocates of public higher education also redoubled their efforts. State universities were established in twenty states before the Civil War. The earliest universities to be set up under state control (but not free of tuition) were in Georgia, North Carolina, and Vermont.

The ideal of freedom as a basis for a state university was most eloquently proclaimed by Thomas Jefferson at the University of Virginia, which opened in 1825. In Virginia, as elsewhere, religious groups were bitterly opposed to the state university and tried to prevent its establishment or to divert public funds to their own institutions.

Federal land grants authorized by the Morrill Act in 1862 gave a significant boost to the state-university movement. Funds from these grants were used by the state to establish agricultural and engineering colleges or to strengthen their state universities.

Despite the advocates of free and equal education for all, the era of republican education tried to get along with common schools at the elementary level, but with secondary and higher institutions divided along denominational lines. In general, while the elementary schools served everyone, the academies and colleges and universities catered to the wealthier and upper social classes rather than to the ordinary people.

The major failure to achieve the reformers' goal of a common universal school was the system of segregated schools for Negroes, which appeared occasionally in the North as well as generally in the South. In fact, it was the Roberts case in the Massachusetts Supreme Court in 1849 which set forth the principle that separate schools for Negroes were permissible so long as their facilities were equal to those of the white schools. Charles Sumner's argument that separate schools violated the equal rights of Negroes was rejected by the court, but, even so, Massachusetts and other Northern states moved soon thereafter to abolish their segregated schools by law.

Turning now to the kind and quality of education achieved in the first century of the Republic, we find the main elements of the common-school curriculum continued to be reading, writing, and arithmetic. These three

R's were supposed to give the elements of literacy and the intellectual tools necessary for acquiring the knowledge and "popular information" of which Madison spoke.

But, said the school reformers, the citizen of the new Republic needed more than this—much more. He needed a knowledge of history and geography to instill feelings of patriotism, loyalty, and national pride. He needed moral teachings to instill habits of "republican" character. And he needed some practical studies, like bookkeeping or manual training, so that he could get and keep a job.

The common school was designed to do more than give intellectual training. It was to provide citizenship training, character education, and a means by which every child might advance up the economic and social scale as far as his talents would carry him.

By providing such equal opportunity, the common school would protect free institutions. It would promote progress and prosperity; it would reduce poverty and prevent crime. This was a big order to hand to the schools, but the optimism, energy, and faith of the times all prodded the schools to try to do their share—sometimes more than their share—in making the American dream come true.

The "new" school had to have new methods as well as new subjects. Such school reformers as Joseph Neef and Horace Mann argued that the customary strict discipline, corporal punishment, and slavish memorizing of textbooks were not good enough to carry the burden the school must carry. They therefore argued for the enthusiasm, excitement, interest, and eager learning that could come with a more humane and sympathetic attitude toward children.

Of course, the conservatives charged that the reformers would spoil the children if they spared the rod, but the reformers persisted despite the opposition.

The main trouble was that the teachers were not trained to deal with small children constructively. Would the liberal-arts colleges provide this training? Some proposals were made—at Amherst, at Brown, at Michigan, and elsewhere—that they should do so, but the colleges were not interested. So, entirely new institutions called normal schools were created to give their whole attention to the training of elementary-school teachers.

The first of these were founded as private normal schools in the 1820's by Samuel R. Hall at Concord, Vermont, and by James G. Carter at Lexington, Massachusetts. The first state normal school was opened in 1839 at Lexington, and the idea eventually spread throughout the country.

The normal schools taught young people of high-school age how to teach the elementary-school subjects. Compared with the better colleges of the day, their quality was low, but they made possible the rapid building of the common school systems in the several states. They raised school teaching above the level of incidental apprenticeship and began the process of making it a profession, narrow though the training was in the beginning. If the colleges of liberal arts had been as much interested in school teaching as they were in law, medicine, or other professions, the quality and status of the elementary-school teacher might have been higher much sooner than they were.

The curriculum of the secondary schools also began to respond to the political and economic progress of the times. The academies, replacing the Latin grammar schools, taught a wider range of subjects. Thus, students began to have some freedom of choice of studies. And some academies opened their doors to girls, a notable victory for freedom. By the 1870's some 6000 academies dotted the educational landscape.

But the common-school reformers felt that the private academies could never do the job that needed to be done. They therefore argued that free public high schools should be created to provide a practical education for those boys and girls who would not or could not go on to college.

Offering a practical nonclassical curriculum to youth who could live at home while attending secondary school, the public high school was destined to become ever more popular after the Civil War. It added to the range of vocations for which the schools prepared and in this way opened up possibilities of self-improvement through careers that had never before been within reach of the majority of youth.

Reformers such as George Ticknor at Harvard and Henry Tappan at Michigan also tried to broaden the curriculum of the colleges to make them serve the commercial, business, and political needs of the rapidly growing nation. They wanted to make real universities out of the small colleges.

Classicists put up great resistance against such reforms. Especially powerful was the report of the Yale faculty in 1828, which condemned practical courses and argued that the colleges should continue to stress the mental discipline to be acquired by strict study of Greek, Latin, mathematics, and philosophy.

Colleges should give a *liberal* education, said the Yale faculty, not a vocational education. Colleges should lay the *foundation* for later professional study; they should not give the professional study itself.

By the 1870's the dominant view of higher education came down to this: Liberal education was the only proper education for a free man, but relatively few young men (and no young women) could profit from such a training. Universal education may be all right for the common man, but college education should be reserved for the uncommon man.

The republican ideal of free universal education had not yet been applied to secondary schools or to colleges. The second century of the Republic, the century of democracy in education, did just this.

III. NEARLY A CENTURY OF DEMOCRATIC EDUCATION (1870's to 1960's)

Whereas the republican ideal had been to provide *some* education for all and *much* education for a few, the democratic goal was to provide *as much education as possible for all.* The keynote of the century of democratic education was "more education for more people." It had its drawbacks, its setbacks, and its ups and downs, but nothing seemed able to stop for long the surge to education as the essence of the search for freedom.

The march to the schools came faster, the lines stretched longer, and the students grew older as the second century of the Republic moved from the 1870's to the 1960's. By 1900 the great majority of children aged six to thirteen were in elementary schools; by 1960 over 99 per cent were in attendance. Universal elementary schooling for all children had been won.

More remarkable, however, was the march to the secondary schools. By 1900 about 10 per cent of children aged fourteen to seventeen were actually in school; in 1930 more than 50 per cent attended; and by 1960 nearly 90 per cent were attending. This comes close to universal secondary education, something not dreamed of by the republican leaders of the first century of nationhood.

In 1760 the average colonist may have had two or three years of schooling; by 1960 the average American had ten to eleven years of schooling. And the end has not been reached. The average years of schooling will probably go to twelve or even to fourteen within a decade or two.

Still more remarkable was the stepped-up tempo of the march to college. In 1910 about 5 per cent of all youth aged eighteen to twenty-one were attending college; by 1960 nearly 40 per cent of all such youth were attending institutions beyond high school. Millions more were attending adult-education classes and courses of instruction being offered by business, industry, labor, the armed services, churches, and voluntary agencies. And education by television and other automatic devices had scarcely begun. The potentials were staggering.

How did all this happen and why? The story is complicated, but a few elements are clear. Republican education may have been sufficient for a society marked by a relatively small population scattered over large areas of rich land and relying mainly upon farming and trading for subsistence. But in a society that relied on science and technology, the situation was radically different.

Not only did the leaders, scholars, experts, and professional men need more and better education, but also the kind of education that *everyone* needed grew steadily greater in quantity and higher in quality. For *this* kind of industrial society, a democratic education would be necessary if freedom were to be maintained.

A society based on steam power, electric power, or nuclear power can be managed and controlled by relatively few people. Technical power leads to political and economic power. To prevent autocratic, dictatorial use of political and economic power by a few, everyone must have an education devoted to freedom. There is no other satisfactory way to limit political or economic power.

So it became increasingly clear that the opportunity to acquire an expanded and extended education must be made available to *all*, to the poor as well as to the rich, to the slow student as well as to the bright, to the South and West as well as to the North and East, to girls as well as to boys, to Negroes as well as to whites, to immigrants as well as to native-born, to Catholic and Jew as well as to Protestant and nonchurchgoer.

The century of democratic education took the doctrines of the common school and applied them almost completely to the secondary school and in part to the college. Equality of opportunity stood alongside freedom as the prime goals of education.

Let us see what happened to the organization and control of education in the age of democratic education:

The nineteenth-century solution to the problem of public and private schools came to this: A system of public institutions ranging from primary school to university, open for everyone as long as his abilities justify, is the best guarantor of a free society based upon equality of opportunity. Private institutions are free to operate alongside the public institutions, but these should be supported voluntarily and should not be given public funds.

In the 1870's a series of court cases (especially the Kalamazoo case in Michigan) agreed that the people of the states could establish and support public high schools with tax funds if they so desired. Thereupon the public high-school movement spread rapidly, and the private academy shrank in importance. Furthermore, all states passed compulsory attendance laws requiring attendance to at least age sixteen. Provision of public secondary schools thereupon became an *obligation* of the states, not just a voluntary matter for the local districts to decide.

Children were permitted to attend properly approved nonpublic schools as a way of meeting state attendance laws. This principle was affirmed by the United States Supreme Court in the Oregon case of 1925 (*Pierce v. Society of Sisters*).

States had the right to supervise, inspect, and set minimum standards for *all* schools and to require children to attend *some* school, but the state could not compel students to attend public schools if their parents preferred private schools. Freedom to have a say in the education of their children was a constitutional right of parents under the Fourteenth Amendment. Besides, private schools were valuable property which could not be destroyed by action of the state without due process of law.

By 1930 the preference of most Americans for public schools was clear; only about 9 per cent of children attended nonpublic schools. The public policy hammered out in the nineteenth century was also clear: Public funds should not be used to support private schools. Beginning in the 1930's, however, the clamor began to rise again that the private schools should be given some public aid. Campaigns to get parents to send their children to private schools began to show results.

Today more than 16 per cent of children are in nonpublic schools, a gain so spectacular that the American people have to face up to certain questions more directly than at any time since the 1830's: Shall we encourage private schools as well as public schools with public money? Is the present balance among public and private schools about right? If not, should we favor private or public schools?

Through the years, much of the controversy over public and private schools has been basically sectarian. Today more than ninety per cent of children attending nonpublic schools are enrolled in parochial schools conducted by the Roman Catholic Church. A whole series of laws and court cases in the nineteenth century decided that religious freedom and separation of church and state meant that the states could not give tax money to support private education. But from 1930 onward, exceptions began to be made.

The Cochran case in 1930 permitted Louisiana to spend tax funds to give free textbooks to children in private as well as public schools; the Everson case in 1947 permitted New Jersey to provide bus transportation for parochial-school pupils; in 1948 the School Lunch Act gave federal money to parochial schools even though state funds could not be so used. Advocates of parochial schools were now arguing that public funds should be used to pay for auxiliary services that benefited the child but were not direct aid to the school as such.

In recent decades, the arguments for diverting public funds to private schools have changed. It is now argued that the states should aid all parents to send their children to the kind of school they wish. This would not aid *schools*; it would aid parents to exercise their freedom of educational choice. So if parents want their children to go to religious schools, they should receive their fair share of tax funds. If they want their children to go to all-white schools, they should receive tax funds to help them do this. Obviously, the whole idea of a common school is now under severe attack.

What the American people will decide in the years to come is in doubt. In fact, the whole idea inherited from republican days that a free society rests upon a common school system maintained and controlled by the free government is in peril.

"Freedom" may come to mean that parents can divide up among themselves the public funds which had originally been designed to support a free educational system which in turn was designed to perpetuate the free society itself. Does freedom of choice for parents mean that the state is obligated to support and pay for that choice?

Such questions as these came to focus sharply in the problem of central and local control. If some towns or regions in a state could not or would not provide good schools for their children, should the children suffer, or should the state try to equalize the burden by giving financial aid to those towns? The answer turned out to be clear: Equalize the burden in fairness to the children.

Most states use tax money, raised all over the state, to support schools in all parts of the state wherever and whenever local property taxes did not provide enough money to operate good schools. Central control in state hands seemed desirable for the purpose.

But what about the federal government? Will the same answer be given? If some *states* cannot or will not provide good schools for their children, should the federal government try to equalize the burden by giving financial aid to the states? If all states try hard, and still some states cannot provide acceptable educational opportunity for all children, should the federal government step in and help out? By and large, the answer thus far has been no; a qualified no, but still no.

To be sure, the Land Ordinances of 1785 and 1787 and other grants gave millions of acres of land to the states for education; the Morrill Act of 1862 helped establish land-grant colleges; the Smith-Lever Act of 1914 supported agricultural and home-economics instruction; the Smith-Hughes Act of 1917 aided vocational education in high schools.

Emergency aid was given in the 1930's and the National Youth Administration and Civilian Conservation Corps helped youth in the depression; a bill was passed to provide aid for federally impacted school districts; the GI Bill of Rights helped millions of veterans of World War II and the war in Korea to get an education; and the National Defense Education Act of 1958 gave loans to students and supported specific programs in foreign-language training, science, guidance, and audio-visual methods.

But up to the present, the idea of federal-state partnership in public-school support has not been squarely faced by the federal government. For nearly a hundred years a whole series of bills had been introduced in Congress to achieve this purpose. Beginning with the Hoar bill, Perce bill, and Burnside bill of the 1870's and the several Blair bills in the 1880's, Republicans were the chief advocates of federal aid, but Democrats of the South were afraid that the federal government was trying to punish them and impose Northern ideas upon them.

In the decade between 1950 and 1960 it was the liberal Democrats from the North and West who tried to achieve federal aid, but were thwarted by economy-minded Republicans and by some Southern Democrats who feared federal imposition of integrated schools upon the South. Throughout the century many Roman Catholic leaders opposed federal aid unless it would help parochial as well as public schools.

The race issue, the religious issue, and the economy issue successfully blocked federal aid for decades. After the close of the Civil War, it was touch and go for a while whether federal action would result in equal educational opportunity for Negroes in the South.

The Fourteenth Amendment (1866) guaranteed "equal protection of the laws" to all citizens, but the federal education bills failed and the Civil Rights Act of 1875 was declared unconstitutional. The Southern states proceeded to set up segregated school systems, one system for Negroes and one for whites. The United States Supreme Court decision in *Plessy v. Ferguson* (1896) was taken to mean that separate school systems were permissible provided they had equal facilities.

In the 1940's a whole series of court cases began the process of gaining access for Negroes to the public institutions of the South—first to the universities and then to the schools. The historic decisions headed by the Brown case of May 17, 1954, reversed the "separate but equal" doctrine of Plessy and declared that segregated schools were inherently unequal even if each had "equal" amounts of money spent on it.

In the following years, case after case was taken to court to require boards of education to admit Negroes to the public schools, on an unsegregated basis.

Violence, often instigated by outside agitators, broke out in Clinton, Tennessee, and a number of other places; and federal troops were called to Little Rock, Arkansas, when the governor interfered with a federal court order to integrate the schools. Gradually, however, desegregation spread through the border states and by 1960 was being faced in the Deep South.

Some Southern governors and legislatures tried to prevent integration by legal devices. Laws were passed to close the public schools, to give public money to parents so they could send their children to segregated private schools, and even to abolish the public-school system itself.

These actions posed the most serious threat to the ideals of both republican and democratic education it was possible to pose. Does a state have the right to abolish its "fourth branch of government?" What *is* essential to a "republican form of government" (as guaranteed in the United States Constitution) if public education is not? Could the principles of a free society withstand this onslaught safely?

If the demands for private religious education and the demands for private segregated education were joined by economy demands for reducing public-school budgets, the result could be a repudiation of the public-school idea itself and a return to the "voluntary" principle of the sixteenth and seventeenth centuries in Europe: Let those have an education who can pay for it; let education be fully private. Or, alternatively: Let us divide up the public moneys among competing racial and religious groups so they can set up their own private schools; let us have many free *private* educational systems.

In either of these cases, the central idea of American education would disappear. An unlimited role for free private enterprise in education would take the place of a limited role for free public enterprise. The freedom of segmented voluntary groups to work at cross purposes would replace the freedom of the people as a whole to work through a system of public schools. The 1960's will doubtless see the struggles heightened. How will the search for freedom come out?

Just as the keynote to *quantity* in education for the century of democratic education has been "more education for more people," so the keynote to *quality* in education has been "better education for all." Each decade has its reformers who demanded better education than the schools were then offering, but there has been little agreement concerning what is "better."

Different reformers have demanded different measures at different times. As the times changed, the schools were behind the times for different reasons. Nowhere else in the world have so many people been so much concerned about education so much of the time—and almost never has everyone been satisfied.

No sooner had the elementary schools been established to start six-year-olds on the road to formal schooling than reformers began to argue that we ought to have a pre-school school called the kindergarten. So, borrowing ideas from Friedrich Froebel in Europe, we began to attach kindergartens to the public schools, beginning in the 1870's. The idea was to help children of four to six years learn by directed play activities.

By 1960 most American cities had kindergartens, and some of them had even established nursery schools for two-to-four-year-olds.

The elementary school itself was subject to recurring reforms. No sooner did it make headway in teaching the three R's to every child than someone, outside the schools or in, would urge it to broaden its curriculum: Add drawing and the arts; add geography and history; add nature study; hygiene and physical training; manual training; domestic science. And these all seemed reasonable.

The famous Swiss educator, Pestalozzi, had said so; Edward A. Sheldon, founder of the Oswego (New York) Normal School, said so; Francis W. Parker, superintendent of schools in Quincy, Massachusetts, said so. And so said a host of others, including such diverse characters as the presidents of Harvard (Charles W. Eliot) and of Columbia (Nicholas

Murray Butler), publicists like Joseph Mayer Rice, social workers like Jane Addams and Lilian Wald, reformers like Jacob Riis and Walter Hines Page.

Social reformers, humanitarians, and philanthropists, especially in the cities of the 1890's, were indignant about the endless memory work that marked most schools. Schools, they said, were far too intellectualistic—they dealt almost exclusively with words and numbers that did not mean very much to the children. They felt that schools should be alive, interesting, exciting, practical and useful.

This seemed fair enough. John Dewey took up the ideas in his experimental school at the University of Chicago, and Teachers College at Columbia University applied them in its experimental Lincoln School. Eventually "progressive" schools mushroomed on the landscape, and "progressive" ideas became popular in the 1920's and 1930's. Chief among the spokesmen after John Dewey was William H. Kilpatrick at Teachers College, Columbia University.

All sorts of plans were devised to loosen up the formal curriculum and give it life and vitality—units, projects, activities, excursions and visits, handicrafts, gardens, laboratories, audio-visual aids, and much else—anything to overcome the slavish drill on the textbook or notebook. There was little doubt that the general quality of learning for most children was raised as the school added vitality and zest to the learning process.

But in the 1940's and 1950's a new set of "reformers" began to charge that the schools were too soft. Schools, they said, were just letting children play and not teaching them anything. Elementary schools were exhorted to return to the three R's and stiffen up discipline and concentrate on intellectual studies.

Many of the criticisms were overdrawn and unfair, but many had some truth in them. Progressive methods *had* been carried to an extreme by a few spokesmen and by a few teachers who assumed that all children learned better by "direct" experiences, by visits, or by physical activities than they did by reading or writing. A general tightening of school methods was evident by 1960.

Sputnik and Russian education strengthened the critics' hands. But how long would it be before "loosening" and flexibility in the curriculum would again be necessary and a new wave of progressive reform to overcome excessive academic formalism be desirable?

Meanwhile, the controversy over religion in the public schools continued. By the beginning of the twentieth century, most public schools had not only dropped sectarian religious teaching but also much of the nonsectarian religious instruction they had attempted in the early nineteenth century. In other words, although the public schools dealt with moral and spiritual values, they no longer tried to deal with religion at all; they were secular. But after World War II the demand arose again that the public schools restore some kind of religious instruction.

Some Protestants proposed that the Bible be read without comment by the teacher, but Catholics and Jews opposed this as really sectarian. It was proposed that students be given time off from regular classes to receive sectarian instruction from their own religious teachers (released time).

In 1948 the United States Supreme Court in the McCollum decision said that released-time religious instructon could not be given inside public-school buildings, but in 1952 (Zorach decision) the Supreme Court said it could be done outside schools if the public teachers did not coerce or persuade students to go to the religious classes. Neither of these decisions has satisfied many people. Some educators have proposed that public schools avoid religious instruction as such but undertake factual study about religion right along with the study of other regular school subjects, but most religious groups have been cool to this proposal. The formula for honoring religious diversity while still promoting social unity through common schools had not been satisfactorily found.

Reform movements stirred through secondary as well as elementary schools. Most revolutionary reform was the very idea of a secondary school which would accept students of the whole range of ability and try to give all a course of study suited to their abilities and their possible vocations in life.

Most other countries divide children at age eleven or twelve, send a few to academic (college-preparatory) schools, others to vocational schools, and the majority directly to work. The American high school, however, has tried to be a comprehensive school, one in which students from all walks of life would study and work and play together. This meant that many new subjects and courses have been added periodically to the high-school curriculum.

The resulting number of elective studies has worried the colleges. As early as 1893 the National Education Association tried to encourage a standardized high-school curriculum. Noteworthy were the efforts of the Committee of Ten (1893) and the Committee on College Entrance Requirements (1899).

These "reforms" stressed those academic studies which should be required for college entrance; namely, four units in foreign language, two in mathematics, two in English, one in history, and one in science. (The relative inattention to science is at least sixty years old.) It was assumed that such studies would be good for all students whether they were headed for college or not. This was fair enough at a time when seventy-five per cent of high-school graduates were going on to college.

But after 1900 the pressures of enrollment on the high schools grew stronger. By 1918 an NEA Committee formulated *The Seven Cardinal*

Principles of Secondary Education, in which preparation for college was definitely less important than it had been twenty years before. Now, the high school's aims were to give attention to health, command of the fundamental processes, worthy home membership, vocational preparation, citizenship, leisure-time activities, and ethical character.

This note continued to be emphasized in the 1930's and 1940's. By 1950 about thirty per cent of high-school graduates were going to college. Preparation for college had actually become a minor function of the high schools.

However, a new wave of reaction (or was it reform?) began to criticize secondary schools for permitting low academic standards, for not stimulating youth to rigorous study, for letting youth take so-called "easy" courses instead of working hard at the regular academic subjects. The success of Russian space flights and the threat of falling behind in the armament race raised fears that American high schools were not doing their jobs.

Many of the critics did not know what they were talking about, but some did. There was little doubt that many high schools could do a better job for college-bound youth than they were doing. Some high-school educators were still assuming that only a small minority of high-school graduates were headed for college. They had not noticed that by 1960 many more high-school students were expecting to go to college.

It might not be long until we would be back where we were in 1900 with 75 per cent of high-school graduates bound for college, but with this vast difference: In 1900 only 10 per cent of youth were in high school; today 90 per cent are there.

The potential enrollments called for a drastic new look at the secondary school, at both the junior-high and senior-high levels. The first thing the schools did was to give more attention to the academic subjects, especially to the foreign languages, science, and mathematics. The time was ripe, however, for a complete overhauling of the junior-high school, which was just about fifty years old and born in a very different age from that of the 1960's.

Undoubtedly the pressure of high-school graduates upon college doors would lead to even further drastic expansion of junior colleges and other two-year institutions. They too were just about half a century old and, in some ways, the epitome of the democratic movement in American education.

It was being estimated that by the decades following 1970 all students with an IQ of one hundred or over would be finishing at least a two-year college. If this proved to be true, standards of admission to some colleges would go up and in others they were bound to go down.

Finally, the upward push of the educational surge left its unmistakable mark on the four-year colleges and universities. In the 1870's most institutions of higher education were relatively small undergraduate colleges. Their curriculums were still largely devoted to the liberal arts of Greek and Latin, mathematics, and philosophy; and these courses were all required of all students.

In a relatively short time, however, new studies, like the modern languages, English, modern history and the social sciences, modern science, and the fine arts found a place in the curriculum. Students had to be given a choice because they could not possibly study all these subjects in four years. So the elective system was instituted.

Meanwhile, graduate study began to change the whole character of higher education. When Johns Hopkins University opened its doors in 1876, it helped to set the pattern for graduate schools devoted to the advancement of knowledge and research in the entire range of the arts and sciences. Professional schools of medicine, law, education, engineering, agriculture, business administration, and the like began to flourish.

This meant that universities were now devoted to direct professional preparation for an ever larger number of vocations rather than for just a few. Some liberal-arts colleges tried to maintain their nonvocational and nonprofessional character, but most were not able or did not care to do so. The democratic surge was too strong.

In the 1920's and 1930's a number of experimental colleges tried to grapple with the overcrowded curriculum and to design new patterns of liberal education. Bennington, University of Wisconsin, Sarah Lawrence, Bard, University of Minnesota were among them.

Critics arose, such as Robert Hutchins and Alexander Meiklejohn, to call for preservation of the liberal-arts college free from professionalism and vocationalism. They were struggling against the tide. Nevertheless, undergraduate colleges did institute a wide variety of programs which, in one way or another, tried to assure that all students would have some acquaintance with the humanities, the social sciences, the sciences and mathematics, and the fine arts. Whatever a liberal education or a general education was supposed to be, it was to deal with these fields of knowledge.

Much criticism was directed at the professional schools for not giving enough attention to the liberal arts. They began to give heed. As the 1960's opened, considerable ferment was evident in medical schools, business schools, engineering schools, and schools of education.

It seemed likely that the teachers college, as a separate institution devoted exclusively to the training of teachers, would disappear. Normal schools had become teachers colleges, and now teachers colleges were becoming state colleges and even state universities. These changes were signs on the road of the march of democratic education.

Higher education was no longer confined to the few nor to the upper classes of wealth or privilege. It was on the way to becoming financially free, as secondary and elementary education had become before it. The opportunity was great.

The question was whether all this educational activity could measure up to the intellectual and moral demands of a free society in the modern world. If individuals used the vast resources of American higher education simply to further their own interests, this was one kind of small freedom all right, but in the long run would it serve the cause of the free society? How to enable American education to serve the cause of the larger freedoms was the paramount question. The answer to this question cannot be rigged. The fate of the nation rides upon it.

At the heart of the answer to the fateful question is the scholarship, the wisdom, the vitality and the freedom of American teachers. If teachers are weak, timorous, or poorly trained, the American idea of education has little chance of success. If powerful or selfish groups demand that teachers conform to *their* ways of thinking or to *their* beliefs, education will be a narrow little thing. And our history here is not too reassuring.

Orthodoxy of belief in colonial days was a prime requirement for teaching. Oaths of loyalty to the crown and to the doctrines of the church were familiar trappings of colonial rule. The American Revolution in its turn demanded that teachers be faithful to the Revolution rather than to the crown; and, similarly, Congress exacted loyalty oaths to the Union in the Reconstruction Period after the Civil War.

Conformity of economic belief, faith in private business enterprise, and opposition to any radical movements were expected of teachers in the nineteenth century. State laws required special loyalty oaths from teachers as early as the 1920's, and as late as 1958 the National Defense Education Act required such oaths from students applying for federal loans.

After World Wars I and II, thirty states passed laws requiring teachers to sign special loyalty oaths. Other laws (notably the Feinberg law of 1949 in New York State) were passed to hunt down and dismiss teachers suspected of belonging to subversive organizations. Many patriotic organizations served as self-appointed censors of school textbooks and complained about outspoken teachers.

The frantic search for communist teachers and others suspected vaguely of "leftist" leaning was fired up by McCarthyism and the wave of legislative investigations that swept the country in the early 1950's.

As a result, a cloud of timidity, suspicion, and fear settled down upon the schools and colleges in what *The New York Times* called "a subtle, creeping paralysis of freedom of thought." Classroom teachers and school administrators tended to avoid acts or ideas that might "cause any trouble" or arouse any criticism.

This general atmosphere of caution and anxiety affecting millions of students did infinitely more damage to the cause of freedom in education than the handful of communist teachers could possibly do. Fortunately, the most active "Red hunts" have now passed, but their revival is an ever-present danger, especially if teachers and students are fearful or are indifferent to the importance of freedom in education.

The first defenses of freedom in education are strong professional organizations of teachers like the American Association of University Professors and the National Education Association. If they do their jobs, they will insist upon high-quality training for teachers, upon fearless and competent scholarship in the classroom, and upon freedom to seek the truth in research and in the publication of findings. They will defend those qualified teachers who come under attack.

The ultimate defenses of freedom in education, however, are the people themselves who will realize that education's main function is to free the minds of the younger generation and to equip them as free citizens and free persons.

The schools and colleges must therefore generate a spirit of intellectual, political, and personal freedom throughout the land. To do this, they must in turn have a genuine measure of self-government resting upon the competent scholarship of the teachers.

The most distinctive mark of a free society is that it specifically delegates to its educational institutions the task of constant study and criticism of the free society itself. No other kind of society dares to permit such a thing. No other kind of society prevents its government from endangering the liberties of the people and at the same time entrusts the government with the obligation to guarantee the rights of the people against attack by powerful groups or individuals in the community.

Just as a free government guarantees the freedom of the press, of association, of religion, and of trial by jury, so must a free government guarantee the freedom of teaching and learning.

A free society knows that its surest foundation rests upon the liberal education of the people — a liberal education available freely and equally to all, beginning with the earliest stages of the elementary school, extending to the highest reaches of the university, and limited only by considerations of talent.

As the fourth century of American history reaches its mid-point and as the second century of the American Republic draws to a close, the search for freedom in American education has just well begun. That is why the story of American education must continue to be, in the future even more than in the past, the unflagging search for freedom.

LAWRENCE A. CREMIN

John Dewey and the
Progressive-Education Movement,
1915-1952

JOHN DEWEY HAD A STORY—IT MUST HAVE BEEN A FAVORITE OF HIS—
about "a man who was somewhat sensitive to the movements of things
about him. He had a certain appreciation of what things were passing
away and dying and of what things were being born and growing. And
on the strength of that response he foretold some of the things that were
going to happen in the future. When he was seventy years old the people
gave him a birthday party and they gave him credit for bringing to pass
the things he had foreseen might come to pass" (1). With characteristic modesty, Dewey told the story autobiographically, using it to describe his own place in the history of American life and thought. And
granted the genuinely seminal character of his contribution, there was a
measure of truth to his disclaimer.

Consider, for example, Dewey's relation to the early progressive-
education movement; it provides an excellent case in point. We know
that the movement arose during the 1890's as a many-sided protest
against pedagogical narrowness and inequity. It was essentially pluralistic, often self-contradictory, and always related to broader currents
of social and political progressivism. In the universities it appeared as
part of a spirited revolt against formalism in philosophy, psychology,

Lawrence A. Cremin, "John Dewey and the Progressive-Education Movement,
1915–1952." *School Review*, *67*, 1959, 160–171. Copyright © 1959 by The University of Chicago Press.

and the social sciences. In the cities it emerged as one facet of a larger program of social alleviation and municipal reform. Among farmers, it became the crux of a moderate, liberal alternative to radical agrarianism. It was at the same time the "social education" demanded by urban settlement workers, the "schooling for country life" demanded by rural publicists, the vocational training demanded by businessmen's associations and labor unions alike, and the new techniques of instruction demanded by *avant garde* pedagogues. Like progressivism writ large, it compounded a fascinating congeries of seemingly disparate elements: the romanticism of G. Stanley Hall and the realism of Jacob Riis, the scientism of Joseph Mayer Rice and the reformism of Jane Addams. Its keynote was diversity, of protest, of protestor, of proposal, and of proponent; it was a diversity destined to leave its ineradicable mark on a half-century of educational reform (2).

There were, needless to say, numerous attempts to portray this remarkable movement in its early decades; but nowhere is its extraordinary diversity more intelligently documented than in Dewey's volume *Schools of To-Morrow*, published in 1915 in collaboration with his daughter Evelyn (3). Over the years, Dewey's continuing interest in pedagogical theory, his widely publicized work at the Laboratory School he and Mrs. Dewey had founded in 1896, his reputation as a tough-minded analyst of pedagogical schemes, and his unfailing support of progressive causes had combined to make him increasingly an acknowledged spokesman of the progressive-education movement. *Schools of To-Morrow* did much to secure this image of him in the public mind. Within ten years the book had gone through fourteen printings, unusual for any book, unheard-of for a book about education.

Written neither as a textbook nor as a dogmatic exposition of "the new," the volume is designed "to show what actually happens when schools start out to put into practice, each in its own way, some of the theories that have been pointed to as the soundest and best ever since Plato" (3: Preface). More than anything, the Dewey of *Schools of To-Morrow* is the man "sensitive to the movement of things about him." The reader is treated to a fascinating collection of glimpses — into Marietta Johnson's Organic School at Fairhope, Alabama, Junius Meriam's experimental school at the University of Missouri, the Francis Parker School in Chicago, Caroline Pratt's Play School in New York, the Kindergarten at Teachers College, Columbia University, and certain public schools of Gary, Chicago, and Indianapolis. In each instance, the guiding educational theory is given and the techniques by which the theory is put into practice are described. The approach is essentially journalistic; Dewey's enterprise is to elucidate rather than to praise or criticize.

Yet there is a very special kind of reporting here, one that bears closer examination. Richard Hofstadter has observed that the Progressive mind was typically a journalistic mind, and that its characteristic contribution was that of a socially responsible reporter-reformer (4). Certainly this was Dewey's central contribution in *Schools of To-Morrow*. For in addition to the who, the what, the when, and the where, Dewey gives us a succession of social whys that quickly transform a seemingly unrelated agglomeration of pedagogical experiments into the several facets of a genuine social movement.

Merely as a record of what progressive education actually was and what it meant to Dewey *circa* 1915, the book is invaluable. The text abounds in vivid descriptions of the physical education, the nature studies, the manual work, the industrial training, and the innumerable "socialized activities" in the schools of tomorrow. Thee is exciting talk of more freedom for children, of greater attention to individual growth and development, of a new unity between education and life, of a more meaningful school curriculum, of a vast democratizing of culture and learning. Nowhere is the faith and optimism of the progressive-education movement more dramatically conveyed.

Moreover, as the analysis proceeds, Dewey's powers as a "socially responsible reporter-reformer" are soon apparent. He points enthusiastically to the concern with initiative, originality, and resourcefulness in the new pedagogy, deeming these qualities central to the life of a free society. He commends the breadth of the new school programs, their attention to health, citizenship, and vocation, arguing that such breadth is not only a necessary adaptation to industrialism but an effort to realize for the first time in history the democratic commitment to equal educational opportunity. He sees the new emphasis on "learning by doing" as a device par excellence to narrow the gap between school and life; and closeness to life is required "if the pupil is to understand the facts which the teacher wishes him to learn; if his knowledge is to be real, not verbal; if his education is to furnish standards of judgment and comparison" (3:294). Even more important, perhaps, a school close to life sends into society men and women "intelligent in the pursuit of the activities in which they engage" (3:249). People educated in this way are inevitable agents of constructive social change, and the schools which educate them are thereby intimately bound to the larger cause of reform (3:226–27). Indeed, it is this very tie that makes progressive education progressive!

Actually, the dialectic between Dewey the observer and Dewey the reformer is probably the most intriguing thing about the volume (5). On the one hand, we know that many of the pedagogical experiments he described grew up quite independently of his own theorizing (6).

On the other hand, we recognize much in *Schools of To-Morrow* that exemplifies the very things he himself was urging in pamphlets going back at least twenty years (7). The only way to reconcile the two Deweys, it seems, is to return to his own disclaimer, that he really was "the man sensitive to the movement of things about him" and to the thesis that his most seminal contribution was to develop a body of pedagogical theory which could encompass the terrific diversity of the progressive-education movement. It is no coincidence that *Democracy and Education* came a year later and wove the diverse strands of a quarter-century of educational protest and innovation into an integral theory (8). The later work has since overshadowed *Schools of To-Morrow*, but the two ought not to be read apart. One is as much the classic of the early progressive-education movement as the other. Their genius was to express a pedagogical age. For their very existence, the movement was infused with larger meaning and hence could never be the same again.

World War I marks a great divide in the history of progressive education. Merely the founding of the Progressive Education Association in 1919 would have changed the movement significantly, since what had formerly been a rather loosely defined revolt against academic formalism now gained a vigorous organizational voice (9). But there were deeper changes, in the image of progressivism itself, that were bound to influence the course and meaning of educational reform.

Malcolm Cowley, in his delightful reminiscence of the twenties, *Exile's Return*, describes these changes well. He notes insightfully that intellectual protest in prewar years had mingled two quite different sorts of revolt: bohemianism and radicalism. The one was essentially an individual revolt against puritan restraint; the other, primarily a social revolt against the evils of capitalism. World War I, he argues, brought a parting of the ways. People were suddenly forced to decide what kinds of rebels they were. If they were merely rebels against puritanism, they could exist safely in Mr. Wilson's world; if they were radicals, they had no place in it (10).

Cowley's analysis provides a key to one of the important intellectual shifts of the twenties. With the end of the War, radicalism seemed no longer in fashion among the *avant garde*, particularly the artists and literati who flocked to the Greenwich Villages of New York, Chicago, and San Francisco. It did not die; it was merely eclipsed by a polyglot system of ideas which combined the doctrines of self-expression, liberty, and psychological adjustment into a confident, iconoclastic individualism that fought the constraints of Babbitry and the discipline of social reform as well. And just as prewar progressivism had given rise to a new educational outlook, one which cast the school as a lever of social change, so this postwar protest developed its own characteristic pedagogical argument: the notion that each individual has uniquely creative potentialities, and that a school in which children are encouraged freely to develop these potentialities is the best guarantee of a larger society truly devoted to human worth and excellence.

Now those who had read *Schools of To-Morrow* must certainly have recognized this essentially Rousseauan stance; it had been at the heart of several of the schools Dewey had described. Yet readers who had troubled to follow Dewey's argument to the end, and who had accepted his analysis incorporating Rousseau's insights into a larger social reformism, must have noted a curious difference of emphasis here (11). For just as radicalism seemed eclipsed in the broader protests of the twenties, so it seemed to disappear from the progressive pedagogy of the decade (12). For all intents and purposes, the *avant garde* pedagogues expanded one part of what progressive education had formerly meant into its total meaning.

Nowhere is this transformation more clearly documented than in the characteristic exegesis of progressive education during the twenties, *The Child-Centered School* (13). Written by Harold Rugg and Ann Shumaker in 1928, the volume attempts for the movement in its time what *Schools of To-Morrow* had done a decade earlier. Its pages teem with pedagogical experiments illustrating the new articles of pedagogical faith: freedom, child interest, pupil initiative, creative self-expression, and personality development. And just as Dewey had seen a central connection with democracy as the crux of the earlier movement, so Rugg and Shumaker saw the relationship with the creative revolution of the twenties as the essential meaning of this one. To grasp the significance of the child-centered schools, they urged, one had to comprehend the historic battle of the artist against the standardization, the superficiality, and the commercialism of industrial civilization. The key to the creative revolution of the twenties was the triumph of self-expression, in art and in education as well. Hence, in creative self-expression they found the quintessential meaning of the progressive-education movement.

Dewey, of course, was not unaware of the continuing ferment in pedagogical circles. His interest in education persisted, but as the decade progressed he became less and less the sensitive observer and interpreter of the progressive-education movement and increasingly its critic. As early as 1926, for example, he attacked the studied lack of adult guidance in the *avant garde* schools with a sharpness uncommon in his writing. "Such a method," he observed, "is really stupid. For it attempts the impossible, which is always stupid; and it misconceives the conditions of independent thinking" (14: 37). Freedom, he counselled, is not something given at birth; nor is it bred of planlessness. It is something to be achieved, to be systematically wrought out in co-operation with experienced teachers, knowledgeable in their own traditions. Baby, Dewey insisted, does not know best! (14)

Two years later, the same year *The Child-Centered School* appeared, Dewey used the occasion of a major address before the Progressive Education Association to reiterate his point. "Progressive schools," he noted, "set store by individuality, and sometimes it seems to be thought that orderly organization of subject-matter is hostile to the needs of students in their individual character. But individuality is something developing and to be continuously attained, not something given all at once and ready-made" (15: 201). Far from being hostile to the principle of individuality, he continued, some systematic organization of activities and subject matter is the only means for actually achieving individuality; and teachers, by virtue of their richer and fuller experience, have not only the right but the high obligation to assist students in the enterprise (15).

His strictures were not heeded, and in 1930 he leveled them even more vigorously in the concluding essay of a *New Republic* series evaluating a decade of progressive education (16). The formalism and isolation of the conventional schoolroom had literally cried out for reform, he recalled. But the point of the progressive revolt had been not to rid the school of subject matter, but rather to build a new subject matter, as well organized as the old but having a more intimate relation to the experience of students. "The relative failure to accomplish this result indicates the one-sidedness of the idea of the 'child-centered' school" (16: 205).

Then Dewey went on to a more pervasive criticism. Progressive schools, he conceded, had been most successful in furthering creativity in the arts. But this accomplishment, however much it contributed to private sensibilities, had hardly met either the social or the aesthetic needs of a democratic-industrial society. A truly progressive education, he concluded, "requires a searching study of society and its moving forces. That the traditional schools have almost wholly evaded consideration of the social potentialities of education is no reason why progressive schools should continue the evasion, even though it be sugared over with aesthetic refinements. The time ought to come when no one will be judged to be an educated man or woman who does not have insight into the basic forces of industrial and urban civilization. Only schools which take the lead in bringing about this kind of education can claim to be progressive in any socially significant sense" (16: 206).

Dewey's comments seemed particularly *à propos* in the summer of 1930. Already the depression which was to envelop the nation and become the central fact of the thirties was very much in evidence. Breadlines were common in the industrial cities, and women could be seen raking through community refuse heaps as soon as garbage trucks departed. Suddenly radicalism was no longer passé; it was bohemianism that appeared a little out of date (17). Socially conscious notions of progressive education, disparaged by the *avant garde* of the twenties as "social efficiency," were now very much to the point (18).

It should be no surprise that Dewey's formulation of the meaning of progressivism in education came once again to the fore. Early in 1932 he accepted membership on a yearbook commission of the National Society of College Teachers of Education dedicated to producing a statement of philosophy of education appropriate to the times. The volume which emerged, *The Educational Frontier*, is, like *The Child-Centered School*, the characteristic progressivist statement of its decade. And while its formulations are essentially collaborative, Dewey's own views are clearly discernible in two chapters he wrote jointly with his student, John L. Childs (19).

The Dewey of these chapters is now the vigorous proponent. His plea is for an educational program conceived in the broadest terms, one which has "definite reference to the needs and issues which mark and divide our domestic, economic, and political life in the generation of which we are a part" (19: 36). As with his educational outlook from the beginning, his call is for a school close to life, one that will send into society people able to understand it, to live intelligently as part of it, and to change it to suit their visions of the better life. Once again, he sees changes through education as "correlative and interactive" with changes through politics. "No social modification, slight or revolutionary, can endure except as it enters into the action of a people through their desires and purposes. This introduction and perpetuation are affected by education" (19: 318).

Dewey held essentially to this position throughout the stormy thirties. To George Counts's provocative question "Dare the school build a new social order?" Dewey replied that in an industrial society with its multiplicity of political and educative agencies, the school could never be the main determinant of political, intellectual, or moral change (20). "Nevertheless," he continued, "while the school is not a sufficient condition, it is a necessary condition of *forming the understanding and the dispositions* that are required to maintain a genuinely changed social order" (21). It would be revolution enough, Dewey once told an NEA audience, were educators to begin to recognize the fact of social change and to act upon that recognition in the schools (22).

Dewey steadfastly opposed indoctrination in the form of the inculcation of fixed social beliefs. But he did contend that for schools to be progressive, teachers would have to select the newer scientific, technological, and cultural forces producing changes in the old order, estimate their outcomes if given free play, and see what could be done to make the schools their ally (23). To some, of course, this was as crass a form of indoctrination as any; and Dewey was criticized on the one hand by those who insisted that his notions would cast the school into an indefensible presentism at the expense of traditional values and verities, and on the other by those in the progressive camp who maintained that any social guidance by adults was really an unwarranted form of imposition.

Dewey replied to both groups in what was destined to be his most important pedagogical work of the thirties, *Experience and Education.* The volume is really a restatement of aspects of his educational outlook in the context of the criticisms, distortions, and misunderstandings which had grown up over two decades. There is little fundamentally new, except perhaps the tone. Progressive educators, he suggests, should begin to think "in terms of Education itself rather than in terms of some 'ism about education, even such an 'ism as 'progressivism.' For in spite of itself any movement that thinks and acts in terms of an 'ism becomes so involved in reaction against other 'isms that it is unwittingly controlled by them. For it then forms its principles by reaction against them instead of by a comprehensive constructive survey of actual needs, problems, and possibilities" (24). By 1938, Dewey the sensitive observer could already note, probably with a measure of sadness, that the movement was devoting too much of its energy to internecine ideological conflict and too little, perhaps, to the advancement of its own cause.

Frederic Lilge, in a perceptive essay he recently published in a volume honoring Robert Ulich, contends that Dewey's pedagogical progressivism embodies a fundamental inconsistency which Dewey never really resolves (25). A theory which seems to harmonize the school with the larger social environment, Lilge argues, and which casts the school as a lever of reform, inevitably faces a twofold difficulty: first in determining which social goals to serve in the school; and second, in deciding whether or not to embark on an ever broader program of political reform outside the school. Thus, "Dewey was confronted by two equally repellent alternatives: pursuing his basic aim of adjusting the schools to the social environment, he could integrate them with institutions and practices whose underlying values he rejected; or he could attempt to withdraw them from being thus corrupted, but at the cost of sacrificing that closeness to actual life which it was one of the main aims of his educational philosophy to establish" (25: 29). Lilge contends that Dewey accepted neither, and that the thirties saw him and a number of influential followers increasingly thrust into a clearly political program of reform, both via the schools and outside them. Their manifesto was Counts's pamphlet, *Dare the School Build a New Social Order*; their statement of educational principles was *The Educational Frontier*; their intellectual organ was the *Social Frontier*, a journal which appeared regularly in the decade following 1934.

Now Lilge himself grants that his analysis is far more relevant to some of Dewey's disciples than to Dewey himself. Even so, some clarification is needed. For to pose the dilemma in the first place is to misread the relationship between progressive education and progressivism writ large, particularly as Dewey perceived it. Dewey had no illusions about the school changing society on its own; that educational and political reform would have to go hand in hand was the progressive view from the beginning (26). Nor did the notion of adjusting the school to society imply that the school would have to accommodate itself to all institutions and practices. Dewey wanted schools to use the stuff of reality to educate men and women intelligent about reality. His notion of adjustment was an adjustment *of* conditions, not *to* them, a remaking of existing conditions, not a mere remaking of self and individual to fit into them (27). And as for the corrupting influence of life itself, Dewey was no visionary; the problem for him was not to build *the perfect society* but a *better society*. To this he thought a school that educated for intelligence about reality could make a unique contribution.

Dewey restated these faiths in the introductory essay he wrote for Elsie Clapp's 1952 volume, *The Use of Resources in Education*; it is probably his last major statement on education (28). Once again, he returns to the role of sensitive observer. "In the course of more than half a century of participation in the theory and practice of education," he writes, "I have witnessed many successes and many failures in what is popularly known as 'progressive education,' but is also known as 'the new education,' 'modern education,' and so on." He sees the triumph of the movement in the changed life-conditions of the American classroom, in a greater awareness of the needs of the growing human being, in the warmer personal relations between teachers and students. But as with all reform victories, he sees attendant dangers. No education is progressive, he warns, unless it is making progress. And he observes somewhat poignantly that in schools and colleges across the country, progressive education has been converted into a set of fixed rules and procedures "to be applied to educational problems externally, the way mustard plasters, for example, are applied." If this ossification continues, he fears progressive education will end up guilty of the very formalism it sought to correct, a formalism "fit for the foundations of a totalitarian society and, for the same reason, fit to subvert, pervert and destroy the foundations of a democratic society."

"For the creation of democratic society," he concludes, "we need an educational system where the process of moral-intellectual development is in practice as well as in theory a cooperative transaction of inquiry engaged in by free, independent human beings who treat ideas and the heritage of the past as means and methods for the further enrichments of life, quantitatively and qualitatively, who use the good attained for the discovery and establishment of something better." Dewey's sentence is involved, complex, and overly long; but it embodies the essence of the movement as he saw it. Those who would understand progressive education would do well to ponder it, as would those who set out to build today's schools of tomorrow.

REFERENCES

[1]*John Dewey: The Man and His Philosophy* (Cambridge, Massachusetts: Harvard University Press, 1930), p. 174.

[2]See my essay, "The Progressive Movement in American Education: A Reappraisal," *Harvard Educational Review*, XXVII (Fall, 1957), 251–70.

[3]John Dewey and Evelyn Dewey, *Schools of To-Morrow* (New York: E. P. Dutton & Co., 1915).

[4]Richard Hofstadter, *The Age of Reform* (New York: Alfred A. Knopf, 1955), p. 185.

[5]Actually, Evelyn Dewey visited the several schools and wrote the descriptive chapters of the volume; but no pun is intended by the phrase — *Dewey the observer.* The larger design of the book — both descriptive and analytical — is obviously the elder Dewey's.

[6]One need only check some of the independent accounts, for example, Marietta Johnson, *Thirty Years with an Idea* (unpublished manuscript in the library of Teachers College, Columbia University, 1939), or Caroline Pratt, *I Learn from Children* (New York: Simon and Schuster, 1948).

[7]The ideas of *My Pedagogic Creed* (New York: E. L. Kellogg & Co., 1897), *The School and Society* (Chicago: University of Chicago Press, 1899), *The Child and the Curriculum* (Chicago: University of Chicago Press, 1902), and "The School as Social Center" (published in the National Education Association *Proceedings* for 1902) are particularly apparent. See Melvin C. Baker, *Foundations of John Dewey's Educational Theory* (New York: King's Crown Press, 1955) for an analysis of Dewey's pedagogical ideas prior to 1904.

[8]John Dewey, *Democracy and Education* (New York: Macmillan, 1916).

[9]The organization was founded by a young reformist educator named Stanwood Cobb, who had come under the influence of Marietta Johnson. Dewey refused a number of early invitations to associate himself with the group, but later served as its honorary president. The best account of the Association's first years is given in Robert Holmes Beck, "American Progressive Education, 1875–1930" (unpublished Ph.D. thesis, Yale University, 1942).

[10]Malcolm Cowley, *Exile's Return* (New York: W. W. Norton & Co., 1934), Ch. 2. Henry F. May contends that the shift toward what Cowley calls bohemianism actually began well before the War. See "The Rebellion of the Intellectuals, 1912–1917," *American Quarterly*, VIII (Summer 1956), 114–126.

[11]The incorporation is most clearly evident in Chapter 12 of *Schools of To-Morrow*. See also Dewey's comments on Rousseau in Chapters 7 and 9 of *Democracy and Education*.

[12]Radicalism even tended to disappear from the pedagogical formulations of many political radicals. See, for example, Agnes de Lima, *Our Enemy the Child* (New York: New Republic, 1925), Ch. 12.

[13]Harold Rugg and Ann Shumaker, *The Child-Centered School* (Yonkers-on-Hudson, New York: World Book Co., 1928).

[14]His essay, originally published in the *Journal of the Barnes Foundation*, is reprinted in John Dewey *et al., Art and Education*, pp. 32–40.

[15]John Dewey, "Progressive Education and the Science of Education," *Progressive Education*, V (July-August-September 1928), 197–204.

[16]John Dewey, "How Much Freedom in New Schools?" *New Republic*, LXIII (July 9, 1930), 204–206. The decade to which the *New Republic* refers is, of course, 1919–1929. The implication, that progressive education really began with the founding of the Progressive Education Association, is oft-repeated but erroneous.

[17]Cowley's "Epilogue" in the 1951 reissue of *Exile's Return* is an interesting commentary on this point.

[18]The common cry was that Dewey had been too much the rationalist to develop an adequate theory of creativity. See, for example, *The Child-Centered School*, pp. 4, 324–325.

[19]William H. Kilpatrick (ed.), *The Educational Frontier* (New York: Appleton-Century, 1933). Dewey actually wrote Chapters 2 and 9, though as joint efforts with Childs. See also "The Crucial Role of Intelligence," *Social Frontier*, I (February 1935), 9–10.

[20]See George S. Counts, *Dare the School Build a New Social Order?* (New York: John Day Company, 1932). The tension between bohemianism and radicalism within the progressive-education movement is dramatically portrayed by Counts in an address in 1932 to the Progressive Education Association, "Dare Progressive Education Be Progressive?" *Progressive Education*, IX (April 1932), 257–263.

[21]John Dewey, "Education and Social Change," *Social Frontier*, III (May 1937), 235–238. Italics mine. See also "Can Education Share in Social Reconstruction?" *Social Frontier*, I (October 1934), 11–12.

[22]John Dewey, "Education for a Changing Social Order," National Education Association *Proceedings*, 1934, pp. 744–752.

[23]John Dewey, "Education and Social Change," *op. cit.*, and "Education, Democracy, and Socialized Economy," *Social Frontier*, V (December 1938), 71–72. The latter article deals with an exchange between John L. Childs and Boyd H. Bode in the previous issue of *Social Frontier*.

[24]John Dewey, *Experience and Education* (New York: The Macmillan Company, 1938), pp. vi–vii.

[25]Frederic Lilge, "Politics and the Philosophy of Education," in *Liberal Traditions in Education*, George Z. F. Bereday (ed.) (Cambridge, Mass.: Graduate School of Education, Harvard University, 1958), pp. 27–49.

[26]Dewey makes the point on page 226 of *Schools of To-Morrow* and in Article V of *My Pedagogic Creed*.

[27]This is a central point in view of contemporary attacks on Dewey. See *The Educational Frontier*, p. 312.

[28]Elsie Ripley Clapp, *The Use of Resources in Education* (New York: Harper & Row, 1952), pp. vii–xi.

JAMES S. COLEMAN

The Concept of Equality
of Educational Opportunity

THE CONCEPT OF "EQUALITY OF EDUCATIONAL OPPORTUNITY" AS HELD
by members of society has had a varied past. It has changed radically
in recent years, and is likely to undergo further change in the future. This
lack of stability in the concept leads to several questions. What has it
meant in the past, what does it mean now, and what will it mean in the
future? Whose obligation is it to provide such equality? Is the concept
a fundamentally sound one, or does it have inherent contradictions or
conflicts with social organization? But first of all, and above all, what is
and has been meant in society by the idea of equality of educational
opportunity?

To answer this question, it is necessary to consider how the child's
position in society has been conceived in different historical periods. In
pre-industrial Europe, the child's horizons were largely limited by his
family. His station in life was likely to be the same as his father's. If his
father was a serf, he would likely live his own life as a serf; if his father
was a shoemaker, he would likely become a shoemaker. But even this
immobility was not the crux of the matter; he was part of the family
production enterprise and would likely remain within this enterprise
throughout his life. The extended family, as the basic unit of social organization, had complete authority over the child, and complete responsi-

James S. Coleman, "The Concept of Equality of Educational Opportunity,"
Harvard Educational Review, *38*, Winter 1968, 7–22. Copyright © 1968 by President
and Fellows of Harvard College.

bility for him. This responsibility ordinarily did not end when the child became an adult because he remained a part of the same economic unity and carried on this tradition of responsibility into the next generation. Despite some mobility out of the family, the general pattern was family continuity through a patriarchal kinship system.

There are two elements of critical importance here. First, the family carried responsibility for its members' welfare from cradle to grave. It was a "welfare society," with each extended family serving as a welfare organization for its own members. Thus it was to the family's interest to see that its members became productive. Conversely, a family took relatively small interest in whether someone in *another* family became productive or not — merely because the mobility of productive labor between family economic units was relatively low. If the son of a neighbor was allowed to become a ne'er-do-well, it had little real effect on families other than his own.

The second important element is that the family, as a unit of economic production, provided an appropriate context in which the child could learn the things he needed to know. The craftsman's shop or the farmer's fields were appropriate training grounds for sons, and the household was an appropriate training ground for daughters.

In this kind of society, the concept of equality of educational opportunity had no relevance at all. The child and adult were embedded within the extended family, and the child's education or training was merely whatever seemed necessary to maintain the family's productivity. The fixed stations in life which most families occupied precluded any idea of "opportunity" and, even less, equality of opportunity.

With the industrial revolution, changes occurred in both the family's function as a self-perpetuating economic unity and as a training ground. As economic organizations developed outside the household, children began to be occupationally mobile outside their families. As families lost their economic production activities, they also began to lose their welfare functions, and the poor or ill or incapacitated became more nearly a community responsibility. Thus the training which a child received came to be of interest to all in the community, either as his potential employers or as his potential economic supports if he became dependent. During this stage of development in eighteenth-century England, for instance, communities had laws preventing immigration from another community because of the potential economic burden of immigrants.

Further, as men came to employ their own labor outside the family in the new factories, their families became less useful as economic training grounds for their children. These changes paved the way for public education. Families needed a context within which their children could learn some general skills which would be useful for gaining work outside the family; and men of influence in the community began to be interested in the potential productivity of other men's children.

It was in the early nineteenth century that public education began to appear in Europe and America. Before that time, private education had grown with the expansion of the mercantile class. This class had both the need and resources to have its children educated outside the home, either for professional occupations or for occupations in the developing world of commerce. But the idea of general educational opportunity for all children arose only in the nineteenth century.

The emergence of public, tax-supported education was not solely a function of the stage of industrial development. It was also a function of the class structure in the society. In the United States, without a strong traditional class structure, universal education in publicly-supported free schools became widespread in the early nineteenth century; in England, the "voluntary schools," run and organized by churches with some instances of state support, were not supplemented by a state supported system until the Education Act of 1870. Even more, the character of educational opportunity reflected the class structure. In the United States, the public schools quickly became the common school, attended by representatives of all classes; these schools provided a common educational experience for most American children — excluding only those upper-class children in private schools, those poor who went to no schools, and Indians and Southern Negroes who were without schools. In England, however, the class system directly manifested itself through the schools. The state-supported, or "board schools" as they were called, became the schools of the laboring lower classes with a sharply different curriculum from those voluntary schools which served the middle and upper classes. The division was so sharp that two government departments, the Education Department and the Science and Art Department, administered external examinations, the first for the products of the board schools, and the second for the products of the voluntary schools as they progressed into secondary education. It was only the latter curricula and examinations that provided admission to higher education.

What is most striking is the duration of influence of such a dual structure. Even today in England, a century later (and in different forms in most European countries), there exists a dual structure of public secondary education with only one of the branches providing the curriculum for college admission. In England, this branch includes the remaining voluntary schools which, though retaining their individual identities, have become part of the state-supported system.

This comparison of England and the United States shows clearly the impact of the class structure in society upon the concept of educational opportunity in that society. In nineteenth-century England, the idea of *equality* of educational opportunity was hardly considered; the system was designed to provide *differentiated* educational opportunity appropriate to one's station in life. In the United States as well, the absence of educational opportunity for Negroes in the South arose from the caste and feudal structure of the largely rural society. The idea of differentiated educational opportunity, implicit in the Education Act of 1870 in England, seems to derive from dual needs: the needs arising from industrialization for a basic education of the labor force, and the interests of parents in having one's own child receive a good education. The middle classes could meet both these needs by providing a free system for the children of laboring classes, and a tuition system (which soon came to be supplemented by state grants) for their own. The long survival of this differentiated system depended not only on the historical fact that the voluntary schools existed before a public system came into existence but on the fact that it allows both of these needs to be met: the community's collective need for a trained labor force, and the middle-class individual's interest in a better education for his own child. It served a third need as well: that of maintaining the existing social order — a system of stratification that was a step removed from a feudal system of fixed estates, but designed to prevent a wholesale challenge by the children of the working class to the positions held for children of the middle classes.

The similarity of this system to that which existed in the South to provide differential opportunity to Negroes and whites is striking, just as is the similarity of class structures in the second half of nineteenth-century England to the white-Negro caste structure of the southern United States in the first half of the twentieth century.

In the United States, nearly from the beginning, the concept of educational opportunity had a special meaning which focused on equality. This meaning included the following elements:

(1)   Providing a *free* education up to a given level which constituted the principal entry point to the labor force.

(2)   Providing a *common curriculum* for all children, regardless of background.

(3)   Partly by design and partly because of low population density, providing that children from diverse background attend the *same school.*

(4)   Providing equality within a given *locality*, since local taxes provided the source of support for schools.

This conception of equality of opportunity is still held by many persons; but there are some assumptions in it which are not obvious. First, it implicitly assumes that the existence of free schools eliminates economic sources of inequality of opportunity. Free schools, however, do not mean that the costs of a child's education become reduced to zero for families at all economic levels. When free education was introduced, many families could not afford to allow the child to attend school beyond an early age. His labor was necessary to the family — whether in rural or urban area. Even after the passage of child labor laws, this remained true on the farm. These economic sources of inequality of opportunity have become small indeed (up through secondary education); but at one time they were a major source of inequality. In some countries they remain so; and certainly for higher education they remain so.

Apart from the economic needs of the family, problems inherent in the social structure raised even more fundamental questions about equality of educational opportunity. Continued school attendance prevented a boy from being trained in his father's trade. Thus, in taking advantage of "equal educational opportunity," the son of a craftsman or small tradesman would lose the opportunity to enter those occupations he would most likely fill. The family inheritance of occupation of all social levels was still strong enough, and the age of entry into the labor force was still early enough, that secondary education interfered with opportunity for working-class children; while it opened up opportunities at higher social levels, it closed them at lower ones.

Since residue of this social structure remains in present American society, the dilemma cannot be totally ignored. The idea of a common educational experience implies that this experience has only the effect of widening the range of opportunity, never the effect of excluding opportunities. But clearly this is never precisely true so long as this experience prevents a child from pursuing certain occupational paths. This question still arises with the differentiated secondary curriculum: an academic program in high school has the effect not only of keeping open the opportunities which arise through continued education, but also of closing off opportunities which a vocational program keeps open.

A second assumption implied by this concept of equality of opportunity is that opportunity lies in *exposure* to a given curriculum. The amount of opportunity is then measured in terms of the level of curriculum to which the child is exposed. The higher the curriculum made available to a given set of children, the greater their opportunity.

The most interesting point about this assumption is the relatively passive role of the school and community, relative to the child's role. The school's obligation is to "provide an opportunity" by being available, within easy geographic access of the child, free of cost (beyond the value of the child's time), and with a curriculum that would not exclude him from higher education. The obligation to "use the opportunity" is on the child or the family, so that his role is defined as the active one: the responsibility for achievement rests with him. Despite the fact that the school's role was the relatively passive one and the child's or family's role the active one, the use of this social service soon came to be no longer a choice of the parent or child, but that of the state. Since compulsory attendance laws appeared in the nineteenth century, the age of required attendance has been periodically moved upward.

This concept of equality of educational opportunity is one that has been implicit in most educational practice throughout most of the period of public education in the nineteenth and twentieth centuries. However, there have been several challenges to it; serious questions have been raised by new conditions in public education. The first of these in the United States was a challenge to assumption two, the common curriculum. This challenge first occurred in the early years of the twentieth century with the expansion of secondary education. Until the report of the committee of the National Education Association, issued in 1918, the standard curriculum in secondary schools was primarily a classical one appropriate for college entrance. The greater influx of noncollege-bound adolescents into the high school made it necessary that this curriculum be changed into one more appropriate to the new majority. This is not to say that the curriculum changed immediately in the schools, nor that all schools changed equally, but rather that the seven "cardinal principles" of the N.E.A. report became a powerful influence in the movement toward a less academically rigid curriculum. The introduction of the new non-classical curriculum was seldom if ever couched in terms of a conflict between those for whom high school was college preparation, and those for whom it was terminal education; nevertheless, that was the case. The "inequality" was seen as the use of a curriculum that served a minority and was not designed to fit the needs of the majority; and the shift of curriculum was intended to fit the curriculum to the needs of the new majority in the schools.

In many schools, this shift took the form of *diversifying* the curriculum, rather than supplanting one by another; the college-preparatory curriculum remained though watered down. Thus the kind of equality of opportunity that emerged from the newly designed secondary school curriculum was radically different from the elementary-school concept that had emerged earlier. The idea inherent in the new secondary school curriculum appears to have been to take as given the diverse occupational paths into which adolescents will go after secondary school, and to say (implicitly): there is greater equality of educational opportunity for a boy who is not going to attend college if he has a specially designed curriculum than if he must take a curriculum designed for college entrance.

There is only one difficulty with this definition: it takes as *given* what should be problematic — that a given boy is going into a given post-secondary occupational or educational path. It is one thing to take as given that approximately 70 per cent of an entering high school freshman class will not attend college; but to assign a *particular child* to a curriculum designed for that 70 per cent closes off for that child the opportunity to attend college. Yet to assign all children to a curriculum designed for the 30 per cent who will attend college creates inequality for those who, at the end of high school, fall among the 70 per cent who do not attend college. This is a true dilemma, and one which no educational system has fully solved. It is more general than the college/noncollege dichotomy, for there is a wide variety of different paths that adolescents take on the completion of secondary school. In England, for example, a student planning to attend a university must specialize in the arts or the sciences in the later years of secondary school. Similar specialization occurs in the German gymnasium; and this is wholly within the group planning to attend university. Even greater specialization can be found among noncollege curricula, especially in the vocational, technical, and commercial high schools.

The distinguishing characteristic of this concept of equality of educational opportunity is that it accepts as given the child's expected future. While the concept discussed earlier left the child's future wholly open, this concept of differentiated curricula uses the expected future to match child and curriculum. It should be noted that the first and simpler concept is easier to apply in elementary schools where fundamental tools of reading and arithmetic are being learned by all children; it is only in secondary school that the problem of diverse futures arises. It should also be noted that the dilemma is directly due to the social structure itself: if there were a virtual absence of social mobility with everyone occupying a fixed estate in life, then such curricula that take the future as given would provide equality of opportunity relative to that structure. It is only because of the high degree of occupational mobility between generations — that is, the greater degree of equality of *occupational* opportunity — that the dilemma arises.

The first stage in the evolution of the concept of equality of educational opportunity was the notion that all children must be exposed to the same curriculum in the same school. A second stage in the evolution of the concept assumed that different children would have different occupational futures and that equality of opportunity required providing different curricula for each type of student. The third and fourth stages in this evolution came as a result of challenges to the basic idea of equality of educational opportunity from opposing directions. The third stage can be seen at least as far back as 1896 when the Supreme Court upheld the southern states' notion of "separate but equal" facilities. This stage ended in 1954 when the Supreme Court ruled that legal separation by race inherently constitutes inequality of opportunity. By adopting the "separate but equal" doctrine, the southern states rejected assumption three of the original concept, the assumption that equality depended on the opportunity to attend the same school. This rejection was, however, consistent with the overall logic of the original concept since attendance at the same school was an inherent part of that logic. The underlying idea was that opportunity resided in exposure to a curriculum; the community's responsibility was to provide that exposure, the child's to take advantage of it.

It was the pervasiveness of this underlying idea which created the difficulty for the Supreme Court. For it was evident that even when identical facilities and identical teacher salaries existed for racially separate schools, "equality of educational opportunity" in some sense did not exist. This had also long been evident to Englishmen as well, in a different context, for with the simultaneous existence of the "common school" and the "voluntary school," no one was under the illusion that full equality of educational opportunity existed. But the source of this inequality remained an unarticulated feeling. In the decision of the Supreme Court, this unarticulated feeling began to take more precise form. The essence of it was that the *effects* of such separate schools were, or were likely to be, different. Thus a concept of equality of opportunity which focused on *effects* of schooling began to take form. The actual decision of the Court was in fact a confusion of two unrelated premises: this new concept, which looked at results of schooling, and the legal premise that the use of race as a basis for school assignment violates fundamental freedoms. But what is important for the evolution of the concept of equality of opportunity is that a new and different assumption was introduced, the assumption that equality of opportunity depends in some fashion upon effects of schooling. I believe the decision would have been more soundly based had it not depended on the effects of schooling, but only on the violation of freedom; but by introducing the question of effects of schooling, the Court brought into the open the implicit goals of equality of educational opportunity — that is, goals having to do with the *results* of school — to which the original concept was somewhat awkwardly directed.

That these goals were in fact behind the concept can be verified by a simple mental experiment. Suppose the early schools had operated for only one hour a week and had been attended by children of all social classes. This would have met the explicit assumptions of the early concept of equality of opportunity since the school is free, with a common curriculum, and attended by all children in the locality. But it obviously would not have been accepted, even at that time, as providing equality of opportunity, because its effects would have been so minimal. The additional educational resources provided by middle- and upper-class families, whether in the home, by tutoring, or in private supplementary schools, would have created severe inequalities in results.

Thus the dependence of the concept upon results or effects of schooling, which had remained hidden until 1954, came partially into the open with the Supreme Court decision. Yet this was not the end, for it created more problems than it solved. It might allow one to assess gross inequalities, such as that created by dual school systems in the South, or by a system like that in the mental experiment I just described. But it allows nothing beyond that. Even more confounding, because the decision did not use effects of schooling as a criterion of inequality but only as justification for a criterion of racial integration, integration itself emerged as the basis for still a new concept of equality of educational opportunity. Thus the idea of effects of schooling as an element in the concept was introduced but immediately overshadowed by another, the criterion of racial integration.

The next stage in the evolution of this concept was, in my judgment, the Office of Education Survey of Equality of Educational Opportunity. This survey was carried out under a mandate in the Civil Rights Act of 1964 to the Commissioner of Education to assess the "lack of equality of educational opportunity" among racial and other groups in the United States. The evolution of this concept, and the conceptual disarray which this evolution had created, made the very definition of the task exceedingly difficult. The original concept could be examined by determining the degree to which all children in a locality had access to the same schools and the same curriculum, free of charge. The existence of diverse secondary curricula appropriate to different futures could be assessed relatively easily. But the very assignment of a child to a specific curriculum implies acceptance of the concept of equality which takes futures as given. And the introduction of the new interpretations, equality as measured by results of schooling and equality defined by racial integration, confounded the issue even further.

As a consequence, in planning the survey it was obvious that no single concept of equality of educational opportunity existed and that the survey must give information relevant to a variety of concepts. The basis on which this was done can be seen by reproducing a portion of an internal memorandum that determined the design of the survey:

> The point of second importance in design [second to the point of discovering the intent of Congress, which was taken to be that the survey was not for the purpose of locating willful discrimination, but to determine educational inequality without regard to intention of those in authority] follows from the first and concerns the definition of inequality. One type of inequality may be defined in terms of differences of the community's input to the school, such as per-pupil expenditure, school plants, libraries, quality of teachers, and other similar quantities.
>
> A second type of inequality may be defined in terms of the racial composition of the school, following the Supreme Court's decision that segregated schooling is inherently unequal. By the former definition, the

question of inequality through segregation is excluded, while by the latter, there is inequality of education within a school system so long as the schools within the system have different racial composition.

A third type of inequality would include various intangible character- istics of the school as well as the factors directly traceable to the com- munity inputs to the school. These intangibles are such things as teacher morale, teachers' expectations of students, level of interest of the student body in learning, or others. Any of these factors may affect the impact of the school upon a given student within it. Yet such a definition gives no suggestion of where to stop, or just how relevant these factors might be for school quality.

Consequently, a fourth type of inequality may be defined in terms of the school for individuals with equal backgrounds and abilities. In this definition, equality of educational opportunity is equality of results, given the same individual input. With such a definition, inequality might come about from differences in the school inputs and/or racial com- position and/or from more intangible things as described above.

Such a definition obviously would require that two steps be taken in the determination of inequality. First, it is necessary to determine the effect of these various factors upon educational results (conceiving of results quite broadly, including not only achievement but attitudes toward learning, self-image, and perhaps other variables). This pro- vides various measures of the school's quality in terms of its effect upon its students. Second, it is necessary to take these measures of quality, once determined, and determine the differential exposure of Negroes (or other groups) and whites to schools of high and low quality.

A fifth type of inequality may be defined in terms of consequences of the school for individuals of unequal backgrounds and abilities. In this definition, equality of educational opportunity is equality of results given *different* individual inputs. The most striking examples of inequality here would be children from households in which a language other than English, such as Spanish or Navaho, is spoken. Other examples would be low-achieving children from homes in which there is a poverty of verbal expression or an absence of experiences which lead to conceptual facility.

Such a definition taken in the extreme would imply that educational equality is reached only when the results of schooling (achievement and attitudes) are the same for racial and religious minorities as for the dominant group.

The basis for the design of the survey is indicated by another segment of this memorandum:

Thus, the study will focus its principal effort on the fourth definition, but will also provide information relevant to all five possible definitions. This insures the pluralism which is obviously necessary with respect to a definition of inequality. The major justification for this focus is that the results of this approach can best be translated into policy which will improve education's effects. The results of the first two approaches (tangible inputs to the school, and segregation) can certainly be translated into policy, but these is no good evidence that these policies will improve education's effects; and while policies to implement the fifth would certainly improve education's effects, it seems hardly possible that the study could provide information that would direct such policies.

Altogether, it has become evident that it is not our role to define what constitutes equality for policy-making purposes. Such a definition will be an outcome of the interplay of a variety of interests, and will certainly differ from time to time as these interests differ. It should be our role to cast light on the state of inequality defined in the variety of ways which appear reasonable at this time.

The survey, then, was conceived as a pluralistic instrument, given the variety of concepts of equality of opportunity in education. Yet I suggest that despite the avowed intention of not adjudicating between these different ideas, the survey has brought a new stage in the evolution of the concept. For the definitions of equality which the survey was designed to serve split sharply into two groups. The first three definitions concerned input resources: first, those brought to the school by the actions of the school administration (facilities, curriculum, teachers); second, those brought to the school by the other students, in the educational backgrounds which their presence contributed to the school; and third, the intangible characteristics such as "morale" that result from the interaction of all these factors. The fourth and fifth definitions were concerned with the effects of schooling. Thus the five definitions were divided into three concerned with inputs to school and two concerned with effects of schooling. When the Report emerged, it did not give five different measures of equality, one for each of these definitions; but it did focus sharply on this dichotomy, giving in Chapter Two information on inequalities of input relevant to definitions one and two, and in Chapter Three information on inequalities of results relevant to definitions four and five, and also in Chapter Three information on the relation of input to results again relevant to definitions four and five.

Although not central to our discussion here, it is interesting to note that this examination of the relation of school inputs to effects on achievement showed that those input characteristics of schools that are most alike for Negroes and whites have least effect on their achievement. The magnitudes of differences between schools attended by Negroes and those attended by whites were as follows: least, facilities and curriculum; next, teacher quality; and greatest, educational backgrounds of fellow students.

The order of importance of these inputs on the achievement of Negro students is precisely the same: facilities and curriculum least, teacher quality next, and backgrounds of fellow students, most.

By making the dichotomy between inputs and results explicit, and by focusing attention not only on inputs but on results, the Report brought into the open what had been underlying all the concepts of equality of educational opportunity but had remained largely hidden: that the concept implied *effective* equality of opportunity, that is, equality in those elements that are effective for learning. The reason this had remained half-hidden, obscured by definitions that involve inputs is, I suspect, because educational research has been until recently unprepared to demonstrate what elements are effective. The controversy that has surrounded the Report indicates that measurement of effects is still subject to sharp disagreement; but the crucial point is that *effects* of inputs have come to constitute the basis for assessment of school quality (and thus equality of opportunity) in place of using certain inputs by definition as measures of quality (e.g., small classes are better than large, higher-paid teachers are better than lower-paid ones, by definition).

It would be fortunate indeed if the matter could be left to rest there — if merely by using effects of school rather than inputs as the basis for the concept, the problem were solved. But that is not the case at all. The conflict between definitions four and five given above shows this. The conflict can be illustrated by resorting again to the mental experiment discussed earlier — providing a standard education of one hour per week, under identical conditions, for all children. By definition four, controlling all background differences of the children, results for Negroes and whites would be equal, and thus by this definition equality of opportunity would exist. But because such minimal schooling would have minimal effect, those children from educationally strong families would enjoy educational opportunity far surpassing that of others. And because such educationally strong backgrounds are found more often among whites than among Negroes, there would be very large overall Negro-white achievement differences — and thus inequality of opportunity by definition five.

It is clear from this hypothetical experiment that the problem of what constitutes equality of opportunity is not solved. The problem will become even clearer by showing graphs with some of the results of the Office of Education Survey. The highest line in Figure 1 shows the achievement in verbal skills by whites in the urban Northeast at grades 1, 3, 6, 9, and 12. The second line shows the achievement at each of these grades by whites in the rural Southeast. The third shows achievement of Negroes in the urban Northeast. The fourth shows the achievement of Negroes in the rural Southeast.

When compared to the whites in the urban Northeast, each of the other three groups shows a different pattern. The comparison with whites in

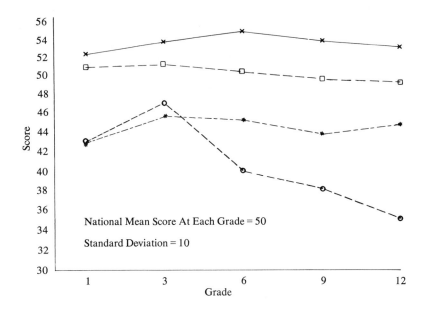

FIGURE 1 *Patterns of Achievement in Verbal Skills at Various Grade Levels by Race and Region*

the rural South shows the two groups beginning near the same point in the first grade, and diverging over the years of school. The comparison with Negroes in the urban Northeast shows the two groups beginning farther apart at the first grade and remaining about the same distance apart. The comparison with Negroes in the rural South shows the two groups beginning far apart and moving much farther apart over the years of school.

Which of these, if any, shows equality of educational opportunity between regional and racial groups? Which shows greatest inequality of opportunity? I think the second question is easier to answer than the first. The last comparison showing both initial difference and the greatest increase in difference over grades 1 through 12 appears to be the best candidate for the greatest inequality. The first comparison, with whites in the rural South, also seems to show inequality of opportunity, because of the increasing difference over the twelve years. But what about the second comparison, with an approximately constant difference between Negroes and whites in the urban Northeast? Is this equality of opportunity? I suggest not. It means, in effect, only that the period of school has left the average Negro at about the same level of achievement relative to whites as he began—in this case, achieving higher than about 15 per cent of the whites, lower than about 85 per cent of the whites. It may well be that in the absence of school those lines of achievement would have diverged due to differences in home environments; or perhaps they would have remained an equal distance apart, as they are in this graph (though at lower levels of achievement for both groups in the absence of school). If it were the former, we could say that school, by keeping the lines parallel, has been a force toward the equalization of opportunity. But in the absence of such knowledge, we cannot say even that.

What would full equality of educational opportunity look like in such graphs? One might persuasively argue that it should show a convergence, so that even though two population groups begin school with different levels of skills on the average, the average of the group that begins lower moves up to coincide with that of the group that begins higher. Parenthetically, I should note that this does *not* imply that all students' achievement comes to be identical, but only that the *averages* for two population groups that begin at different levels come to be identical. The diversity of individual scores could be as great as, or greater than, the diversity at grade 1.

Yet there are serious questions about this definition of equality of opportunity. It implies that over the period of school there are no other influences, such as the family environment, which affect achievement over the twelve years of school, even though these influences may differ greatly for the two population groups. Concretely, it implies that white family environments, predominantly middle class, and Negro family environments, predominantly lower class, will produce no effects on achievement that would keep these averages apart. Such an assumption seems highly unrealistic, especially in view of the general importance of family background for achievement.

However, if such possibilities are acknowledged, then how far can they go before there is inequality of educational opportunity? Constant difference over school? Increasing differences? The unanswerability of such questions begins to give a sense of a new stage in the evolution of the concept of equality of educational opportunity. These questions concern the *relative intensity* of two sets of influences: those which are alike for the two groups, principally in school, and those which are different, principally in the home or neighborhood. If the school's influences are not only alike for the two groups, but very strong relative to the divergent influences, then the two groups will move together. If school influences are very weak, then the two groups will move apart. Or more generally, the relative intensity of the convergent school influences and the divergent out-of-school influences determines the effectiveness of the educational system in providing equality of educational opportunity. In this perspective, complete equality of opportunity can be reached only if all the divergent out-of-school influences vanish, a condition that would arise only in the advent of boarding schools; given the existing divergent influences, equality of opportunity can only be approached and never fully reached. The concept becomes one of degree of proximity to equality of opportunity. This proximity is determined, then, not merely by the *equality* of educational inputs, but by the *intensity* of the school's influences relative to the external divergent influences. That is, equality of output is not so much determined by equality of the resource inputs, but by the power of these resources in bringing about achievement.

Here, then, is where the concept of equality of educational opportunity presently stands. We have observed an evolution which might have been anticipated a century and a half ago when the first such concepts arose, yet one which is very different from the concept as it first developed. This difference is sharpened if we examine a further implication of the current concept as I have described it. In describing the original concept, I indicated that the role of the community and the educational institution was relatively passive; they were expected to provide a set of free public resources. The responsibility for profitable use of those resources lay with the child and his family. But the evolution of the concept has reversed these roles. The implication of the most recent concept, as I have described it, is that the responsibility to create achievement lies with the educational institution, not the child. The difference in achievement at grade 12 between the average Negro and the average white is, in effect, the degree of inequality of opportunity, and the reduction of that inequality is a responsibility of the school. This shift in responsibility follows logically from the change in the concept of equality of educational opportunity from school resource inputs to effects of schooling. When that change occurred, as it has in the past few years, the school's responsibility shifted from increasing and distributing equally *its* "quality" to increasing the quality of its *students'* achievements. This is a notable shift, and one which should have strong consequences for the practice of education in future years.

HENRY STEELE COMMAGER

Education and the International Community

WE ARE CONFRONTED, AT THE VERY THRESHOLD OF OUR INQUIRY, BY
a problem of far-reaching importance and of no little difficulty. Are we
concerned, here, primarily with education or with the conduct of international relations? Clearly, they are almost inextricably related: Those
who study international relations are likely to get involved in them; those
who conduct them must study them first. Yet the objectives of the two
approaches are different, and so too, therefore, their methods and their
philosophies.

If our concern is education, then the center of gravity of our inquiry
must be the educational system at every level but chiefly at the level of
the university. If our concern is the conduct of international relations,
then we must inevitably look to government and to those institutions that
serve government for progress. The nature of the difference emerges at
once if we consider the approach to a common concern: war — one of
the major functions of international relations. The university approach
to the study of war is — or should be — scholarly, judicious, impartial,
and scientific. It is no more interested in the Korean War, let us say, than
in the Peloponnesian, and it cannot, if it is true to its nature, take sides on
wars, past or present. But inquiry into war by, let us say, the Rand
Corporation or the Hudson Institute or the Department of Defense is

Henry Steele Commager, "Education and the International Community." *Phi
Delta Kappan, 51*, 1970, 230–34. Reprinted by permission of the author and
publisher.

very much directed to current wars, and into wars in which the United States is involved, and does not pretend to be aloof or impersonal in its inquiries or its conclusions. Where the university should take a long view, to the past and to the future, government and its agencies want immediate answers to urgent questions, and answers that are usable. The same principles apply to the study of foreign policy in general: The attitude here of the Kennedy Institute, let us say, is, or should be, very different from that of the school of experts who serve the purposes of the CIA.

The distinction is familiar enough. There is a century-old tradition that the academy concerns itself not with what is immediate and parochial but with what is permanent, universal, and philosophical: Leave aside the question whether the academy invariably lives up to this high standard. Certainly the distinction is taken for granted in most of those areas where the university makes contributions — law, medicine, science, and politics, for example. A university that turned out practicing lawyers but did not concern itself with jurisprudence, that produced practicing physicians but did not sponsor research into the causes of cancer or other diseases, that trained potential civil servants but ignored political philosophy, would not only betray its own character but would fail even the professions of law, medicine, chemistry, and politics.

Obviously, the conduct of the business of government and of international relations, on all levels — political, economic, cultural — has its own importunate claims, and society is bound to provide the institutions that will satisfy them. A sensible society wants the best services it can get even for practical day-by-day affairs, and it turns therefore to whatever institutions promise these services — universities, for example — or it creates new institutions to do what it wants done: the Rand Corporation, the Office of Strategic Services, the military service institutes, and so forth. Fortunately, our society boasts a great variety of institutions, ranging from the private to the public, to conduct the far-flung and intricate operations that involve foreign policy. Government conducts its own training program, formal and informal. It draws on the products of academic training schools such as the Woodrow Wilson at Princeton, the Fletcher at Tufts, the Johns Hopkins in Washington and Bologna, and others. It uses the scores of quasi-private organizations that our culture has developed — developed more efficiently than any other: the Foreign Policy Association, the Council on Foreign Relations, the American Scandinavian Foundation, the Institute of International Education, and so forth, almost ad infinitum. It profits from the wisdom, and the largesse, of great foundations like the Rockefeller, the Carnegie, the Ford — how odd that it now seems bent on weakening or paralyzing these beneficent institutions!

In the past quarter century government itself has invented, or created, three remarkable institutions that have played, and may continue to play, a major role both in education and in foreign relations: the Fulbright program, the AID programs, and the Peace Corps. Two of these, certainly, represent creativity of a high order: the Fulbright program, which in a quarter century has enlisted some 125,000 scholars and students in the enterprise of creating a new community of learning; and the Peace Corps, which each year sends some 10 or 12 thousand young men and women on what are both welfare and educational missions. A Congress which prefers to spend money on war rather than on peace is now starving both of these benevolent enterprises; let us hope that its present mood of despair will in time give way to confidence.

Though all three of these programs for international education originated in government and are financed by government, they draw from and depend upon the academy for their effectiveness. The university, in short, remains the vital center of the enterprise of international education. It is the universities that provide the Fulbright Scholars who go abroad and welcome those who come here; it is the colleges that are the nurseries and the training grounds for members of the Peace Corps; it is the universities that are responsible for the far-flung programs of AID that have made invaluable contributions to agriculture, engineering, teacher training, and similar programs in some 30 underdeveloped countries.

It is inevitable that the American university should play a large role in the development of science, technology, and education in these countries, and inevitable, too, that it should furnish something of a model for higher education. For the new nations of Asia and Africa — and to some extent of Latin America — are seeking in one or two generations to catch up with the progress of the West over the past four centuries. They are going through something of the same crises that the United States itself went through during the first century or so of its existence, hence they require from universities what the United States required in the nineteenth century. Because Americans had few other institutions to do the tasks that Old World societies placed upon a score of ancient institutions, they turned to their colleges and universities and required them to do everything that they wanted done: Thus the beginnings of the "multiversity." Because the American was an equalitarian society, it took for granted that all subjects and disciplines that served society were of equal interest and equal dignity, and saw no reason why teacher training, nursing, agriculture, library science, and business administration should not be taught at and by the university alongside the ancient and orthodox subjects. Because American society and economy were growing with unprecedented rapidity, it was taken for granted that the universities would respond by a comparable expansion of their student bodies. All of this flew in the face of Old World tradition; it created a new tradition on which the new nations of the globe can draw with some confidence.

Thus the American university cannot avoid a special responsibility towards education overseas — a responsibility which inevitably (as in the AID programs) involves it in foreign relations. But the experience of some universities whose enterprises were corrupted by the CIA and of others whose effectiveness was paralyzed by involvement in politics, by too lively a readiness to respond to governmental importunities, warns us against an association of government and the university that is one-sided or uncritical. The unhappy experience of so many of our universities with Department of Defense contracts stands as a warning here. Students, outraged at the readiness of universities to lend their facilities to government even for purposes of an immoral war, have called for a complete separation of the university and the federal government. Needless to say, that is not the answer, nor the solution. It is not a complete separation that is required — indeed, such a separation is palpably injurious to the community of science and of learning. It is, rather, independence. The university must educate government itself to respect the integrity of science and education, and it must devise methods of sterilizing governmental support of its obnoxious features.

These objectives are not difficult to attain. After all, society needs its universities and research institutions as it needs government. Government cannot impose its will upon universities — not unless it is prepared to settle for second-rate institutions. It can enlist universities in research on terms acceptable to the academic community, or it can carry out its own research in its own bureaus and departments. And what are the terms that are acceptable to the academic community? They are essentially simple: First, no secrecy in research; all the findings of scholars, in every field, must be available to all. Second, the university itself must be in complete charge of research of all kinds; in charge of the particular projects, in charge of the personnel engaged in the research, and in control of the conduct of the research and of its findings. These elementary safeguards will both advance research itself and preserve the integrity of the academy.

Something should be said of one now widely discussed proposal for using the university as an instrument for advancing international understanding: the founding of "world" universities. And what should be said is that the notion, generous and hopeful as it is, is quite irrelevant to reality. For universities are by their very nature world institutions; or if they are not, they should be. Happily, most of them are: Paris is a world university, and so too are London and Edinburgh, Oxford and Cambridge, Göttingen, and Heidelberg; Columbia, California, Harvard, Michigan, Wisconsin, and a dozen other major American institutions are both in their constituency and in their programs and their objectives world universities. Some of these institutions — like Paris — have 15 or 20 thousand foreign students, and great American universities number from one to three thousand foreigners in their student bodies. Faculties are drawn from every country and every culture; libraries are stocked with volumes from every country and every age; the activities of the universities spread out to embrace the interests of every society. Most important of all, the university is, by its nature, not parochial or even national but universal; it is part of the great community of learning and, if it is true to itself, serves primarily that community. We do not need to create new "world" universities; we need to make sure that all of our universities are indeed global institutions.

So far we have been discussing education with primary emphasis on its international function and with special concern for governmental policies and programs. If we consider our problem as primarily educational, we see at once that it has other dimensions than those we have so far drawn.

If our purpose is to develop an enlightened attitude toward the rest of the world, create a sympathetic understanding of other peoples and cultures, foster tolerance and advance peace — as surely it must be — we must deal with more than formal education for international relations; we must deal with education as a whole.

Education is, as we know, a seamless web. It begins in infancy, it is formalized in the elementary school, it continues through the most advanced graduate and professional study. It embraces not only what goes on in the classroom and the library but in the home, on the playing fields, and through the newspapers, magazines, and television. It is not too great an exaggeration to say that every book, every magazine article, every television broadcast is part of the child's international education.

How then is education at every level and through every medium to encourage an enlightened view of the world and promote an enlightened foreign policy?

The problem is intractable and perhaps insoluble, but let us discuss it in terms of schools.

For the past half century American schools and universities have attemped to educate the young to a sense of their membership in the whole human race and their global responsibilities. They have introduced children to other civilizations at a very early age; they have taught world history and literature in the high schools. In the last quarter century they have provided for "non-Western" studies at both high school and college levels. Nor is it the schools alone that have been involved in this laudable undertaking. Every day the popular press provides a broader spectrum of news about foreign nations than any previous generation enjoyed; every day television spreads a global spectacle, even a cosmic, before the fascinated gaze of children.

All this should have produced the most cosmopolitan, sophisticated, and magnanimous generation in our history. It should have erased intolerance with peoples of different color, culture, faith, and political ideologies. It should have ushered in an era when we would, infallibly, resort to the counsels of reason, not the weapons of war, to resolve international difficulties; when we would not exacerbate divisions but work for universal unity; when we would pin our hopes not on the might of our armies and the size of our stockpile of nuclear weapons but on great international organizations like the United Nations and the World Court.

Alas, that is not the way it has turned out.

Clearly education is not getting the results that all of us deeply want and desperately need. Is this the fault of education or is the notion that these results are obtainable a delusion? Is prejudice so deep, interest so compulsive, zeal for power so ineradicable, that no education can counter or overcome their importunate demands? Or have we, perhaps, relied overmuch on misguided educational philosophy and inadequate educational methods?

There are, in a broad way, two obvious educational approaches to the problems of our relations with the rest of mankind that glare upon us so relentlessly: the modern and the traditionalist. The modern approach, cultivated more assiduously in the United States than elsewhere, is to expose the young to foreign cultures early and persistently. It relies not so much on the study of literature, philosophy, and history as on the study of sociology, economics, and politics; its aim is not so much qualitative understanding as quantitative coverage; its preferred technique is that of "problem solving." This sovereign philosophy of education operates vertically on the whole body of our children through formal schooling from elementary school through college, and horizontally on the whole of our population through mass media such as television, newspapers, and magazines.

Never in history, it can be confidently asserted, have so many been exposed to so much with results so meager. For if we judge by results — and by what other standards are we to judge? — this pervasively American method of teaching about the rest of the world has been a stunning failure. After half a century of exposure to world cultures and politics and of problem solving, we are culturally more alienated and politically more isolated than at any time in the past, and we seem totally unable to solve any of our major problems, foreign or domestic. Who can deny that the American people are today more nationalistic, chauvinistic, militaristic, parochial, and intolerant in their attitude toward other nations and cultures than at any time in the past century?

The traditionalist philosophy of education assumes that it is quite impossible to anticipate the needs, the demands, the crises of the future, and just as impossible to predict the interests or idiosyncrasies of the individual, and that it is therefore impossible to prepare the young for their future by trying to teach the whole of the contemporary, or the future, world. It places its faith in an education designed to familiarize students with the great ideas and institutions that have molded the minds of Western man for centuries. It is not much interested in exposing the young to large quantities of information — much of it miscellaneous — but seeks instead to excite the imagination, stir the sentiments of emulation, and deeper judgment when confronted with the spectacle of greatness. It assumes — not with any confidence, to be sure — that with such a training and with such a stimulus, the young will somehow grow in tolerance, sympathy, and wisdom.

In the past this concept of education has concentrated not on the study of current events or on the attempt to solve current problems but on familiarity with the classics of literature, history, and philosophy, with languages and mathematics, confident that students deeply immersed in the classics, skilled in languages, and disciplined by mathematics will be resourceful enough to adjust to almost any situation that arises. Thus, confronted by the crisis of the Cold War, students might find it more profitable to study the history of the Wars of Religion of the sixteenth and seventeenth centuries than to study the labyrinthine details of current Soviet-American relations. Thus, confronted by the crisis of the cities, they might prefer to start with Pericles' Funeral Oration and move on through literature to Zimmern's *Greek Commonwealth* or Lewis Mumford's philosophical interpretations of cities, rather than confront the immense literature of urban problems pouring from our presses today. Thus, when confronted by the Vietnam War, they might conclude that a study of the long war between Athens and Sparta, or of the decline of the Roman Empire, might better prepare their minds to understand the nature of that war than would a study of the confused origins of our Asia policy. None of this, needless to say, applies to training or scholarship at the higher levels. The traditionalists believe quite as firmly in technical training as do the modernists, but they would build it on the foundation of traditionalist education.

This is the educational philosophy which has been pretty generally accepted in Britian, and of which Winston Churchill was both a product and a protagonist. To this day English university and governmental examinations are directed not so much toward testing candidates on their expertise in particular fields as toward discovering how broad and how deep is their knowledge of history or literature or science, how well they express themselves, how critical is their judgment. Where the university and government led, even industry and finance followed; until recently a graduate with a "First" in classics or philosophy or history stood a better chance of getting a job with Barclay's Bank or Imperial Chemicals than students who had concentrated on finance or chemistry but achieved a lesser distinction.

But we should perhaps not go to contemporary England for our illustrations: There are doubtless too many imponderables here to make comparisons very useful. It is, however, not without interest to contrast the educational philosophy and techniques of the past two generations with those of the generation of the Founding Fathers.

The men who fought the Revolution; won independence; made a nation; wrote state and national constitutions; launched America on the path of self-government, federalism, and popular enlightenment; and solved every major problem but one — and that one still unsolved — were not formally trained to politics, economics, sociology, or even science. All of them had what we would call a "general" education; none enjoyed a specialized training or education. All were groomed on the classics (Latin, Greek, and occasionally Hebrew), on history (mostly ancient), on mathematics and philosophy and a smattering of "natural philosophy," which we would call science. Most of them entered college very young — 13 or 14 was not uncommon — and graduated at 18 or 19. They did not attend specialized schools, for there were none, though a few "read" law at the Inns of Court or studied medicine at Edinburgh or Leyden.

Insofar as men are ever the "product" of education, the Founding Fathers and those who supported them were the product of an education that was traditionalist, classical, and — certainly in our eyes — antiquarian. When they thought about wars — and fought them — it was the wars of the Greeks and the Persians or of the Romans and the Carthagenians. When they thought about constitutions — and wrote them — it was in terms of the constitutional principles of Greece and Rome and seventeenth-century England. When they pondered the problems of federalism — and created a federal system — it was to the confederations of ancient Greece, of the Italian city states, and of the Swiss and the Dutch that they turned, if not for relevant provisions then for inspiration. In some areas there were no classical antecedents: popular education, for example, or the new colonial system, or penal reform. Even here their approach was philosophical rather than technical; that is no doubt why we still turn to what they wrote for guidance today.

In their dealings with foreign nations — the subject which particularly concerns us — they were wholly without formal training or preparation; indeed, it has often been observed that, in all probability, neither Jefferson nor Gallatin nor John Quincy Adams, our three greatest diplomat-statesmen, could qualify for entrance into the U.S. foreign service today. But somehow they did manage to avoid destructive wars which would have ended the career of the new nation, to conclude agreeable treaties with foreign nations, to win the respect of the rest of the world, to formulate doctrines which have survived to our own day, and even, *mirabile dictu*, to keep the military in its place.

It would be folly to suggest that we might solve the problems that crowd about us by a return to the classics, or to the deadly drill to which eighteenth-century youngsters were exposed. But it may not be irrelevant to recall that our earlier philosophy of education was associated with a political and international system that was affluent and successful, and that our contemporary technical and problem-oriented education is not.

It is impossible to assert that any system of education will surely give us a more humane culture, a more cosmopolitan society, a more tolerant citizenry, a more enlightened civil service, a more statesmanlike government, a more generous foreign policy. But is it not clear that the educational philosophy we have has failed to produce these qualities so deeply needed, those policies so desperately desired?

PART III

Philosophical
Foundations

For the teacher and educator, the primary value of an
inquiry into the philosophical foundations of education is to
provide a theoretical or intellectual foundation for both the
guidance of educational practice and the analysis of the data
of educational experience. A well-defined philosophy of
education offers the educator a frame of reference out of which
he can construct and give meaning to his teaching activities
and interpret the learning behavior of his pupils. Without
the guidance of philosophical principles, classroom decisions
tend to become random, based upon a moment's expedience,
and the goal of a consistent educational process — lending
itself to prediction and long-range planning — is
hardly possible.

Of more importance to the teacher, however, is the fact that learning is enhanced when classroom activities can be perceived by the student as possessing a coherent pattern. The student needs to see the relationship between means and ends, and to see these relations extending beyond the present moment to other days, months and years. Further, consistence in educational planning provides the atmosphere of security so necessary for effective learning.

The "doing" of philosophy of education and what is done with the results of philosophizing about education requires clarification. The results of the efforts of educational philosophers do not, and are not intended to, tell the teacher what to do. It is the teacher himself who must formulate his theory of educational practice: what philosophers of education "do" is provide guidance to those educators who wish to develop and articulate their own ideas and formulae; and never, it seems, has the alliance between teacher and philosopher been more necessary. At no time in our history have educational practices seemed so fragmented and so lacking in any unity of purpose. The pressing need is to establish some clearly defined goals, and the contribution of philosophy will be, not to provide answers, but a wider range of alternatives — not merely alternative goals, but alternative methods for determining them.

Philosophers of education also contribute to enhancing the decision-making and problem-solving capacities of the teacher. By increasing teachers' awareness of options in decision-making situations, a familiarity with theory of education increases freedom of choice and the teacher's sensitivity in handling and applying the means that he chooses.

And, so important in this time of cultural transition, a thorough background in the philosophical foundations of education helps to facilitate educational change, both in the expansion of teaching options and in the direction that philosophy may give to larger decision-making processes in the schools and communities. It is in the history of educational thought that the teacher and administrator may find a perspective upon which new patterns of education may be based. Without knowing where we have been, it is difficult to determine where we *are* and impossible to decide rationally where we ought to go.

One final matter deserves emphasis. Change in educational practice is not brought about by educational philosophy. It is the decisions of individuals, whose choices are revealed in their actions, that bring about change. The following selections in the philosophy of education are offered to students and teachers who are now, or soon will be, making the decisions that will determine the future of American education.

In his "Challenge to Philosophize about Education," John S. Brubacher draws attention to the fact that conflict or tensions within educational theory and practices reflect the deeper conflicts that run through society as a whole. He illustrates this by recounting the conflicts associated with the progressive education movement and their sources in twentieth-century American society. Brubacher then examines those issues which he sees as the primary challenge to the teacher and the field of education. While they are described in educational terms, these issues are shown to be part of the more universal considerations of philosophy and social change.

Jonas F. Soltis' article presents the reader with an analysis of the various methods of "doing" educational philosophy. His particular form of analysis establishes categories or "dimensions" into which the various specific examples of educational philosophy can be assigned, and then focuses upon the characteristic way in which each dimension deals with educational theories and practices. Soltis offers a simplified view of the entire field in order to show how individual philosophers of education may be working within a particular mode contained within the discipline of educational philosophy.

We then see one of those philosophers, Jacques Maritain, deducing a set of prescriptive educational values from one fully developed philosophical position, that of the Thomist school. In addition to examining the aims and purposes inherent in his philosophical stance, Maritain describes those practical applications that may be made from a Thomist theory of liberal education.

And then, from this example of specific philosophizing, we conclude with Kenneth D. Benne's illustration of a philosophical argument which carries in it important educational implications. His argument proceeds from the premise that there exists today a social disorientation in the United States of such magnitude as to constitute a crisis. From his analysis of this crisis, the author concludes that the concept of education must radically change if we are to avoid social chaos.

Taking the conclusion that education must change, Benne analyzes the resistance to such a change, a resistance that centers around fear arising from those conflicts that are a necessary component of the existing discontinuities of social crisis. The discontinuities themselves present a major obstacle to needed change; our present mechanistic, bureaucratized way of viewing social functions poses *the* major barrier to the effective adaptation of social institutions — especially educational institutions. Benne outlines what desirable changes are possible and how they may be facilitated.

JOHN S. BRUBACHER

The Challenge to Philosophize About Education

EDUCATIONAL THEORY IN RELATION TO SOCIAL TENSIONS

THE STUDY OF EDUCATIONAL PHILOSOPHY HAS FLOURISHED IN THE twentieth century as never before in the whole history of education. Earlier centuries, no doubt, produced a fair share of famous essays on education, but relatively few of these essays were philosophical in exposition and intent. Comenius' *Didactica Magna*, Locke's *Thoughts Concerning Education*, and Rousseau's *Émile* were notable publications, but none of the three was explicitly a philosophy of education. Perhaps a philosophy of education was implicit in these essays, but certainly none was systematically set forth. Philosophers like Aristotle, St. Thomas, Kant, and Hegel gave passing attenion to education, but in no case did one of them give it rounded treatment. Herbart took education much more seriously, but even he limited himself to its moral and psychological aspects. Only Plato of pre-twentieth-century philosophers produced a notable philosophy of education (in his *Republic*). The twentieth century, by contrast, has produced almost a plethora of publications on philosophy of education, mostly American. Indeed, only half over, it has

John S. Brubacher, "The Challenge to Philosophize About Education." In N. B. Henry (Ed.), *Modern Philosophies and Education*. National Society for the Study of Education, Fifty-Fourth Yearbook, Part I. Chicago: The University of Chicago Press, 1955, 4–16. Copyright © 1955 by The University of Chicago Press.

already produced not only one major philosophy of education, Dewey's *Democracy and Education*, but a dozen or more minor ones as well.[1]

What is the reason for this greatly augmented interest in educational philosophy? Perhaps the simplest answer is the rise of "progressive education" as a *cause célèbre*. At first, the newer educational procedures of this movement were a protest against the rather formal educational practices inherited from the nineteenth century. As the protest gained momentum, people began to see that the newer educational practices were not just an amendment to traditional practice but involved a fundamental departure from it. In the early phases of the movement, "progressive education" met no more opposition than the inertia of convention. While the progressive concepts had difficulty in overcoming this inertia in practice, the advocates of reform won easy victories over such opposition in the field of theory during the 1920's. As theoretical victories led to more and more victories in the field of practice, the defenders of traditional and conventional education finally took pen in hand to defend their own practices and even to go over to the offensive to attack progressive education during the 1930's. Then war intervened, causing an interlude in the strife of educational systems, and our whole energies were mobilized to resolve the international strife of political and economic ideologies. Now that there is an interlude after that war, we have returned to the conflict of educational ideologies again.

It is no doubt an oversimplification to ascribe the great interest of the twentieth century in educational philosophy to just the contest between progressive and traditional educational practices. The issue really lies much deeper. The experimental schools which made up progressive education were but the vanguard of that larger twentieth-century endeavor to assume more and more intentional control of the social process. Traditional methods of cultural transmission and renewal, once left to automatic processes, now became the object of conscious consideration. Progressive schools, for instance, deliberately fashioned their practices on scientific findings. As these often were in conflict with cherished traditional convictions there was an urgent demand for a fresh philosophical approach to resolve the conflict.

Thus, while traditional education has been based on a metaphysical psychology, "progressive education" has taken its cue from a psychology recently become scientific. Techniques of measurement devised by the new psychology have demanded a different conception of human nature, a conception which traditional education has often found repugnant to its metaphysical psychology. Again, the interpretation of biological findings, especially the theory of organic evolution, has widened the differences between traditional and "progressive" education. To attach the adjective "progressive" to education can mean quite different things depending on whether one uses an Aristotelian or a Darwinian conception of development. Further educational complications have arisen from a third scientific area, anthropological and sociological studies. The cultural relativity frequently espoused by these disciplines has stood in sharp contrast to fixed conceptions of the curriculum, especially in moral education, held by adherents of the old school. Underlying all these issues are conflicting assumptions which only careful and systematic philosophizing can clarify.

It must be remembered, too, that these disagreements over educational policy took place in the twentieth century in a matrix of political and economic upheaval. This century has witnessed a rising struggle for political power between varieties of autocracy — monarchic at first, fascistic later, and communistic currently — and varieties of democracy — laissez-faire individualism, benevolent paternal new-dealism, and a pragmatic liberalism strongly supported by many professional leaders of teachers. The resulting confusion over political ideals obviously has obscured the precise nature of citizenship as a dominating aim of education. The strife of political systems has been underscored by the further strife of economic systems, notably capitalism and communism. If, as some philosophers allege, the quality of education varies according to the way in which a man earns his bread, then the road ahead for education is anything but clear, for the rise of the working classes the world over is already making unprecedented demands for the reform of education.

The strife of political and economic ideologies has also greatly aggravated nationalistic rivalries. To the rational arguments which can be adduced for each ideology has been added the organized forces of national states. Consequently, national schools have taught these ideologies with patriotic fervor. The threat this provides to amicable settlement of international disagreements brings nearer the resulting danger of war. Just how to harness national resources to provide added educational opportunities and yet how at the same time to avoid irreconcilable rivalries is obviously another problem driving educators to philosophy. Their problem takes on complication as well as inspiration as they seek an educational policy to undergird the efforts of UNESCO, a policy which will respect diverse national, political, economic, and religious factors in education and yet will find a common denominator for them all.

Naturally, conflicts such as these have placed tremendous strain on the moral texture of twentieth-century culture. To teach children how to maintain moral integrity and integrated personalities in the face of all these conflicting demands is no simple task. The main trouble is that it is so difficult to tell in a period of accelerated social transition whether new departures in well-accepted customs are a weakening of former standards or a step toward new and better ones. It is even difficult to tell whether the ills which beset us presently are the result of changing social conditions or the changes brought about in the schools by "progressive education." On the assumption that it is the secularism of "progressive education" that is to blame, some in the twentieth century have demanded a renewed emphasis on religion in public education. This demand, of course, requires a re-examination of the nineteenth-century policy of the divorce of church and state in matters of education, to say nothing of rethinking the whole problem of religious and moral education in the light of the foregoing forces.

In view of the contradictory, often confusing, issues presented, it should not be surprising that men have resorted to philosophizing about education in this century as never before. This does not mean that it is anything new for men to be in a quandary about which direction education should take. Men have confronted many such crises in civilization's long history. Plato, for instance, wrote his *Republic* partly in response to the unstable social conditions of his day. Still, the present tensions seem more acute for education than previous ones. The principal difference between present and past eras seems to be that today education is consciously used as a tremendous instrument of public policy. Formerly, only the privileged classes benefited by an extended education. But today most states aim at universal education, the education of all classes. Consequently, alterations in educational direction caused by shifting configurations of tension among the forces mentioned above have a far greater outreach than ever before in the world's history.

PROGRESSIVE VERSUS TRADITIONAL
AIMS IN EDUCATION

While aggravated tensions— political, economic, religious, scientific — are probably at the bottom of the proliferation of educational philosophies in the twentieth century, it should not escape notice that one philosophical endeavor to resolve these tensions is itself also a major cause of this proliferation. Except for the emergence of John Dewey and the persistent challenge of his pragmatism to every phase of contemporary education, it is unlikely that educational philosophy would have had anywhere near the rise to prominence it has had in this century. His writings were not only the inspiration for others who wrote in the same vein but, much more important for richness and breadth in professional literature, he provoked opponents of his view to make explicit a variety of philosophical defenses of traditional or conservative educational practices which had only been implicit thitherto. This was particularly true of the Catholic position.

Since Dewey's pragmatism has been the principal philosophical proponent of "progressive education" and since the launching of "progressive education" was the immediate, if not ultimate, cause of so much writing in educational philosophy, it may be well, before sharpening and stating the issues to which the contributors of this yearbook will address themselves, to give some exposition of the nature of the attack that Dewey and pragmatism have made on conventional educational practices. Perhaps before doing that, however, we should take a look at the theory and practice of the sort of education which Dewey sought to reform when he inaugurated his experimental school at the University of Chicago.

Perhaps the briefest and at the same time the most accurate description of the conventional school of the late nineteenth and early twentieth centuries is to be found in the Lynds' *Middletown*.[2] "The school like the factory," ran their sociological description of Middletown, "is a thoroughly regimented world. Immovable seats in orderly rows fix the sphere of activity of each child. For all, from the timid six-year-old entering for the first time to the most assured high-school senior, the general routine is much the same. Bells divide the day into periods. For the six-year-olds the periods are short (fifteen to twenty-five minutes) and varied; in some they leave their seats, play games, and act out make-believe stories, although in 'recitation periods' all movement is prohibited. As they grow older the taboo upon physical activity becomes stricter, until by the third or fourth year practically all movement is forbidden except the marching from one set of seats to another between periods, a brief interval of prescribed exercise daily, and periods of manual training or home economics once or twice a week. There are 'study periods' in which children learn 'lessons' from 'textbooks' prescribed by the state and 'recitation periods' in which they tell an adult teacher what the book has said; one hears children reciting the battles of the Civil War in one recitation period, the rivers of Africa in another, the 'parts of speech' in a third; the method is much the same."

No one in the nineteenth century explicitly expounded the philosophy behind this practice. Yet an educational philosophy it surely had. The spirit of this school fairly breathes rigidity, formalism, and regimentation. These qualities may have been due to the shortcomings of unselected and poorly trained teachers of which there is an oversupply at any time. But over and above that, there were many educators, lay and professional people, who justified this formalism because it afforded a valuable discipline for children. By subduing their natural spontaneity and subjugating it to a fixed routine, to screwed-down seats and desks, to a logically organized subject matter, children learned to conform to the way things are. And things did exist in a definite order and fashion. This was particularly true in the moral order and the scientific order of nature. In this order, human nature was composed of faculties, and it was the role of the school to sharpen them by grinding them against the abrasive whetstone of the hard facts of life. If that seemed disagreeable, Mr. Dooley was at hand to humor critics by stating ironically that it did not really matter what children studied so long as they didn't like it. Consequently, interest was neglected and children were urged to put forth effort in the sheer performance of abstract duty. The teacher's authority, even for those so fortunate as to be trained along Herbartian lines, was omnipresent to enforce this duty.

At a little deeper level most thoughtful nineteenth-century educators, and many twentieth-century educators as well, whether Catholic or Protestant, subscribed to a humanistic theory of education. They held with Aristotle that the distinctive nature of man which set him off from other animals was his rationality. The principal function of education, therefore, was to develop this rationality. This was to be sought as a worth-while end in itself for, as Aristotle said, "The activity of God, which surpasses all others in blessedness, must be contemplative; and of human activities, therefore, that which is most akin to this must be most of the nature of happiness. . . . Happiness extends, then, just as far as contemplation does, and those to whom contemplation more fully belongs are more truly happy, not as a mere concomitant but in virture of the contemplation; for this is itself precious."[3] Or, as Cardinal Newman put it centuries later with educational bearings more definitely in mind, "Surely it is very intelligible to say, and that is what I say here, that Liberal Education, viewed in itself, is simply the cultivation of the intellect as such, and its object is nothing more or less than intellectual excellence."[4]

The experimental schools of the twentieth century, of which Dewey's was merely one of the earlier and better known, made a definite departure from the type of education compositely described in *Middletown*. In these new schools the last thing school resembled was a factory. Instead of mechanical uniformity, school was characterized by flexibility and spontaneity. School furniture was movable and the length of periods was measured by the work in hand to be done. Pupil activity, far from being taboo, became the central feature of the progressive school. Indeed, its curriculum became known as an "activity" curriculum. Children still dug subject matter out of texts but not isolated from life and for the mere formal purpose of reproducing it on examinations. On the contrary, they undertook projects in which they were interested and searched subject matter for suggestions for activities to be undertaken to insure the successful outcome of their projects.

Obviously, the spirit or philosophy of this school stood in marked contrast to that of *Middletown*. The features of this spirit which impressed observers most were its emphasis on pupil interest and pupil freedom in a school atmosphere where the teacher was less a taskmaster and more a friendly guide. Children were free to select tasks they were interested in and free to move about in search of resources from the library, laboratory, field, and shop which might promote the completion of what they had undertaken. Naturally, such a school had need to be rich in resources so that no side of child development would be neglected. If such a regime developed individuality, initiative, self-reliance, and a moral autonomy in its pupils, it was but the normal expectation.

Parenthetically, it might be mentioned that this far even conservative and traditional educators had generally moved by the middle of the twentieth century. By that time, indeed, they had so absorbed many progressive practices that the Progressive Education Association had spent much of its driving protest force from the 1920's. Yet, while copying many progressive practices, conservatives and traditionalists still refused to support them theoretically with Dewey's pragmatism.

At a still more penetrating level, progressive educators themselves split on the theoretical underpinning of their practices. One group followed the lead of Rousseau and Froebel. They took the romantic view of natural development. Reverencing the essential goodness of child nature, they held it their duty as parents and educators to let nature express itself freely and to interfere with its laws as little as possible. Because they reverenced the unique in child nature as well as the universal, they insisted on giving a high priority to the individual interests of the child in organizing the school program. Romantic progressives derived further support for their theory from G. Stanley Hall and Sigmund Freud. Hall's theory, that the child must "recapitulate" racial experience just as his foetal development recapitulated organic evolution, led to the further theory of catharsis. According to this theory, if the child acts like a little savage when passing through and recapitulating the aboriginal stage of culture, adults must let him behave that way to get it out of his system. Even more recently the romantic progressives have leaned mistakenly on Freudian psychoanalysis to support their theory of freedom for child nature. From seeing the warped personalities which result from abnormal repression of natural drives, they have justified a system of education which encouraged uninhibited expression of native impulses.

The romantic wing of progressive education has attracted so much public attention, mostly unfavorable, that it has almost eclipsed the more sober and stable wing which drew its support largely from the leadership of John Dewey. Dewey, too, favored the activity program with its attendant pupil interest and freedom. But instead of grounding this program in a theory of child nature, he grounded it in his pragmatic theory of knowledge. Knowledge, he claimed, is the outcome of action. Confronted with a problem, an adult or child constructs in imagination a theory or hypothesis of how it might be solved. The truth or falsity of the proposed solution develops from whether or not the consequences of acting on the hypothesis corroborate it. Under such a regime freedom and interest are necessary conditions for selecting appropriate ends and means in solving the child's project. The progressive in contrast to the traditional school, then, according to Dewey, allows the child freedom to engage in interesting activities, not just because the child's active nature demands it (although that is important) but also because only by initiating activities and noting their consequences is an investigator or learner warranted in asserting when knowledge is true.

In Dewey's conception of the progressive school, the role of intelligence is clearly instrumental. Taking his cue from Darwinian evolution, he regards human intelligence as a relatively latecomer on the world scene. Consequently, the school cultivates intelligence as a tool to solve problems. This is very different from Aristotle and Newman, who would have education cultivate intelligence as an end in itself. For Dewey, taking his cue further from Darwinian evolution, there are no final educational ends in and of themselves. The ends of education are always subject to further reconstruction in the light of an uncertain and contingent future.

Not everyone has the talent, or what is more necessary, the economic leisure to join that stratum of society known as the intelligentsia which cultivates intelligence as an end in itself. Yet everyone can employ intelligence in the managment of his daily affairs. In the one case, the cultivation of intelligence leads to the education of the few; and in the other, to the education of the many. Consequently, progressives claimed their educational philosophy to be more democratic than that of the traditionalists. Both philosophies, of course, supported the idea of education for all, but they differed on the quality of the education to be so given. Thus, progressives further claimed that their more pupil-centered practices were more democratic than the teacher-centered practices of the traditional school.

With the coming of the great economic depression of the 1930's, the romantic individualists in the "progressive-education" movement were severely taken to task for lack of a social orientation. Spurred on by the vital sense of direction fascist and communist education seemed to possess, many progressives turned social-planners and championed the notion that the school should take the initiative in bringing about a new social order cured of the defects of the present. The idea that progressive education should take a position in the van of social progress seemed entirely logical to many of its supporters. As a matter of fact, however, the left-wing group who captured "progressive education" for this cause received as much, if not more, unfavorable notice from the conservatively minded public as had the romantic individualists of the preceding decade. The traditional school considered itself the creature of the existing social order, not the creator of a new one!

Those who thought that the school should take a position of leadership in reconstructing the social order were in constant need of the protection of academic freedom. When the ship of state rocked violently to and fro

during the depression, conservatives were afraid that progressive educators might rock it just the bit further which would cause it to founder.
Loyalty oaths, designed at this time to lessen the lurch by screening out
"radical" teachers, became much more formidable threats to schools
after the war when the world settled down to the prolonged cold war
between the communist East and the democratic West.

CONTEMPORARY ISSUES IN
AMERICAN EDUCATION

We have been at some pains to recount briefly the principal points of the
controversy between traditional and "progressive education" — all against
the twentieth-century background of world political, economic, religious,
and scientific tensions — not only to account for the great interest of this
century in educational philosophy but also to point up the main issues in
contemporary education to which the contributors of this yearbook will
address themselves. It is mainly because these issues remain unresolved
as we return to them again after the war and because we need fresh
insight into their solution in the second half of the century that we invite
a group of academic philosophers to bring their talents to bear on them
in this yearbook.

Now to summarize and restate the issues. Unfortunately, to state them
in the detail they deserve is out of the question in a volume of this size.
In the short space at the disposal of each contributor, it will only be
possible to indicate the main issues.

1. *There is a current anxiety that modern education is adrift without
rudder, chart, or compass.* Is there a frame of reference by which we can
defendably orient ourselves and thus regain a sense of direction? It is all
well and good to flatter ourselves that in the twentieth century we are sub-
stituting conscious and deliberate transmission and renewal of the culture
for the automatic selection of the folkways. Yet we could easily deceive
ourselves without a reliable point of reference. For instance, shall we take
a monistic or pluralistic view of the culture we seek to screen and renew?
Can we detect any enduring structures in culture quite relativistic? By
what standard of truth shall we judge our culture? Shall we teach young
people that there is just one standard or that there are several standards:
religious, metaphysical, and scientific?

2. *There is a current anxiety that, of the educational aims we have,
too many are vague or conflicting and too few generate strong loyalty.*
By what standard can we validate our aims and values? By the ordinances
of some deity? By aptness to human nature? By some subrational measure
like "blood and soil"? By fitness to some particular time and place? Of
course learning involves the continual reconstruction of experience but

should that include a constant reconstruction of the aims of education as well? Or are there some aims of education which are not merely proximate ends but ultimate and perennial? Without answers to questions such as these, how can we tell which studies in the curriculum are the solid ones and which the fads and frills? Are social studies, such as the college-preparatory ones, inherently and intrinsically valuable while others, like vocational ones, are only instrumentally valuable?

3. *There is a current anxiety that there has been a serious letdown in standards of instruction as a result of modern educational procedures.* In part, this anxiety grows out of an apprehension that too much attention is paid to the motivation of studies. All agree that no learning takes place without some motivation or interest. But should we go so far as to say that subjects in the curriculum derive their value from being liked by children, or do subjects on occasion have values independently of being liked so that children can be told they ought to learn them even though they are not interested in them? Must standards necessarily fall unless we take this latter position? Is it good discipline to study what you do not like? Does such study result in greater force of moral character?

In part, the above anxiety grows out of the authority of instruction. How shall we regard the deposit of truth in the curriculum? Does the truth antedate instruction or is it the outcome of activities undertaken in the classroom, in school shops or laboratories, or on field trips? Is the problem-solving method, predicated on the scientific method, the best way of teaching and learning the truth? Would a student meet higher standards if his instruction depended on other methods as well, e.g., intuition, pure reasoning, or the acceptance of authority?

4. *There is a current anxiety that we are unsure of our democratic conception of education and that we have only fainthearted faith in it anyhow.* Just what does the democratic regard for the individual mean? Does it mean a laissez-faire, almost romantic freedom for each student to design his own house of knowledge? Does it mean a benevolent paternalism wherein the school authorities determine what is best for children and then see that they get it? Or does it involve a situation in which children, together with adults and other children, learn to share decisions and their consequences even though this may mean testing out many things for themselves and sometimes reaching conclusions at variance with tradition? If the latter, should we expect the school to include controversial social issues in its curriculum? In that event, should the school take a neutral stand between the contending views, slant the outcome of instruction toward accepted democratic values, or encourage children to think in terms of a progressive reconstruction of the social order? This raises a question of the extent of our commitment to academic freedom as a preparation for the civil liberties of American life.

5. *There is a current anxiety that the social framework of the school accords the child too much freedom and does not subordinate him sufficiently to authority and control.* This statement stirs the inquiry whether parents and teachers yield children too much initiative and are too prone to assign priority to children's interests. Would it be better if children's interests were more frequently subordinated to those of adults, if adults would exert more control over children again? If more external control is restored in education, how at the same time shall we build initiative, self-reliance, and moral autonomy in children? And if the authority of the adult regains some of its former importance, how at the same time shall we preserve education from becoming authoritarian and undemocratic?

6. *There is a current anxiety that the public schools, overanxious to avoid sectarianism, are neglecting religion and becoming too secular.* Is there a religious dimension to education which is being neglected? Would more attention to such a dimension give current education a much-needed stability and sense of direction? Will more attention to religion in the public school confuse the proper spheres of God and Caesar? Should we re-examine the nineteenth-century tradition of the divorce of church and state in the field of public education?

THE ROLE OF PHILOSOPHY IN EDUCATIONAL PROGRESS

No doubt, as already stated, more issues could be listed. No doubt, too, the issues listed could have been drawn up under different categories. In terms of where we are in the middle of the twentieth century, however, the foregoing seem to be the areas in which the major contemporary issues lie. The issues have been stated largely in educational rather than bald philosophical terms. But the underlying philosophical issues are not far to seek. The usual problems of philosophy lie just beneath the surface of these educational terms. The nature of knowledge, of value, of man, of society, and of the world must each be met before a satisfactory conclusion can be formed of what to do next in our present predicament.

---

[1] For a bibliography of these writings, see John S. Brubacher's *Modern Philosophies of Education*, pp. 299n, 303n, 314n, 317n, 320n. New York: McGraw-Hill Book Co., 1950 (revised edition).

[2] R. S. Lynd and H. M. Lynd, *Middletown*, pp. 188–89. New York: Harcourt, Brace & Co., 1929.

[3] Aristotle, *Ethics*, Bk. X, chap. viii.

[4] J. H. Newman, *The Idea of a University*, p. 121. London: Longmans, Green & Co., 1910.

JONAS F. SOLTIS

Philosophy of Education:
A Fourth Dimension

PERCEPTIVE OBSERVERS OF CONTEMPORARY CULTURE HAVE SOUNDED urgent warnings of impenetrable walls abuilding between scholar and scholar, scholar and layman. The cement of technical vocabulary is applied to blocks of sophisticated theory, and towering cubicles of isolation arise across the academic terrain. Inside each structure narrow, intricate passageways are built which separate those inside from one another and tend to obscure their view of the whole. Meanwhile, those standing outside behold the massive, solid exteriors and feel powerless to probe the inner forms. It is the purpose of this essay to provide a blueprint of one such modern academic structure called "philosophy of education" so that a schematic view of its basic dimensions may be shared by insiders and outsiders alike.

As a vehicle for exposition, the figure of "dimensionality" readily lends itself to my purposes, for it connotes a view of the whole considered from its basic perspectives; and it is with providing such a view of the tasks engaged in by philosophers of education that I am primarily concerned. The three dimensions I will first describe are the familiar and generally recognizable dimensions of world-view, valuation, and philosophical analysis; but I would also like to take this opportunity to point to what

Jonas F. Soltis, "Philosophy of Education: A Fourth Dimension." *Teachers College Record, 67,* 1966, 524–31. Reprinted by permission of the author and publisher.

I take to be a new dimension in the philosophy of education, a fourth dimension whose exploration has barely begun and whose philosophical mapping promises new vistas for modern educational theory and practice. Finally, the use of the theme of "dimensionality" will allow me to display my belief that the various tasks performed by philosophers of education are complementary rather than antithetical, each involving inquiry into the different philosophical dimensions of education and each potentially worthy of pursuit.

THE SYNTHETIC-SYNOPTIC

The first dimension to be sketched is older than Plato and newer than Dewey. It is distinguished by its central concern with a systematic and comprehensive view of the Universe into which the education and life of Man is fitted. The task of the philosopher of education operating in this dimension may be characterized as either *original* or *derivational*. There are many well-known philosophers like Dewey and Plato, original thinkers who have produced a comprehensive view of Reality which includes a corresponding detailed picture of education. Less generally known, perhaps, and certainly in the majority are those philosophers of education who utilize the world-view of some philosopher or school of philosophy to derive a full-blown concept of education consistent with the basic tenets of that philosopher or school. Frequently they bridge the gap between philosophers who are not centrally concerned with education and the work of those philosophers which has direct relevance to educational theory and practice. The work of a realist like Harry S. Broudy or of an idealist like Donald Butler, both contemporary philosophers of education, is generally known to the readers of this journal and is representative of the derivational function. The task taken on by such men is to place educational theory and practice into the larger context of some traditional philosophical system and thereby to produce a comprehensive view of education.

Whether original or derivational, however, philosophers who operate in this dimension see a need to answer the perennial philosophical questions about Reality, Knowledge, Value and the Nature of Man as a prerequisite to intelligent discourse about education and its role in human life. Such a search for meaning and total context is not new to philosophy nor to educators. It is a powerful theme repeated throughout the intellectual history of Man and as such cannot easily be rejected out of hand. It can be done well or poorly, but it cannot be denied its potential to provide perspective, meaning and inspiration to those who educate. It is a viewing of education straight on in its broadest dimension—that of breadth.

THE PRESCRIPTIVE-PROGRAMMATIC

If the synthetic-synoptic dimension can be visualized as that of breadth, then we can liken the prescriptive-programmatic dimension to that of height. The traditional association of "good" with "higher" and "bad" with "lower" may simply be an accidental result of our civilization's preoccupation with heaven and hell; but, nevertheless, the task assumed by philosophers of education working in this dimension does appear to be one of pointing upward to the "heights" to be reached through education. This is the value dimension of philosophy of education wherein judgments of worth are made and descriptions of the Good created. Just as human beings have always speculated about the nature of the cosmos, so they have also been eternally searching for the principles of the Good Life. Even though philosophers have consistently failed *logically* to bridge the gap between what is and what ought to be, *practically* the fact remains that men are constantly faced with decisions of value. This is also true for those working with educational theory and practice; and it is in response to this practical need to make decisions of value in education that some philosophers turn their minds and talents to the prescriptive-programmatic dimension.

Broadly speaking, one might distinguish between two types of tasks performed in this dimension: the *judgmental* and the *descriptive*. Some turn their energies to judging the worth of existing educational theories and practices. Others focus on identifying and describing what they feel are the proper goals for education and the proper means for attaining them. All are concerned with the traditional philosophical questions about values seen in the context of the purposeful human activity called education. Thus, on the descriptive side we find educational philosophers such Philip Phenix, attempting in much of his work to identify and describe the values relevant to the "prescription" of a proper "program" for education. Or we find such men as William Heard Kilpatrick providing and describing a "program" for "character education" in the value context of a social democracy. On the judgmental side, we find in contemporary America critics such as Hutchins and Adler, who function as gadflies questioning the goals, values, choices and procedures which presently exist. At times their judgment is harsh, at times benevolent, at times merely the prelude to their own prescriptions and programs.

It should be apparent also that neither the descriptive nor judgmental valuational functions are the sole possession of philosophers of education, as any Bestor, Conant, Rickover, Koerner, Martin Mayer or PTA member will attest. There is no escape from this value dimension in education. Choices must be and are made every day. But the philosophers of education come to this dimension uniquely armed with a tradition of scholarly concern with ethical systems and a disciplined mode of inquiry for examining problems of value. For this reason, the task taken on by philosophers of education in the prescriptive-programmatic dimension has great potential. Once again, however, it may be performed poorly or well, but to deny the potential of intelligent inquiry into the valued and valuable seems ludicrous.

THE ANALYTIC-EXPLICATIVE

Of the three ordinary dimensions, we have only that of "depth" left. However, it is most appropriate to use the notion of depth as a descriptive term for the analytic-explicative dimension of philosophy of education. Philosophers of this bent look deeply into the technical language of educational theory and practice seeking clarity and precision of meaning. They probe through the surface of philosophizing about education in an attempt to locate underlying assumptions; and they search beneath educational arguments and ideas for their logical underpinnings.

Just as we have divided the first two dimensions considered into two sub-types of tasks performed in each, we might fruitfully attempt to view the analytic-explicative dimension as having both a *critical* and a *constructive* aspect. One need not look far to find a representative of the critical aspect of philosophizing in this dimension. D. J. O'Connor in his *Introduction to the Philosophy of Education (2)* is quite critical of attempts to philosophize about education in terms of what have been called here its synthetic-synoptic and its prescriptive-programmatic dimensions. He argues

> that the traditional philosophers promised more than they were able to deliver and that their claims to interpret the universe on a grade scale must be rejected for the same reason that the claims of alchemists, astrologers or magicians are now rejected . . . [because their results are not] publicly testable, reliable and coherent with the rest of public knowledge.

With respect to values and moral principles, O'Connor refuses to make judgments concerning values until he can find a way to justify such judgments. He concludes his examination of this dimension of philosophizing by saying:

We still do not know all it means to say that a certain moral principle is 'right' or 'valid' or 'justifiable'. . . . For this reason the problem of how to justify our value judgments is still an unsolved problem of philosophy. To realize this will save us from dogmatism and at the same time encourage us to go on looking for the answer [to the questions of how to justify value judgments].

Of course, the critical aspect of the analytic-explicative dimension can take a narrower tack. Rather than taking on the basic assumptions or questioning the validity of the approaches utilized in the other dimensions of educational philosophy, one may examine particular theories or particular concepts imbedded in theories of education for ambiguities, logical function and coherence with an eye to showing their weaknesses.

In terms of what I have called the constructive aspect of the dimension called analysis-explication, one can point to examinations in depth of such key educational ideas as "learning by experience," "needs and the needs-curriculum," "subject matter," "mastery," and "teaching" or to the analysis of "metaphors," "slogans" and "definitions" as they operate in the *Language of Education (4)*. I consider such efforts to be constructive because generally they not only pull apart central concepts of education but in doing so they also make clearer and more precise our use of these ideas in theory and practice. Being clear about our ideas is a prerequisite to putting them into effective practice.

In essence then, the task taken on by those who operate in the dimension of analysis-explication is one which takes ideas basic to educational theory and practice apart and unfolds their meaning and logic for all to see clearly. Traditionally, philosophy has never been free from critical examination of others' theories—a glance at Plato and Aristotle will surely bear this out—nor free from scrutinizing in depth the meaning of central concepts as again Plato (the meaning of justice), Aristotle (of substance), Augustine (of time) *et al.*, will amply demonstrate. Man, throughout civilized times, has sought out the power behind ideas, arguments and theories. There seems to be no reason to deny the worthiness of such an enterprise in the narrower sphere of philosophizing about the theory and process of education.

A PAUSE FOR PERSPECTIVE

Before going on to describe the fourth dimension of philosophy of education, a few reservations about the views thus far presented ought to be offered in an attempt to provide a truer perspective. Although I think that the rough categories and distinctions offered thus far can be justified and that there are those philosophers of education who can be neatly pigeon-holed as operating within a single dimension and even within a particular aspect of it, I would hasten to indicate that the device I've constructed for showing parts of a whole is not meant to indicate that these parts ought to be taken as mutually exclusive. At different times and in different works any particular philosopher may address himself to problems in any of these three dimensions. In fact, one might cogently argue that no philosopher of education can operate in any one dimension without carrying with him certain submerged views with respect to the other dimensions.

Moreover, a cursory reading of a philosopher like John Dewey would show that even in a single work, such as *Democracy and Education*, one can deal effectively and in depth with all three dimensions and their sub-areas. His view of Reality as sketched therein is certainly in great part original, but parts of it are also derivational (from Darwin and James). He is not unwilling to prescribe a program for educating in his description of the learning process, growth and the democratic society; nor is he reluctant to critically judge the value systems of others (such as Plato, Rousseau, Locke, Froebel, *et al.*). Finally, one may point to his analysis and explication of such concepts as "experience," "social democracy," "learning," "thinking," "subject matter," etc., and see his effort to clarify ideas central to the process of educating.[1]

Given such exceptions, I should hastily add in the spirit of my endeavor to paint as true a picture as possible of the current state of philosophy of education that there is a growing tendency to specialize in the investigation of a single dimension. Perhaps the greatest impetus for this is what has been called the "revolution in philosophy" in the 20th century. The referent for this "revolution" is the growth of sophisticated methods of analyis developed in England and America and the consequent emergence of what is loosely termed linguistic or analytic philosophy. But this is another story and one which cannot be told here. Let us turn instead to the newer and inviting fourth dimension of the philosophy of education.

THE FOURTH DIMENSION

If, as I believe, the three dimensions discussed thus far do fairly describe the activities currently carried on by philosophers of education, it still seems legitimate to ask just what these dimensions actually encompass. A moment's reflection should reveal that the three dimensions described focus on and treat the process of educating from different perspectives. In simpler terms, philosophers of education are concerned with visions, evaluations and analyses of the whole or part of education as a process. Some are even concerned with an examination of what philosophers do when they turn their philosophical attention to any dimension of inquiry into that process of educating.

But omitted from even this broad view of what is contained by the three dimensions already described is the "field of education" itself. In one sense it is there, but in a much more profound sense it is not. In that philosophers of education are specialized inquirers into the process of educating, they are thus operating *within* the "field of education." Without terrible distortion, one could generally describe the "field of education" as encompassing those areas of inquiry, examination and study of the process of educating as are dealt with by philosophers, historians, anthropologists, economists, curriculum specialists, administrative specialists, psychologists, etc. What binds all of these scholars and inquirers together is their focus on the process of educating and their theoretical or scholarly interest in some one or other aspect of that process.[2] Thus the "field of education" can be isolated as another dimension different from those already described. In this way, the total "field of education" taken as a composite of various techniques of inquiry into the educational process provides a fourth dimension in which philosophers of education may also operate.

However, by designating the "field of education" as the fourth dimension of philosophy of education, I do not mean to imply that no one ever has dealt philosophically with this dimension. I will, in fact, cite some examples of philosophers who have done so in a preliminary way. Rather, my purposes in pointing to the "field of education" as a fourth dimension are threefold. First, I believe there is logical justification for distinguishing this dimension as a unique entity worthy of study and investigation much as the other dimensions have been distinguished and pointed to as rich potential areas for philosophical inquiry. Second, although some have indeed tackled problems in this dimension, there seems to have been no overt realization by philosophers of education that the "field of education" is a unique dimension different in important logical respects from the others designated in this essay, and so I hope this designation as a fourth dimension will correct the situation. Third, the "field of education" is a relatively recent historical phenomenon which has grown and developed extensively in this century and, I believe, as such presents many new philosophical avenues of inquiry which have yet to be explored or traveled by philosophers of education.

THE FIELD OF EDUCATION

In what follows, I will try to characterize this dimension of the philosophy of education much as I have done with the other dimensions except that I would prefer to be more nebulous (if that is possible) about its boundaries than I have been with the others. I do this because I feel that a tight drawing of limits would narrow the possibilities for inquiry, and this would in turn negate my reason for suggesting that this fourth dimension is one which provides a heuristic area rich in potential for philosophizing.

Two central forms of philosophizing in this dimension seem apparent to me. There may be, and I hope there are, others. First, one may examine the total field itself looking for the logical glue which holds it together, or for a clear and adequate structural description of its various activities or functions. This we may call the *structural* aspects as opposed to the *component* aspect which turns the focus of investigation into the relevant philosophical parts of individual non-philosophical components of the total field.

Indeed, some philosophers have looked into the fourth dimension from the structural point of view. Ralph Barton Perry in his *Realms of Value (3)* briefly discusses the "science of education" and its "explanatory, normative and technological methods." Marc Belth has recently published a work called *Education as a Discipline (1)* in which his avowed purpose is to inquire ". . . into the developing discipline of education in the form of a logical analysis of the structure of the activity itself . . ." But as with other types of philosophical areas of investigation, philosophers are hardly agreed with respect to the structural question of what the field of education is from a philosophical point of view.[3] Although some work has been done in this aspect of the fourth dimension, more, it seems, is possible.

The component aspect of this dimension by contrast seems to have attracted less attention and has not been pursued in any systematic fashion. Here I will not offer examples from the literature because I myself am only familiar with those probings of philosophers that concern the philosophical component of the field of education and have already mentioned them as part of the task performed in the analytic-explicative dimension.[4] But it seems to me to be legitimate not only to distinguish the scholarly study and examination of the theory and practice of the process of educating from this process itself, but also to distinguish scholarly inquiry into the forms taken by studies of the process of educating from those studies themselves. More simply, questions about the kind of questions put to the educating process by non-philosophical inquirers are legitimate questions of a philosophical nature in the same sense that philosophers raise questions about what the practitioners of science, history, law, etc., do when they operate on a theoretical level in their own areas of interests.

PROPOSALS FOR INQUIRY

Obviously, there are many components in the field of education besides philosophy, and philosophical questions can be asked of these components. One may, for instance, turn to that component designated as "comparative education" and ask structural, procedural or methodological questions of it. Recent work in the philosophy of the social sciences would seem to be relevant here at least in a derivational way as it would also seem applicable directly to those sub-components of comparative education called "educational sociology, anthropology, political science, etc." More original work might take on philosophical analysis of the concept of "comparison" or "generalization" as it pertains to the methodology of the comparative educator. Or, one might look for the ethical problems inherent in the component called "guidance" or "counseling." There also may be philosophical work in the philosophy of history which is relevant to the historian of education and his special task, or ideas developed in the philosophy of law which have relevance to educational inquiries of the scholars of educational administration. Such examples of philosophical inquiry into the components of the "field of education" could easily be multiplied.

But, in essence, I think it can be seen that the fourth dimension of the philosophy of education as described here is focused on both the total structure and the scholarly components of the field of education. It is an area just as worthy of investigation as the others in that it forces reflection back on what assumptions and ideas scholars in the field of education utilize in their study of education. It is a new dimension just beginning to be developed and, by separating it from the other dimensions of philosophy of education, I hope to have made its uniqueness clear to philosophers and non-philosophers alike. For the one, it beckons with virgin lands to explore; for the other, it holds the promise of a fruitful harvest which will provide essential sustenance to the study and understanding of the process of educating.

ONE LAST LOOK

In this essay I have tried to do two things. First and foremost my purpose was to provide a blueprint for viewing the structure of philosophy of education as it is currently being practiced and developed for those outside its technical and scholarly confines. I have done this in the hope that they might obtain a complete schematic view of philosophy of education, while also hoping that this effort might stimulate others to provide such a view of their structures for an *Auslander* like myself. My second task was directed more at my colleagues in philosophy of education and was an attempt to suggest an area invitingly ripe for inquiry whose examination would be relevant to all scholars of education. In using the device of dimensionality (and perhaps over-using it at times), I also hope that

I have provided a convenient framework for putting before my non-philosophical readers the four main stances taken by philosophers of education as they inquire into the synoptic-synthetic, the prescriptive-programmatic, the analytic-explicative aspects of the process of education and into the field of education itself. If the potential of these various approaches is recognized, then, I believe, philosophers of education can learn much from each other's work. And if those outside that specialized tower of educational inquiry called philosophy of education can see what philosophers of education are currently about, then they may bring more appropriate questions to them and also better know what kinds of answers to expect from them. Finally, I hope that this essay has done more than provide a blueprint; that it has in fact cut a side door into the technical structure built by philosophers of education allowing for ease of entrance and exit, and has also provided a few windows which may be used both for looking in *and* for looking out.

---

[1] These and other similar topics are dealt with in Smith & Ennis, (eds.), *Language and Concepts in Education* (Chicago: Rand McNally, 1961).

[2] Of course, the field of education also has its practical side; that of preparing and initiating students into the tasks of educators, those who carry on the process of educating itself. But this "professional" aspect of the field of education ought not to be confused with theoretical and investigatory aspects.

[3] See the report of a symposium edited by John Walton and James L. Kuethe, *The Discipline of Education* (Madison: University of Wisconsin Press, 1963), in which philosophers not only disagreed on what the field of education is, but also on whether it can be called a discipline.

[4] Now with this aspect of the fourth dimension of philosophy of education described, such inquiries and conclusions as O'Connor's above, re the synoptic-synthetic and prescriptive-programmatic dimensions might be more fruitfully categorized in this dimension when they focus on philosophical problems which arise directly from the nature of the activity undertaken by a scholar in the field of education.

REFERENCES

[1] Beth, Marc. *Education as a Discipline.* Boston: Allyn & Bacon, 1965.

[2] O'Connor, Donald J. *Introduction to the Philosophy of Education.* London: Routledge & Kegan Paul, 1957.

[3] Perry, Ralph B. *Realms of Value.* Cambridge: Harvard Univer. Pr., 1954; reprinted in I. Scheffler (Ed.) *Philosophy of Education.* Boston: Allyn & Bacon, 1958.

[4] Scheffler, Israel. *The Language of Education.* Springfield, Ill.: Chas. D. Thomas, 1960.

JACQUES MARITAIN

Thomist Views
of Education

EDUCATION AND THE INDIVIDUAL

Concerning Philosophical Principles

AMONG THE MANY QUESTIONS WHICH CAN BE DISCUSSED UNDER THIS
heading, the one I shall point out is the essential question: Who is the
"principal agent" in the educational process?

The teacher exercises a real causal power on the mind of the pupil, but
in the manner in which a doctor acts to heal his patient; by assisting nature and co-operating with it. Education, like medicine, is *ars co-operativa
naturae*. The contention of Thomist philosophy is that in both cases nature
(the vital energies of nature in the patient, the intellectual energies of
nature in the pupil) is the principal agent, on whose own activity the process primarily depends. The *principal agent* in the educational process is
not the teacher, but the student.[1]

CONCERNING PRACTICAL APPLICATION

This basic truth was forgotten or disregarded by the advocates of education by the rod. Here we have the fundamental vice of the "Middletown"

Jacques Maritain "Thomist Views of Education." In N. B. Henry (Ed.), *Modern
Philosophies and Education*. National Society for the Study of Education, Fifty-
Fourth Yearbook, Part I. Chicago: The University of Chicago Press, 1955, 70–83.
Copyright © 1955 by The University of Chicago Press.

162

conception of the school. Into whatever exaggeration it may have fallen, progressive education has had the merit of putting the forgotten truth in question in the foreground. The "principal agent" is not able to give himself what he does not have. He would lead himself astray if he acted at random. He must be taught and guided: But the main thing in this teaching process is that his natural and spontaneous activity be always respected and his power of insight and judgment always fostered, so that at each step he may master the subject matter in which he is instructed. In this perspective, what matters most is to develop in the child the "intuitivity" of the mind and its spiritual discriminating and creative energies. The educational venture is a ceaseless appeal to intelligence and free will in the young person.

The most precious gift in an educator is a sort of sacred and loving attention to the child's mysterious identity, which is a hidden thing that no techniques can reach. Encouragement is as fundamentally necessary as humiliation is harmful. But what must be specially stressed is the fact that the teacher has to center the acquisition of knowledge and solid formation of the mind on the freeing of the learner's intuitive power.

The liberation of which I am speaking depends essentially, moreover, on the free adhesion of the mind to the objective reality to be seen:

> Let us never deceive or rebuke the thirst for seeing in youth's intelligence! The freeing of the intuitive power is achieved in the soul through the object grasped, the intelligible grasping toward which this power naturally tends. The germ of insight starts within a preconscious intellectual cloud, arising from experience, imagination, and a kind of spiritual feeling, but it is from the outset a tending toward an object to be grasped. And to the extent that this tendency is set free and the intellect becomes accustomed to grasping, seeing, expressing the objects toward which it tends, to that every extent its intuitive power is liberated and strengthened.[2]
>
> In asking a youth to read a book, let us get him to undertake a real spiritual adventure and meet and struggle with the internal world of a given man, instead of glancing over a collection of bits of thought and dead opinions, looked upon from without and with sheer indifference, according to the horrible custom of so many victims of what they call "being informed." Perhaps with such methods the curriculum will lose a little in scope, which will be all to the good.[3]

SCHOOL AND SOCIETY

The Teaching of the Democratic Charter

Concerning Philosophical Principles. A society of free men implies agreement between minds and wills on the bases of life in common. There are, thus, a certain number of tenets—about the dignity of the human person, human rights, human equality, freedom, justice, and law—on which democracy presupposes common consent and which constitute what may be called the democratic charter. Without a general, firm, and reasoned-out conviction concerning such tenets, democracy cannot survive.

But these basic tenets and this charter of freedom are of a strictly *practical* character—at the point of convergence of the theoretical approaches peculiar to the various, even opposite, schools of thought which are rooted in the history of modern nations. No common assent can be required by society regarding the *theoretical justifications*, the conceptions of the world and of life, the philosophical or religious creeds which found, or claim to found, the practical tenets of the democratic charter. A genuine democracy cannot impose on its citizens or demand from them, as a condition for their belonging to the city, any philosophic or any religious creed.

As a result, as I have pointed out elsewhere:

> The body politic has the right and the duty to promote among its citizens, mainly through education, the human and temporal—and essentially practical—creed on which depend national communion and civil peace. It has no right, as a merely temporal or secular body, to impose on the citizens or to demand from them a rule of faith or a conformism of reason, a philosophical or religious creed which would present itself as the only possible justification of the practical charter through which the people's common secular faith expresses itself. The important thing for the body politic is that the democratic sense be in fact kept alive by the adherence of minds, however diverse, to this moral charter. The ways and the justifications by means of which this common adherence is brought about pertain to the freedom of minds and consciences.[4]

Since education (one of the essential, though secondary, aims of which is to prepare for life in society and good citizenship) is obviously the primary means to foster common conviction in the democratic charter, a particularly serious and difficult problem arises at this point for educational philosophy.

On the one hand, the educational system has a duty to see to the teaching of the charter of freedom. Yet it can do this only in the name of the common assent through which the charter in question is held true by the people. And thus — since in actual fact the body politic is divided in its fundamental theoretical conceptions, and since the democratic state cannot impose any philosophical or religious creed — the educational system, in seeing to the teaching of the common charter, can and must cling only to the common practical recognition of the merely practical tenets upon which the people have agreed to live together, despite the diversity or the opposition between their spiritual traditions and schools of thought.

On the other hand, there is no belief except in what is held to be intrinsically established in truth nor any assent of the intellect without a theoretical foundation and justification. Thus, if the educational system is to perform its duty and inculcate the democratic charter in a really efficacious way, it cannot help resorting to the philosophical or religious traditions and schools of thought which are spontaneously at work in the consciousness of the nation and which have contributed historically to its formation.

Adherence to one or another of those schools of thought rests with the freedom of each person. But it would be sheer illusion to think that the democratic charter could be efficiently taught if it were separated from the roots that give it consistency and vigor in the mind of youth, and if it were reduced to a mere series of abstract formulas — bookish, bloodless, and cut off from life. Those who teach the democratic charter must stake on it their personal convictions, their consciences, and the depth of their moral lives. They must, therefore, explain and justify its articles in the light of the philosophical or religious faith to which they cling and which quickens their belief in it.

> Now, if every teacher does thus put all his philosophical or religious convictions, his personal faith, and his soul, into the effort to confirm and vivify the moral charter of democracy, then it is clear that such teaching demands a certain spontaneous adaptation between the one who gives and the one who receives, between the aspiration animating the teacher and the basic conceptions that the student holds from his home circle and his social milieu and that his family feels the duty of fostering and developing in him.[5]

The conclusion is obvious. For the very sake of providing unity in the adherence to the democratic charter, a sound pluralism must obtain in the means. Inner differentiations must come into force in the structure of the educational system, which must admit within itself pluralistic patterns enabling teachers to put their entire convictions and most personal inspiration in their teaching of the democratic charter.

Concerning Practical Application with Respect to the Teaching of the Democratic Charter. After having put forward general views quite akin to those I just mentioned, Mahan states:

> I think we can set down one principle as basic: that public schools must recognize and acknowledge the various influences, both religious and areligious, which inspired our democratic ideal. . . . That principle is very broad and gives rise to seemingly insurmountable problems. How are we going to insure unbiased exposition of influence? There are several ways—none of them very practical.[6]

I am ready to admit that no perfectly satisfactory solution can be found. In such a complex matter, some inherent difficulty or questionable aspect may always be pointed out. Nevertheless I keep on believing that prudential wisdom can invent and apply solutions which — though more or less imperfect in some respect — will prove to be the best possible under given circumstances.

I would like, first, to remark that any teacher entrusted with the teaching of the democratic charter should possess two complementary qualities: On the one hand, he should be animated, as we have seen, by deep personal convictions, in which his whole philosophy of life is engaged — for no teaching deprived of conviction can engender conviction; on the other hand, he should have such intellectual openness and generosity as to foster a sense of fellowship with respect to those who justify the democratic creed through other theoretical approaches — this is required, as we have seen, by the very nature of the thing taught. And this, moreover, is of a nature to lessen to some extent the difficulty of our problem, when it comes to minorities which do not share in the philosophical or religious outlook of the teacher, and which, of course, must not be discriminated against.

Now there are, in my opinion as regards practical application, three possible ways which might be submitted for consideration.

In the first place, we might imagine that when the schools are located in communities each one of which is homogeneous as to its spiritual traditions, the teachers who are in charge of the democratic charter could be allotted such or such a particular area, according to their own wishes as well as to the moral geography of the local communities, so that their own personal religious or philosophical convictions would roughly correspond to those which prevail in the social environment.

In the second place, when the local communities in which schools are located are heterogeneous as to their spiritual traditions, the teaching of the democratic charter might be divided among a few different teachers whose respective personal outlooks correspond in broad outline to the main religious or philosophical traditions represented in the student population.

In the third place, instead of having the democratic charter taught as a special part of the curriculum, we might have it embodied in a new discipline which would be introduced into the curriculum and which, being merely historical, would permit the teacher, while giving a free rein to his own personal inspiration, to put less emphasis on the theoretical principles which justify for him the secular democratic faith. The new discipline in question would bring together, in the basic framework of national history and history of civilization, matters pertaining to the humanities, human sciences, social philosophy, and philosophy of law, all these to be centered on the development and significance of the great ideas comprised in the common charter. Thus, this charter would be taught in a concrete and comprehensive manner, in the light of the great poets, thinkers, and heroes of mankind, of our knowledge of man, and of the historical life of the nation.

Would the three ways I just mentioned answer all the requirements of the practical issue under discussion? They are, it seems to me, at least worthy of being tentatively tried and tested. They are the only ways I am able to conceive of, but I hope that other and better ones can be proposed. In any case the fact remains that the teaching of the democratic charter is, today, one of the chief obligations of education and no practical solution is possible except along the lines of some pluralistic arrangement.

> Americans may disagree as to why American democracy is right, but
> they must agree that there are reasons why it is right. I do not know how
> public education can meet the demand upon it to insure that conviction.
> I do know that, if the public schools are allowed to swallow the philoso-
> phy of scientific humanism because of its purported neutrality, they will
> fail to meet their obligations to further the common good.[7]

Concerning Practical Application with Respect to School Life. From the point of view of practical application, there are other considerations whose relevance should be stressed as regards the preparation of the youth for a real understanding of the democratic way of life. These considerations no longer have to do with the teaching, they have rather to do with the very life of the school and the college.

There, in the life of the school and the college, the beginnings of the habits and virtues of freedom and responsibility should take place in actual exercise. In other words, the students should not be a merely receptive element in the life of that kind of republic which is the school or the college. They should, to some extent, actively participate in it. The best way for this would obtain, in my opinion, if they were freely organized in teams, responsible for the discipline of their members and their progress in work.

Such an experiment was made in some places with surprisingly good results. The teams are formed by the students themselves, without any interference from school authorities; they elect their own captains; they have regular meetings — which no teacher attends — in which they examine and discuss how the group behaves and the questions with which it is confronted. Their captains, on the other hand, as representatives of each team, have regular contacts with the school authorities, to whom they convey the suggestions, experiences, and problems of the group. So the students are actually interested in the organization of studies, the general discipline, the "political life" of the school or the college, and they can play a sort of consultative part in the activity of the educational republic.

With such methods, the youth become concretely aware of, and attached to, the democratic way of life, while a sense of dignity and self discipline, collective autonomy, and collective honor develops in them. In a manner adapted to the age and capacity of students, schools and universities should be laboratories in the responsibilities of freedom and the qualities of the mind proper to democratic citizenship. It can hardly be stated that no improvement is needed in this respect. Displays of oratory, making students proud of their skill in airing opinions, and intoxicated with words, seem to me to be only illusory compensations for the lack I just alluded to.

LIBERAL EDUCATION FOR ALL

Concerning Philosophical Principles. Education directed toward wisdom, centered on the humanities, aiming to develop in people the capacity to think correctly and to enjoy truth and beauty, is education for freedom, or liberal education. Whatever his particular vocation may be, and whatever special training his vocation may require, every human being is entitled to receive such a properly human and humanistic education.

Liberal education was restricted in the past to the children of the upper classes. This very fact reacted on the way in which it was itself conceived. Liberal education for all obliges us, I believe, to undertake a double reconsideration.

In the first place, a serious recasting of the very concept of the humanities and the liberal arts has been made necessary by the development of human knowledge in modern centuries. The notion of the humanistic disciplines and the field of liberal arts must be enlarged so as to comprise physics and the natural sciences, the history of sciences, anthropology and the other human sciences, with the history of cultures and civilizations, even technology (in so far as the activity of the spirit is involved), and the history of manual work and the arts, both mechanical and fine arts.

I would like to insist, in particular, that physics and the natural sciences must be considered one of the chief branches of the liberal arts. They are mainly concerned with the mathematical reading of natural phenomena, and they insure in this way the domination of the human spirit over the world of matter, not in terms of ontological causes but rather in terms of number and measurement. Thus they appear, so to speak, as a final realization of the Pythagorean and Platonist trends of thought in the very field of that world of *experience* and *becoming* which Plato looked upon as a shadow on the wall of the cave. Physics and the natural sciences, if they are taught not only for the sake of practical applications but essentially for the sake of knowledge, provide man with a vision of the universe and a sense of the sacred, exacting, unbending objectivity of the humblest truth, which play an essential part in the liberation of the mind and in liberal education. Physics, like mathematics, if it is viewed in the creative power from which great discoveries proceed, is close to poetry. If it were taught as it demands to be, in the light of the spiritual workings of man, it should be revered as a liberal art of the first rank and an integral part of the humanities.

As to the human sciences, the positivistic bias with which, as a rule, they are cultivated today makes their humanistic value rather questionable indeed. Yet this is an abnormal situation, for which they themselves are not responsible. It would be a great misfortune, and a blunder, to exclude from the realm of the humanities the sciences of man, even though developed at the level of empiriological knowledge. The problem for them, as for physics and the other sciences of phenomena, is to be set free, in the minds of scientists, from the pseudophilosophical prejudices which have preyed upon them as parasites. They should be taught, in so far as they are a part of a program in the humanities, from a philosophical point of view, with reference to the particular epistemological approach they involve, and with a constant concern, either for the understanding of human nature and the development of its potentialities, or for the understanding of the ways in which the human mind functions.

We have also to stress the crucial importance of the history of sciences with respect to humanistic education. In the perspective of the humanities, the genesis of science in the human mind and its progress, adventures, and vicissitudes in the course of history have as much illuminating power as the results that science attains and the changing disclosures on the universe of nature that it offers us in various periods of its development. Knowledge of the succession of scientific theories, of the inner logic, and also of the part of chance and contingency, that can be observed in their evolution, and of the actual ways through which scientific imagination proceeds from discovery to discovery can alone give the student a real understanding of scientific truth and its authentic range. The history of sciences is the genuine instrument through which physical sciences can be integrated in the humanities and their humanistic value brought out in full light.

In the second place, it has become indispensable to give full recognition to the concept of basic liberal education and to the typical requirements it involves. I have just indicated the necessary *broadening* of the *matters* comprised within the scope of the liberal arts and the humanities. What I am now emphasizing is the necessary *restriction* of the burden imposed on the student, and of the curriculum, as concerns the very *ways and perspective* in which the matters in question have to be taught.

Let us refer to the considerations laid down in a previous section on natural intelligence and basic liberal education.[8] On the one hand, the objective of basic liberal education is not the acquisition of science itself or art itself, along with the intellectual virtues involved, but rather the grasp of their *meaning* and the comprehension of the truth and beauty they yield. We grasp the meaning of a science or an art when we understand its object, nature, and scope, and the particular species of truth or beauty it discloses to us. The objective of basic liberal education is to see to it that the young person grasps this truth or beauty through the natural powers and gifts of his mind and the natural intuitive energy of his reason backed up by his whole sensuous, imaginative, and emotional dynamism.

On the other hand, as concerns the content of knowledge, of the *things* that the young person has to learn, this content is to be determined by the very requirements of the grasp in question. Many things which were taught in the past in liberal education are useless; many things which were not taught in the past in liberal education are necessary in this regard. But in any case, the subjects and methods which are proper to graduate studies have no place at this level. In short, the guiding principle is less factual information and more intellectual enjoyment. The teaching should be concentrated on awakening the minds to a few basic intuitions or intellectual perceptions in each particular discipline, through which what is essentially illuminating as to the truth of things learned is definitely and unshakably possessed. The result would be both a rise in quality of the teaching received and an alleviation of the material burden imposed by the curriculum.

Concerning Practical Application. If all the preceding remarks are true, we see that the distinction between basic liberal education and higher learning or graduate studies should be emphasized: because the first deals with a world of knowledge appropriate to natural intelligence, the second with a world of knowledge appropriate to intellectual virtues.

When he enters this world of knowledge proper to higher learning, or the world of technical and professional studies, or the world of practical activity in a given job — the youth will specialize in a particular field. At the same time he will have the opportunity, either by means of the university or the technological institutions, or by his own initiative, to pursue and improve his humanistic education. This would be simply impossible if he were not previously equipped with an adequate basic liberal education.

Basic liberal education should cover both high school and college. During high-school years, the mode of teaching would be adapted to the freshness and spontaneous curiosity of budding reason, stirred and nourished by the life of the imagination. When it come to college years, we would have to do with natural intelligence in a state of growth, with its full natural aspirations to universal knowledge — and, at the same time, with its normal tendency to develop some more perfect *habitus* or disposition relating to preparation for a particular field of activity. So the college would have to insure both basic liberal education in its final stages and the development of a particular state of capacity. The best arrangement for this purpose would be to have the college divided into a number of fields of concentration or fields of primary interest, each one represented by a given school (or "*institut*," in the French sense of this word). In effect, this would be to have the college divided into a number of *schools of oriented humanities*, all of which would be dedicated to basic liberal education, but each of which would be concerned with preparatory study in a particular field of activity, thus dealing with the beginnings and first development of a given intellectual virtue or a given intellectual skill. And basic liberal education rather than this preparatory study would be the primary aim. But precisely in order to make basic liberal education fully efficacious, the manner in which it would be given, and the teaching organized, would take into consideration the particular intellectual virtue, or the particular intellectual skill, to be developed in the future scientist or businessman, artist, doctor, newspaperman, teacher, lawyer, or specialist in government.

I mean that all the students would have to attend courses in all the matters of the curriculum in basic liberal education; but, on the one hand, the apportionment of the hours given to certain of these courses might be different for the students in the various schools of oriented humanities; and, on the other hand, special courses in each of these schools would enlighten the student on the vital relationship between the particular discipline being taught and the chief disciplines of the common curriculum.

Thus, the essential hierarchy of values inherent in liberal education would be preserved, with the main emphasis, as to the disciplines, on philosophy; and, as to the ways and methods, on the reading of great books. But the practical arrangement of the curriculum would be attuned, in the manner I just indicated, to what will be later on, in actual fact, the principal activity of the person who is now a student. In this way it would be easier to insure the unity and integration of the teaching, especially if the teachers of each school of oriented humanities co-operated in a close and constant manner so as to elaborate and enforce a common educational policy. And the students would receive a kind of preprofessional training (unavoidable as it is in actual existence) which, instead of impairing liberal education and worming its way into it like a parasite, would serve to make the young person more vitally interested in liberal education and more deeply penetrated by it.

The notion of basic liberal education, with the kind of recasting of the list of liberal arts and the method of teaching the humanities we have considered, is of a nature, it seems to me, to give practical and existential value to the concept of *liberal education for all*. On the one hand, basic liberal education, dealing only with the sphere of knowledge and the educational approach appropriate to natural intelligence and respecting the need of natural intelligence for unity and integration, avoids any burden of pseudoscience to be imposed on the student and feeds on the spontaneous, natural interests of his mind. On the other hand, given the broadening of the field of liberal arts and humanities, on the necessity of which I have laid stress, liberal education would cease being considered an almost exclusively literary education. Since the humanities in our age of culture require articulate knowledge of the achievements of the human mind in science as well as in literature and art, and since it is normal to attune, during college years, the common teaching of the humanities, essential for all, to a particular preparatory training diversified according to the various prospective vocations of the students, basic liberal education is adapted to all the real needs which the liberal education of the past was reproached with being unable to satisfy.

Basic liberal education does not look upon students as future professors or specialists in all the branches of knowledge and the liberal arts taught in the curriculum. It does not look upon them as future gentlemen or members of the privileged class. It looks upon them as future citizens, who must act as free men and who are able to make sound and independent judgments in new and changing situations, either with respect to the body politic or to their own particular task. It is also to be expected that these future citizens would educate their children and discuss with them competently the matters taught in school. Moreover, it is assumed that they would dedicate their own leisure time to those activities of rest through which man enjoys the common heritage of knowledge and beauty, or those activities of superabundance through which he helps his fellowmen with generosity.

---

[1]Cf. Thomas Aquinas, *Sum. theol.*, I, q. 117, a. 1; *Contra Gent.*, Bk. II, chap. lxxv; *De Verit.*, q. 11, a. 1.

[2]Jacques Maritain, *Education at the Crossroads*, p. 44. New Haven, Connecticut: Yale University Press, 1943.

[3]*Ibid.*, pp. 44–45.

[4]Jacques Maritain, *Man and the State*, pp. 111–12. Chicago: University of Chicago Press, 1951.

[5]*Ibid.*, pp. 121–22.

[6]Thomas W. Mahan, "The Problem of a Democratic Philosophy of Education," *School and Society*, LXXVI (September 7, 1952), 193–96.

[7]Thomas W. Mahan, *loc. cit.*, p. 196.

[8]See *supra*.

KENNETH D. BENNE

Continuity and Discontinuity in Educational Development

"DEVELOPMENT" HAS BECOME A GOD-TERM IN THE THINKING AND rhetoric of theorists and practitioners of the contemporary arts of politics, economics and education. It points to an area of thought and action which links theorizing and research on the one hand with needed alterations — hopefully, improvements — in economic, political, social and educational practices on the other. This mid-ground between basic and disinterested investigations of phenomena and customary and traditional arts of practice is, of course, the domain of technology and engineering. The products of developmental research are technologies, principles and strategies of making, doing and organizing which, on the one hand, are knowledge-based and also are shaped relevantly to the improvement of practice, to the better meeting of unmet or inadequately met human and social needs.

It may be a remnant of a lingering colonial mentality within us that when we project developmental activities into the economic or educational systems of non-Western nations, we tend to speak of the *development* of *underdeveloped* countries. When we think of applying knowledge in the improvement of the far from satisfactory life of our own cities, we speak of urban *redevelopment*. We may, thus, be more willing to grant that practitioners of life in our urban ghettoes are already developed, that they have a going set of rationales and theories to support their

Kenneth D. Benne, "Continuity and Discontinuity in Educational Development." *Journal of Educational Thought*, 2, 1968, 133–49. Reprinted by permission of the author and publisher.

present strategies of living and technologies of survival and adaptation to environment, in short that they are already possessed of a culture. If we grant this, we, outside the ghettoes, cannot sanely develop new practices of life for ghetto dwellers, in a one-way imperialistic thrust of do-gooding, out of our own cultural frameworks, although at times we may try to do so. Their present strategies, rationales, theories, including value systems, must be jointly and collaboratively *interaccommodated* to strategies and technologies of practice which are based on scientific research and are imbued with the world views and value assumptions of the scientific enterprise and of middle-class culture, if developmental changes in ghetto life are to occur at all.

I might say in passing that we tend to deal with student protests against academic culture more in the image of developing *underdeveloped* countries, rather than as a joint task of *redevelopment* through creative bargaining. Actually, I believe that all developmental work with human systems, in which the participants are more than a few months old, is *redevelopment* and needs to be approached as a collaborative transaction rather than as a one-way imperialistic thrust of do-gooding on the part of the developers. This belief will color all of the observations on developmental work in education which follow.

Why has "development" or, if I am right, "redevelopment," become a god-term in the language of contemporary managers in various institutions of social practice? It is, I think, because of a growing realization among these managers that the maintenance and stability of contemporary institutions can come, not through preventing or forestalling change but rather through more or less deliberate changing in the service of newly emergent values, along with the values inherent in institutional stability and continuity. Where *conservation* was once the figure in the manager's perceptual field and *changing* the ground, today changing is tending to become his central responsibility and stabilization a peripheral one. Continuity with past values is now, so many have come to accept, impossible to achieve without taking the risks of discontinuity with past practices, norms and patterns. *The service of continuity through planned discontinuity with past traditions is at the core of many of the difficulties in the contemporary management of change.* And it is around this theme that I wish to organize my further comments on educational development.

The centrality of "development" as a term in the current language of managers of institutions and organizations is based on a growing realization of a contemporary condition which Robert Oppenheimer has described succinctly and eloquently.

> In an important sense this world of ours is a new world, in which the unity of knowledge, the nature of human communities, the order of ideas, the very notions of society and culture have changed and will not

return to what they have been in the past. What is new is new not because it has never been there before, but because it has changed in
quality. One thing that is new is the prevalence of newness, the changing
scale and scope of change itself, so that the world alters as we walk in
it, so that the years of man's life measure not some small growth or
rearrangement or moderation of what he learned in childhood, but a
great upheaval. To assail the changes that have unmoored us from the
past is futile, and in a deep sense, I think, it is wicked. We need to recognize the change and learn what resources we have.[1]

If each of us were to "free associate" to the word "change," along with
positively affective terms like "challenge," "opportunity," "growth" and
"progress," we would find "loss," "destruction," "disorder," "tension,"
"struggle," "conflict" coming into our minds — into the same minds into
which the positively affective terms also came. We are ambivalent about
"change," however fully we grant cognitively and intellectually Oppenheimer's observation that today's "world alters even as we walk in it."
And, since "development" is a synonym for change and [changing]
most of us are affectively ambivalent about "development" too. It is
true that "development" suggests a sequential pattern to be found or
created in processes of personal and social change. It connotes an orderly
process for maintaining continuity between the goods of the past and the
actualized values of a future which, we can be sure, will also be fraught
with shocks and surprises.

"Development" is thus an optimistic term for describing and analyzing
changes of various sorts. There is solace for liberal optimists — and
most educators are heirs of the liberal-optimistic tradition — in using the
term "development." For, although they can no longer have faith rationally in the idea of inevitable progress which fathered their world view,
liberals still fervently hope for the possibility of its attainment if proper
plans are made and steps taken. And "development" incorporates the
hope for such attainment. There is nothing wrong with using optimistic
terms in discussing prospects and processes of change in our "time of
troubles." In fact, there are advantages in using terms which maximize
human hope. For hope is itself a factor in quickening efforts to find and
nourish seeds of growth and progress within the flux of change within
which we live. But hope is silly and misleading if it diverts us from
facing and dealing with the contemporary realities of conflict, tension,
destruction, discontinuity out of which growth and progress must emerge
today, if they are to come at all.

So as we grapple with issues of educational and social development and
seek to generate rationally hopeful commitments to a better future, we
should recognize and accept, we should not deny, the pains elicited by
change, transition and discontinuity within our own experiences — the
sense of loss and grief for old loyalties, old circles of closeness and security,

old friends which achievement of "progress" and "bettering ourselves," with their attendant physical and social mobilities, bring into our lives: the sense of rootlessness which moving out of provincial securities into the challenge and excitement of more cosmopolitan ways of life brings to any or all of us when we listen to our hearts or, as a "mod" organ analogue, our guts; the sense of homelessness when we discover that we talk a different language from the language of our parents or our children; the desperately sad gaiety of the class reunion; the muted range, accompanied by self-doubt, when we discover that our reasons for our favored way of life, convincing though these may be to us, are not convincing at all to people once under our power and control but now free to strike out on their own — be these other people's children or young people or newly liberated minorities, red or black or yellow. These suggest some of the inner feelings and emotions which define the human meaning of encounter with discontinuity in change or development — feelings which we must learn to recognize, acknowledge and manage, with all due respect for the maintenance of traditional goods and values, if development is ever to become for us a way of life and education.

Alfred North Whitehead recognized more than a generation ago the ineptness of our traditional mentalities to deal wisely with a qualitatively different social world in which perforce we must live today.

> Our sociological theories, our political philosophy, our practical maxims of business, and our doctrines of education are derived from an unbroken tradition and practical examples from the age of Plato. . . . The whole of this tradition is warped by the vicious assumption that each generation wil substantially live amid the conditions governing the lives of their fathers and will transmit these conditions to mold with equal force the lives of its children. We are living in the first period of human history for which this assumption is false.[2]

It is difficult to know, a generation after he wrote, how far Whitehead's "vicious assumption" still operates in efforts to plan and manage change in various institutions of Western societies, as well as in societies in which methods of scientific research and technological innovation, major dynamic elements in continuously changing and rechanging the conditions of Western life, have not taken such deep root. But it is probably fair to say that in most institutions the "vicious assumption" still operates side by side with alternative assumptions more in keeping with the image of an institution or association or society continually renewing and developing itself by creative adaptation of its forms and controls and relationships to changing external and internal environments.

Let me make this schizoid quality in the management of change, which characterizes many institutions of our society, more clear through an example. A typical industry will spend millions of dollars in support of a research and development department charged with discovering, testing and evaluating *new* products, *new* processes and *new* technologies. Yet the production department in the same industry may well be run on the basis of hierarchical prescription and control of standardized job descriptions, roles and role relationships and procedures. Deviations from prescribed and standardized ways of behaving and relating within the organization are treated as discipline problems, as breaches of "traditionally sound" ways of maintaining the social system of the industry, even though the traditions may be no older than some recent upheaval and reorganization. When new products, processes and technologies from the R & D department are introduced into such a production department, calling for new job descriptions, new role relationships, new forms of human organization, the changeover is marked by resistance, conflict and lowered morale. Finally, some new *correct* norms for operating the human system will be imposed again. And these norms will be centrally maintained and controlled with much energy going into their policing and enforcement until further notice. The technical side of change tends to be handled by methods of inquiry, testing, experimentation; the human side of change is handled by prescription, fiat, "engineered consent." This schizoid quality in managing change permeates many institutions of Western industrialized societies. We tend to assume that the latest model of automobile or household appliance is best because it has the most recent research, inquiry and applied knowledge built into it. But we tend to judge the best political constitution, laws or ways of organizing human effort by its age and precedents — the older the better — by its pedigree, and by the prestige and status of its originator or present defenders. This discontinuity between ways of dealing with conflicts, with variations from established norms, of confronting differences among groups in adjacent areas of life which are actually inter-dependent, drives wedges between persons and groups in the same institutions and blocks wholeness and sanity of response in planning for and managing our changing environments.

It is true that some industrial organizations, as well as other organizations, are now establishing R & D departments to develop and facilitate experimentation with new forms of human organization and relationships, thus moving away from the "vicious assumption" on the social and human as well as the technical side of system change. Such efforts ordinarily include opportunities for re-education and training of organization members in self-understanding and self-management, in ways of building and rebuilding groups and organizations, and in creatively managing and resolving human conflicts.

In a society where changes in roles, relationships and associations have become the expectation — rather than stability in roles, relationships and associations after adolescence, when persons have settled down — in such a society, socialization processes which shape character, value orientation and life style cannot rationally be considered complete at any chronological age. Organizational development programs such as I have described above recognize this fact. And the opportunities for continuing reeducation and retraining which they provide for members of organizations are not limited to the acquisition of knowledge and skills required for mastery of new technologies and new work procedures. The training rather offers opportunities for resocialization as well. Or, what is more important, the training is designed to help persons learn how to manage their own continuing resocialization, using their own resources along with those of other persons — peers, bosses, subordinates as well as experts — in creating and recreating relationships, orientations and roles adequate to shifting and changing personal and organizational requirements. I will have more to say about the goals of organizational redevelopment later.

Actually, some industrial organizations have moved further in replacing Whitehead's "vicious assumption" with assumptions more in keeping with contemporary social and cultural realities than most educational institutions have done. An alternative assumption, as we have seen, is that education and re-education, socialization and re-socialization, are life-long processes. Persons must have access to help in creating new and adaptive responses to changing, expanding or decreasing, personal needs and powers, and to changing and novel social requirements as long as they live. This alternative assumption has not permeated the management or organization of educational opportunities or our systems of educational practice in schools, colleges or universities. The education of children and young people is still typically seen as preparatory for life in some settled state beyond adolescence — a settled career, a settled family role, fixed and stable political and civic orientations and roles, settled aesthetic and literary tastes. In this mythical settled state, men and women will begin to make "real" choices and to act upon these, in short to do. Up to that magic time, children and young people, so far as formal election is concerned, have only been learning to do. Learning, on this view, is detached from the responsibilities of informing, guiding and humanizing ongoing choices and actions. And doing and action after formal schooling tend to be divorced from continuing learning, and indeed show only limited effects from previously crammed information and advices which were, after all, acquired not primarily for the illumination and guidance of personal and collective decisions and actions, but rather for examination purposes.

On this preparatory view of education, quite in keeping with the assumption about life which Whitehead called vicious for our time and place, teachers, parents and other adults are thought to know what children and young people will need to know and be able to do when they grow up. Actually, of course, they do not and can not know. And protesting students often sense the unconvincingness of the reasons which adults offer for the prescribed, adult-selected content which makes up the curriculum as usually defined. Students' interests tend to be seen as motivational sales points, to be manipulated, circumvented, or appeased in selling the adult-selected curriculum. They are not seen as points of potential growth in a developing person coping with a developing environment. They are not typically respected.

When interests are respected, educators and students alike see them as possible directions in the development of a growing self. Intrinsic motivations, when they are respected and handled educationally, are to be self-criticized, with the collaboration of others, including adults. Interests are to be self-tested and evaluated. If affirmed, they are to be cultivated, informed, disciplined, under the responsible management of the student, or, in most cases, of a group or community of learners, with whatever help adult resources can give. Such treatment of student interests is, unfortunately as I see it, more often advocated in text books in educational philosophy than practiced in actual teaching processes.

Kenneth Boulding once made a distinction between human systems which develop to support, sustain and control human life and behavior and mechanical systems which human beings set up to accomplish tasks and to achieve goals with a maximum predictability and a minimum surprise with respect to the outcomes of the operation of the system. The predictable and standardized outcome is the mark of an effective mechanical system. Human systems, when they are permitted and helped to develop, are inherently evolutionary systems. "Surprise," unpredictable outcomes, system breaks, periods of chaos, regression and reintegration on some novel basis, characterize the histories of human systems, whether families, classrooms, industries, churches or nations. Human systems have histories. A mechanical system, if perfect enough as a mechanical system, has no history. Time, surprise, creative distortion, innovation are foreign to the ideal model of the mechanical system.[3]

Yet it is all too clear that modern men, enamored of their own invention, the mechanical system, have tried widely to impose the virtues of that system — standardized and predictable outcomes and lack of novelty and surprise — upon the organization of human effort and activity. It is ironic, and to me sad, that in the human systems where novelty, variety, surprise, should be most at home, in places nominally dedicated to the stimulation, support and facilitation of human learning, in schools, colleges and universities, this image of the mechanical system as the right model for organizing human efforts and relationships has made great headway. It is reflected not alone in the adult imposed curriculum already discussed, but in other hierarchical patterns of administrative control, in the departmentalization of instruction, in rigid age grouping for purposes of instruction and of much recreation as well, in standardized examination systems, in the impersonalization of teacher-student, student-student, and administrator-teacher-student relationships — an impersonalization which is always tending to pass over into depersonalization, in the typical treatment of atypical or surprising behavior as norm-violating behavior to be controlled and brought into line rather than as a subject for joint inquiry, as an opportunity for possible creative adaptation in which the onus for adaptation and change may rest as much with the system as with the individual or group deviants from established norms.

I fear that educational systems have much redevelopment to do in their own internal organizational patterns and relationships if they are to become laboratories in which younger and older people together can practice and learn the arts and sciences necessary to develop and redevelop other institutions and associations in our society, national and transnational.

I have already suggested that our current crisis in industrialized and urbanized societies — the crisis which prescribes the major tasks of current social redevelopment — is basically a struggle between rival principles for ordering life and learning, not a struggle between order and chaos, with defenders of the traditional social order cast as the good guys and protesters and challengers of that order cast as the bad guys. This melodramatic way of defining contemporary crisis is one which fearful reactionaries tend to embrace. I know of no more eloquent delineation of the rival principles of order now struggling for men's allegiance than that made by W. C. Behrendt in discussing modern building and city planning. Behrendt, one of the Bauhaus designers and architects out of pre-World War II Germany, found this struggle between clashing principles of ordering in his own field of work and, by extension, in society at large.

Our time, there is no doubt, must be characterized as a period of crisis. The fundamental change of economic conditions under the insignia of industrialization and mechanization has shaken social order to its foundations. A complete transformation of life is taking place. Wherever we look, at the state or the people, at economics or society, at science or art, fundamental changes are in process. A world of obsolete forms and institutions is coming to an end, another slowly struggles into existence. With violent concussions, that everlasting spectacle of dying and growing is taking place . . . on the stage of the world. With combat and convulsion the old forms of order are broken to pieces. With intense resistance the emancipation from traditional habits of law is carried though; emancipation from forms that once were original and full of life, but which in the course of historical evolution have lost their primary meaning and relationship to life. Reluctantly, but at last, the discussion is opened on the changed reality that forms our environment. . . .

Whether regular or irregular, static or dynamic, all form is a final result
of a desire for order. To build is to make a plan. To plan is to follow a
definite concept of order.
In building, we find . . . two different principles of order: one takes the
structure of an organism: growing on its own according to the immutable law of its individual existence; adapted to its function and environment, as a plant or any other living organism grows, developing in its
proper life-space. Then, in contrast to this principle, we find another idea
of order taking the structure as mechanism, composed of various elements put into order according to the immutable law of a system *a
priori.* Viewing these two different concepts of the problem of structure,
we speak of organic order as opposed to mechanical order. . . .
The disastrous conditions into which an excessive rationalism and a
humiliating mechanism have forced our rational existence have awak-
ened a new . . . desire to be nearer to the sources of life. A complete
reversal of outlook on life is taking place in these times: we see another
approach of man to nature, this time, however, not in the sentimental
spirit of a Rousseau, but in accordance with the strict teachings of
science and technique which have revealed the idea of organism, and
have opened to us, in this way, the wonder of creation and life anew.[4]

I agree with Behrendt that there are signs and seeds of personal growth
and social progress within the challenges to an outmoded social order
which often present themselves today as confrontations and encounters,
sometimes violent, always disturbing. The challenges come from people,
persons and groups, who are alienated from participation in the processes
which give form to the transactions of their lives, from people who are
now limited in power to shape their own destinies within the limits of
contemporary reality, not the reality of established status or convention,
which they have come to distrust, but some more fundamental reality,
the limits of which are not yet clearly defined. The protesters may batter
at established forms of order, seeking in various ways to subvert or de-
potentiate these, or they may seek to drop out of the conventionally
proper round of life.

It is difficult for these of us over thirty to see hope and a dynamic for
redeveloping life and society in young people — students many of them —
who express their distrust of us and our intentions openly and often
belligerently, who label our generation hypocritical as we profess the
values of peace, an abundant life for all, and democratic participation and
yet support a social order which creates wars, maintains inequalities, re-
veres the material symbols of status above all else, and demonstrates
powerlessness and/or unwillingness to redistribute power in the interest
of a better life for all peoples. It is difficult for us to find hope and a
dynamic for an improved future in protesting students because we are
afraid — even when we grant they have a point, though overstated, in
their indictment of us.

We are afraid because we see chaos outside the presently established forms of social order, not a developing alternative order to be invented, experimented with, brought into being partly through our own efforts, perhaps mainly through the efforts of those younger than we. In the not-too-clear manifestoes of protesting students, we fear discontinuity with the things and goods we genuinely cherish in the present. We fear the yawning gap of non-relationship between the generations which we have felt uneasily before but which now can not be denied. And rage gets mixed with our fears. And our rage is even greater toward the Hippie types who withdraw from encounter than with the militant student leftists who seek conflictual encounter. For conflict is a form of relationship which is less frustrating than no relationship at all. Part of our anger comes from a self-admission that is playing the game of the system, we have compromised needlessly with the needs of our own persons for growth and fulfillment. Part of our anger is thus anger against ourselves — an anger turned out against those who enact values which we have suppressed, against those who remind us of our failures and needless compromises with ourselves. The breakdown of communications across the chasm between generations represents one of the fearful discontinuities of culture which threatens the redevelopment of current institutions and associations toward more organic structures of relationship and toward more adaptive and self-renewing ways of coping with changing internal and external environments. The immediate threat to institutional re-development is the augmenting of unrealistic conflict between young and old — a wild growth of fantasy and stereotypy in the definition of the terms of the conflict and of each others' motivations which makes creative bargaining concerning the real differences among young and old more and more difficult to achieve. The immediate threat is greatest in institutions of education. The researches of men like James Coleman and Edgar Friedenberg and the brilliant pamphleteering of Paul Goodman show that their positing of the existence and operation of a youth sub-culture within, and inceasingly in non-communication with, adult culture, and nowhere more apparently than in schools and colleges, is not an exaggeration of our current social reality.[5]

Only creative bargaining with respect to the realistic differences that now divide young and old in their interests and orientations can bridge this discontinuity and move the structures of educational institutions and, in turn, other institutions, toward more organic, more participative and more self-renewing forms of relationship and operation. But the feelings of fear, rage, and ingratitude, such as I have described above, must be clarified and worked through before the realistic bases of conflict can be commonly identified and mutually dealt with. This calls for joint participation by young and old in semi-therapeutic groups and communities to accomplish the clarification of feelings toward each other and to dissipate the fantasies about each other which now make common definition or effective resolution of the realistic conflicts between them virtually impossible to achieve.

I do not mean that the whole burden of change and adaptation rests with the older generation. It cannot and should be so. The building of new relationships between estranged parties calls for mutual exchange and interaccommodation between both parties. But there are good reasons to believe that adults will need to take the lead in getting processes aimed at reconciliation started. Adults usually find it harder than young people in expressing their feelings openly, in "leveling" with each other and with young people, as the latter might say it, especially when such leveling violates conventional canons of politeness and propriety. And adults are in positions of control in most institutions, including schools and colleges. The redistribution of power necessary to accomplish mutual re-education and creative bargaining and negotiation must come as a concession from adults to young people, not the other way around. These reasons perhaps justify my emphasis on adult responsibility in opening up processes of bridging the discontinuity between generational sub-cultures and in redeveloping the institutions to support continuing adult-youth communication and collaboration as a necessary condition of accomplishing this mission.

Another kind of social and cultural discontinuity which at once blocks the ready development of an organic ordering of life in contemporary urban and suburban systems and which also furnishes a point of useful tension and conflict in redeveloping the outmoded traditional order of life is, historically speaking, a remnant of a lingering colonial mentality among people of North-European origins in their relations with various minority groups. I do not know whether the term "WASP" has acquired a non-entomological usage in Canada as it has in the U.S.A. WASP is often used to refer to people of White, Anglo-Saxon, Protestant origins or, by extension, to people whose dominant reference group is White, Anglo-Saxon-Protestant, whatever their racial, ethnic and religious origins. It is nearly as hard for WASPS to hear hope for a better social order in the current pressures of various minority groups against WASP hegemony in economic and educational affairs, as it is for beleaguered parents and teachers to hear the voice of progress in the sometimes raucous and belligerent cries of student power advocates. WASPS have been the dominant group in countries like the U.S.A. and Canada. It is WASP values and orientations which have been taken as the criterion values and orientations in judging the relevance and importance of other ways of life that have been carried by immigrants of various sorts into our polyglot cultures and societies. Although we have voiced doctrines of democratic pluralism in the past, doctrines which advocate that sub-cultural differences should be prized and honored, our dominant institutions, political, economic and educational, have been controlled by WASPS, as loosely defined above. Sub-cultural differences have been tolerated when they have remained quaint manifestations of some foreign past; and they have been frequently feared, shunned or repressed when they have threatened to make important differences in the direction and control of economic, political and educational affairs. Now that WASP hegemony has been effectively challenged, now that cultural pluralism has become a fact, the challenges are coming from fresh articulations of various sub-cultural groups seeking their places in the sun. It is hard to locate the mainstream of social and cultural life as eddies of red, yellow or black power become more visible, or comparable eddies along ethnic lines — French or Italian or Slavic (or less often along "purely" religious lines: Roman Catholic, Jewish or Muslim) — or sometimes the more traditional protests of the poor against those with adequate means, become articulated and articulate. One way of stating the question which this fact of resurgent pluralism raises for educational institutions is — whose values shall be taught in schools and colleges? The answer cannot be, even though "scientistic" school men often make it, that no values will be taught. The very organization of a common effort, in schools or elsewhere, embodies values and value orientations as part of its normative system. And people who participate significantly in an organization incorporate these norms as candidate values for their allegiance, whether values become a part of the formal curriculum or not. The old answer — WASP values will be taught as natural and right — is no longer tenable. WASPS who are also liberals and democrats can not accept this answer, let alone the clamant minorities. Nor is the answer of parallel schools teaching different values to different subcultural groups, with no planned and effective linking or bridging between the parallel trends, a viable answer in the long run. The only viable answer, apart from continued fruitless and destructive struggles for domination among groups, or the desperate short-run "peace" of a police state, seems to lie in efforts to make our factual pluralism into a democratic pluralism in deed as well as in profession. New bases of community must be hammered out jointly and collaboratively through creative resolution of conflicts among struggling groups. Again, as in the case of generational discontinuity, members of disconnected racial or ethnic or religious and economic class groups must make and use opportunities to work through the feelings and fantasies about each other which now becloud the realistic bases of their conflicts and of their possible and desirable collaboration. The common bases must be worked out through creative bargaining and problem-solving. Differences will remain but these will come to be prized as sources of strength and good rather than tolerated as unavoidable evils. In this process, more viable, more organic forms of institutional and associational life will be worked out and developed, though no golden age of non-conflict will be attained. And organizational redevelopment will remain a continuing challenge to human ingenuity. In processes of redevelopment, the availability and use of persons who sustain multiple memberships and allegiances and who can maintain integrity and autonomy, while sustaining the internal conflicts which multiple allegiances often involve them in, are extremely important. Without such bridging and linking persons, who trust themselves and who are trusted and respected by both or all sides of a conflict, the prospect of creative compromise of confronting differences and the forging of new common bases of value of orientation is dim indeed. The development of autonomous, bridging persons is a major mission of educational processes in a developing democratic pluralism.

A third set of discontinuities which poses a central and continuing problem for educational redevelopment is in the fragmentation of our contemporary knowledge-building and knowledge utilization enterprises. This fragmentation has come from the specialization of research and scholarship and the bureaucratized organization which segregates departmentalized work in modern university structures. The departmentalization and compartmentalization of disciplines and sub-disciplines has been copied organizationally by the helping professions and by the sub-professions and para-professions each of these has spawned as these have found their way into the university. As academic and professional persons have come to overinvest their personal identities in their academic and professional roles, creative compromise among disciplinary and professional persons and groups in the interest of effective and inventive uses of their resources in solving human problems becomes more and more difficult to achieve. The need for communication and collaboration among men of knowledge and for communication and collaboration among men of knowledge and men of practice and action has never been greater than at present. And the *difficulties* in accomplishing the needed communication and collaboration have never been greater. The general answer to the difficulty lies in the reorganization of the university toward the model of more organic community and away from the model of the mechanically ordered bureaucracy which now underlies the conversion of desirable specialization into non-communicating and autistically hostile fragmentation. But where will the human dynamic for such reorganization come from? Such a dynamic usually arises from disaffected persons and groups who press for the reorganization of a society which excludes their interests and their persons from respectful recognition and which excludes them from effective participation in the shaping of their destinies. We have found such a dynamic in increasingly articulated pressures from disaffected youth and from various clamant minorities, including the poor. But where is the equivalent dynamic for organizational change among men and women of the professions and of academia?

There is no adequate substitute for reorganization of university life if education is to become an important factor in the redevelopment of society. I believe we can get help in solving the problems of society and of its institutions from more adequate computerized systems of storage and retrieval of information from various disciplines and professions. I do not reject this at all. This represents the renovation and refinement of the library system as an aid to knowledge utilization in the light of modern technology. But this is not enough. I believe that we can also develop new skills in bridging between academic and professional specializations and confronting human problems, and can educate human relations experts or change agents — call them what you will — who are skilled in linking systems of knowledge building with systems for developing knowledge into technology and with systems of institutionalized practice, and, eventually, with articulated consumer needs and demands. The mission of the Human Relations Center, where I spend a good bit of my time at Boston University, can be described in this way. But these efforts are not enough if universities and, in turn, colleges and school systems are to play their essential part in redeveloping other institutions and associations of our society toward more organic, more creatively adaptive, more self-renewing forms of life and practice. The organizational life of universities must be redeveloped in the image of community and away from the mechanical model of bureaucracy, if educational systems are to play their indispensable part in the redevelopment of contemporary societies.

Since I put so much stress on organizational development as an important key in gearing educational systems to their part in wider social redevelopment, perhaps I should be more concrete about what an organic ordering as over against a mechanical ordering of organizational life and work would be like. And, if I turn to an account of industrial organizations which are seeking to move beyond bureaucracy for my model, it is, as I have said before, because industrial organizations have often grappled more forthrightly and more vigorously with the invention of forms of organizations in tune with contemporary realities than educational and service organizations have typically done. The principles developed in the redevelopment of industrial organizations apply to other organizations of human effort as well, whatever differences their differing missions may make in the detailed forms of organization. I will draw on the work of Bennis, Shepard and Blake, as well as on my own experiences with organizations like the Aluminum Company of Canada in my characterization of an organic ordering of organization life.[6]

First, an organic structure does not locate the source of needed communication, control or decision-making at any one point in the system, particularly not at the top of a pyramidal structure. Networks of communication follow the lines wherever the linkage of resources and of needs and resources arise and where exchange of information, ideas and feelings is required. Decision-making and problem-solving take place at points in the organization where some particular concentration of resource and need can be brought together. Control is diffused and is designed to facilitate cooperation among people with special resources needed in getting the mission of the organization accomplished and organizational problems solved as they arise. Second, the cement of organic systems is mutual trust and confidence among members, rather than fixed and sanctioned authority-obedience relations. Third, the structure of the organization is not legally defined by lines of pre-assigned responsibilities attached to fixed positions in the hierarchy of the system. Structure corresponds to the networks of interdependence among members, networks which grow out of the requirements of the organization's mission or task. Within each network, interdependence is defined in terms of shared responsibility. Fourth, linkage of parts of the organization is accomplished through authoritative supervision vested in a fixed supervisory role in command of sanctions of reward and punishment to insure compliance with a centrally prescribed plan. Fifth, conflicts of interests and goals do not disappear from an organic structure. Rather, people are encouraged to bring their conflicts out into the open as points of potential growth and innovation in the organization. And organization members are trained to use creative bargaining and problem-solving as a way of managing and resolving their conflicts, rather than to resort to duplicity, repression, arbitration or war. Sixth, a research and development function is recognized as essential on both the human and the technical sides of the enterprise. Data are collected continually concerning existing conditions, particularly conditions relevant to issues and conflicts; scientific expertise is used in collecting and processing information, but the meaning of the data and information for changes in practice or organization is determined through shared decision-making among those concerned with the change. In this sense, development and redevelopment are not seen as periodic crisis readjustments but as a continuing way of organization life.

In this view of organizational form, practice and action are not divorced from research, education and reeducation, but are linked together in an interdependent effort to make valid the judgments and choices with respect to continuity and discontinuity which are inescapable in the planning and management of change in the forms and practices of life. A self-renewing system must learn as it acts concerning the consequences of and the alternatives to its present forms of action, and it must organize or reorganize itself to act effectively on what it has learned about consequences and alternatives. I believe that an educational system whose mission is not the production of goods and services but of learning on the part of its participants, whether through research, instruction or evaluated action and practice would multiply its learning production a hundredfold if it could move from a mechanical system of organizing relationships among its members toward the kind of organic structuring just described. And participants in such educational systems would develop the orientations, skills and commitments to develop organic structures in the other associations and institutions in which they periodically went out from the educational system to live and to work.

SUMMARY

I can summarize the rather diffuse argument implicit in my previous remarks in eight principal points.

1. Development refers to deliberate changing of the instrumentation and goals of practice and related forms of human organization through the utilization and application of valid knowledge. Development of human systems, since it involves the interaccommodation of new patterns and rationales of practice with already existing patterns and rationales is always redevelopment. Collaboration between men of knowledge, practitioners and consumers — those affected by changed modes of practice — is the method for planning redevelopment best calculated to reduce resistance and to accomplish the reeducation of persons which redevelopment always requires.

2. Since we must now assume that the conditions of human life for man will be different from those of the present and past, reality oriented education can no longer be conceived of as the transmission of the cultural heritage to the young. Education must be conceived of as a lifelong process, not complete at any age, and education must be deepened to include continuing resocialization as well as the communication of relevant new information and skills to learners. Value orientations and patterns of relationship, as well as skills and knowledge, become obsolescent in a developing society. Education for redevelopment must be conceived of as empowering, supporting and equipping men and women to invent and reinvent their own futures.

3. The fears of adopting redevelopment as a way of life center on the threats of discontinuity which change always involves — discontinuity

with present and past values, with present and past securities, with present and past associations and relationships. Yet it is at points of discontinuity within culture that redevelopment efforts need most to be focused. For points of discontinuity mark areas of experience where fresh and novel continuities need to be built, rationally — by creative bargaining and problem-solving — if possible. And it is at points of discontinuity in culture where a dynamic for change, growing out of the dissatisfactions of those alienated or dispossessed by present forms of order, is available to give power to redevelopment efforts.

4. The struggle at points of conflict in our soicety and culture is between rival principles of ordering human efforts, human making and doing, human relationships — not a clash between order and chaos. I have called the current struggle a clash between mechanical principles for ordering human life and relationships according to the model of bureaucracy and organic principles of ordering according to the model of community. Mechanical principles of ordering learning efforts and relationships among learners have taken over the organization of most educational systems. This form of organization prevents the joining of learning and action in developing habits and expectations adequate to the management of surprise, conflict and discontinuity in humane and competent ways. The redevelopment of educational organizations according to organic principles of ordering is a necessity for an education which will contribute significantly to the continuing redevelopment of other institutions in a self-renewing society.

5. Feeling and fantasies grow in people around points of discontinuity and disease in society. Negative stereotypy of each other by parties to the conflicts which signal discontinuity makes conflicts unrealistic and prevents the rational identification of the realistic differences among conflicting parties and the joining of communication in the creative resolution of realistic conflict. Reeducative efforts which go to the depth of therapy are necessary to work through distorting feelings, fantasies and stereotypes so that conflicts can be joined realistically and adequate mutual trust generated to make creative resolution of conflict possible.

6. Several discontinuities in contemporary industrialized and urbanized societies offer appropriate points of focus in redevelopment work in educational and other social systems. There is the discontinuity between youth and adult sub-cultures signalized by student protests. There are the various discontinuities between formerly dominant WASP sub-cultures and the growing aspirations and pressures of various minorities against WASP hegemony, whether these challenges are articulated along the lines of race, ethnicity, religion or economic class. There is the fragmentation of knowledge stemming from the segregated organization of research and professional specializations, and the isolation of disciplines,

and professions from people in need of the resources which research, knowledge and professional expertise can provide. These represent foci for redevelopment work in educational systems and in other institutions and associations of contemporary life as well.

7. Efforts in organizational redevelopment toward more organic principles of ordering human effort and relationships, particularly in industrial organizations, furnish models which need to be instituted in the redevelopment of universities, colleges and school systems. In brief, these efforts seek to facilitate and support innovation and experimentation through relating persons or parts of the organization in ways which advance the organization's mission through inquiry and problem-solving rather than to focus on system maintenance, often at the expense of personal growth and organizational innovation, as mechanical systems tend to do.

8. Ideally, educational systems should function as laboratories for developing and testing novel linkages between life and learning, between research, instruction and action, and should provide demonstrations of such linkages to the society surrounding the educational system. In the process, such educational systems will develop persons oriented to, skilled in and committed to the redevelopment of various institutions in the model of creative community. If you ask, where will educational systems get the time and energy to do the redevelopment work which you suggest?, I can only answer that thoughtful participation in wholehearted efforts to redevelop educational systems will provide the education for children, young people and adults which is most needed today. Let the traditional programs go and get on with the redevelopment task.

[1]Robert Oppenheimer, "Prospects in the Arts and Sciences," *Perspective* USA, II (Spring 1955), pp. 10–11.

[2]A. N. Whitehead, *Adventures of Ideas* (New York: Macmillan, 1933), p. 117.

[3]Kenneth Boulding in *Prospective Changes in American Society by 1980 Vol. I of Designing Education for the future,* edited by Morphet, Edgar L. and C. O. Ryan (Denver, Colo.: Citation, 1966).

[4]W. C. Behrendt, *Modern Building* (New York: Harcourt, 1937), pp. 11–12, 15.

[5]James Coleman, *The Adolescent Society* (Glencoe, Ill.: The Free Press, 1961). Edgar Friedenberg, *The Vanishing Adolescent* (New York: Dell, 1962). Paul Goodman, *Growing Up Absurd* (New York: Random House, 1960).

[6]Warren Bennis, *Changing Organizations* (New York: McGraw-Hill, 1966). Robert Blake and Herbert Shepard, "Changing Behavior through Cognitive Change," *Human Organization,* 21 (Summer, 1962).

PART IV

Psychological Foundations

The psychological foundations of education cover as broad a field as psychology itself, and encompasses an equally broad range of topics. This fact should come as no surprise to the reader, for the educator is naturally concerned with the growth and development of the individual student. However, the relevance of psychological data to educational practices is by no means direct. Psychological data are usually derived from a laboratory, and not from a classroom setting. Such data pertain to individuals behaving in an isolated situation rather than in a group situation. A large amount of teaching time is spent directing group behavior by methods appropriate to group processes. Thus individual psychological data needs to be translated, wherever possible, into methods for diagnosing, analyzing, and treating group behavior before the teaching profession can be served by its results. Less "translation" is required to render psychological data valuable for the diagnosis and treatment of individual learning difficulties. What stands in need of translation is what we may call the environmental component, that is, a translation from a laboratory situation to a classroom situation.

The following selections reflect to some extent the wide topics of concern to both the teacher and psychologist. They include a discussion of the method of operant conditioning, a consideration of IQ and its relation to cultural deprivation, the educational implications of the work of a major experimental psychologist, and, finally, a psychological look at personality and creativity. The psychological foundations of education cannot really be defined; rather, they are best described in terms of what psychologists are doing and discovering that has educational significance.

In the first selection, B. F. Skinner describes the method of operant conditioning and its attendant problems and prospects. The study of operant behavior and the role of reinforcement in the management of behavior provides the data upon which much current educational technology is based. Programmed learning, computer-aided instruction, and similar developments reflect the educational application of this approach to research in psychology. Even further "translations" of this methodology are to be found in the growing trend toward performance contracting in education.

Jean Piaget is primarily an experimental psychologist. Yet his work is probably more widely discussed by educators than by psychologists. Piaget's work, being experimental, rarely explicates its educational implications. Piaget is concerned with empirically establishing a theory of knowledge and not with educational practices. Therefore, we include in this group of selections a chapter from David Elkind's recent work on Piaget, in which he draws out the educational significance of Piaget's theories. Professor Elkind examines Piaget's work for its contribution to philosophy of education, learning processes and teaching practices, revealing in essence Piaget's belief in education as a growth encouraging process, with the teacher functioning as a model.

Finally, Donald W. MacKinnon describes for us the personality correlates of creativity. Studies of creativity and creative behavior have assumed greater importance in recent years. This is in part due to the increasing concern over the dehumanizing aspects of a technological society, and in part due to the social demands for ever more innovative applications of technology itself. A wide variety of methods are employed in studies of creativity, and these methods themselves worthy of note, constituting as they do important clues to ways in which creativity is being defined. The author provides his readers with an explicit definition of creativity; other investigators are not always so considerate. Nevertheless, the results of a wide variety of studies, employing a wide variety of methods, are beginning to produce pictures of creative behavior which are amazingly similar. MacKinnon's "traits" of creative people are in line with this growing consensus. All these traits, as the author indicates, have great implications for the educational process.

B. F. SKINNER

Operant
Behavior

WE ARE INTERESTED IN THE BEHAVIOR OF AN ORGANISM BECAUSE OF ITS
effects on the environment. (One effect on the social environment is, of
course, the arousal of our interest.) Some effects seem to throw light on
the behavior which produces them, but their explanatory role has been
clouded by the fact that they follow the behavior and, therefore, raise
the specter of teleology.

An attempt has been made to solve the problem by creating a contemporary surrogate of a given effect. A quality or property of purpose is
assigned to behavior to bring "what the organism is behaving for" into
the effective present, or the organism is said to behave in a given way
because it intends to achieve, or expects to have, a given effect, or its
behavior is characterized as possessing utility to the extent that it maxi-
mizes or minimizes certain effects. The teleological problem is, of course,
not solved until we have answered certain questions: What gives an
action its purpose, what leads an organism to expect to have an effect,
how is utility represented in behavior?

The answers to such questions are eventually to be found in past
instances in which similar behavior has been effective. The original problem can be solved directly in the same way. Thorndike's Law of Effect

B.F. Skinner, "Operant Behavior." *American Psychologist, 18,* 1963, 503–15.
Copyright © 1963 by the American Psychological Association, and reproduced by
permission.

was a step in that direction: The approximately simultaneous occurrence of a response and certain environmental events (usually generated by it) changes the responding organism, increasing the probability that responses of the same sort will occur again. The response itself has passed into history and is not altered.

By emphasizing a change in the organism, Thorndike's principle made it possible to include the effects of action among the causes of future action without using concepts like purpose, intention, expectancy, or utility. Up to that time, the only demonstrable causes of behavior had been antecedent stimuli. The range of the eliciting stimulus was later to be extended by Pavlovian conditioning, and the concept could be broadened to include the releasers of the ethologists, but only a small part of behavior can be predicted or controlled simply by identifying or manipulating stimuli. The Law of Effect added an important new class of variables of which behavior could be shown to be a function.

Thorndike's solution was probably suggested by Darwin's treatment of phylogenetic purpose. Before Darwin, the purpose of a well developed eye might have been said to be to permit the organism to see better. The principle of natural selection moved "seeing better" from the future into the past: Organisms with well developed eyes were descended from those which had been able to see better and had therefore produced more descendants. Thorndike was closer to the principle of natural selection than the above statement of his law. He did not need to say that a response which had been followed by a certain kind of consequence was more likely to occur again but simply that it was not less likely. It eventually held the field because responses which failed to have such effects tended, like less favored species, to disappear.

Thorndike was concerned with how animals solved problems rather than with the concept of purpose, and his Law of Effect did not end purposive formulations. The devices used for the study of behavior during the next quarter of a century continued to emphasize an intentional relation between behavior and its consequences. The relation was represented spatially. In mazes, runways, and open fields, for example, organisms ran *toward* their goals. In discrimination apparatuses they chose the door which led *to* food. They escaped *from* the dangerous side of shuttle boxes or pulled *away from* sources of dangerous stimulation. They drew objects *toward* them with rakes or strings. The experimenter could see the purpose of an action in the spatial relation of the organism and the objects toward which it was moving or from which it was receding. It was even asserted that the organism itself should see a purposive relationship in some such form in order to behave effectively. Köhler, for example, criticized Thorndike on just this score.

The spatial representation of purpose, expectancy, or intention obscured one of the most important features of the relation emphasized by Thorndike. The process he identified remained unexplored for 30 years, and during that time was confused with rote habit formation and with various formulations of Pavlovian conditioning. In the late 1920s, however, the consequences of behavior began to be studied with devices of another sort. Pavlov's technique for the study of conditioned reflexes contributed to their development, even though Pavlov himself was not primarily concerned with consequences as such. In his basic studies, indeed, it might be said that the organism did not receive food *for* doing anything; the salivation elicited by the conditioned stimulus did not produce the food which followed. The experimental design, however, called for food to be introduced at a given moment automatically. Once the procedure was familiar, it was no great step to arrange devices in which a response "produced" food in a similar fashion. Ivanov-Smolensky (1927), one of Pavlov's associates, studied an experimental arrangement, close to Thorndike, in which a child squeezed a rubber bulb and delivered candy into his mouth. Miller and Konorski (1928) devised an apparatus in which a shock to the foot of a dog elicited flexion of the leg, and the resulting movement was followed by the presentation of food; the leg eventually flexed even when the foot was not shocked. In America D. K. Adams (1929) used a similar arrangement with cats, and in England Grindley (1932) with guinea pigs. The essential features may be seen in an apparatus in which depression of a level operates a food dispenser (Skinner, 1932). Pressing a lever is not a natural or unconditioned way of getting food. The response produces food only in the sense that food follows it — a Humean version of causality. Behavior is nevertheless altered. The consequences of action change the organism regardless of how or why they follow. The connection need not be functional or organic — as, indeed, it was not in Thorndike's experiment.

PRACTICAL ADVANTAGES

These early devices were not designed to eliminate spatial representations of purpose, but they all did so, and the fact had far-reaching consequences. Some of these were practical. The experimenter could choose a response which was conveniently recorded, or one which the organism could execute rapidly and without fatigue for long periods of time, or one which minimized the pecularities of a species and thus furthered a comparison between species with respect to properties not primarily related to the topography of behavior. In particular, it was possible to choose a response which was relatively free of extraneous variables and not likely to be confused with responses elicited or evoked by them. When a shuttle box, for example, is used to study the effect of the postponement or termination of a shock, the behavior affected (running or jumping from one side to the other) is topographically similar to unconditioned responses to the shock, such as startle or jumping into the air, and to more elaborate patterns of escape from a space in which shocks have been received. It may also resemble response of both these sorts conditioned in the Pavlovian manner and elicited by the warning stimuli. The inevitable confusion can be avoided by making the postponement or termination of a shock contingent on an arbitrary response, such as pressing a lever in the Sidman arrangement, which is not otherwise related to the variables at issue (Sidman, 1953).

A response which is only temporally related to its consequences could also be conveniently studied with automatic equipment. Instruments were developed which permitted the investigator to conduct many experiments simultaneously, particularly when unskilled technical help was available. It is true that automatic mazes and discrimination boxes had been or were soon to be built, but most modern programming and recording equipment can be traced to research on responses with arbitrarily arranged consequences for the very good reason that the conditions are easily instrumented. The availability of automatic equipment has helped to standardize experiments and has facilitated the study of relations between responses and consequences too complex to be arranged by hand or followed by eye.

Another practical result was terminological. The concept of the reflex made no reference to the consequences of a response. Reflexes were often obviously "adaptive," but this was primarily a phylogenetic effect. The term "operant" was introduced to distinguish between reflexes and responses operating directly on the environment (Skinner, 1937). The alternative term "instrumental" suggests the use of tools. To say that a rat "uses a lever to obtain food" has purposive overtones, and where nothing can be identified as an instrument, it is often said that the organism "uses a response" to gain an effect. For example, verbal behavior is interpreted as "the use of words," although the implication that words exist as things apart from behavior unnecessarily complicates an analysis (Skinner, 1957). Another change was from "reward" to "reinforcement." Reward suggests compensation *for* behaving in a given way, often in some sort of contractual arrangement. Reinforcement in its etymological sense designates simply the strengthening of a response. It refers to similar events in Pavlovian conditioning, where reward is inappropriate. These changes in terminology have not automatically eliminated purposive expressions (such as, "The pigeon was reinforced *for* pecking the key"), but a given instance can usually be rephrased. Comparable teleological expressions are common in other sciences, as Bernatowicz (1958) has pointed out.

RATE OF RESPONDING AS A DATUM

A more important result of studying an arbitrary connection between a response and its consequences, together with the simplified procedures which then become available, has been to emphasize rate of responding as a property of behavior. Earlier devices were almost always used to study responses from trial to trial, where rate of responding was controlled by the experimenter and hence obscured as a datum. When the organism can respond at any time, its rate of responding varies in many subtle ways over a wide range. Changes in rate comprise a vast and previously largely unsuspected subject matter. (The changes are made conspicuous with a cumulative recorder, the ubiquity of which in the study of operant behavior is no accident. In a cumulative record, rate and changes in rate are visible at a glance over substantial periods of time. The "on-line" record permits the experimenter to note changes as they occur and take appropriate steps.)

Rate of responding is important because it is especially relevant to the principal task of a scientific analysis. Behavior is often interesting because of what might be called its character. Animals court their mates, build living quarters, care for their young, forage for food, defend territories, and so on, in many fascinating ways. These are worth studying, but the inherent drama can divert attention from another task. Even when reduced to general principles, a narrative account of *how* animals behave must be supplemented by a consideration of *why*. What is required is an analysis of the conditions which govern the probability that a given response will occur at a given time. Rate of responding is by no means to be equated with probability of responding, as frequency theories of probability and comparable problems in physics have shown. Many investigators prefer to treat rate of responding as a datum in its own right. Eventually, however, the prediction and control of behavior call for an evaluation of the probabilty that a response will be emitted. The study of rate of responding is a step in that direction.

Rate of responding is one of those aspects of a subject matter which do not attract attention for their own sake and which undergo intensive study only when their usefulness as a dependent variable has been discovered. Other sciences have passed through comparable stages. The

elements and compounds studied by the chemist also have fascinating
characters — they exist in many colors, textures, and states of aggregation and undergo surprising transmutations when heated, dissolved,
combined, and so on. These are the characteristics which naturally first
attract attention. They were, for example, the principal concern of the
alchemists. In contrast, the mere weight of a given quantity of a substance
is of little interest in its own right. Yet it was only when the weights of
substances entering into reactions were found to obey certain laws that
chemistry moved into its modern phase. Combining weight became important because of what could be done with it. Rate of responding has
emerged as a basic datum in a science of behavior for similar reasons —
and, hopefully, with comparable results.

Rate of responding differs from the measures derived from earlier
devices and procedures, such as the time required to complete a task or
the effort expended or the number of errors made in doing so, and the
two kinds of data have led to different conceptions of behavior as a
scientific subject matter. We like to believe that basic processes are
orderly, continuous, and significant, but the data obtained from mazes,
memory drums, shuttle boxes, and so on, vary "noisily" from trial to trial
and depend for their dimensions on particular tasks and apparatuses.
Orderly and significant processes are therefore sought elsewhere — in
some mental, physiological, or merely conceptual inner system which by
its nature is neither directly observed in, nor accurately represented on any
given occasion by, the performance of an organism. There is no comparable inner system in an operant analysis. Changes in rate of responding are directly observed, they have dimensions appropriate to a scientific
formulation, and under skillful experimental control they show the uniformity expected of biological processes in general. Those accustomed to
the older formulation have nevertheless found them difficult to accept as
an alternative subject for analysis.

BEHAVIORAL PROCESSES

One difficulty is that changes in rate do not closely resemble the behavioral processes inferred from earlier measures. A few examples may be
cited from the field of learning. By arranging a reinforcing consequence,
we increase the rate at which a response occurs; by eliminating the consequence, we decrease the rate. These are the processes of operant conditioning and extinction. Topographical properties of the response depend
on the contingencies. The force with which a lever is pressed, for example,
is related to the force required to operate the food dispenser. An initial
moderate force can be increased indefinitely, within physiological limits,

by progressively requiring greater forces. A complex topography can be "shaped" with a series of changing contingencies, called a program, each stage of which evokes a response and also prepares the organism to respond at a later stage. A shaping program can be mechanically prescribed in advance, but the process is most easily demonstrated when the experimenter improvises contingencies as he goes.

The behaviors evoked by mazes, puzzle boxes, memory drums, and so on, are also shaped, but almost always without specific programing of contingencies. The organism is usually exposed at once to a set of *terminal* contingencies, for which it possesses no adequate behavior. Responses occur, however — the rat explores the maze, the subject guesses at the next nonsense syllable — and some of these may be reinforced in ways which lead at last to a terminal performance. What can we conclude from the series of stages through which this comes about?

Such data are usually plotted in so-called learning curves showing, let us say, the times required to complete a task or the number of errors made in doing so, by trials. These are facts and in some sense quantifiable. From such a curve we may predict within limits how another organism will behave in similar circumstances. But the shape of the curve tells us little or nothing about the processes of conditioning and extinction revealed in an operant analysis. It merely describes the rather crude overall effects of adventitious contingencies, and it often tells us more about the apparatus or procedure than about the organism.

Similar discrepancies appear in the analysis of stimuli. In so-called stimulus-response theories, a stimulus is broadly defined as something which customarily precedes a response — the eliciting stimulus in a conditioned reflex, the "cue" to more complex behavior, or even an internal "drive state." The term is little more than synonym for cause, and various relations between cause and effect are usually not distinguished. The stimulus control of an operant, on the other hand, has been carefully analyzed. Although we can shape the topography of a response without identifying or manipulating any anterior stimulus, stimuli enter into a more complex type of contingency in which a response is reinforced in the presence of a stimulus and is therefore more likely to be emitted in its presence. The relations among the three terms in this contingency — stimulus, response, and reinforcement — comprise a substantial field for investigation.

One property of the control acquired by a stimulus when a response is reinforced in its presence is shown in the so-called stimulus generalization gradient. Hypothetical gradients in mental, neurological, or conceptual inner systems have been discussed for years, but thanks to the work of Guttman (1963) and his students, and others, behavioral gradients are now directly observed. A pigeon, reinforced when it pecks a circular key of a given color and size, will peck keys of other shapes, colors, or sizes at lower rates depending upon the differences in the properties. When the response is reinforced in the presence of one property and extinguished in the presence of others — the well-known process of discrimination — a very sensitive and powerful control is established. In a classroom demonstration a response is brought under the control of a red as against a green key. So long as the key is green, no response is made; when it turns red, the pigeon pecks it immediately. The power of the stimulus can be dramatically shown by changing from red to green just as the pigeon's beak moves toward the key. The pecking response will be interrupted in mid-air, even though stopping probably requires more energy than following through. Stimulus control can also be shaped by changing relevant stimuli in a program which leads the organism into subtle discriminations, often without "errors," as Terrace (1963) has recently shown. Very little of this is seen in traditional studies of sensory learning, however. In using a classical multiple-choice apparatus, for example, the organism is exposed at once to a set of terminal contingencies. Its progress toward an appropriate performance is represented in a curve showing, say, the number of errors made or the times required to reach a criterion, over a series of trials, but the dimensions of these measures are again arbitrary, and the behavior is obviously the product of shifting, largely adventitious contingencies.

Classical studies of learning have emphasized the process of *acquisition*, presumably because one can easily see that an organism is doing something new or is responding to a new stimulus, but reinforcement is also responsible for the fact that an organism goes on responding long after its behavior has been acquired. The fact has usually been attributed to motivational variables, but an experimental analysis has shown that various schedules of intermittent reinforcement are usually involved. The nature or quantity of reinforcement is often much less important than the schedule on which it is received. Programing is again important, for many schedules can take effect only when the organism has passed through intervening contingencies. To take a very simple example — an apparatus which reinforces every hundredth response will have no effect at all if 100 responses are never emitted, but by reinforcing every second, then every fifth, then every tenth response, and so on, waiting until the behavior is well developed at each stage, we can bring the organism under the control of the more demanding schedule. The pathological gambler and the dedicated scientist both show terminal behavior resulting from a special history of reinforcement on a related ("variable-ratio") schedule — a history which society attempts to prevent in the former case and encourage in the latter.

The history which brings a complex terminal schedule into control is not, of course, visible in the terminal performance. A scientist once borrowed an apparatus to demonstrate the use of a multiple fixed-interval fixed-ratio schedule in assessing the effects of certain drugs. When one of the pigeons lent with the apparatus was accidentally killed, he purchased another, put it into the apparatus, and was surprised to find that nothing happened. We make the same mistake when we attempt to explain conspicuous effects of reinforcement on human behavior by examining only *current* schedules.

Complex terminal contingencies involving multiple stimuli and responses, in sequential or concurrent arrangements, are often called problems. An organism is said to have solved such a problem when it comes under the control of the terminal contingencies. Its capacity to respond appropriately under such contingencies must, however, be distinguished from its capacity to reach them through a given series of intervening stages. Whether an organism can solve a problem in this sense is as much a question of the program through which it passes — and the skill of the programmer who constructed it — as of any so-called problem solving ability. Whether an organism can solve a problem without the help of a prepared program depends on the behavior initially available and the more or less accidental contingencies which follow from it. Apparent differences in problem solving ability among species or among organisms of different ages or other properties within a species must be interpreted accordingly. Solving a problem, like learning, is again often attributed to an inner system, although the supposed inner processes, like the facts they explain, are more complex. Those committed to sequestered faculties and thought processes are not likely to feel at home in an analysis of the behavior itself and may, therefore, find it inacceptable as an alternative enterprise.

STATISTICS

Another difficulty is methodological. Processes taking place in some inner system can usually be investigated only with "statistics." If learning is never accurately represented in one performance, performances must be averaged. If statements about the inner system cannot be directly confirmed, hypotheses must be set up, and theorems deduced and tested, following established practices in logic and scientific method. If some properties of the inner system are meaningful only with respect to larger sets of facts, a procedure such as factor analysis may be needed. It is not surprising that research on this pattern has come to be judged by the sophistication of its statistical and logical techniques. Confidence in an experiment is proportional to the number of subjects studied, an experiment is good only if properly "designed," and results are significant only at a level determined by special tests.

Much of this is lacking in the experimental analysis of behavior, where experiments are usually performed on a few subjects, curves representing behavioral processes are seldom averaged, the behavior attributed to complex mental activity is analyzed directly, and so on. The simpler procedure is possible because rate of responding and changes in rate can be directly observed, especially when represented in cumulative records. The effect is similar to increasing the resolving power of a microscope: A new subject matter is suddenly open to direct inspection. Statistical methods are unnecessary. When an organism is showing a stable or slowly changing performance, it is for most purposes idle to stop to evaluate the confidence with which the next stage can be predicted. When a variable is changed and the effect on performance observed, it is for most purposes idle to prove statistically that a change has indeed occurred. (It is sometimes said in such a case that the organism is "used as its own control," but the expression, borrowed from a basically different methodology, is potentially troublesome.) Much can be done in the study of behavior with methods of observation no more sophisticated than those available to Faraday, say, with his magnets, wires, and cells. Eventually the investigator may move on to peripheral areas where indirect methods become necessary, but until then he must forego the prestige which attaches to traditional statistical methods.

Some traditional uses must also be questioned. Learning curves remain inadequate no matter how smooth they are made by averaging cases. Statistical techniques may eliminate noise, but the dimensions are still faulty. A curve which enables us to predict the performance of another organism does not therefore represent a basic process. Moreover, curves which report changes in variables having satisfactory dimensions can often not be averaged. The idiosyncracies in a cumulative record do not necessarily show caprice on the part of the organism or faulty technique on the part of the experimenter. The complex system we call an organism has an elaborate and largely unknown history which endows it with a certain individuality. No two organisms embark upon an experiment in precisely the same condition nor are they affected in the same way by the contingencies in an experimental space. (Most contingencies would not be representative if they were precisely controlled, and in any case are effective only in combination with the behavior which the organism brings to the experiment.) Statistical techniques cannot eliminate this kind of individuality; they can only obscure and falsify it. An average curve seldom correctly represents any of the cases contributing to it (Sidman, 1960).

An analysis which recognizes the individuality of the organism is particularly valuable when contact is made with other disciplines such as neurology, psychopharmacology, and psychotherapy, where idiosyncratic sets of variables must also be considered. The rigor of the analysis is not necessarily threatened. Operant methods make their own use of Grand Numbers: Instead of studying 1,000 rats for 1 hour each, or 100 rats for 10 hours each, the investigator is likely to study 1 rat for 1,000 hours. The procedure is not only appropriate to an enterprise which recognizes individuality, it is at least equally efficient in its use of equipment and of the investigator's time and energy. The ultimate test of uniformity or reproducibility is not to be found in method but in the degree of control achieved, a test which the experimental analysis of behavior usually passes easily.

The study of operant behavior also seldom follows the "design of experiments" prescribed by statisticians. A prior design in which variables are distributed, for example, in a Latin square may be a severe handicap. When effects on behavior can be immediately observed, it is most efficient to explore relevant variables by manipulating them in an improvised and rapidly changing design. Similar practices have been responsible for the greater part of modern science. This is not, however, the tenor of R. A. Fisher's *Design of Experiments*, which, as Lancelot Hogben (1957) has said, gives the reader the impression that recourse to statistical methods is prerequisite to the design of experiments of any sort whatever. In that event, the whole creation of experimental scientists from Gilbert and Hooke to J. J. Thomson and Morgan has been groaning and travailing in fruitless pain together; and the biologist of today has nothing to learn from well-tried methods which have led to the spectacular advances of the several branches of experimental science during the last three centuries [p. 29].

Statistics, like logic and scientific methodology in general, emphasizes the verbal behavior of the scientist: How reliable are his measures, how significant are the differences he reports, how confident can we be that what he says is true? His nonverbal behavior is much less easily codified and analyzed. In such considerations, what the scientist *does* takes second place to what he *says*. Yet the a priori manipulation of variables, guided by directly observed effects, is superior to the a posteriori analysis of covariation in many ways. It leads more rapidly to prediction and control and to practical recombinations of variables in the study of complex cases. Eventually, of course, the experimenter must behave verbally. He must describe what he has done and what he has seen, and he must conduct his research with this obligation in mind. But a compulsive preoccupation with validity or significance may be inimical to other, equally important obligations.

A nonstatistical strategy may also be recommended for its effect on the behavior of the investigator, who is perhaps as strongly reinforced during a successful experiment as the organism he studies. The contingencies to which he is submitted largely determine whether he will continue in similar work. Statistical techniques often inject a destructive delay between the conduct of an experiment and the discovery of the significance of the data — a fatal violation of a fundamental principle of reinforcement. The exceptional zeal which has often been noted in students of operant behavior is possibly attributable to the immediacy of their results.

THE CIRCUMVENTION OF AN OPERANT ANALYSIS

By accepting changes in rate of responding as basic behavioral processes and by emphasizing environmental variables which can be manipulated with the help of automatic equipment, research on operant behavior has been greatly simplified. But it has not been made easy. Technical advances have been offset by the demand for increasing rigor, by the problems which arise in studying one organism at a time, and by the attack on more and more complex arrangements of interrelated operants. Behavior — human or otherwise — remains an extremely difficult subject matter. It is not surprising that practices which seem to circumvent or simplify an operant analysis are common. In particular, verbal communication between subject and experimenter is widely used in lieu of the explicit arrangement of contingencies of reinforcement and the objective recording of behavior. The practice goes back to the study of mental life and is still favored by psychologists who formulate their subject matter in mental terms, but it survives as if it were a labor-saving device in many essentially behavioristic formulations.

The manipulation of independent variables appears to be circumvented when, instead of exposing an organism to a set of contingencies, the contingencies are simply described in "instructions." Instead of shaping a response, the subject is told to respond in a given way. A history of reinforcement or punishment is replaced by a promise or threat: "Movement of the lever will sometimes operate a coin dispenser" or ". . . deliver a shock to your leg." A schedule of positive or negative reinforcement is described rather than imposed: "Every response to the right lever postpones the shock but increases the number of responses to the left lever required to operate the coin dispenser." Instead of bringing the behavior under the control of a stimulus, the subject is told to behave as if a discrimination had been established: "Start when the light goes on, stop when it goes off." Thus instructed, the subject is asked either to behave appropriately or to describe behavior he might emit under such circumstances. The scope of the verbal substitute can be estimated by considering how a nonverbal organism, human or otherwise, could be similarly "instructed."

Descriptions of contingencies are, of course, often effective. Hypothetical consequences are commonly used for practical purposes ("Will you do the job if I pay you $50?" or "How would you feel about going if I told you that X would be there?"), and the subject is worth studying. Verbal instruction may be defended when the resulting behavior is not the primary object of interest; for example, the experimenter may show a subject how to operate a piece of equipment rather than shape his behavior through reinforcement so long as he is not concerned with the acquisition of the response but with what happens to it later. Verbal communication is not, however, a substitute for the arrangement and manipulation of variables.

There is no reason why a description of contingencies of reinforcement should have the same effect as exposure to the contingencies. A subject can seldom accurately describe the way in which he has actually been reinforced. Even when he has been trained to identify a few simple contingencies, he cannot then describe a new contingency, particularly when it is complex. We can scarcely expect him, therefore, to react appropriately to descriptions by the experimenter. Moreover, the verbal contingencies between subject and experimenter must be taken into account. Instructions must in some way promise or threaten consequences not germane to the experiment if the subject is to follow them.

The other major task in an operant analysis may seem to be circumvented when, instead of recording behavior so that rate or probability of response can be observed or inferred, the experimenter simply asks the subject to evaluate his tendency to respond or to express his preference for responding in one way rather than another. The subject may do so by describing his "intentions" or "plans" or by reporting "expectations" regarding the consequences of an action. Such behavior may be worth investigating, but it is not a substitute for the behavior observed in an operant analysis. Only in the simplest cases can a person correctly describe his ongoing behavior. The difficulty is not linguistic, for he may be given an operandum and permitted to "model" the behavior — for example, to generate a cumulative record. It is practically impossible to construct a curve closely resembling the curve one would generate if actually exposed to a specified set of contingencies, or even a curve one has already generated when so exposed. Changes in rate of responding are not easy to describe. They necessarily take place in time, and even a second observer cannot "see" them until they have been reduced to graphic form. The subject's own behavior presents other difficulties, which are not overcome by permitting him to be less specific. If we ask him to say simply whether he will be more or less likely to respond or will respond more or less rapidly, we have increased his chances of being right only by asking him to say less. Any report, no matter how specific, is also subject to the verbal contingencies which induce him to describe his behavior and possibly by similar contingencies elsewhere which may classify his behavior, for example, as right or wrong.

Verbal substitutes for arranged or observed variables may be used at different points in an investigation: Contingencies may be described and the subject's behavior then actually observed, the subject may be exposed to a set of contingencies and then asked to evaluate the nature or probability of his responses, and so on. Similar practices are used to evaluate the reinforcing or aversive properties of a given event or procedure, to predict the outcome of several variables operating at once, and so on, and are subject to the same criticism.

To those interested primarily in mental processes, verbal communication may not be an attempted circumvention or shortcut. On the contrary, an operant analysis may seem to be the long way around. The position is sometimes defended by insisting that the student of behavior always begins with an interest in mental life — possibly his own — and designs his experiments essentially to test hypotheses about it. Whatever the case may once have been, operant research has long since passed the point at which the experimenter can be guided by considering possible effects of variables on himself. The introspective vocabulary used in circumventing an experimental analysis is hopelessly inadequate for the kinds of facts currently under investigation. If one field is to borrow from the other, the debt will henceforth almost certainly be in the other direction: From the study of the behavior of other organisms, the experimenter is most likely to come to understand himself. In some theories of knowledge, introspective observations may be regarded as primary data, but in an analysis of behavior they are a form of theorizing which is not required or necessarily helpful (Skinner, 1963).

FORMAL ANALYSES OF CONTINGENCIES OF REINFORCEMENT

The consequences of action and their effects on behavior also enter into theories of probability, decision making, conflict, and games. The classical urn containing a given proportion of black and white balls may, like other sample spaces, be analyzed without reference to behavior, but it would be of little interest if the consequences of drawing either a black or white ball were not in some way reinforcing. (There has always been a close connection between probability theory and gambling, where every play is punished to the extent of its cost and some plays are also reinforced.) Probability theory also often takes into account the fact that this reinforcement will occur on an intermittent schedule, and that as a consequence the drawer will experience a given subjective or felt probability, or exhibit a given probability of drawing again.

The probability that the drawer will draw again is usually assumed to be related to the probability function of the sample space. A relation is implied when it is said that a subject who has sufficient knowledge about a given system, possibly inferred from his experience with it, can behave "rationally." A relation is also implied when it is argued that irrational behavior requires explanation. For example, the fact that intermittent reinforcement raises the probability of responding above the value generated when all responses are reinforced has recently occasioned surprise (Lawrence & Festinger, 1962). Any such relation is, of course, an empirical fact, to be determined experimentally. Standard operant equipment can be used to set up contingencies of reinforcement which have the effect of classical sample spaces. A schedule could, if necessary, be programed by actually drawing balls from an urn. An organism can then be exposed to the schedule and the effect on its behavior observed. In such a procedure the status of the probability function of the sample space (the schedule of reinforcement arranged by the programing equipment) is clear. The probability that the organism will respond at a given time is inferred from its rate.

The relation between the two probabilities is complicated by the fact that rate of responding under a given schedule depends, as we have seen, on previous exposure to the schedule. When introduced into an experimental space for the first time, an organism may be said to show a certain "prior probability" of responding — the so-called operant level. A first response is or is not reinforced, and the rate rises or falls accordingly. This brief history contributes to what is now a different situation. When the organism responds again and is again possibly reinforced, the situation changes still more substantially. A given set of contingencies yields a performance which combines with the programing equipment to generate other contingencies which in turn generate other performances, and so on.

Many of these interactions between behavior and programing equipment have been carefully studied. Under a variable-interval schedule of reinforcement, for example, the organism often responds at a nearly constant rate for long periods of time. All reinforcements therefore occur when it is responding at that rate, *although this condition is not specified by the equipment.* The rate becomes a discriminative and, in turn, a reinforcing stimulus, which opposes any change to a different rate—such as would otherwise be induced by, say, a psychopharmacological agent. As another example, when only the first response after the passage of a fixed interval of time is reinforced, the organism comes to exhibit a fairly stable performance in which the number of responses emitted during an interval approaches constancy. The organism is then being reinforced not only after a constant interval of time but after emitting a constant number of responses. The latter condition, *which is not specified by the equipment,* is characteristic of a fixed-ratio schedule, and it generates a much higher rate of responding. As rapid responding breaks through, the stability of the fixed-interval performance is destroyed, the number of responses per reinforcement is no longer constant and a stable interval performance is restored, as another cycle begins (Ferster & Skinner, 1957).

A third example is closer to probability theory. A schedule in which a response is reinforced upon completion of an appreciable fixed or variable number of responses must often be reached through a program, as we have seen. The number must first be small, but the schedule favors reinforcement when the organism is responding at a high rate, and it is soon possible to "stretch" the requirement. When a hungry rat is reinforced with food for running in a wheel, the required distance can be increased until more energy is consumed than is available in the food received (Skinner, 1938). The behavior of the gambler, which almost always shows a similar "negative utility," is the result of the same kind of stretching. The variable-ratio schedules inherent in gambling systems maintain behavior only after a history of reinforcement in which behavior has combined with the programing equipment to generate certain powerful terminal contingencies.

In summary, a scheduling system has no effect until an organism is exposed to it, and it then no longer fully determines the contingencies. Still other interactions between equipment and performance arise when a second response is introduced in order to study choice or decision making. Suppose, for example, that a subject may press either of two keys, A and B, on which reinforcements are independently scheduled. The performance on either key can be accounted for only by examining the combined action of equipment and earlier performances *on both keys.* For example, if reinforcements are programed on interval schedules, responding to A after B is more likely to be reinforced than responding to B after B since the equipment may have set up a reinforcement on A while a response was being made to B. The behavior of changing from A to B or from B to A may be favored to the point at which the performance becomes a simple alternation (Skinner, 1950). This yields the same rate on both keys, even though the schedules may be substantially different. The interaction may be corrected with a "change-over delay" in which, for example, a response to B is not reinforced if a response to A has been made during the preceding second, or in which the first response to either key after changing over is never reinforced (Herrnstein, 1961). The contingencies on the two levers are nevertheless still subject to other interactions. (A word of caution: By manipulating the change-over delay and other characteristics of the schedules it may be possible to generate rates of responding on the two keys which would be predicted from some hypothesis of rationality or utility. It is tempting to regard these as optimal conditions and possibly to stop the research when they have been discovered.)

Interactions between performance and programing system are still more complex if the performance changes the system, as in the so-called "adjusting" and "interlocking" schedules (Ferster & Skinner, 1957). Many examples are to be found in the theory of games and conflict, where the behavior of one organism alters the contingencies affecting another, and vice versa. The rules of any game can be represented by programing equipment which is subject to modification by the performances of the players, but the actual contingencies of reinforcement are still more complex, for they include conditions not specified by the equipment but generated by the earlier performances of all parties.

(That there is a limitation inherent in formal analyses is suggested by the fact that mathematical inquiries into probability, decision making, conflict, and games confine themselves almost exclusively to ratio schedules. The contingencies defined in sample spaces and rules practically always specify reinforcement as a function of a number of responses, a restraint traceable perhaps to practical issues involving winning, losing, and ultimate utility. Yet the interactions between equipment and performance are the same when reinforcement is scheduled by clocks or speedometers rather than by counters, and the same processes are involved, as an experimental analysis has abundantly shown.)

The formal properties of sample spaces, like the various conditions under which choices are made, games played, or conflicts resolved, may be analyzed without taking behavior into account or, at most, by assuming selected performances. Those interested primarily in a formal analysis are likely to approach behavior, if at all, by setting up hypotheses. The research which follows has the nature of hypothesis testing and is wasteful if the data collected lose their value when a hypothesis has been disproved or abandoned for other reasons. An experimental analysis of the behavior generated by the contingencies in sample spaces may be conducted without guessing at the results.

THE USE OF FORMAL ANALYSES

Formal analyses of contingencies of reinforcement are related to behavior in another way when they are used as guides. The behavior of a person who has calculated his chances, compared alternatives, or considered the consequences of a move is different from, and usually more effective than, the behavior of one who has merely been exposed to the unanalyzed contingencies. The formal analysis functions as a discriminative stimulus. When such a stimulus is perfectly correlated with reinforcement, the behavior under its control as maximally reinforced. On an interval schedule and in the absence of related stimuli, an organism emits unreinforced or "wasted" responses, but if the apparatus presents a conspicuous stimulus whenever a reinforcement becomes available, the organism eventually responds only in the presence of that stimulus and no responses are wasted. Clocks provide stimuli of this sort in connection with events occurring on interval schedules and are built and used for just that reason. Stimuli less closely correlated with reinforcement yield lesser improvements in efficiency. If a given setting on a clock cannot be sharply discriminated, for example, some responses will be emitted prior to "the time to respond" and some potentially effective responses may be delayed, but performance is nevertheless improved. A speedometer serves a similar function when reinforcement depends on a given rate of responding.

Formal analyses of sample spaces serve the same function as imprecise clocks and speedometers. Not every response under their control is reinforced, but there is still a net gain. When a man learns to play poker under the contingencies arranged by the cards and rules, his sampling of the possible contingencies is necessarily limited, even in prolonged play. He will play a more successful game, and after a much shorter history, if he consults a table showing his chances of success in making given plays. The contingencies in poker also depend upon the behavior of other players, and prior stimuli correlated with that behavior are therefore also useful. They are particularly important in such a game as chess. Chess playing may be shaped by the unanalyzed contingencies generated by the rules of the game and by the performances of opponents, but a player will play a better game, after a shorter history, if he can consult standard gambits, defenses, end games, and so on, which show some of the likely consequences of given moves.

A stimulus commonly correlated with reinforcement and hence useful in improving efficiency is the record left by previous behavior. When a man finds his way from one place to another, he may leave traces which prove useful when he goes that way again. He wears a path which supplements the change taking place in his behavior and may even be useful to others who have not gone that way before. A path need not be constructed because it serves this function, but the advantages gained may reinforce the explicit leaving of traces. A trail is "blazed," for example, precisely because it is more easily followed. Comparable reinforcing advantages have led men to construct pictures and verbal descriptions of paths.

Many proverbs and maxims are crude descriptions of contingencies of social or nonsocial reinforcement, and those who observe them come under a more effective control of their environment. Rules of grammar and spelling bring certain verbal contingencies of reinforcement more forcefully into play. Society codifies its ethical, legal, and religious practices so that by following a code the individual may emit behavior appropriate to social contingencies without having been directly exposed to them. Scientific laws serve a similar function in guiding the behavior of scientists.

A person could, of course, construct rules of grammar and spelling, maxims for effective personal conduct, tables of probabilities in the games he plays, and scientific laws for his own use, but society analyzes the predictable contingencies for him. He constructs comparable stimuli for himself when he makes resolutions, announces intentions, states expectations, and formulates plans. The stimuli thus generated control his behavior most effectively when they are external, conspicuous, and durable — when the resolution is posted or the plan actually drafted in visible form — but they are also useful when created upon occasion, as by recalling the resolution or reviewing the plan. The gain from any such discriminative stimulus depends upon the extent to which it correctly represents the contingencies which led to its construction.

Discriminative stimuli which improve the efficiency of behavior under given contingencies of reinforcement are important, but they must not be confused with the contingencies themselves, nor their effects with the effects of those contingencies. The behavior of the poker player who evaluates his chances before making a given play merely resembles that of the player whose behavior has been shaped by prolonged exposure to the game. The behavior of one who speaks correctly by applying the rules of a grammar merely resembles the behavior of one who speaks correctly from long experience in a verbal community. The efficiency may be the same, but the controlling variables are different and the behaviors are therefore different. Nothing which could be called following a plan or applying a rule is observed when behavior is a product of the contingencies alone. To say that "the child who learns a language has in some sense constructed the grammar for himself" (Chomsky, 1959) is as misleading as to say that a dog which has learned to catch a ball has in some sense constructed the relevant part of the science of mechanics. Rules can be extracted from the reinforcing contingencies in both cases, and once in existence they may be used as guides. The direct effect of the contingencies is of a different nature.

The distinction bears on two points already made. In the first place, the instructions used in circumventing an operant analysis also have the status of prior stimuli associated with hypothetical or real contingencies of reinforcement, but behavior in response to them is not the behavior generated by exposure to the contingencies themselves even when, on rare occasions, the two are similar. When subjects report that they understand instructions and hence know what to expect, it does not follow that comparable reportable states are generated by the contingencies themselves. In the second place — to return at last to the point with which this paper began — when a man explicitly states his purpose in acting in a given way he may, indeed, be constructing a "contemporary surrogate of future consequences" which will affect subsequent behavior, possibly in useful ways. It does not follow, however, that the behavior generated by the consequences alone is under the control of any comparable prior stimulus, such as a felt purpose or intention.

THE CONTINGENCIES OF REINFORCEMENT

The Law of Effect specifies a simple temporal order of response and consequence — the relation implied by the term operant. The contingencies of reinforcement currently under investigation are much more complex. Reinforcement may be contingent, not only on the occurrence of a response, but on special features of its topography, on the presence of prior stimuli, and on scheduling systems. An adequate analysis must also reach into the traditional fields of motivation and emotion to determine what is reinforcing and under what conditions. Interrelated systems of operants raise other problems.

The techniques of an experimental analysis have fortunately remained commensurate with the increasing complexity of the subject. Rate of responding has come to be examined over a much wider range and in much greater detail. Cumulative records have been supplemented by distributions of interresponse times and, very recently, by "on-line" computer processing. Better measures of topographical properties have become available. Independent variables have been effectively controlled over a wider range and in more complex patterns. Arrangements of operants resembling many of the behaviors attributed to higher mental processes have been successfully constructed and studied.

The experimental space has been improved. Brief daily experimental periods have given way to continuous observation for many hours, days, weeks, or even months. More of the behavior exhibited in the experimental space has been controlled, recorded, and analyzed. Total control of the environment from birth is within range. As in the study of animal behavior in general, the hundreds of thousands of extant species are still far from adequately sampled, but problems of instrumentation have been solved for a fairly wide range of anatomical and behavioral differences.

The contingencies of reinforcement which define operant behavior are important in the analysis of variables of other sorts. The stimulus control of behavior is central to a kind of nonverbal psychophysics, where interest may be primarily in the action of receptor mechanisms. Operant techniques are important in defining the behavioral effects of physiological variables — surgical, electrical, and chemical — in specifying what aspects of behavior are to be attributed to hereditary endowment, in tracing features of mature behavior to early environment, and so on. They are important in clarifying the nature of defective, retarded, or psychotic behavior. As Lindsley (1963) has pointed out, the important thing about a psychotic is often not what he is doing but what he is not doing, and in such a case it is important to be able to predict normal performances under standard conditions.

Contingencies of reinforcement are also valuable in interpreting behavior not easily submitted to a laboratory analysis. Verbal behavior, for example, can be defined just in terms of its contingencies: Its special characteristics are derived from the fact that reinforcement is mediated by other organisms. In education the instructional programing of reinforcement is the *raison d'être* of teaching machines, the future of which is much brighter than current activities may suggest. It is too early to predict the effect of comparable analyses in other branches of the social sciences — for example, economics and government — but if the history of physical technology is any guide, the knowledge and skills derived from an experimental analysis will become increasingly important.

In short, in the field of human behavior as a whole, the contingencies of reinforcement which define operant behavior are widespread if not ubiquitous. Those who are sensitive to this fact are sometimes embarrassed by the frequency with which they see reinforcement everywhere, as Marxists see class struggle or Freudians the Oedipus relation. Yet the fact is that reinforcement *is* extraordinarily important. That is why it is reassuring to recall that its place was once taken by the concept of purpose; no one is likely to object to a search for purpose in every human act. The difference is that we are now in a position to search effectively. In its very brief history, the study of operant behavior has clarified the nature of the relation between behavior and its consequences and has devised techniques which apply the methods of a natural science to its investigation.

REFERENCES

Adams, D. K. Experimental studies of adaptive behavior in cats. *Comp. Psychol. Monogr.*, 1929, 6(1, Whole No. 27).

Bernatowicz, A. I. Teleology in science teaching. *Science*, 1958, 128, 1402–1405.

Chomsky, N. Review of Skinner's *Verbal behavior. Language*, 1959, 35, 26–58.

Ferster, C. B., & Skinner, B. F. *Schedules of reinforcement.* New York: Appleton-Century-Crofts, 1957.

Grindley, G. C. The formation of a simple habit in guinea pigs. *Brit. J. Psychol.*, 1932, 23, 127–147.

Guttman, N. Laws of behavior and facts of perception. In S. Koch (Ed.), *Psychology: A study of a science.* Vol. 5. New York: McGraw-Hill, 1963. Pp. 114–178.

Herrnstein, R. J. Relative and absolute strength of response as a function of frequency of reinforcement. *J. exp. Anal. Behav.*, 1961, 4, 267–272.

Hogben, L. *Statistical theory.* London: Norton, 1957.

Ivanov-Smolensky, A. G. On methods of examining conditioned food reflexes in children and in mental disorders. *Brain*, 1927, 50, 138–141.

Lawrence, D. H., & Festinger, L. *Deterrents and reinforcement.* Stanford, Calif.: Stanford Univer. Press, 1962.

Lindsley, O. R. Direct measurement and functional definition of vocal hallucinatory symptoms. *J. nerv. ment. Dis.*, 1963, 136, 293–297.

Miller, S., & Konorski, J. Sur une forme particulière des réflexes conditionnels. *CR Soc. Biol., Paris*, 1928, 99, 1155–1157.

Sidman, M. Avoidance conditioning with brief shock and no exteroceptive warning signal. *Science*, 1953, 118, 157-158.

Sidman, M. *Tactics of scientific research.* New York: Basic Books, 1960.

Skinner, B. F. Drive and reflex strength: II. *J. gen. Psychol.*, 1932, 6, 38-48.

Skinner, B. F. Two types of conditioned reflex: A reply to Konorski and Miller. *J. gen. Psychol.*, 1937, 16, 272-279.

Skinner, B. F. *Behavior of organisms.* New York: Appleton-Century-Crofts, 1938.

Skinner, B. F. Are theories of learning necessary? *Psychol. Rev.*, 1950, 57, 193-216.

Skinner, B. F. *Verbal behavior.* New York: Appleton-Century-Crofts, 1957.

Skinner, B. F. Behaviorism at fifty. *Science,* 1963, 134, 566-602.

Terrace, H. S. Discrimination learning with and without "errors." *J. exp. Anal. Behav.*, 1963, 6, 1–27.

DAVID ELKIND

Piaget and
Education

THE PAST DECADE HAS BORNE WITNESS TO A PHENOMENAL GROWTH OF interest in Piaget's work and thought. While this interest is widespread among psychologists, psychiatrists, pediatricians, sociologists, and philosophers, it is particularly prominent among educators. As a consequence, books and articles dealing with Piaget's work and directed toward educators are appearing in ever increasing numbers (e.g., 2, 6, 8, 18).

Before proceeding a few cautionary remarks are in order. Piaget is not an educator, nor is he principally concerned with problems of education. In its primary intent, his work has been philosophical, and designed to provide a theory of knowledge and of knowing based upon empirical evidence. Philosophies of knowledge, however, have always had considerable impact upon educational theory and practice. This was as true for the philosophies of Plato and Aristotle as it was for those of Descartes, Locke, and more recently the Vienna Circle, but in each case educators have had to draw their own implications with respect to educational theory, the processes of learning, and methods of instruction.

The same holds true for Piaget's work. He has provided a new and empirically based conceptual framework and schema from which to view educational problems. What we see from that framework or within those concepts, however, is very much determined by our own predilections, attitudes, and biases. It is necessary to state this at the outset because this chapter reflects my interpretation of the implications of Piaget's work for education. Put differently, if there are any ideas of value they most assuredly are attributable to Piaget while the commonplaces must remain my own responsibility.

THE PHILOSOPHY OF EDUCATION

Every philosophy of education presupposes, in addition to a set of values and a theory of instruction, a particular image of the child which dominates the other components. When, for example, Calvinistic theology postulated that the child was imbued with original sin, the corresponding educational values and teaching practices were oriented accordingly. Puritan education aimed at developing self-control and discipline with the use of fear, threat, and punishment as motivational aids. Centuries later, when Freud described childhood as the period of neurotic and psychotic formations, a different educational philosophy arose which aimed at freeing the child from inhibitions and repressions, and the educational mode was permissiveness and freedom from constraint.

Piaget's impact upon educational philosophy will probably derive from the unique image of the child that his work projects. Once that image is clearly formulated, the educational philosophy which the image suggests will be easy to adumbrate. To uncover this image we need to recall briefly Piaget's unique methodology and his discoveries regarding the development of children's thinking.

Like other investigators in the child area, Piaget has used observation and testing in his investigations of children's thinking. Unlike other investigators, however, he also employed an analytic tool that might be called *empathic inference*. Starting from his observations of child behavior, or from the child's test responses, Piaget proceeded then to infer how the child *must have experienced the world in order to behave as he did*. To illustrate, Piaget (20) observed that his infant son, Laurent, who was crying vigorously at the sight of his bottle, showed no distress and ceased crying when the bottle disappeared from view. Piaget empathically inferred from this datum that Laurent had no awareness of the fact that objects continue to exist when they do not impinge upon his senses.

It was with the aid of empathic inference, and a multitude of ingenious experiments that Piaget made his most important discoveries about children's thinking. In a very real sense Piaget discovered what amounts to the "dark side" of the child's mind, namely, those beliefs and concepts foreign to the adult intellect and which were hitherto both unknown and unsuspected. To illustrate, Piaget discovered that young children believe that the sun and moon follow them when they walk, that dreams come in through the window at night, and that everything that moves is alive. In other domains he found that young children believe that number, length, amount, and area change with a change in their appearance.

Now the image of the child suggested by these discoveries is that of a person who, relative to adults, is a *cognitive alien*. That is to say, the child, like the person from a foreign country, thinks differently and, figuratively at any rate, speaks a different language. It is useful to contrast this image of the child with that promulgated by Freud. For Freud (5) the child was, relative to adults, an *emotional alien*. In Freud's view the child was, at least potentially, polymorphous perverse and incestuously enamoured of the parent of the opposite sex. On the other hand, however, Freud imbued the child with cognitive capacities in infancy which were in many ways comparable to those of the adult.

To compare these two images of the child more succinctly we might say that, for Freud, the child is similar to adults in his thinking but different from them in his feelings which for Piaget just the reverse holds true. In Piaget's work the child is similar to adults in his feelings but different from them in his thoughts.

There are several rather general principles of education implicit in Piaget's image of the child as an intellectual alien in the adult world. First of all, it implies that the foremost problem of education is *communication*. According to the Piaget image, the child's mind is not an empty slate. Quite the contrary, the child has a host of ideas about the physical and natural world, but these ideas differ from those of adults and are expressed in a different linguistic mode. The first prerequisite, then, for educating children, is developing effective modes of communication with them. That is to say we must learn to comprehend what children are saying and to respond in the same mode of discourse.

A second implication is that the child is always unlearning and relearning as well as acquiring entirely new knowledge. The child comes to school with his own ideas about space, time, casualty, quantity, and number. His ideas in these areas are, however, incomplete in comparison with those of adults. The concept of education must, therefore, be broadened to encompass aiding children in the modification of their existing knowledge in addition to helping them to learn new material.

Still a third implication for educational philosophy implicit in the view of the child as a cognitive alien in that the child is by nature a knowing creature. If the child has ideas about the world which he has not been taught (because they are foreign to adults) and which he has not inherited (because they change with age) then he must have acquired these notions through his spontaneous interactions with the environment. This means that the child is trying to construct a world view on his own and is limited only by his abilities and experience. Education need not, then, concern itself with instilling a zest for knowledge within the child since the desire to know is part of his makeup. Rather, education needs to insure that it does not dull this eagerness to know by overly rigid curricula that disrupt the child's own rhythm and pace of learning.

The image of the child held at any particular point in history must reflect and be reflected by events in the society as a whole. This was certainly true in Calvin's day as well as Freud's. Accordingly, one test of the validity and viability of Piaget's image of the child is the extent to which the cognitive alienation that Piaget posits for the child, holds for the larger society as well.

It is probably fair to say that a major characteristic of contemporary modern societies is the breakdown of interpersonal communication. While there have always been failures to communicate between labor and management, the difficulties are greatly increased today as businesses have grown enormously large and chains of command correspondingly longer. The same holds true for government where the "credibility gap" is but another name for the breakdown in communication that seems endemic today. Easily the most dramatic indications of the communication problems in modern society are the evidences of the "generation gap" and the campus revolts. Even in the university, the citadel of reasoned communication, the gaps in understanding between students and faculty, between faculty and administration, and between students and administration are everywhere evident. If communication is difficult in the university, what must it be like in other domains?

Likewise, it is probably not too far-fetched to interpret some of the current movements in the theater and in literature as attempts to redress the balance and to re-establish communication even if this has to be at the most primitive body level. The current emphasis upon sensitivity training in business and in education is still another evidence of the recognition that something needs to be done to get people to understand one another. In all of these activities, a common element is an attempt to penetrate the impersonalization and dehumanization of a highly technological and automated society. People want to be recognized as individuals rather than numbers or statistics, and such recognition must come from interpersonal communication.

Piaget's image of the child as cognitively but not affectively alien to adults is thus entirely in keeping with a dominant problem of our time. Specialization, the meteoric increase in available knowledge, and the proliferation of media has intellectually alienated us from all but small groups of people. Our commonality rests in our emotional reactions, and artists and writers work increasingly on our most basic ones to produce some consensus of understanding. It is probably fair to say that cognitive alienation is becoming a symptom of our times, and Piaget's image of the child as cognitively alien from adults reflects, in part at least, a phenomenon of our society at large.

THE PROCESS OF LEARNING

In his essays on learning (21, 22) Piaget makes a distinction between learning in the strict sense (modifications of behavior and thought as a result of experience) and learning in the broad sense (modifications of behavior and thought which result from experience *and* from processes of equilibration or complex feedback activities between maturation and experience). For our purposes we will consider only his discussion of learning in the narrow sense because learning in the broad sense covers the whole of human development.

Within the realm of learning in the strict sense Piaget again distinguishes between two different modes of experience that result in behavior modification. One mode occurs when things act upon us which Piaget calls physical (P) experience. Another occurs as a result of our actions upon things which Piaget labels logico-mathematical (LM) experience. Piaget attaches considerable importance to this distinction and it is the focus of much of his discussion of learning. Indeed, the major implications of Piaget's work for the process of learning derive from the differences between P and LM experiences.

In the first place, P learning involves the discovery of the qualities and properties of things. Shape, color, and form are results of energies emanating from things and acting upon us. Such experiences are, moreover, arbitrary in the sense that they are devoid of logical necessity. There is no logical reason for cherries to be red, sweet, and juicy; they simply are that way. In addition, the modifications of behavior and thought which result from physical experience are for the most part extrinsically motivated. A child learns that candy is sweet and that certain berries are sour by tasting them; properties of the objects or their consequences facilitate learning.

LM experience on the other hand involves learning about the properties and relations which belong not to things but rather to our actions upon things. Concepts such as "right" and "left," "causality," "quantity," and "number" all derive from our actions upon things.[1] LM experiences have a logical necessity not present in physical experience. When a child discovers that number is conserved—remains unchanged across a transformation in its appearance—he asserts that this will hold true across all transformations. Conservation is based on deductive reasoning (44), and hence the conclusion is generalized as a logical necessity. Finally, LM experiences are intrinsically motivated in that the discovery of, say, conservation is self-satisfying. The discovery or realization of logical truth does not need to be rewarded in any physical way because the exercise of reason is pleasurable in of itself. We shall return to this motivational issue later and deal with it in more detail.

Piaget's distinction between P and LM learning is not unlike the distinction between associative and insightful learning made by Gestalt psychologists (15, 16). Insight learning also involves the action of the subject upon things (the reorganization of the field) and is self-rewarding (the "aha" experience). For the Gestalt psychologists, however, the *laws* of organization are not derived from the subject's actions upon things but are rather inherent in the organism. For the Gestalt psychologist (25, 26) the task is to get the subject to utilize the principles and laws of organization appropriately. For Piaget, in contrast, principles of organization and relations are not inherent in the organism but must be learned or abstracted from his actions upon things.

In Piaget's view, all learning can be shown to manifest a logical form which brings us to a last and all important distinction between P and LM learning. The logic manifested in P learning is of a more primitive and less complete form than that manifested by LM learning. When a subject learns (by association) a list of words, he has in fact organized a series which might be described as A before B before $C > D > E$ and so on. This is a primitive seriation because the subject cannot, without relearning, reverse the series. When, however, a child learns to seriate a set of size-graded blocks, the capacity to seriate them from smallest to largest implies the capacity to seriate the objects in the opposite direction. The difference in the two modifications is that the child learned the seriation as a consequence of his own actions whereas in the case of the word list, the order was imposed by the activity of the experimenter.

The practical implications of Piaget's distinction between physical and logico-mathematical experience and learning can be limited to a discussion of the LM mode of experience since we are all familiar with P learning from elementary texts in psychology and education. Certain aspects of LM learning are of particular relevance to education.

ASPECTS OF LM LEARNING

There are several important features of LM learning that are in some ways unique in comparison with P learning. These aspects have to do with: a) the relation of LM learning to maturation and development; b) the unique content of LM learning; c) the effects of LM learning upon the child's perception of the world and d) the relation of LM learning to motivation and reinforcement.

Learning and Development. If P learning is regarded as primarily an associative process then such a process can clearly be observed at and possibly even prior to birth (24). Changes in this process as the child grows older would lie, from this point of view, in the area of increased rapidity or efficiency of functioning. In recent years, however, even investigators concerned with P learning have suggested that there may be changes in the learning process itself as the child grows older (28). Investigators have attributed such changes to neurophysiological growth (12), to learning to learn (10), to verbal mediation (14), and to cumulative learning (7).

These approaches differ from Piaget's view in that they try to attribute changes in the learning process to the learning process in question. Harlow's (10) notion of "learning sets," for example, ascribes the ability to discriminate to practice in discrimination. Likewise the "verbal mediation" suggested by the Kendlers (14) and the hierarchies described by Gagné (7) presupposes associative learning processes; any new learning process derived from associative processes is of necessity "associative" in nature and hence not really "new." Even though there may not be any really new proceses which emerge with age there is the possibility that P learning may be influenced by developmental changes in LM learning.

LM learning, in contrast, involves induction and deduction rather than association; the modes of induction and deduction change with age and development. These changes can be described in terms of the number of variables or factors that the child can integrate or deal with at any given age level for, while the basic logical operations are present in rudimentary form even in infancy, their coordination and hierarchical integration changes with age.

During the first two years of life, the infant can learn about objects by comparing them in a rather global and undifferentiated fashion. A stranger's face, for example, is discriminated on the basis of its global configuration rather than upon a specific characteristic. During early childhood (2–7 years), children begin to single out various dimensions and qualities but deal with them one at a time without integration. Number is thought of in terms of the length or the density of a collection but the child does not think of number as involving the coordination of these two dimensions. During middle and late childhood, the elementary school years, the child begins to coordinate and integrate two variables or dimensions at the same time. He understands that a friend can be a boy and a child at the same time and that the amount of liquid in a container depends upon both the container's height and its width. It is only in adolescence, however, that children can learn and make discoveries by taking many different variables into account simultaneously; the adolescent can discover all the sixteen possible combinations of five chemical agents and reagents that will color water a particular color and make it clear again (13).

The changes in learning ability described above clearly express in somewhat different form the mechanisms available to the child at Piaget's sensory-motor, pre-operational, concrete operational and formal operational stages. Piaget's task is to explain how these stages and their corresponding learning processes come about. It is at this point that the distinction between learning in the broad sense and learning in the narrow sense becomes all important. We have been talking about changes in LM learning—learning through the abstraction of our actions upon things, which is a form of learning from experience alone. To explain these changes in learning in the narrow sense, Piaget invokes the concept of learning in the broad sense, namely, learning that involves the complex feedback activity of maturation *and* experience; he calls this process equilibration.

By invoking the notion of learning in the broad sense, Piaget has avoided the difficulty encountered by those who attempt to explain age changes in P learning. Piaget has recognized that it is not possible to get a new process out of the continuous utilization of an old one, without invoking another higher order process. It is equilibration between maturation and experience that determines the changes in the LM learning process and not the mere functioning of that process itself. Consequently, the changes in LM learning that come about with age are not simply more of the same (as in P learning), but rather are qualitatively distinct processes.

For Piaget, then, learning in the broad sense of the modification of behavior as the result of the *equilibration* of maturation and experience determines the nature of learning in the narrow sense of a modification of behavior due to experieince *alone*. Or, since learning in the broad sense corresponds to what we usually mean by development, and learning in the narrow sense refers to what we usually mean by learning, we might simply say that for Piaget, development determines learning.

Content and LM Learning. Whenever we talk about the content of learning we generally have in mind a body of knowledge or facts which might be called P content. To learn geography, for example, is to learn some facts about the political and physical features of the earth. LM content must also be learned but is more general in nature and serves to organize the more discrete factual information. Such contents have to do with our ideas of space, time, causality, and number that serve in the organization and relation of all particular facts. In school, for example, the teacher assumes that the child knows such categories as "same" and "different," and such spatial relations as "right" and "left" and "top" and "bottom." She uses words like "more" and "less" as well as "because" without thinking to explain them. These LM concepts are, however, not innate and must themselves be learned.

An essential difference between P contents and LM contents is that the P contents a child has learned are relatively unaltered by his progressive mental growth whereas the LM contents are radically transformed. A child may learn his birthdate when he is six or seven and that P content, or date, is retained without alteration throughout his life. In contrast a child may first learn about "left" and "right" when he is four or five but the meaning of these terms will continue to evolve until he reaches the age of 11 or 12 (3; 19). LM learning changes with age and the products or contents of that learning can be expected to change as well.

To make concrete the change in LM contents that occurs as a consequence of growth in LM learning processes, consider the development of the child's conception of "right" and "left" mentioned earlier. The infant has a concept of "right" and left" in the sense that he can orient to sound or sights coming from particular directions. His sense of direction is, however, part of a total bodily orientation and is not yet differentiated from the objects or stimulation which produce the orientation reaction. At the pre-school level, the child can label his "right" and "left" hands but he does not recognize their relational character. When an adult stands opposite him he says the adult's "right" and "left" hands are directly opposite his own. During the elementary school period the child can take another person's point of view and designate that person's "right" and "left" hands correctly even when the person is opposite him. It is, however, only toward adolescence that young people understand that one and the same element can, at the same time, be on the right of one thing and on the left of another.

This example of how LM contents are transformed in accordance with changes in LM learning illustrates another important difference between LM contents and P contents. The child has P content or he does not— either he knows that Independence Day is celebrated on the 4th of July or he does not. With LM contents, however, the situation is different. As the example given above demonstrates, even the infant has a global conception of "right" and "left." What is important about LM contents is that the child has a *different* conception of right and left at successive age levels. LM contents can, then, never be evaluated as present or absent or as right or wrong. In evaluating LM contents all we can say is that the infant's concept of right and left is *different* from that of the young child whose conception is *different* from that of the adolescent and the adult.

Piaget describes two mechanisms by which LM contents evolve. One of these mechanisms is *integration* and the other is *substitution*. Most quantitative and relational conceptions such as "number" and "right" and "left" evolve by integration. In the evolving conception of right and left, for example, the earlier absolutistic notions are incorporated in, and made part of, the later more relational conception. The same holds true for number. The young child's idea of number as a single dimension is later integrated into a conception of number as two dimensions in combination.

Substitution, in contrast, is much more common among concepts that deal with causality and the living world. Although most of us, as we grow older, substitute an abstract conception of life for the animistic views we held in childhood, backsliding is frequent. Whenever we kick a car because it fails to start or curse a television set for fading at the wrong moment, we have reverted to animistic thinking. When the content of a given concept changes by means of substitution, therefore, there is always the possibility of reversion to the earlier level of conceptualization and understanding.

Piaget's description of LM contents as changing with age either by integration or substitution as a consequence of changes in LM learning has important consequences for education. In the pedagogical literature two emphases have alternated down through the ages. One of these was the emphasis upon teaching facts and more facts while the other emphasis was upon training children in certain logical thought processes (formal discipline). The implication in Piaget's work is that this emphasis upon content *or* process is, at least with respect to LM learning, a false dichotomy. In LM learning, content cannot be taught without affecting process and vice versa. If a child is taught about "right" and "left," he is also being taught to abstract from his own actions and hence the process of LM learning is affected as well.

From an educational standpoint, therefore, Piaget's work suggests that much more attention ought to be paid to LM contents, to the basic concepts within which experience is arranged and organized. The value of instruction in these domains is twofold. First, training of LM contents will affect both process *and* content so that the instruction will have broader impact. Secondly, since LM contents serve as the framework for P learning, the learning of P contents might be facilitated as well.

LM Learning and the Child's Perception of the World. A very important characteristic of LM learning has to do with its effects upon the subject's views of the world about him. In general P learning tends to be analytic in that it enables us to better differentiate among various features in the environment. LM learning is, on the contrary, synthetic in the sense that it helps us to organize events into larger wholes. Such organization is possible because LM learning derives from our actions upon things — which actions are infinite in their variety — and not directly from the things themselves. Accordingly, while P learning takes us closer to things by making us more aware of their properties, LM learning takes us farther from things by stressing their relations to other things. Put rather more simply we might say that P learning changes *what* we see whereas LM learning changes *how* we see what we do.

A few examples of the effects of LM learning on perception may help to make the foregoing ideas more concrete. Whenever a stimulus is more or less unstructured it provides an opportunity for us to act and impose an organization upon it, that is to say, to utilize LM learning. The well-known Rorschach inkblots provide such an unstructured stimulus. When subjects look at the blots they are completely unaware of their own activity in organizing the material. That they are organizing the material is, however, clear from the fact that one subject will see a "bear" where another will see a "tree" or "threatening clouds." What is significant about responses to the Rorschach is that: a) the subject organizes the stimulus and b) he is unaware of having done so and assumes that the "bear" or "tree" is present in the blot.

Roughly the same holds true for cognitive organizations mediated by LM learning. When the child discovers that a row of pennies contains the same number as are present in a pile, he acts as if the equality were present in the pennies themselves and as if he had nothing at all to do with finding their equality. As in the case of the Rorschach response, the child organizes the stimulus but is aware only of the result and not of the act of organization. In contrast to the Rorschach response, however, the child's response to conservation problems (apparent but not real changes in properties, qualities, and relations) does not reflect individual or personal organizations but rather the mental operations characteristic of all "normal" children of about that age.

This difference between the Rorschach type of response and the conservation type of response is all important. It is easy to recognize the subjectivity of the Rorschach response because individuals vary so much in the kinds of responses they give. Conservation responses, on the contrary, are so uniform, indeed so universal, beyond a certain age that their subjectivity had been overlooked until Piaget discovered it. This discovery means that much in the world about us which we regard as "out there" is really, in part at least, a product of our own mental actions. We are not aware of our part because all adults externalize the products of their mental actions in the same fashion and hence view the world in the same way. To detect such universal externalizations one has to study their development in the child.

An important educational implication in the discovery of the partial subjectivity of apparently objective knowledge is that just as children differ from adults in their thinking so too do they literally as well as figuratively *see* the world differently than do adults. The adult, moreover, is frequently unaware of this difference (for the same reason a subject is unaware of his part in producing the Rorschach response). Because he externalizes the products of his own mental activity and takes the world as independent of thought he often fails to comprehend how the child can view it differently. Children's infamous "why" questions are a case in point. When a child asks "why is the light green?" he does not want a physical explanation dealing with the wave lengths of light. On the contrary, he wants to know the purpose of the green light, namely, to allow the cars to go.

This difference (frequently unacknowledged) in viewpoints between children and adults is particularly pernicious in education. Most good teachers intuitively recognize the unique world view of the child and gear their instruction and verbalizations accordingly. Those who do not, fail to understand the child at crucial moments in the educational process and they in turn may not always make themselves understood. It seems reasonable to expect that teacher education should include instruction as to how children at different age levels view the world and how this view differs from that of adults.

LM Learning and Motivation. In recent years increasing attention has been paid by psychologists and educators to the self-rewarding quality of many types of learning and behavior. The existence of "competence" motivation (27) and of curiosity drives (1) are such obvious features of human behavior it is a wonder it took psychology so long to recognize them. While the positing of these types of motivation greatly broadens the forces propelling P types of learning, they are still of little relevance to the logicomathematical learning described by Piaget because even the "intrinsic" motivations described by White and Berlyne are seen as something separate from and as acting upon the learning process itself. Curiosity and competence motivation lead to the "stamping in" or to the "stamping out" of behavior but are separate from the stamping process itself.

In the case of LM learning, however, any distinction between the process of learning and its motivation is false and artificial. For Piaget, the motivation of the LM learning process is inherent in the process itself and can be discerned only when that process is looked at from a particular point of view. Piaget's position can be made a little less abstract by an analogy. Ordinarily we do not ask "Why does the heart beat?" or "Why does the stomach digest food?" because "why" is usually employed in the psychological or intentional sense. Since the heart and the stomach have no separate ego, to ask why they behave as they do in the intentional sense is absurd. If, however, we ask for the physical or physiological reasons for their activities the question is not absurd and can be given a reasonable answer.

This analogy was not selected at random because for Piaget the mind is an organ of the body whose fundamental processes (assimilation, accommodation, and equilibration) are common to all organs. The mind functions as it does because of these processes and because of the way it is constructed. When we ask "why" a child learns conservation, then, we have to look at the mind from the standpoint of its structure and function. It is only in terms of mental structures and functions that the "why" question about conservation can be answered. The infant does not consciously set out to discover the conservation of the object nor is he driven to it by hunger or thirst. Likewise, the concrete operational child does not consciously set out to discover the conservation of number, of mass, weight, and volume, of length, area, time, and speed. The child's discovery of these various conservations is as natural a product of the mind's structures and functions as are the products of the heart's beating or the stomach's digestion. Indeed, the apparently universal attainment of many of these conservations (9) attests to the status of these attainments as products of structures and processes common to most children. From the Piaget perspective, then, the question as to why the child attains conservation has to be answered in a particular way. The answer cannot include reference to motives, intentions, or rewards, but must describe the structures and processes which govern the functioning of the mind. Current computer simulations of human intelligence (17; 23) take just this approach to the "explanation" of human cognition.

For education this view of mental functioning means that some of the most important ideas the child acquires, those which structure his experience in general, are not taught but are spontaneously (unintentionally) acquired. In addition, it means that learning is going on *all of the time*. Learning in Piaget's broad sense is coextensive with life processes and the child learns every moment of his waking life. The child who sits watching a fly move along the sill is learning something. Likewise, the youngster who creates chaos in the classroom may not be learning the curriculum but he is learning how to create chaos. And the child who sits quietly doing nothing is learning how to withdraw from the world without antagonizing it. Learning then is an ongoing activity for every child.

This point cannot be overemphasized. Too often we take a rather narrow view of learning and assume the child is learning only when he is acquiring what we want him to learn; a "slow learner" is one who does not acquire the curriculum at a "normal" rate. But it is a big mistake to identify learning ability with curriculum acquisition. The slow learner is fast to learn that he is slow. He learns quickly how to mask his deficiencies either by memory (so that he appears to be reading) or by defensive maneuvers such as becoming the class clown or bully. What the child learns about himself may, in the long run, be more important to his educational progress than what he learns from the curriculum. In summary, then, perhaps the most important implication of Piaget's views regarding motivation and learning is that we need to conceive of learning more broadly and to recognize that it is an ongoing life process. Once we acknowledge that children are learning something, all of the time — even if it is not what we set out to teach them — then we have considerably broadened our options for reaching children and for directing their mental growth.

THE PRACTICE OF TEACHING

Effective teaching is still more of an art than it is a science. This does not mean that teaching cannot be taught; but the acceptance of teaching as art means that it cannot be reduced to sound knowledge of subject matter or to skill in handling curriculum or audio-visual materials. The successful teacher needs, in addition to technical skill and certain fundamental personality traits, an orientation toward teaching and toward children that will guide her in the effective and appropriate use of her technical skills. Although Piaget has not spoken to the problem of teaching directly, his work does suggest an orientation that might be of value to those who are not born teachers but who have become teachers or have had teaching thrust upon them. This orientation involves the three principles of communication, valuation, and dedication.

Communication. It has already been suggested that an important implication of this image was that effective education presupposes meaningful communication between teacher and pupil. Later, in the discussion of LM learning, it was pointed out that externalization (the process by which we take our own mental productions as given in the environment) is an important hindrance to effective communication between adults and children. The teacher who knows about the differences between adult and child world views is likely to communicate and educate more successfully than one not so prepared. Communication with children then requires that the teacher be trained in the vagaries and vicissitudes of children's thinking and that she be willing to discourse at that level.

Equally important is the understanding of the child's non-verbal communications. The way in which a child sits and moves, the tone of his voice, and his nervous habits are as much communications as his verbal productions. The teacher must be sensitive to all levels of communication if she wishes truly to understand and relate to her charges. Training in the non-verbal as well as the verbal communications of children is particularly important in working with children who come from different socio-economic backgrounds. Each ethnic and socio-economic group has its own non-verbal signals which must be read if true communication is to occur. Here again, the implication of Piaget's work is that teachers be trained in understanding the child's verbal as well as non-verbal productions as a prerequisite to effective instruction.

Valuation. Education and applied psychology have long tended to be test oriented. One characteristic of tests is that they presuppose "right" and "wrong" answers. So long as we are dealing with P type learning, this kind of dichotomy makes sense. Columbus did discover America in 1492 and 1493 just as two and two make four and not six. When we come to LM learning, however, the issue is not so clear. As pointed out earlier, the child has a progression of concepts of space, time, causality, and quantity which differ from one another in their completeness and adequacy.

In the case of LM concepts, therefore, it would be misleading to say that the four year old who conceives of "right" and "left" as attributes has a "wrong" conception of these terms for we, as adults, use such terms in a variety of senses, some of which are coincident with the way in which the child uses them. Althrough "right" and "left" are usually employed in the relative sense they are also used in the absolute sense when we speak of our "right arm" or our "left arm." The child's use of "right" and "left" as absolute designations is thus not wrong, it is merely limited. To describe less differentiated concepts as "wrong" thus ignores the fact that such usages are "right" even for adults in particular circumstances.

Accordingly, when we deal with LM type concepts we must not *evaluate* them as right or wrong but rather *value* them as genuine expressions of the child's budding mental abilities. When we deal with spatial, temporal, causal, or quantitative concepts, we need to explore the kinds of meanings children give to such terms. Such exploration reveals the level and reference frame of the child's understanding and makes clear the next step needed to broaden this understanding. More importantly, such exploration avoids the inhibiting suggestion that the child's incomplete (but partially correct) understanding of such terms is "wrong." A teacher who sees a child's productions as having value, as meaning something, avoids putting the child on the track of always seeking "right" answers. More importantly, perhaps, her orientation conveys to the child a sense of her attempt to understand him and her respect for his intellectual productions.

Dedication. The ability to communicate adequately with children and to value their responses will have little impact if the teacher lacks dedication to certain values. Implicit in the Piaget conception of education is the premise that the teacher must be dedicated to growth, to her personal growth as well as to the growth of her pupils. Education is, after all, adults and children interacting, and personal, social, and intellectual growth is what the interaction is all about.

A dedication to growth means, in the first place, that learning is living and that no matter what the child is doing, he is learning something. The teacher dedicated to growth will attempt to surmise what even her "worst" pupils are learning and will try to counteract the negative self-images, the feelings of failure and inadequacy that accompany poor academic achievement. (This is not to say that a teacher must be a psychotherapist — far from it. The emotionally disturbed child has no place in the classroom if he so distracts the students or so preoccupies the teacher as to disrupt the educational process.)

A teacher dedicated to growth must also be dedicated to her own personal growth. She must be willing to try new things, to evaluate their effectiveness objectively, and to discard and modify as the situation warrants. As the teacher matures in her own life, as she marries, has children, and sees them mature, her attitudes toward her students will also change. What the teacher learns as a wife and mother are invaluable in her role as teacher if she is willing to use her experience in this way.

Example is still the most effective tutor. The teacher who is curious to learn, who is willing to be innovative, to evaluate and be critical, and to try again will instill similar values in her young charges. A teacher cannot really expect her pupils to be creative, objective, and critical if she is not. Children do model themselves after the teacher's behavior (11); teacher resourcefulness, dictatorialness, and punitiveness had significant effects upon such pupil behavior as involvement, achievement, and concreteness.

Teacher dedication can be manifested in an infinite variety of ways, and sets no limits on the teacher's individuality and uniqueness of expression. Likewise, a true dedication to growth involves a commitment to helping every child find his own abilities in his own way and in his own time. In addition it involves the recognition that growth, like life in general, involves conflict, constant change, and no end of problems. The teacher who reflects, in her own behavior, a dedication to growth and the courage to live in a teacher in the best and most comprehensive sense of that word.

---

[1]The concept of "action upon things" must be broadly construed to include not only motor manipulation but also perceptual exploration and judgment. It is the abstraction from motor and perceptual actions that is the basis of LM learning.

REFERENCES

[1]Berlyne, D. E. *Conflict Arousal and Curiosity*. New York: McGraw-Hill, 1960.

[2]Brearly, Molly, and Hitchfield, Elizabeth. *A Guide to Reading Piaget, 1968*. New York: Schocken, 1968.

[3]Elkind, D. "The Child's Conception of Right and Left." *Journal of Genetic Psychology*, 1961, Vol. 99, 269–76.

[4]Elkind, D. "Piaget's Conservation Problems." *Child Development, 1967*, Vol. 38, 1967, 15–27.

[5]Freud, S. "Three Contributions to the Theory of Sex." In A. A. Brill (ed.), *The Basic Writings of Sigmund Freud*. New York: Modern Library Edition, 1938, 553–632.

[6]Furth, H. G. *Piaget and Knowledge*. Englewood Cliffs, New Jersey: Prentice-Hall, Inc., 1969.

[7]Gagné, Robert M. "Contributions of Learning to Human Development." *Psychological Review*, 1968, Vol. 75, 177–91.

[8]Ginsberg, H., and Opper, Sylvia. *Piaget's Theory of Intellectual Development: An Introduction*. Englewood Cliffs, New Jersey: Prentice-Hall, Inc., 1969.

[9]Goodnow, Jacqueline J. "Problems in Research on Culture and Thought." In D. Elkind and J. H. Flavell (eds.), *Studies in Cognitive Development*. New York: Oxford University Press, 1969, 439–64.

[10]Harlow, H. F. "The Formation of Learning Sets." *Psychological Review*, 1949, Vol. 56, 51–65.

[11]Harvey, O. J., Prather, Misha, White, B. J., and Hoffmeister, J. K. "Teacher's Beliefs, Classroom Atmosphere, and Student Behavior." *American Educational Research Journal*, 1968, Vol. V, 151–66.

[12]Hebb, D. O. *The Organization of Behavior*. New York: Wiley, 1949.

[13]Inhelder, Bärbel and Piaget, J. *The Growth of Logical Thinking from Childhood to Adolescence*. New York: Basic Books, 1958.

[14]Kendler, Tracy S., and Kendler, H. H. "Reversal and Non-Reversal Shifts in Kindergarten Children." *Journal of Experimental Psychology*, 1959, Vol. 58, 56–60.

[15]Koffka, K. *Principles of Gestalt Psychology*. New York: Harcourt, Brace, 1935.

[16]Köhler, W. *Gestalt Psychology*. New York: Liveright, 1947.

[17]Newell, A., and Simon, H. A. "Computer Simulation of Human Thinking." *Science*, 1961, Vol. 134, 2011–17.

[18]Phillips, J. L. *The Origins of Intellect: Piaget's Theory*. San Francisco: W. H. Freeman, 1969.

[19]Piaget, J. *Judgment and Reasoning in the Child*. London: Routledge & Kegan Paul, Ltd., 1951.

[20]Piaget, J. *Les relations entre l'affectivité et l'intelligence dans le développement mental de l'enfant*. Paris: C. D. U., 1954 (mimeographed and bound lectures given at the Sorbonne).

[21]Piaget, J. "Apprentissage et connaissance (première partie)." In P. Greco and Piaget (eds.), *Études d'épistémologie génétique.* Vol. 7, *Apprentissage et Connaissance.* Paris: Presses Universitaires de France, 1959, 21–67.

[22]Piaget, J. "Apprentissage et connaissance (seconde partie)." In M. Goustard *et al.* (eds.), *Études d'épistémologie génétique.* Vol. 10, *la logique des apprentissages.* Paris: Presses Universitaires de France, 1959, 159–88.

[23]Reitman, W. R., Grove, R. B., and Shoup, R. G. "Argus: An Information Process Model of Thinking." *Behavioral Science,* 1964, Vol. 9, 270–81.

[24]Spelt, D. K. "The Conditioning of the Human Fetus *in utero.*" *Journal of Experimental Psychology,* 1948, Vol. 38, 338–46.

[25]Wertheimer, M. *Productive Thinking.* New York: Harper, 1945.

[26]Wertheimer, M. *Productive Thinking.* New York: Harper, 1959 (2nd edition).

[27]White, R. W. "Motivation Reconsidered: The Concept of Competence." *Psychological Review,* 1959, Vol. 66, 297–333.

[28]White, S. H. "The Hierarchical Arrangement of Learning Processes." In L. P. Lipsitt and C. C. Spiker (eds.), *Advances in Child Development and Behavior, II.* New York: Academic Press, 1965, 187–220.

DONALD W. MacKINNON

Personality Correlates
of Creativity

. . . I SHALL, IN DESCRIBING THE PERSONALITY CORRELATES OF CRE-
ativity, pass rather quickly over matters of research design and the methods whereby we were able to determine the traits of creative persons in
order to discuss at greater length the implications of our findings for the
fostering of creative talent and the encouragement of productive thinking.
The findings to which I refer were obtained in studies of creativity conducted during the past six years in the Institute of Personality Assessment
and Research on the Berkeley campus of the University of California and
supported in large part by the Carnegie Corporation of New York (5).

The major method employed in the execution of these studies was the
assessment method. It involved bringing the creative persons whom we
would study to Berkeley, where — in the Institute building, a remodeled
fraternity house — we worked with them, 10 at a time, for several days,
most often over a three-day weekend. These people were studied intensively by a variety of means — by the broad problem posed by the assessment situation itself; by problem-solving experiments; by tests designed
to discover what a person does not know or is unable to reveal about
himself; by tests and questionnaires that permit a person to manifest
various aspects of his personality and to express his attitudes, interests,

Donald W. MacKinnon, "Personality Correlates of Creativity." In M.J. Aschner,
and C.E. Bish (Eds.), *Productive Thinking in Education*. Washington, D.C.: National Education Association, 1965, 159–171. Copyright © 1965 by National Education Association. Reprinted by permission of the author and publisher.

and values; and by searching interviews. These methods will be described in greater detail later in the conference in Dr. Barron's discussion of methods of assessing creative ability in adults.

A DEFINITION OF "CREATIVITY"

Before undertaking our studies we had to agree upon what we would consider creativity to be. This was a first requirement, since creativity has been so variously defined and described. We agreed that true creativeness fulfills at least three conditions. It involves a response that is novel or at least statistically infrequent. But novelty or originality of thought and action, while a necessary aspect of creativity, is not sufficient. If a response is to lay claim to being a part of the creative process, it must to some extent be adaptive to, or of, reality. It must serve to solve a problem, fit a situation, or accomplish some recognizable goal. And, thirdly, true creativeness involves a sustaining of the original insight, an evaluation and elaboration of it, a developing of it to the full. Creativity, from this point of view, is a process extended in time and characterized by originality, adaptiveness, and realization.

The acceptance of such a conception of creativity had two important consequences for our researches. It meant that we would not seek to study creativity while it was still potential but only after it had been realized and had found expression in clearly identifiable creative products — buildings designed by architects, mathematical proofs developed by mathematicians, and the published writings of poets and novelists. Our conception of creativity forced us further to reject as indicators or criteria of creativeness the performance of individuals on so-called tests of creativity. While tests of this sort — that require that the subject think, for example, of unusual uses for common objects and the consequences of unusual events — may indeed measure the infrequency or originality of a subject's ideas in response to specific test items, they fail to reveal the extent to which the subject, faced with real life problems, is likely to come up with solutions that are novel and adaptive and which he will be motivated to apply in all of their ramifications.

The professional groups chosen for study, some more intensively than others, were writers, painters, architects, mathematicians, research workers in physical science and engineering, independent inventors, and senior college women. It may be noted that in so choosing our samples we have been able to study artistic creativity, scientific creativity, as well as creativity which requires that its practitioners be at one and the same time both artists and scientists. Thus, we shall be in a position to say something about what characterizes the creative worker most generally, regardless of his special field of endeavor and type of creativity, as well as to be able to delineate the characteristics of the creative worker and his mode of work in each of the areas studied.

However, I shall limit my remarks here to presenting a few of the most salient characteristics of all the creative groups we have studied, emphasizing what is most generaly true of creative persons, and suggesting ways in which we might nurture creativity, while it is still potential, by ourselves creating social environments and intellectual climates which are appropriate to the encouragement of creative talent and its realization.

TRAITS OF CREATIVE PERSONS

Creative people are intelligent. I shall begin by reporting what you all know — namely, that creative persons are intelligent. But this, I believe, is not the most important thing to say about them. It is not surprising that no feeble-minded subjects turned up in any of our samples, but it is worthy of note that in our various groups, intelligence — as measured by the Terman *Concept Mastery Test* (7) — is not significantly correlated with creativity. Among creative architects the correlation of the two variables is −.08, among research scientists −.07 — values not significantly different from zero. Obviously, this does not mean that over the whole range of creative endeavor there is no relation between intelligence and creativity. It signifies, rather, that a certain amount of intelligence is required for creativity; but, beyond that point, being more or less intelligent does not determine the level of a person's creativeness, and the level of intelligence required for creativity is sometimes surprisingly low.

What is more important than the level of intelligence as measured by an intelligence test is the effectiveness with which one uses whatever intelligence he has. In a study of leisure-time inventors, I discovered that the inventor who held more patents than anyone else in the group earned a score of 6 on the Terman *Concept Mastery Test!* By way of comparison, incidentally, average scores on this test are 156 for creative writers, 118 for research scientists, 113 for architects, and 60 for Air Force captains. Let me add, though, that these are not IQs, and, obviously, the inventor in question is not so dumb as his score of 6 would suggest.

The Terman *Concept Mastery Test*, which consists of synonyms, antonyms (essentially a vocabulary test of intellience), and analogies (a test of word knowledge, general information, and reasoning ability), is scored number right answers minus number wrong answers. One who guesses on such a test when he is not certain of his answer is apt to be penalized and will, of course, be penalized if his guess is wrong. If, for example, we count only the correct responses which our inventive inventor gave, he scores 87 rather than 6! He clearly has a fair amount of correct knowledge which he can record, but also a good deal of wrong information which he does not hesitate to give. Our inventor thus reveals, in taking an intelligence test, a willingness to take a chance, to try anything that might work; and this attitude also characterizes him in his inventory activity. He is typical of many who make up for what they lack in verbal intellectual giftedness with a high level of energy, with a kind of cognitive flexibility which enables them to keep coming at a problem using a variety of techniques from a variety of angles; and, being confident of their ultimate success, these people persevere until they arrive at a creative solution.

This kind of person should remind us that creative giftedness is not to be equated with high verbal intelligence, and while the creativity of such persons may not be of the highest order, it is nevertheless worthy of respect and encouragement. It is easy to be impatient with persons of this type, but patient waiting for their solutions and sympathetic understanding of their persistence in arriving at them may well result in the appearance of creative behavior in the most unlikely individuals.

For those, on the other hand, who are truly intellectually gifted, there is nothing, I believe, that will contribute so much to their creativity as will holding them to the highest standards of performance and repeatedly setting problems for them — or, better still, encouraging them to set problems for themselves that are on the borderline of the limits of their performance. To work just this side of frustration — when every bit of one's ability is required — is the best way I know of to maximize the creativeness of solutions which will be achieved.

Creative persons are original. The statement that creative persons are original will strike you as a tautology if, like many, you conceive creativity to be essentially a matter of novelty or originality of response. With such a notion I would strongly disagree, for, as I have already indicated, originality as I see it is only a part of true creativeness.

Originality of response, if we focus upon that for a moment, has two aspects which must be distinguished: the quantity or number of original responses which one can give vs. the quality or goodness of these responses. In our investigations we find that, in general, those who are most fluent in suggesting new solutions tend also to come up with the better ones. The quantity and quality of original responses correlate .53 in one test (consequences) and .78 in another (unusual uses).

These correlations are low enough, however, to suggest — and indeed this is our finding — that some persons tend to make many original responses which are not very good, while others make fewer but generally better or more fitting ones. These findings point to individual differences in creativity, some persons being strong in just those aspects of the creative process in which others are weak. The implications are obvious: There is no single method for nurturing creativity; procedures and programs must be tailor-made, if not for individual students, at least for different types of students.

To nurture the fullest creativity in those most fertile with new ideas, greater emphasis must be placed upon seeking the implications and deeper meanings and possibilities inherent in every idea. This is a matter of pursuing ideas in depth and in scope, not of criticizing and rejecting — which is so easy to do and which is so crippling to creativity. Insights, however fresh and clever they may seem, do not enter the stream of creative solutions to urgent problems unless their consequences are tested in application and revised and extended to meet the requirements of the situation for which they were first devised. What I am suggesting is that mere fluency in unusual ideas will not alone make for fresh and creative solutions to problems, but, in some persons, rather to "freshness" in its worst sense.

Getzels and Jackson cite the story given by one of their subjects in response to a picture as evidence of creativity (albeit creativity which they concede might drive a teacher dotty). The story reads as follows: "This man is flying back from Reno where he has just won a divorce from his wife. He couldn't stand to live with her any more because she wore so much cold cream on her face at night that her head would slide across the pillow and hit him in the head. He is now contemplating a new skidproof face cream." (Reported in *Time*, October 31, 1960.)

Unlike Getzels and Jackson (4), I would not interpret this story as indicative of "a mind that solves problems by striking out in new directions." Such fresh ideas as one finds in this story are not likely to lead to creative solutions, for they reveal too much freshness for freshness' sake, too much striving for shock effect, and insufficient concern for reality problems. Students with this kind of originality, which I refuse to call creativity, need to be taught to pay more attention to the demands of reality and to sacrifice some of their fluency for greater attention to the quality and appropriateness of their ideas.

On the other hand, students who have few original ideas, but whose ideas are usually of a high order of excellence, may well be encouraged to seek to increase their output. These individuals tend to be rather the shy, withdrawn, relatively more introverted persons than the "fresh and fluent" types. They, more than the fluent individual, are in need of understanding and encouragement if their original ideas are to be made known to others. Indeed, there is some evidence to suggest that persons who produce few original ideas, but whose ideas are uniformly high in quality, actually experience many more ideas than they are willing to make public.

Creative persons are independent in thought and action. Independence is a trait so characteristic of creative individuals that it is difficult to believe it was acquired *after* the school years. According to their own reports, this independence of spirit was already theirs in high school though it tended to increase in college and thereafter.

One can well believe that many creative students chafe under the discipline of group activities and requirements of the classroom. It is not that they are lazy, or that their level of aspiration is low, or that in their rebellious attitudes they are "rebels without a cause." The problem (if we permit it to become a problem) derives from their high level of energy which they seek to channel into independent, nongroup-coordinated strivings for extremely high goals of achievement — goals which they set for themselves and which may well conflict with goals that have been set for the group.

It is thus a fundamental characteristic of creative subjects that they are strongly motivated to achieve in situations in which independence of thought and action is called for and that they have much less interest or motivation to achieve in situations which demand conforming behavior. Since this is the case, I can only conclude that teachers who are genuinely interested in nurturing creativity must be prepared to grant more autonomy to their abler students and even reward them for behaviors which at times may be disturbing of classroom harmony.

For the most part, though, students with creative potential will not so much actively disrupt classroom activities as they will passively, and at times stubbornly, resist efforts to integrate them into the group. Not infrequently, students having creative potential — concerned with their own experiences of both inner life and outer world, more introvert than extrovert and more isolate than social — will pursue projects of their own making.

Here one comes up against the paradox and the problem: At just the time when increasing emphasis is being placed on the identification and development of creative talent — which demands that the student be given more individual treatment, if not attention — the student-teacher ratio, both in school and in college, is almost certainly bound to increase as a result of the explosion in our population.

A partial answer may lie in the use of automated teaching techniques which have the merit that they permit the student to pace himself. The very personality of the potentially creative student is almost ideally suited to self-instruction. At this suggestion, I can hear howls of dismay, that it is just the creative student — with his disposition to separateness and aloneness — who needs, for his own sake and for his healthy psychological development, the special, personal ministrations of another human being, his teacher, and who needs more association with his peers if he is to develop into a well-rounded person.

To this problem-paradox I can only answer that many of the highly creative persons we have seen are not especially well rounded. They have one-sided interests, sharp edges to their personalities, and marked peaks and dips on their personality-test profiles. We will not create our able students in the image of the highly creative if we always insist upon their being well rounded.

Here we come face to face with a sharp conflict of values in our society and in our schools today: The emphasis, on the one hand, upon togetherness, the integration of the individual into the group and its activities, good group dynamics, and smooth interpersonal relations; and, on the other hand, the nurturing of creative talent. All our evidence points to the incompatibility of these opposed values and goals. On one test of interpersonal behavior, the subjects of a nationwide sample of creative architects revealed even less desire to be included in group activities than that expressed by the naval and civilian personnel who volunteered to man the Ellsworth Station outpost in Antarctica during the International Geophysical Year.

It is conceivable, of course, that outstandingly creative persons develop their desire for aloneness and time apart from others for contemplative thinking as a result of the strong distaste for group participation which they have acquired in being forced into group activities. If this is indeed the case, then we may actually be depriving able students of much of their motivation for creative activity if we free them from participation in group activities and grant them more time for their individual pursuits, including learning. This, I must say, seems unlikely to me, and so I continue to think that one of the best methods for nurturing creativity is to de-emphasize group participation, with its demands for conformity, and to provide maximum opportunity for the able student to work out his own interests.

In recent years, it has been fashionable in industry — and, I understand, in some schools — to think that "brainstorming" is one of the more effective ways to stimulate fresh and creative thinking. The method consists in having persons in a group suggest ideas in as rapid succession as possible. Under the rules of the game criticism is taboo. Wild ideas are welcome. Quantity is sought, though there is some attempt to build upon and improve each other's suggestions. But a recent controlled study (6) has found that this type of group process does not yield proportionately more ideas, more unique ideas, or ideas of higher quality. In fact, it appears that the group process under these conditions inhibits creative thinking.

It is not easy for a teacher, or for anyone else who always has to deal with groups of individuals, to welcome nonconforming behavior; and this is, of course, especially anxiety provoking for the inexperienced person. It is not nonconformity *as such* that deserves respect or even acceptance — and certainly not nonconformity that is carried on for nonconformity's sake (which ends by being conformity in reverse) — but rather, that kind of nonconforming, independent behavior merits respect which is an expression of the wholehearted commitment of the individual to truly creative goals.

Lest I seem to be urging too much freedom for the student, let me say that the lives of our creative subjects indicate that discipline and self-control are also necessary. It would appear that these abilities must be learned if one is to be truly creative; but it is important that discipline and self-control not be overlearned. Furthermore, there is a time and a place for their learning; but having been learned, self-discipline and control should be used flexibly, not rigidly or compulsively.

Creative persons are especially open to experience, both of the inner self and of the outer world. As between perceiving (becoming aware of something) and judging (coming to a conclusion about something), creative persons are on the side of perception — they are open to and receptive of experience and seeking to know as much as possible about life. The perceptive attitude expresses itself in curiosity and is the hallmark of an inquiring mind.

The open mind can, of course, become cluttered and may — until it goes to work ordering the multiplicity of experiences which it has admitted — reveal a good deal of disorder. Moreover, having to deal with confusion and disorder in one's own mind may be sufficient cause for anxiety, especially in the young, until at last they find some higher-order integrating and reconciling principles.

At such times, a parent or a teacher or a friend may be of the greatest help in communicating an empathetic understanding of the turmoil going on in the youngster and in conveying to him a quiet, even unspoken, confidence that the anxiety which he is experiencing will pass. The other way, the noncreative way, is the rigid control of experience — of repressing impulse and imagery, of blinding oneself to great areas of experience, and never coming to know oneself.

To grow creatively is not the easiest way to develop, and for some it may be too risky and dangerous an undertaking. Those who succeed reveal a richness and actualization of the self which the judgmental person, who in the extreme case prejudges experience and thus becomes the prejudiced person, can never achieve. More than most, creative persons are able to recognize and give expression to most aspects of inner experience and character, including the feminine in the case of the male and the masculine in the case of the female, admitting into consciousness and behavior much that others would repress, integrating reason and passion, and reconciling the rational and irrational.

Young adolescents obviously will not often show these traits of open-hearted expressiveness and balance which are so characteristic of the mature creative person. Moreover, it can be safely assumed that many youngsters who will eventually be characterized by these traits are, during adolescence, troubled and disturbed, experiencing conflicts of role, crises in religious belief, uncertainty with respect to a multiplicity of possible life goals, and so on.

It is in respect to this aspect of creativity — the openness to experience and the necessity of finding integrating and reconciling symbols — that the subtlest and wisest skills of the parent and teacher as counselor are needed. My own thought is that, when counsel of this sort can be given inconspicuously or casually in the directing of the teen-ager to more and more sources of knowledge out of which he can find the answers which he needs, such counsel will be most conducive to his creative development. Such nondirective counseling, of course, is not suited to all students, but it is, I believe, the type of guidance indicated for those with creative potential.

Creative persons are intuitive. Having stressed the perceptiveness of the creative person, I would now emphasize the intuitive nature of his perceptions. In perceiving, one can focus upon what is garnered by the senses, the sense perception of things as they are, the facts; and in the extreme case, one can unimaginatively remain stuck there, bound to the stimulus, the presented material, or the situation. This I shall call simply *sense perception.* On the other hand, one may in any perception be imaginatively more alert and responsive to the deeper meanings, to the implications, and to the possibilities for use or action of that which is experienced by way of the senses. This immediate grasping of the real as well as the symbolic bridges between what is and what can be, I shall call *intuitive perception.*

One would expect creative persons not to be stimulus- and object-bound, but to be alert to the as-yet-not-realized. In other words, these individuals are characterized by their capacity for intuitive perception. And that is exactly how we find them to be in all our studies. Whether the disposition to sense perception or to intuitive perception is constitutionally or temperamentally determined, I cannot say with certainty. It is my impression that the preference in perception is at least in part so determined. But I also believe that the style of one's perceptions can also, at least in part, be learned and trained.

Rote learning, learning of facts for their own sake, repeated drill of material, too much emphasis upon facts unrelated to other facts, and excessive concern with memorizing can all strengthen and reinforce sense perception. On the other hand, an emphasis upon the transfer of training from one subject to another, upon the searching for common principles in terms of which facts from quite different domains of knowledge can be related, the stressing of analogies, similes, and metaphors, an eager seeking for symbolic equivalents of experience in the widest possible number of sensory and imaginal modalities, exercises in imaginative play, training to stand back from the facts in order to see them in larger perspective and thus in broader context — these and still other emphases in learning would, I believe, strengthen the disposition to intuitive perception and to intuitive thinking as well.

If the widest possible relationships among facts are to be established, and if what Bruner (2) has called the structure of knowledge is to be grasped, then the student must command a large body of facts and also master a large array of reasoning skills. You will see, then, that what I am proposing is not that in teaching we should neglect acute and accurate sense perception but that we should use it to build upon, leading the student always toward an intuitive understanding of that which he experiences.

The creative person has strong theoretical and aesthetic interests. On a test of values, the Allport-Vernon-Lindzey *Study of Values* (1) — which measures in the individual the relative strength of the theoretical, the economic, the aesthetic, the social, the political, and the religious values as described by the German psychologist and educator, Eduard Spranger — all of our creative subjects hold most dear the theoretical and aesthetic values. A prizing of theoretical values is congruent with a preference for intuitive perception; for both orient the person to seek some deeper or more meaningful reality which lies beneath or beyond that which is actually present to the senses. Both set one to seek truth which resides not so much in things themselves as in the relating of them one to another in terms of identities and differences and in terms of overriding principles of structural and functional relationships.

Theoretical interests are carried largely in abstract and symbolic terms. In science, for example, they change the world of phenomenal appearances into a world of scientific constructs. One is not on such firm ground in dealing with theoretical concepts and issues as one is in dealing with concrete objects. Accordingly, to be forced to deal with ideas rather than things can be an anxiety-provoking experience for the student. Here the role of the parent and teacher in helping the youngster to gain self-confidence in dealing with "theory" rather than with "fact" can be of the greatest importance. A concern with theoretical ideas will appear as "unrealistic" to less gifted and tougher-minded students (and, of course, there is a sense in which they are right). Those who are developing such interests may experience another source of insecurity: the at-times hostile and rejecting attitudes of their less gifted peers. At such times they may find themselves more extreme "isolates" than even they wish to be. The parent or teacher who in his or her own mature and effective person shows a high evaluation of the theoretical provides the young person with a model with which he can identify and thus helps him more confidently to permit within himself the development of his own theoretical interests.

Although there may appear to be some conflict between the theoretical value with its cognitive and rational concern with truth and the aesthetic value with its concern with form and beauty, these two values, as already indicated, are the two strongest values in our creative subjects. That they are both emphasized suggests that for the truly creative person the solution of a problem is not sufficient: There is the further demand that it be elegant. The aesthetic viewpoint permeates all of the work of a creative person, and it should find expression in the presentation of all subjects if creativity is to be nurtured in the home and in the school. Aesthetic values are stressed in art and music and perhaps to a lesser degree in the language arts; it is no less important that they be recognized and emphasized in mathematics, in physics and chemistry, in history, in shop work — indeed, in all subjects.

The creative person has a strong sense of destiny. With a marked degree of resoluteness and almost inevitably a measure of egotism, the creative person typically considers himself to be destined to do what he is doing, or intends to be doing, with his life. But over and above these traits there is a belief in the foregone certainty of the worth and validity of his creative efforts. This is not to say that our creative subjects have been spared periods of frustration and depression when blocked in their creative striving, but only that overriding these moods there has been a steady, unquestioning commitment of these individuals to their own creative endeavors. Another, probably related, characteristic of the creative person is that he knows who he is, where he wants to go, and what he wants to achieve. In Erikson's (3) phrase, the creative person has solved the problem of his own identity.

In Erikson's theory of ego development, however, the major problem of puberty and adolescence is to find one's own identity instead of losing oneself in a diffusion of conflicting roles. Ego identity and sense of destiny, though characteristic of the mature creative person, are not often likely to characterize even the most able students whom, on other grounds, one may believe to have great creative potential. One of our creative architects had already, at the age of four, decided that he would become an architect; but he was the exception. It was much more common to find our creative subjects struggling with the identity problem during the high school years, in conflict about themselves and their life goals, and even troubled by the fact that they possessed so many skills and interests. As a consequence, they were pulled in many directions and tempted by the possibility of several quite different careers. What the student needs in the face of such conflicts is a tolerance for ambiguity, and support in remaining tentative with respect to his life career and in resisting the dangers of premature closure which may cut off forever certain avenues of future development. Some of our creative subjects found their identity in high school, others not until after college.

Our several investigations suggest that there is no domain of interaction between student and teacher in which the teacher can more effectively nurture the creative potential of the student than in supporting him
in his tentativeness and openness to career possibilities and in protecting
him from pressures to solve prematurely his identity problem. Parents,
too, often enough play an important role in shaping the identities which
their children achieve. But with respect to the career aspect of the
identity and whether it is followed creatively or banally, the life histories
of our subjects testify repeatedly to the signal importance of some one
teacher during the high school or college years.

This teacher — by his devotion to a field of study, by exhibiting the
excitement and satisfaction which accompany a deep absorption in the
problems and challenges of a field of study, by stirring the imagination
of the student with a clear exposition of the structure of knowledge in
the subject, and in his own seeking to respond creatively to its still
unsolved problems — offers the student a model with which he can
identify. Often it is not with the profession of teaching that the identification is made but with the field of study that is taught with so much
skill, devotion, and excitement, or with the professional field to which
it may later lead — e.g., medicine, law, or a host of others.

From his association with this kind of instructor, a true exemplar, the
student learns something of the delight and joy and fresh insights which
come from a sense of confidence in one's competence and in the exercising of one's skill. Such experience can motivate the student to acquire
through study and hard work the knowledge, skills, and competence that
alone can provide grounds for a confident setting of one's own goals, and
a zestful attacking of ever more difficult problems in the field of one's
interest.

The parent or teacher who does not try to force interest, but who
instead encourages the youngster to explore many different paths until he
has found the right one for himself, will have — more often than not —
played a crucial role in bringing into realization and fruition that creativity which was only a potentiality within the youngster when he was
seeking his self-identity during his high school and college years.

In these remarks I have wandered far from our research data, discussing their implications for teaching and for learning in much too
direct and positive terms. Nevertheless, my assertions have not been
conjured out of the blue; they find support in the traits of our creative
subjects and in what they have told us about their early years, and
especially about their experiences as students. Yet I would be remiss
if I did not in closing remind you that what I have offered here are not
proved prescriptions for action but only hypotheses worthy of testing.

REFERENCES

[1]Allport, G. W.; Vernon, P. E.; and Lindzey, G. *Study of Values: Manual of Directions.* (Revised edition.) Boston: Houghton-Mifflin Co., 1951.

[2]Bruner, Jerome S. *The Process of Education.* Cambridge, Mass.: Harvard University Press, 1960. 97 pp.

[3]Erikson, E. H. *Childhood and Society.* New York: W. W. Norton & Co., 1950. 397 pp.

[4]Getzels, J. W., and Jackson, P. W. *Creativity and Intelligence.* New York: John Wiley & Sons, 1962. p. 39.

[5]MacKinnon, David W. "The Nature and Nurture of Creative Talent." *American Psychologist* 17: 484–95; July 1962.

[6]Taylor, D. W.; Berry, P. C.; and Block, C. H. "Does Group Participation When Using Brainstorming Facilitate or Inhibit Creative Thinking?" *Administrative Science Quarterly* 3: 23–47; 1958.

[7]Terman, L. M. *Concept Mastery Test, Form T Manual.* New York: Psychological Corporation, 1956.

PART V

Socio-Cultural Foundations

Socio-cultural foundations refer to those factors in the environment that influence individuals and groups. In terms of education, they refer to those factors in the environment that influence the individual student and various groups of students in school and how and what they learn. Socio-cultural foundations in education call for a knowledge of cultural values, norms and behavior patterns, as well as the process of assimilation and acculturation. They call for an understanding that the school is an agent of society that helps to socialize the student and teaches him to conform in the ways deemed best by the society — or, more precisely, by the middle-class society. For the greater part, school does not change society (though it may help improve it); it mirrors society.

It must be understood that the schools are middle-class

institutions, where middle-class teachers and administrators help per-petuate middle-class values. The schools assimilate and acculturate stu-dents who do not fit into the "American way": immigrant, minority, poor, and working-class children and youth. Since the schools are middle-class in nature, they tend to favor those students who are middle-class or who easily fit the mold. There is nothing unusual about this analysis; to some extent the reader himself is a product of this molding process. In fact, he is one of the successful products by virtue of entering college in order to obtain the "proper credentials" deemed necessary by the larger society. In short, the schools serve as a means of transmitting and preserving the culture of the larger society.

By viewing education as an outgrowth of culture and society, it is pos-sible to become aware of the controls and limitations of the school, the way the school conflicts with the culture of the poor, the problems of equal educational opportunity, the problems of deprivation and how it affects the learning process, the problems of assimilation and accultura-tion as manifested in the classroom, the way race and racism are reflected in schools, how student alienation affects the student's performance in school, and the gap between our cherished ideals and actual practices. In this connection, some of the objectives of this section are to try to understand the changing patterns of society and how they affect children and youth, the needs and problems of youth as they engage school and society and in turn how school and society affects youth, how culture affects the learning process, and what might be done to improve the school situation which students must face.

In the first article, Margaret Mead points out the changing patterns and influences of society, and how these forces affect youth and adults. She distinguishes three types of culture: *post-figurative* (in which children learn from adults), *cofigurative* (in which children and adults learn from their peers), and *prefigurative* (in which adults also learn from children). According to Mead, we are approaching the third type of culture. She goes on to examine the reasons for the dissonance among today's youth on a global basis and the way they view adults as corrupting the environ-ment, mismanaging their tasks, and groping for answers. Although youth do not have the answers, they feel they can no longer trust adults to work out the solutions; youth feel they must find the answers before it is too late and adults wreck the world. As youth tell us and the author warns, "The future is now."

Since the 1960s, there has been growing concern for the children com-monly referred to as the "disadvantaged" or "deprived." The social, psychological, and cognitive problems of these children have been keenly described by several investigators. The way school and society discrimi-nate against the disadvantaged, as well as the problems of race, poverty, and equal educational opportunity, have also been described in detail.

In the next article, Allan C. Ornstein directs attention to the central question of "Who Are the Disadvantaged?" and in doing so systematizes the research on this topic. He first describes the disadvantaged in terms of the traditional view, pointing out their negative characteristics and limitations, then proceeds to outline several other descriptions of children who could be considered disadvantaged. For educational purposes, however, Ornstein concludes that any student who falls behind the academic norm (especially in reading) will probably be disadvantaged in school.

Throughout the ages, societies have wasted their talented and gifted youth. Today, as a result of our technological society, we are forced to search for talented youth, to encourage them to develop their skills and abilities and to utilize them effectively when they become adults. During the post-sputnik years, the search for talent was most evident in the fields of science, mathematics, and engineering. Today the talent search seems to be directed toward human service fields. In our search to find and develop the talented and gifted, we often lose sight of the fact that these youth are often exploited for the sake of their parents' egos and their school's reputation; pushed to the breaking point; discriminated against in school by less talented and gifted teachers, who therefore resent them; isolated by their peers, who also resent such youth; and manipulated and bribed by society, so it can meet its challenges.

Edgar Z. Friedenberg examines the plight of gifted youth in school. The teachers dislike them because of their spontaneity, their novel answers, and the fact they may show them to be incompetent. From this discussion, the author goes on to examine the reasons why teachers enter the profession, as well as their attitudes and behaviors, most of which seem to be negative to Friedenberg. According to the author, teaching is a second-rate profession, which the teachers know and feel ashamed of. Coupled with their feelings of impotence and anger in teaching, they vent their *ressentiment* on students, and especially the gifted.

In terms of school and society, what rights do students have? Do adults have the right to deprive students of their rights because of their age or immaturity? Do schools have the right to deprive students of their rights because of the nature of mass education? Granted youth must be socialized if society is to perpetuate itself, and students must learn to conform to certain rules if the school is to function effectively, but what if the socializing process or school rules are unconstitutional? Surely the constitution applies to youth and carries over in the schools.

The principles set forth in the next article have been adopted by the American Civil Liberties Union (ACLU) and are geared for secondary students in both public and private schools. Although the application of the specific principles may be modified according to individual situations, the central ideas have general application. Some of the principles set forth may seem contrary to common sense; however, it is the contention of the

ACLU that the student has the right to "the principle of law" and his rights should be accorded so long as the health or safety of the other students are not endangered or the educational process imminently threatened. The ACLU also maintains that only by promoting some of their rights as citizens can students grow into politically wise and mature adults — a vital concern for our democratic society.

MARGARET MEAD

Youth Revolt:
The Future Is Now

OUR PRESENT CRISIS HAS BEEN VARIOUSLY ATTRIBUTED TO THE OVER-
whelming rapidity of change, the collapse of the family, the decay of
capitalism, the triumph of a soulless technology, and, in wholesale repudiation, to the final breakdown of the Establishment. Behind these attribu-
tions there is a more basic conflict between those for whom the present
represents no more than an intensification of our existing cofigurative
culture, in which peers are more than ever replacing parents as the
significant models of behavior, and those who contend that we are in fact
entertaining a totally new phase of cultural evolution.

Most commentators, in spite of their differences in viewpoint, still see
the future essentially as an extension of the past. Edward Teller can still
speak of the outcome of a nuclear war as a state of destruction relatively
no more drastic than the ravages wrought by Genghis Khan, and historians
can point out that time and again civilization has survived the crumbling
of empires. Similarly, many authorities treat as no more than an extreme
form of adolescent rebellion the repudiation of present and past by the
dissident youth of every persuasion in every kind of society in the world.

Theorists who emphasize the parallels between past and present in their
interpretations of the generation gap ignore the irreversibility of the
changes that have taken place since the beginning of the Industrial Revolu-

tion. This is especially striking in their handling of modern technological development, which they treat as comparable in its effects to the changes that occurred as one civilization in the past took over from another such techniques as agriculture, script, navigation, or the organization of labor and law.

One urgent priority, I believe, is to examine the nature of change in the modern world, including its speed and dimensions, so that we can better understand the distinctions that must be made between change in the past and that which is now ongoing. To do so, I make distinctions among three different kinds of culture: *post-figurative,* in which children learn primarily from their forebears; *cofigurative,* in which both children and adults learn from their peers, and *prefigurative,* in which adults learn also from their children.

Although it is possible to discuss both post-figurative and cofigurative cultures in terms of slow or rapid change without specifying the nature of the process and to compare past and present situations when the focus is kept on generation relationships and on the type of modeling through which a culture is transmitted, it is only when one specifies the nature of the process that the contrast between past and present change becomes clear.

The primary evidence that our present situation is unique, without any parallel in the past, is that the generation gap is world-wide. The particular events taking place in England, Pakistan, the United States, New Guinea, or elsewhere are not enough to explain the unrest that is stirring modern youth everywhere. Recent technological change or the handicaps imposed by its absence, revolution or the suppression of revolutionary activities, the crumbling of faith in ancient creeds or the attraction of new creeds — all these serve only as partial explanations of the particular forms taken by youth revolt in different countries.

Concentration on particularities can only hinder the search for an explanatory principle. Instead, it is necessary to strip the occurrences in each country of their superficial, national, and immediately temporal aspects. The desire for a liberated form of communism in Czechoslovakia, the search for "racial" equality in the United States, the desire to liberate Japan from American military influence — these are particularistic forms. Youthful activism is common to them all. The key question is this: What are the new conditions that have brought about the revolt of youth around the world?

The first of these is the emergence of a world community. For the first time human beings throughout the world, in their information about and responses to one another, have become a community that is united by shared knowledge and danger. As far as we know, no such single, interacting community has existed within archaeological time. The largest clusters of interacting human groups have always been fragments of a still larger unknown whole, and the idea that all men are, in the same sense, human beings always has been either unreal or a mystical belief.

The events of the past twenty-five years changed this drastically. Exploration has been complete enough to convince us that there are no humanoid types on the planet except our own species. World-wide air travel and globe-encircling TV satellites have turned us into one community, in which events taking place on one side of the earth become immediately and simultaneously available to peoples everywhere else. No artist or political censor has time to intervene and edit as a leader is shot or a flag is planted on the moon. The world is a community, though it still lacks the forms of organization and the sanctions by which a political community can be governed.

Men who are the carriers of vastly different cultural traditions are entering the present at the same point in time. It is as if, all around the world, men were converging on identical immigration posts, each with its identifying sign: YOU ARE NOW ABOUT TO ENTER THE POST-WORLD-WAR-II WORLD AT GATE 1 (GATE 23, etc.). Whoever they are and wherever their particular points of entry may be, all men are equally immigrants into the new era. They are like the immigrants who came as pioneers to a new land, lacking all knowledge of what demands new conditions of life would make upon them. Those who came later could take their peer groups as models. But among the first comers, the young adults had as models only their own tentative adaptations and innovations.

Today, everyone born and bred before World War II is such an immigrant in time as his forebears were in space — a pioneer struggling to grapple with the unfamiliar conditions of life in a new era. Like all immigrants and pioneers, these immigrants in time are the bearers of older cultures, but today they represent all the cultures of the world. And all of them, whether they are sophisticated French intellectuals or members of a remote New Guinea tribe, land-bound peasants in Haiti or nuclear physicists, have certain characteristics in common.

Whoever they are, these immigrants grew up under skies across which no satellite had ever flashed. Their perception of the past was an edited version of what had happened. Their perception of the immediate present was limited to what they could take in through their own eyes and ears and to the edited versions of other men's sensory experience and memories. Their conception of the future was essentially one in which change was incorporated into a deeper changelessness. The industrialist or military planner, envisaging what a computer, not yet constructed, might make possible, treated it as another addition to the repertoire of inventions that have enhanced man's skills. It expanded what men could do, but did not change the future.

When the first atom bomb was exploded at the end of World War II, only a few individuals realized that all humanity was entering a new age. And to this day the majority of those over twenty-five have failed to grasp emotionally, however well they may grasp intellectually, the difference between any war in which, no matter how terrible the casualties, mankind will survive, and one in which there will be no survivors. They continue to think that a war, fought with more lethal weapons, would just be a worse war. Our thinking still binds us to the past— to the world as it existed in our childhood and youth.

We still hold the seats of power and command the resources and the skills necessary to keep order and organize the kinds of societies we know about. We control the educational systems, the apprenticeship systems, the career ladders up which the young must climb. Nevertheless, we have passed the point of no return. We are committed to life in an unfamiliar setting; we are making do with what we know.

The young generation, however — the articulate young rebels all around the world who are lashing out against the controls to which they are subjected — are like the first generation born into a new country. They are at home in this time. Satellites are familiar in their skies. They have never known a time when war did not threaten annihilation. When they are given the facts, they can understand immediately that continued pollution of the air and water and soil will soon make the planet uninhabitable and that it will be impossible to feed an indefinitely expanding world population. As members of one species in an underdeveloped world community they recognize that invidious distinctions based on race and caste are anachronisms. They insist on the vital necessity of some form of world order.

No longer bound by the simplified linear sequences dictated by the printed word, they live in a world in which events are presented to them in all their complex immediacy. In their eyes the killing of an enemy is not qualitatively different from the murder of a neighbor. They cannot reconcile our efforts to save our own children by every known means with our readiness to destroy the children of others with napalm. They know that the people of one nation alone cannot save their own children; each holds the responsibility for all others' children.

Although I have said they *know* these things, perhaps I should say that this is how they *feel*. Like the first generation born in a new country, they listen only half-comprehendingly to their parents' talk about the past. For as the children of pioneers had no access to the landscapes whose memories could still move their parents to tears, the young today cannot share their parents' responses to events that deeply moved them in the past. But this is not all that separates the young from their elders. Watching, they can see that their elders are groping, that they are managing clumsily and often unsuccessfully the tasks imposed on them by the new conditions.

The young do not know what must be done, but they feel that there must be a better way and that they must find it.

Today, nowhere in the world are there elders who know what the children know, no matter how remote and simple the societies are in which the children live. In the past there were always some elders who knew more than any children in terms of their experience of having grown up within a cultural system. Today there are none. It is not only that parents are no longer guides, but that there are no guides, whether one seeks them in one's own country or abroad. There are no elders who know what those who have been reared within the last twenty years know about the world into which they were born.

True, in many parts of the world the parental generation still lives by a post-figurative set of values. From parents in such cultures children may learn that there have been unquestioned absolutes, and this learning may carry over into later experience as an expectation that absolute values can and should be re-established.

There are still parents who answer such child's questions as why he must go to bed, or eat his vegetables, or learn to read with simple assertions: Because it is *right* to do so, because *God* says so, or because *I* say so. These parents are preparing the way for the re-establishment of post-figurative elements in the culture. But these elements will be far more rigid and intractable than in the past because they must be defended in a world in which conflicting points of view, rather than orthodoxies, are prevalent.

Most parents, however, are too uncertain to assert old dogmatisms. They do not know how to teach these children who are so different from what they themselves once were, and most children are unable to learn from parents and elders they will never resemble. In the past, in the United States, children of immigrant parents pleaded with them not to speak their foreign language in public and not to wear their outlandish foreign clothes. They knew the burning shame of being, at the same time, unable to repudiate their parents and unable to accept simply and naturally their way of speaking and doing things. But in time they learned to find new teachers as guides, to model their behavior on that of more adapted age mates, and to slip in, unnoticed, among a group whose parents were more bearable.

Today, the dissident young discover very rapidly that this solution is no longer possible. The breach between themselves and their parents also exists between their friends and their friends' parents and between their friends and their teachers.

These young dissidents realize the critical need for immediate world action on problems that affect the whole world. What they want is, in some way, to begin all over again. They are ready to make way for something new by a kind of social bulldozing — like the bulldozing in which every tree and feature of the landscape is destroyed to make way for a new community. Awareness of the reality of the crisis (which is, in fact, perceived most accurately not by the young, but by their discerning and prophetic elders) and the sense the young have that their elders do not understand the modern world, because they do not understand their children, has produced a kind of rebellion in which planned reformation of the present system is almost inconceivable.

Nevertheless, those who have no power also have no routes to power except through those against whom they are rebelling. In the end, it was men who gave the vote to women; and it will be the House of Lords that votes to abolish the House of Lords — as also, in the final analysis, nations will act to limit national sovereignty. Effective, rapid evolutionary change, in which no one is guillotined or forced into exile, depends on the co-operation of a large number of those in power with the dispossessed who are seeking power.

These, in brief, are the conditions of our time. These are the two generations — pioneers in a new era and their children — who have as yet to find a way of communicating about the world in which both live, though their perceptions of it are so different. No one knows what the next steps should be. Recognizing that this is so is, I submit, the beginning of an answer.

I believe we are on the verge of developing a new kind of culture, one that is as much a departure in style from cofigurative cultures as the institutionalization of cofiguration in orderly — and disorderly — change was a departure from the post-figurative style. I call this new style "prefigurative," because in this new culture it will be the unborn child, already conceived but still in the womb — not the parent and grandparent — that represents what is to come. This is a child whose sex and appearance and capabilities are unknown, but who will need imaginative, innovative, and dedicated adult care far beyond any we give today.

No one can know in advance what the child will become — how swift his limbs will be, what will delight his eye, whether his tempo will be fast or slow. No one can know how his mind will work — whether he will learn best from sight or sound or touch or movement. But knowing what we do not know and cannot predict, we can construct an environment in which a child, still unknown, can be safe and can grow and discover himself and the world.

Love and trust, based on dependency and answering care, made it possible for the individual who had been reared in one culture to move into another, transforming, without destroying, his earlier learning. It is seldom the first generation of voluntary immigrants and pioneers who cannot meet the demands of a new environment. Their previous learning carries them through. But unless they embody what is new post-figuratively, they cannot pass on to their children what they had acquired through their own early training — the ability to learn from others the things their parents could not teach them.

Parents, in a world where there are no more knowledgeable others to whom they can commit the children they themselves cannot teach, feel uncertain and helpless. Still believing that there should be answers, parents ask how they can tell their children what is right. So some try to solve the problem by advising their children, very vaguely, that they will have to figure it out for themselves. And some parents ask what the others are doing. But this resource of a cofigurative culture is becoming meaningless to parents who feel that the "others" — their children's age mates — are moving in ways that are unsafe for their own children to emulate, and who find that they do not understand what their children figure out for themselves.

It is the adults who still believe that there is a safe and socially approved road to a kind of life they have not experienced who react with the greatest anger and bitterness to the discovery that what they had hoped for no longer exists for their children. These are the parents, the trustees, the legislators, the columnists and commentators who denounce most vocally what is happening in schools and colleges and universities in which they had placed their hopes for their children.

Today, as we gain a better understanding of the circular processes through which culture is developed and transmitted, we recognize that man's most human characteristic is not his ability to learn, which he shares with many other species, but his ability to teach and store what others have developed and taught him. In the past men relied on the least elaborate part of the circular system — the dependent learning by children — for continuity of transmission and for the embodiment of the new. Now, with our greater understanding of the process, we must cultivate the most flexible and complex part of the system: the behavior of adults. We must, in fact, teach ourselves how to alter adult behavior; we must create new models for adults who can teach their children not what to learn, but how to learn, and not what they should be committed to, but the value of commitment.

In doing this we must recognize explicitly that the paths by which we came into the present can never be traversed again. The past is the road by which we have arrived where we are. Older forms of culture have provided us with the knowledge, techniques, and tools necessary for our contemporary civilization.

The freeing of men's imagination from the past depends on the development of a new kind of communication with those who are most deeply involved with the future — the young who were born in the new world. In the past, in cofigurational cultures, the elders were gradually cut off from limiting the future of their children. Now the development of prefigurational cultures will depend on the existence of a continuing dialogue in which the young, free to act on their own initiative, can lead their elders in the direction of the unknown. Then the older generation will have access to the new experiential knowledge, without which no meaningful plans can be made. It is only with the direct participation of the young, who have that knowledge, that we can build a viable future.

Instead of directing their rebellion toward the retrieval of a grand-parental utopian dream, as the Maoists seem to be doing with the young activists in China, we must learn together with the young how to take the next steps. Out of their new knowledge — new to the world and new to us — must come the questions to those who are already equipped by education and experience to search for answers. The children, the young, must ask these questions that we would never think to ask, but enough trust must be re-established so that the elders will be permitted to work with them on the answers.

I feel that we can change into a prefigurative culture, consciously, delightedly, and industriously, rearing unknown children for an unknown world. But to do it we must relocate the future.

Here we can take a cue from the young who seem to want instant utopias. They say the future is now. This seems unreasonable and impetuous, and in some of the demands they make it is unrealizable in concrete detail; but here again, I think, they give us the way to reshape our thinking. We must place the future, like the unborn child in the womb of a woman, within a community of men, women, and children, among us, already here, already to be nourished and succored and protected, already in need of things for which, if they are not prepared before it is born, it will be too late. So, as the young say, the future is now.

ALLAN C. ORNSTEIN

Who Are The Disadvantaged?

INTRODUCTION

EDUCATORS WHO SPEAK OF OR WRITE ABOUT THE DISADVANTAGED TEND
to categorize them somewhat arbitrarily into one or more of the following
areas of deprivation: economic, racial, social, psychological, intellectual
and/or geographical. The descriptions of each category focus on their
weaknesses and cumulative deficits. This is the prominent school of
thought, based on the writings of the 1940s and 1950s which described
the plight of lower-class youth and black youth and emerged as "common wisdom" by the early 1960s — when references to these groups of
youth began to appear interchangeably with the term "disadvantaged."

Although this author tends to agree that lower-class and minority-group
youth are disadvantaged in our schools and society, he sees the danger of
creating an oversimplified relationship: the labeling of all students as
lower or middle class, and the categorizing of all minority groups as lower
class, all whites as middle class. Similarly, it invites stereotyping, reinforces a segregated rather than an integrated view of society, and reflects
in part, a culture bias.

Reprinted with permission from *Young Children,* Vol. XXVI, No. 5, May 1971.
Copyright © 1971, National Association for the Education of Young Children, 1834
Connecticut Ave., NW, Washington, D.C. 20009.

THE TRADITIONAL VIEWPOINT

In describing the disadvantaged, Havighurst (1964, 1970) tends to follow the traditional approach. He refers to their family, personal and social group handicaps, and tends to categorize them into "observable groups," mainly in terms of low income, as well as "in racial and ethnic groups": in this way, trapping the uncritical reader into thinking of the disadvantaged solely in terms of income and race.

Clift (1969) depicts perhaps the most dismal image of the disadvantaged, enumerating 169 negative traits related to factors of personality, cognitive functioning and educational values. Although he claims that the successful teacher needs to be aware of such traits in order to ameliorate the learning problems of the disadvantaged (and there is no doubting the need for this knowledge), there is a danger that teachers and schools may invariably view the students' life styles and values to be in conflict with learning, and under the guise of trying to educate the disadvantaged will systematically undermine their self-worth and dignity. In enumerating as many negative traits, the students tend to be perceived in terms of group characteristics, and also as an uneducable group, rather than as individuals.

In general, the traditional approach for describing the disadvantaged leads to three related cognitive theories: the (1) "deprivation theory," (2) "critical period theory," and (3) "cumulative intellectual deficit theory." Briefly, the "deprivation theory" explains the importance of environment, especially in the early years of child development — the theory that a child who is deprived of a quantity and quality of environmental stimuli will lack sufficient experiences required for adequate development of the central processes necessary for acquiring intellectual skills and abilities. The "critical period theory" points out that if the child is deprived of the necessary stimulation during a period in which he is maximally susceptible to learning, some degree of permanent cognitive retardation ensues. This leads to the "cumulative intellectual deficit theory," that is, a child who has an intellectual deficit from a past period is less able to advance to new levels of intellectual development. The deficits become cumulative and lead to the student continually falling further behind as he is passed from grade to grade. The outcome is that he often drops out of school or graduates as a functional illiterate.

It might be argued that the three theories constitute a scholarly mode for describing the disadvantaged in terms of being "stupid." Although the objective is to make the teacher aware of the intellectual factors related to learning, as well as to counteract the child's limited environmental stimulation with compensatory programs and proper teaching practices, the continuous listing of negative traits and supporting cognitive theories may be used to "alibi" the teachers' and schools' ineffectiveness. It may also be alleged that the social scientists themselves, by delineating these traits and theories, unwittingly contribute to the teachers' acquiring negative attitudes about the disadvantaged students' inability to learn. The teachers, to some degree, probably adopt these attitudes by reading about and discussing such negative traits and cognitive theories. Nevertheless, if one is unwilling to realistically examine the economic, racial and cognitive theories related to educating the disadvantaged, it is premature, as Clift (1969) points out, to expect the teacher to successfully teach them.

THE POSITIVE VIEWPOINT

What may be considered as a reaction to the negative literature on the disadvantaged is the attempt to define and enumerate the positive, sometimes overlooked, characteristics and strength of the disadvantaged, as exemplified by the writings of Eisenberg (1963-1964), Hickerson (1966), Riessman (1962, 1964, 1966) and McCreary (1966). This treatment tends to romanticize the disadvantaged and imply that their teachers have no real respect for or understanding of them. Comparing both schools of thought, the literature that portrays the disadvantaged negatively implies that the student, or his family and environment, is mainly to blame for his school failure; that which presents a positive viewpoint of the disadvantaged blames the teachers and schools.

Riessman (1962, 1964, 1966) is perhaps the most noted authority who expresses the new and growing trend toward describing the disadvantaged as having many positive characteristics — a physical orientation, hidden verbal ability, creative potential, group cohesiveness, informality, sense of humor, etc. But by using the words "deprived" and "disadvantaged" in his writings which describe these positive characteristics, Riessman unintentionally endorses the standards of middle-class school and society which he criticizes. Perhaps for this reason, Riessman currently uses the term "poor" youth, with the mistaken conviction that it is a more positive term, in referring to the "deprived" or "disadvantaged."

THE "CULTURE OF POVERTY"

An extension of the positive portrayal of the disadvantaged is the contention that these children and youth are not culturally deprived, that they have their own culture, and that most of us fail to recognize this because of our middle-class biases and the use of our middle-class standards in measuring and judging them. Those who argue this viewpoint — Coles, (1965, 1970), Gans (1962), Harrington (1963), Lewis (1961,

1966b, 1968) and Padilla (1958) — to name a few — outline or refer to the concept of the "culture of poverty," and in so doing tend to go further than romanticizing, often glorifying the poor — which seems almost ludicrous, for slums are ugly and slum life is painful. Also, there is a propensity to claim the poor do not want to become like the middle-class. This seems equally ludicrous, for the poor, even those who are trapped in the "culture of poverty," wish to break their chains of penury, which connotes a striving toward a middle-class-income level.

Lewis (1961, 1966b, 1968) is best known for popularizing the concept. However, he did not write directly for an educational audience (but mainly for an anthropological and sociological audience) or about the disadvantaged in America (but mainly about Latin Americans). His concept of the "culture of poverty" reflects his deep respect and concern for the poor, and is the basis of the writings in which the term "culturally deprived" is rejected and poverty is ennobled. For Lewis, the "culture of poverty" is a way of life shared by poor people, transcending rural-urban, regional and national differences. Poverty, throughout the globe, is more than just a story of deprivation, disorganization and dispirit. It has a structure, organization and rationale — a sense of community and group values. Although the poor are marginal and helpless now, Lewis warned that they have a deep resentment toward the establishment, the "haves," and they represent a potentially powerful and worldwide political force. Lewis (1966a) claimed that about 10 million Americans live in the "culture of poverty." Although blacks are not the only group that constitute this bottom aggregation, according to this author, their liberation movement — from chattel to black power — perhaps represents both ends of the continuum of the "culture of poverty," the emerging fist of the "third world."

WORKING-CLASS YOUTH

Cohen (1960), Havighurst et al. (1962), Hollingshead (1949), Warner, Havighurst and Loeb (1944), and Whyte (1943) have all written books which describe the problems of working-class or "street-corner" adolescents. They are the children of "Mr. Smith" and "Mr. Jones" — anonymous, hardworking, everyday people. Their fathers are policemen, truck drivers, mechanics, clerks and construction workers — mainly of eastern and southern European descent.

Many of their parents have managed to save enough money to move from their old neighborhoods and they may now live on the fringes of or near a middle-class, white-collar, better educated group of neighbors. Because of this proximity, these youth are apt to attend schools with students who are more socioeconomically advantaged. In school (and in the adjoining "better" neighborhood), they find they are disliked and disparaged by adult authority and by their more advantaged counterparts; they find they are at the bottom of the status hierarchy, helpless, powerless, unable to organize together, as black youth are doing today, and collectively challenge and change the system that discriminates against them.

Schrag's (1970) recent analysis of life on "Mechanic Street" reveals that the social order has not changed much for these youth within the last 10 or 20 years, since the studies of the aforementioned authors. Schrag describes the obscure existence and ambivalent future of these youth. Although most of them graduate from high school, "they are academic losers"; they get their Cs and rarely go to college.

SUBURBAN YOUTH

Many educators, among them Dodson (1958, 1968), Keniston (1965, 1968), Fantini and Weinstein (1968), Meyer (1969), Miel (1967), and O'Reilly (1970), now contend that middle-class, suburban youth can no longer be taken for granted either. Many are in revolt against their parents and against the technological aspects of society — bigness, bureaucratization, impersonality and careerism. For the most part, they feel aimless, useless, cynical and alienated — deeply worried about their future —or even questioning if there will be one.

His slum counterpart may live in a fatherless home, but the suburban adolescent may also be seriously lacking parental attention: often both parents work in the day, attend social activities in the evening, and vacation without the children for a month or so. The sons and daughters (and schools, too) are pressured by parents who are obsessed with grades and their children getting into Harvard or Radcliffe.

From the elementary-school level on, the suburban description is blemished. The average suburban elementary child, according to Miel's (1967) findings, is bigoted and hypocritical about racial, religious, ethnic and socioeconomic groups. Materialism, selfishness, conspicious consumption, cheap abundance and conformity reflect in the child's behavior. By the time these students enter college, Keniston (1965, 1968) points out that many of them wind up rejecting the values and life styles of their parents, rootless and alienated from their middle-class backgrounds.

THE MALE STUDENT

The writings of Fantini and Weinstein (1968), Goldman (1967), Goodman (1964), Mayer (1961), and Sexton (1969) indicate that the schools are largely staffed by females— especially on the elementary level, which is a critical age for the child's development. The schools are dominated by female norms of politeness, cleanliness and obedience. The curriculum, texts and classroom activities are female-oriented — safe, nice, antiseptic, sweet. The school frowns on vulgar language and fighting; it suppresses the boy's maleness and often fails to permit action-oriented, tough sports. The problem is apt to be magnified in the poor and minority-group home by the fact that the male partner is often missing or too economically powerless and psychologically handicapped by society to provide a positive model to emulate; the home is usually female-dominated which deprives the boy of a desirable behavioral pattern and which often ignores his needs and emasculates him.

Comparing the above group of authors, Sexton's (1969) analysis is perhaps the most controversial and well documented, showing how the feminized schools discriminate against the male and subvert his identity. Her data show that approximately three out of four students regarded as "problems" are boys, and since teachers tend to fail "problem" students, approximately two out of three students who fail subjects are boys. Boys who do poorly in scholastics are not necessarily less intelligent than many of their male peers, but governed by values and interests of athletics, sex and group loyalty — which conflict with the teachers who are predominantly female (and with the male teachers, too, who by virtue of their role tend to enforce and reinforce the feminized school norms). Sexton maintains that the schools' values and resulting discrimination and injuries against the boys are cumulative, and are one reason for boys largely outnumbering girls in school dropout rate, deviant and delinquent acts, mental illness and suicides. Whereas Sexton's book has wide appeal for men, Millet's (1970) book, which is discussed below, serves almost the same purpose for women, especially for those who feel discriminated against by males.

THE FEMALE

The male dominates both public attention and the literature. The problems of childhood and adolescence are usually discussed in terms of the male. We often fail to recognize that the young girl struggles with equally pressing and perhaps more complicated problems of growing up, because of the females' secondary role in society and the conflicting demands of education, career fulfillment and marriage. This concern is expressed in the writings of Bettelheim (1962), Erikson (1968), and Fisher and Noble (1960), and more recently with the popular writings of Bird and Briller (1970), Firestone (1970), and Millet (1970).

Erikson (1968) asserts that starting with early adolescence the girl is at odds with her womanhood and the permanent inequality to which she is seemingly doomed. The girl who is devoted to an education and a career often feels the pressure of the marriage market. From early childhood she is taught that she cannot have a complete identity until she marries, nor can she fulfill her womanhood until she has a child. Erikson goes on to point out that the female lacks equal rights and equal representation. In graduate school and on the job, especially in fields in which she competes against the male, she is discriminated against. While Erikson assures us that their status is changing, he fails to point out that some women do not feel the need for equal rights or would not know what to do with them. With all due respect for Women's Liberation, some females would prefer to remain in their so-called second-class position and be submissive.

CREATIVE AND INTELLIGENT STUDENTS

Some educators, such as Coleman (1965), Friedenberg (1966), Getzels and Jackson (1962), Taylor (1964), Torrance (1965, 1970) and Wallach and Kogan (1965, 1967), contend that creative and intellectually gifted students are discriminated against in school. They are often poorly motivated in school and their teachers often fail to support and encourage them; in fact, many teachers are threatened by their superior knowledge, novel solutions and nonconforming behavior. The schools, under the guise of enhancing the democratic process and operating under egalitarian rules, often squash their talents and diversity. Also, these students are often the victims of their parents' aspirations and the school's reputation.

Getzels and Jackson (1962), in their study of students at the University of Chicago Lab School, attended mainly by children of professors and graduate students, pointed out that creative and high IQ students were often labeled as "problem" students and punished for their originality. In turn, these students learned to repress their talents and abilities. By being too creative or intelligent, they often invited social ostracism from their peers, as well as resentment and hostility from their teachers. The students felt anxiety, frustration, anger and repression. One can only hypothesize that if these students were handicapped in the Lab School, they would fare worse in a regular public school.

ALL STUDENTS

While most of us realize that the inner-city student is often disadvantaged not only by his environment but also by his teachers and schools, a view suggested by Dennison (1969), Friedenberg (1965, 1966), Henry (1955, 1963), Holt (1964, 1967, 1969, 1970), Goodman (1964), Gross and Gross (1969), and Neill (1960) extends the concept of the

disadvantaged to include *all* students. No matter what their class, color
or geographical location, most students are short-changed by teachers
and schools; they are unable to fulfill their learning potential. Thus, students do not fail school; teachers and schools fail them.

Holt (1964, 1969) is perhaps the most radical of the group, or at least
he seems to have the largest following. He points out the way students
adopt strategies of fear and failure. The longer the student goes to school,
the more bored, answer-centered and stifled he becomes; he learns how
to bluff, fake and cheat; he learns how not to learn; he learns not to do
anything unless he is bribed or "conned"; he learns to escape from reality;
he learns that very little is worth doing, or at least worth doing in school.
According to Holt, the only things the teachers and schools are doing
successfully are the wrong things. Indeed, the reader cannot take a middle
of the road view of Holt. Either he is in deep sympathy with him or he is
incensed by him.

YOUTH

Dodson (1968), Friedenberg (1962, 1965, 1966), Goodman (1960,
1970), Kelly (1962), McCabe (1967) and Ornstein (1970, 1971) contend that all youth — boys and girls, from all socioeconomic classes,
whether they are academic winners or losers, whether they are in school
or roaming the streets — are disadvantaged because of their age; they
occupy a subordinate position in school and society, and live under the
tutelage of their parents and teachers, as well as adult authority in general. They are powerless, impotent, exploited and manipulated by parents,
the school and society.

In this connection, Friedenberg (1962, 1965, 1966) affirms that the
adult world is badly frightened by youth; the adult reaction to them is
"a kind of panic response" to the liquidation of adult authority and control over them. The school is the official agent of adult society which
manipulates and castigates youth. In school, youth have relatively no legal
rights; their teachers often are jealous of, resent and/or fear their new
values and spontaneity; their teachers attempt to make them submit to
the mold of school and society by abrogating their initiative and identity.
Those who refuse to conform are labeled as "troublesome" or, even
worse, as "disturbed."

In the past, students decided it was easier to accept than to rebel, and
allowed the school to define and mold them until they either dropped
out or were graduated. The overt rebellious students were either tamed
or expelled. The school was unable to conceive that its functioning may
have needed adjusting, only that the students needed adjusting. Today,

students are confronting the school and trying to change their status from victim to shaper.

CONCLUSION

The term "disadvantaged" is somewhat nebulous, as well as relative to one's biases; educators would do well to agree upon and define the term. It should be noted, also, labeling a group as "disadvantaged" can be patronizing, if the group is being defined according to the norms and standards of another part of American culture.

For the author's purposes, and he makes no "liberal" or "fashionable" pretense about it, any student who falls below the school standard is disadvantaged. In this connection, the research shows that there is a substantially high positive correlation between (1) low school achievement and low-income youth and (2) low school achievement and minority-group youth. Similarly, there is a high positive correlation between low-income and minority groups, which is rooted in American discriminatory practices toward nonwhites — boxing them into substandard education, employment and housing — making it nearly impossible for the majority to escape from their poverty and ghetto, creating a "structurally" poor and second-class citizenry among racial minorities.

To the author's knowledge, there is as yet no school in which low-income or minority-group students are not discriminated against — where they have an "equal educational opportunity," regardless of the amount of compensatory educational input or quota of school interracial mixing. The school, by its nature and function, is a middle-class, white-oriented institution because it reflects the dominant culture. Regardless of their race, most teachers, because of the level of their education and income, tend to adopt and mirror middle-class white values. Similarly, achievement and IQ tests, school texts and curriculum objectives still reflect a middle-class, "fair-skinned" world — despite our notions about (nonexistent) culture-free tests, token-integrated primers, and token-black history courses.

All our schemes about reorganizing the schools and redistributing power (say, through integration, decentralization or local control) will unlikely change the schooling process: bright students will be siphoned off from slow students; the former will continue to be awarded gold stars while the latter receive demerits. Unless society reforms, which is unlikely in the near future, a large percentage of poor and minority-group students, because of their handicapped environment, will continue to come to school educationally disadvantaged, and unless curtailed by viable compensatory programs and quality teaching practices (however, both of these types of programs and practices seem scarce), these disadvantages will most likely continue to snowball as these students are passed from grade to grade.

For purposes of school achievement, it does little good for the student not to possess adequate cognitive skills, but instead other skills and "positive" strengths, or a different culture — unless the schools change. Granted, the middle-class, white student may reject school and society; but, when all the other variables are considered (although we may not all agree on a specific list), he has more of an equal chance than the poor and/or minority-group student for eventually obtaining the "proper" credential — a college degree — and becoming a part of the very power structure and society he may condemn. He may decide to accept or reject the myth of the dominant culture, but at least he has this choice.

Thus our concern should be realistically directed toward those students who seem destined to drop out of school or to graduate as functional illiterates. Although I may be accused of stereotyping, I contend that American low-income and minority-group children and youth are more prone to fall into the schools' ignorant wasteland — of becoming educationally disadvantaged. While some readers might feel the pendulum of discussion has made a complete cycle and has returned to the traditional school of thought, a difference should be noted: whereas, the traditional school blames the student for his school failure, the author is saying that the school is at fault, too.

REFERENCES

Bettelheim, B. The problems of generations. *Daedalus*, 1962, 91, 68–69.
Bird, C. & Briller, S. W. *Born Female*. New York: McKay, 1970.
Clift, V. A. Curriculum strategy based on the personality characterisitcs of disadvantaged youth. *J. Negro Ed.*, 1969, 38, 94-104.
Cohen, A. *Delinquent Boys*. Glencoe, Ill.: Glencoe Free Press, 1960.
Coleman, J. S. *Adolescents and the Schools*. New York: Basic Books, 1965.
Coles, R. The poor don't want to be middle class. *New York Times Magazine*, Dec. 19, 1965, 7, ff.
_____. *Uprooted Children*. Pittsburgh: Univ. of Pittsburgh Press, 1970.
Dennison, G. *The Lives of Children*. New York: Random House, 1969.
Dodson, D. W. Suburbanism and education. *J. ed. Sociology*, 1958, 32, 2–7.
_____. The uncivilized right to revolt. Unpublished manuscript, 1968.
Eisenberg, L. Strengths of the inner city child. *Baltimore Bull. Ed.*, 1963–64, 41, 10–16.
Erikson, E. H. *Identity, Youth and Crisis*. New York: Norton, 1968.
Fantini, M. D. & Weinstein, G. *The Disadvantaged*. New York: Harper & Row, 1968.
Firestone, S. *Dialectic of Sex*. New York: Morrow, 1970.
Fisher, M. B. & Noble, J. *College Education as Personal Development*. Englewood Cliffs, N. J.: Prentice-Hall, 1960.
Friedenberg, E. Z. *The Vanishing Adolescent*. (Paper ed.) New York: Dell, 1962 (originally published in 1959).

————. *Coming of Age in America.* New York: Random House, 1965.

————. *The Dignity of Youth and Other Atavisms.* Boston: Beacon Press, 1966.

Gans, H. *The Urban Villager.* New York: Free Press, 1962.

Getzels, J. W. & Jackson, P. W. *Creativity and Intelligence,* New York: Wiley, 1962.

Goldman, H. The schools and the disadvantaged. In H. Goldman (Ed.), *Education and the Disadvantaged,* Milwaukee: Univ. of Wisconsin, Aug. 1967, 111-126.

Goodman, P. *Growing Up Absurd.* New York: Random House, 1960.

————. *Compulsory Mis-education.* New York: Horizon, 1964.

————. *New Reformation.* New York: Random House, 1970.

Gross, R. & Gross, B. (Eds.), *Radical School Reform.* New York: Simon & Schuster, 1969.

Harrington, M. *The Other America.* New York: Macmillan, 1963.

Havighurst, R. J. Who are the socially disadvantaged? *J. Negro Ed.*, 1964, 33, 210–217.

————. Minority subcultures and the law of effect. *Am. Psychologist,* 1970, 25, 313–322.

Havighurst, R. J. et al. *Growing Up in River City.* New York: Wiley, 1962.

Henry J. Docility, or giving teacher what she wants. *J. soc. Issues,* 1955, 11, 33–41.

————. *Culture Against Man.* New York: Random House, 1963.

Hickerson, N. *Education for Alienation.* Englewood Cliffs, N. J.: Prentice-Hall, 1966.

Hollingshead, A. B. *Elmstown Youth.* New York: Wiley, 1949.

Holt, J. *How Children Fail.* New York: Pitman, 1964.

————. *How Children Learn.* New York: Pitman, 1967.

————. *The Underachieving School.* New York: Pitman, 1969.

————. *What Do We Do on Monday?* New York: Dutton, 1970.

Kelley, E. C. *In Defense of Youth.* Englewood Cliffs, N. J.: Prentice-Hall, 1962.

Keniston, K. *The Uncommitted.* New York: Harcourt, Brace & World, 1965.

————. *Young Radicals.* New York: Harcourt, 1968.

Lewis, O. *Children of Sanchez.* New York: Random House, 1961.

————. Culture of poverty. *Scientific American.* 1966. 215, 19–25 (a).

————. *La Vida.* New York: Random House, 1966 (b).

————. *Study of Slum Culture.* New York: Random House, 1968.

Mayer, M. *The Schools.* New York: Harper & Row, 1961.

McCabe, J. (Ed.). *Dialogue on Youth.* Indianapolis: Bobbs-Merrill, 1967.

McCreary, E. Some positive characteristics of disadvantaged learners and their implications for education. In S. W. Webster (Ed.), *The Disadvantaged Learner.* San Francisco: Chandler, 1966, 47–52.

Meyer, J. A. Suburbia: A wasteland of disadvantaged youth and negligent schools? *Phi Delta Kappan,* 1969, 50, 575–578.

Miel, A. *Children of Suburbia.* New York: Human Relations, 1967.

Millet, K. *Sexual Politics.* New York: Doubleday, 1970.

Neill, A. S. *Summerhill.* New York: Hart, 1960.

O'Reilly, J. Notes on the new paralysis. *New York,* Oct. 26, 1970, 28–36.

Ornstein, A. C. On high school violence: The teacher-student role. *J. sec. Ed.,* 1970, 45, 99–105.

————. On high school violence: Anomic and alienated student. *J. sec. Ed.,* 1971, 46, 9–15.

Padilla, E. *Up from Puerto Rico.* New York: Columbia Univ. Press, 1958.

Riessman, F., *The Culturally Deprived Child.* New York: Harper & Row, 1962.

————. Overlooked positives of disadvantaged groups. *J. Negro Ed.,* 1964, 33, 225–231.

————. *Helping the Disadvantaged Pupil to Learn More Easily.* Englewood Cliffs, N. J.: Prentice-Hall, 1966.

Schrag, P. Growing up on Mechanic Street. *Saturday Rev.,* Mar. 21, 1970, 59–61, ff.

Sexton, P. C. *The Feminized Male.* New York: Random House, 1969.

Taylor, C. W. *Creativity*. New York: McGraw-Hill, 1964.

Torrance, E. P. *Gifted Children in the Classroom*. New York: Macmillan, 1965.

_____. *Encouraging Creativity in the Classroom*. Dubuque: W. C. Brown, 1970.

Wallach, M. A. & Kogan, N. *Modes of Thinking in Young Children*. New York: Holt, Rinehart & Winston, 1965.

_____. Creativity and intelligence in children's thinking. *Trans-action*, 1967, 4, 38–44.

Warner, W. L., Havighurst, R. J. & Loeb, M. B. *Who Shall Be Educated?* New York: Harper & Row, 1944.

Whyte, W. F. *Street Corner Society*. Chicago: University of Chicago Press, 1943.

EDGAR Z. FRIEDENBERG

The Gifted Student
and His Enemies

ONE OF THE MOST HEAVILY EMPHASIZED THEMES IN CURRENT DIS-
cussions of education in the United States is the search for potential
excellence. In the past we have tended to equate academic promise with
high intelligence, and to infer that the most serious wastage of young
people in school resulted from the school's failure to recognize and
reward high academic aptitude in lower-status youngsters. The search for
excellence, on these terms, became an extension of the traditional American quest for equality of opportunity, which served as its moral justification. But this defines the issue far too narrowly. Of perhaps more fundamental importance is the effect of the school on kinds of giftedness that
may be useless or even disadvantageous in earning good grades and high
recommendations in a typical high school milieu. High IQ and diligence
do not exhaust the possibilities of superior capacity. Originality and
insight, disciplined but impassioned sensitivity, and a highly personal
and unique quality of mind contribute as indispensably to human
achievement.

In the school, as in much of our society, creative youngsters seem
usually to arouse a specific animus. Teachers dislike them, and the students learn quite early that the spontaneity and subjectivity they prize in
themselves cannot be expected to lead to success in school or in later life.

Edgar Z. Friedenberg, "The Gifted Student and His Enemies." *Commentary*,
33, 1962, 36–44. Reprinted from *Commentary*, by permission; copyright © 1962
by the American Jewish Committee.

What is the source of the animus, and why is the creative student so likely to encounter it? Particularly useful in answering these questions is a concept which, though explicitly introduced by Friedrich Nietzsche, has only recently had much impact on American social thought. This is the concept of *Ressentiment*.[1] The word sounds like a French translation of "resentment," and this does approximate the meaning. But only imprecisely. *Ressentiment* is less completely conscious than resentment, and less focused on the particular real experiences that are its actual causes. In contrast, it is usually rationalized, covert, diffuse, and largely unconscious. Just as one may legitimately refer to "free-floating anxiety" as a decisive element in certain kinds of personality, *ressentiment* is a kind of free-floating ill-temper. It is the syndrome produced by intense hostility intensely repressed over long periods of time. As such, it is familiar enough. Why then is it worth discussing as a *social*, rather than a psychological, disorder? Because of the peculiar and devastating ways in which *ressentiment* has become institutionalized in twentieth-century mass culture.

The conditions of contemporary life have reified *ressentiment* into a massive social and political reality. The operation of democratic political institutions — and especially their underlying egalitarian value assumptions — has greatly increased the political influence of the most *ressentient* social groups while weakening the will of more affirmative individuals to resist them.

Public education is one of the social institutions most strongly affected by *ressentiment*. The public schools attract, as teachers, administrators, and counselors, individuals from groups in the population that are particularly subject to it, and for reasons which are likely to influence the selection of the more *ressentient* from among such groups. The school is the traditional avenue — and arena — for social mobility, which many of its clientele appear to conceive as its sole *raison d'être*; one goes to school in order to get ahead, or one drops out; few youngsters are held in school by any real commitment to the cultural values represented by education, and few public schools in fact represent those values adequately. But those who are most anxious about social mobility are also most likely to be *ressentient*.

Those social groups are most prone to *ressentiment* whose members are especially subjected to frustration in their position in life, but who feel so impotent that they do not dare to get consciously angry and rebel and hit back, or strike out for themselves against the actual source of their frustration. Generally, they dare not even recognize it. Instead they identify with and accommodate to the very individuals or social forces undermining their position, and whose strength they tend to admire and exaggerate. By thus exercising their impotence, they increase it; what a less threatened individual would have felt as rage becomes resentment, then a kind of small-shopkeeper's fearful and self-pitying distrust, and finally, perhaps, merely an unconscious predisposition to sanctimonious spitefulness.

Ressentiment therefore ravages most seriously the rootless lower-middle or white-collar classes who give up most in order to be respectable and get least real deference and security in return. The threat to them is much more serious now that Western life permits its lower-level personnel to develop so few real skills. Yet, they cannot attack the system that has made their lives meaningless, for they are in collusion with it and want to rise within it.

It is not merely the economic threat that leads to *ressentiment*, for *ressentiment* is not simply anxiety. The *ressentient*, rather, are those who have given up important human potentialities in making deals with the system, and are now faced with mounting evidence that this is not going to pay off. Thus the German inflation of the twenties, wiping out the savings of millions of petty bourgeois who for a lifetime had slaved to confuse thrift and order with decency, helped pave the way to Nazism, which epitomized *ressentiment* in its Eichmannesque combination of sadism and alienation. The essence of the Nazi position, after all, is that its motives were worthy of the highest traditions of the civil service; one likes to think that the executioners of Joan of Arc, by comparison, at least felt that there was something cheerful about a nice fire. Even hatred is too strong an emotion for the highly authoritarian, who can handle feeling only by bureaucratizing it, so that it emerges as prejudice against classes of individuals rather than open hostility. Good authoritarians never get personal.

But the rigidity, hostility, and alienation that reveal the authoritarian personality in face-to-face relationships are not peculiar to adherents of the political far right. In the presence of the doctrinaire young liberal, the professional Negro or Zionist, the militant opponent of atomic warfare, one often senses the existence of the same animus however strongly one may agree with their views. It does not seem to matter very much — it does matter somewhat — whether humanitarian issues are themselves a central part of the ideology. The aggressively poor young college instructor, flaunting his radical views, minority status, and undisciplined children as explanations of his lack of recognition and status, is no fascist. But he does seem to run on the same fuel. Such a person, feeling helpless to begin with, becomes frightened lest his resentment provoke further punishment, and rationalizes it as a more positive emotion: Christian love, the desire to protect the weak, or to secure social justice. All these are perfectly real emotions that may and do arise as spontaneous responses to real human experiences. It is perfectly possible to wish, through love or compassion, to help a suffering fellow being, whether the cause of his misery be poverty, disease, sheer misfortune, or any combination of evils. It is likewise possible to be moved by his plight to genuine and fierce anger at the persons or circumstances that have brought it about, and to commit oneself wholeheartedly to fight the good fight on his behalf. But this is a very different attitude, and expresses a very different character, from that represented by *ressentiment* — which prizes the victim *because* he is a victim, and loves the suffering while covertly exploiting the sufferer.

No one has expressed this difference more clearly, or evaluated it more precisely, than Thoreau in the following passage from *Walden:*

> I would not subtract anything from the praise that is due to philanthropy, but merely demand justice for all who by their lives and works are a blessing to mankind . . . I want the flower and fruit of a man; that some fragrance be wafted over from him to me, and some ripeness flavour our intercourse. His goodness must not be a partial and transitory act, but a constant superfluity, which costs him nothing and of which he is unconscious. This is a charity that hides a multitude of sins. The philanthropist too often surrounds mankind with the remembrance of his own castoff griefs as an atmosphere, and calls it sympathy. We should impart our courage, and not our despair, our health and ease, and not our disease, and take care that this does not spread by contagion. From what southern plains comes up the voice of wailing? Under what latitudes reside the heathen to whom we would send light? Who is that intemperate and brutal man whom we would redeem? . . .
>
> I believe that what so saddens the reformer is not his sympathy with his fellows in distress, but, though he be the holiest son of God, his private ail. Let this be righted, let the spring come to him, the morning rise over his couch, and he will forsake his generous companions without apology. . . . There is nowhere recorded a simple and irrepressible satisfaction with the gift of life, any memorable praise of God. . . . All health and success does me good, however far off and withdrawn it may appear; all disease and failure helps to make me sad and does me evil, however much sympathy it may have with me or I with it. . . . Do not stay to be an overseer of the poor, but endeavour to become one of the worthies of the world.

In the contemporary American high school, *ressentiment* is much more effectively institutionalized in its "philanthropic" than in its authoritarian form. Individual teachers and administrators representing either tendency are common, but one way of expressing a major change in the climate of American education over the past half-century is by saying that authoritarianism has been placed in a thoroughly defensive position, while the "philanthropic" attitude has become dominant.[2]

Teachers and administrative officials of schools come primarily from lower-middle-class backgrounds. Many come from families of somewhat higher status, but the folkways of the schools are lower-middle-class folkways: the official language, the customs and regulations governing dress— even the food in the school cafeteria. All these tend to be shabby-genteel. They are not forthright expressions of the actual limitations of the schools' financial, intellectual, and social resources, such as peasant life and art express, but cheap reproductions of corporate or academic life, as imperfectly conceived. Schoolteachers by and large have likewise notably resisted, even more than most white-collar workers, identifying with the working class in their own financial interests, as by unionization. One may, of course, dislike joining a union and refuse to do so on a variety of grounds from social ideology to personal taste. But the actual circumstances of the public school teacher's background and vocational life make union membership a promising device for achieving his legitimate economic aspirations. The difficulty seems to be that teachers' economic aspirations are regularly subordinated by their middle-class identifications. Unionization is inconsistent with their insistence that they practice a profession. Fully established professions, like medicine and law, have of course evolved militant organizations to advance and safeguard their economic interests, though these are not called unions. But teachers have not so far created any organization suited to the purpose of direct economic action on their behalf.[3] The life-style of the public high-school teacher remains, characteristically, that of the dutiful subordinate awaiting preferment in a niggardly bureaucratic structure.

Such a life is the very breeding ground of *ressentiment*. The teacher is linked to his principal, his superintendent, and his peers by a pretense of professional equality that prevents him from either demanding the perquisites of status or the liberty to scoff at it. Within a bureaucratic structure in which one depends not merely for advancement but for personal gratification as well on the endorsement of one's peers and subordinates, open conflict generates intolerable anxiety. Frustration and anger degenerate into malicious gossip, and are absorbed into the general ambience of wariness and cynicism. Ultimately, the consequence is alienation; in such people there is no longer direct connection between their actual experiences, their feelings, and their actions.

Nothing about this is peculiar to the career of teachers in contemporary America; this is rather the familiar catalogue of complaint about life in the organized system. *Ressentiment* probably is less prominent among teachers than among many social groups like waiters or cab drivers, whose work keeps them in constant contact with people visibly enjoying a higher standard of life than they can achieve in a culture that makes it impossible to take pride in performing personal service well — or like social workers, whose "philanthropic" enterprise puts them in a position of unparalleled opportunity to intervene in the lives of other people whose poverty and tendency to act out conflicts make them both particularly tempting and particularly vulnerable to the *ressentient*. And there are many other social groups in which *ressentiment* has become institutionalized under somewhat different conditions: yellow journalism and the pornography of violence, for example. But there are further reasons that are peculiar to the education establishment why the public high school should be the locus of strong *ressentiment*.

The official function of the schoolteacher is still defined in academic and intellectual terms, however irrelevant the definition may be to the daily work a teacher in a slum school actually does. And in academic and intellectual terms, the public secondary school teacher is inferior. This, moreover, is a fact he must consciously face. The elementary school teacher can avoid facing it — if indeed it is a relevant judgment to apply to her — because she is not graded in her professional training in direct competition with people who are going into other work. In other words, she is likely to be — in many states she virtually has to be — an "ed major." High school teachers are not; they are math majors or English majors or history majors and, generally speaking, they are the ones who made poorer grades than those who head into industry, the professions, or higher education on the basis of their specialized study. In graduate school such direct comparisons are again inapplicable, but the norms for graduate students in education on standardized intelligence tests (like the Miller Analogies) are substantially lower than those for graduate students in other academic disciplines.

Students are forced into secondary school teaching because they are not able to make the grade in a specialized or scholarly discipline. Finding themselves comparatively impotent academically, they are unwilling to relinquish respectable intellectual pretensions altogether, and settle for something that, in their own view, is decidedly second-rate. It is perfectly possible, of course, to define the function of a high school teacher as an honorable and extremely significant specialty in its own right; and it is also perfectly possible that, if it were so defined, it would have a rather low correlation with conventional academic and intellectual achievement. If high school teaching *were* so defined, the people who go into it would not have a sense of partial failure, and there would be no reason for their academic situation to lead to *ressentiment*. Certainly, neither the early-childhood nor the primary grade school teacher seems so prone to it. The public image of such a teacher as a constricted and punitive spinster has disappeared — though, as usual, more slowly than the reality — to be replaced by the image of the young woman who thinks of herself as, and very often really is, a professional emissary to the private world of childhood. She may not be especially scholarly or analytical-minded, but she knows her job and does it well. The children know that she does; and there is a good deal of mutual respect and affection. Jules Henry's observations in *Culture Against Man*[4] suggest I may be a little fatuous about this.

In the later grades and in junior high and high schools the situation is much worse.[5] Subject matter has begun to matter, and so has the fact that the teacher is often incompetent to handle it. There is more to this incompetence than relative ignorance or stupidity. There is also the fact that the school has begun to deal with controversial content and controversial purposes. High school civics, social studies, and biology courses are no place for people who do not know their history, economics, or biology. But they are also not the place for timid or insecure people, for people who are especially anxious to make a good impression on the community or to keep out of trouble. These are, of course, exactly the kinds of people that a principal or superintendent who is timid or insecure himself will try to keep there.

Again, in this context, the feeble persistence of identification with academic norms contributes to the high school teacher's *ressentiment*. The identification is not strong enough to make him a hero.[6] But it is strong enough to make him ashamed of himself, and to add to his feeling of impotence. His impotence is real enough; he generally just does not *know* enough to defend an unpopular position on scholarly grounds even if he had the courage. But until he abandons the professional stance, or ceases to link it to academic competence, he cannot accept himself as a part of the local propaganda apparatus either. The statement "You shall know the truth, and the truth shall make you free" is quite false; knowledge can be a dreadful burden. But like pregnancy, knowledge to a teacher is a form of commitment no longer subject to voluntary abridgment without a sense of catastrophic guilt, and to have only a little is no help at all.

I have stated that the most serious consequence of *ressentiment* is alienation. The *ressentient* individual loses the connection between his feelings and the situation in which he is actually living. His emotions, and even his perceptions of reality, are channelled in the directions that cause least anxiety rather than toward the experiences that actually arouse them, either in the past or in the immediate present. All neurosis, of course, has this effect, but *ressentiment* is especially effective because it is the emotion itself—anger, rage, impotence, and fear of retribution—that is the source of anxiety and that must be repressed. So *ressentient* individuals are especially clumsy and insensitive, in contrast to those with other sorts of neurotic difficulty, in using their feelings to help them understand the meaning of their lives and to discipline their moral conduct. This is why they become sentimental; they prefer fake experiences that decorate the actual situation to symbolic evocations of its actuality. This kind of sentimentality has become a negative status symbol, evoking the atmosphere of lower-middle-class life as surely as a whiff of H_2S brings back freshman chemistry: the plastic flowers in the apartment house lobby, which insist that this is a place in the sun; the conventional cuteness of the mass-produced mock-hostile office signs and mock-boastful chef's aprons. The worst thing that could happen, obviously, is that a genius really should be at work.

What happens when one is—even an embryonic one? The essential quality of the creative student, as he is beginning to be defined in the literature, is that his thought is divergent. He doesn't arrive at right answers by deducing them from established premises, but by an intuitive understanding of how the problem he is dealing with really works, of what actually goes into it, and the right answers he arrives at may not be right in the textbook; they will not be, if the textbook has been carefully edited to make it as widely acceptable as possible. He works hard when the problem requires it, and respects facts as a part of reality. But for the creative student, facts are not right answers but tools and components for building original solutions.

How will the high school teacher react to this? If he is a high school teacher because the job gives him joy, and is competent intellectually, he will react with astonished delight. But to the degree that he is *ressentient,* with defensive hostility. Consider the poor mathematician, who manages to salvage enough math to become a high school teacher, or the ninth-grade teacher who hates mathematics and never meant to have any traffic with it at all. Such teachers manage by knowing a set of answers, and a conventional procedure for arriving at them. They maintain their self-esteem by convincing themselves that this is really enough; and the student who really understands mathematics puts them in a dilemma. On the one hand, he may show them up as incompetent. On the other, they don't know but that he may be cheating somehow, and laughing at them for being taken in. They dare not commit themselves either way. If they are authoritarian, they bully him into solving the problems "the way I show you as long as you are in my class." If they are "philanthropic," they respond with studied tolerance and amusement to Johnny's "attention-getting behavior." But in either case they try to make sure that he doesn't embarrass them again by actually getting up and doing mathematics in front of the whole class.

In the humanities the creative student is both more threatening and more vulnerable. He is more vulnerable because there aren't any right answers to support him. He is more threatening because the humanities, if truthfully handled, are themselves threatening to the *ressentient.* It is the job of the humanities to get to the root of human experience, which at best means hewing austere beauty out of some very ugly blocks in such a way that their real character is revealed. This is just what the alienated cannot tolerate. What happens to the adolescent boy or girl who writes a theme about an experience that had deep meaning for him—at this age it will probably be in part a sexual experience—as it really was? For that matter, how does the well-indoctrinated professional educator, suffused with the benign values underlying his course in child development and his belief in the wholesomeness of family living, handle either Medea or Salome?

The position of the social science teacher is more ambiguous. *Ressentiment* is not always such a handicap in the social sciences, which provide a superb eminence from which to look down on one's neighbors while discharging one's scholarly obligations. The convention of objectivity keeps the *ressentient* social scientist from having to face the full responsibility for his hostility and destructiveness; after all, he is just doing his job. The creative student in social studies may therefore get an additional chance. Besides the possibility common to all fields of encountering a superior, *ressentiment*-free instructor, there is the possibility in social studies of finding an instructor who does not clobber the creative even though he is *ressentient,* but identifies with their undisciplined or rebellious disjunctivity and accepts and encourages it as an expression of his own *ressentiment*—taking refuge in academic freedom and his obligation to the truth if detected.

But such teachers are inevitably rare; they are selected out in the process of teacher-training, which requires the candidate to suffer a great deal of nonsense without protest; and administrators get rid of them if they find them out in time as likely to get the school in trouble with intransigent groups in the community. The creative student is far less likely to encounter a social critic on the high school staff than he is teachers with whom he will quickly establish a mutual loathing and who are continually reminded by his freshness of perception that they have consented to devote their lives to teaching what they know to be false or irrelevant; to denying in class that the fundamental experiences of his life can even have occurred. Hundreds of high school teachers can, and do, spend several hours a day trying to teach slum children in civics courses the official syllabus on the American Way of Life. If the children are creative, the questions they raise are difficult to answer, especially after they have given up trying to ask them verbally, and express them directly through their attitudes and behavior in class. One gets used to it, in time, and learns to maintain order. But the job of an assistant warden in a custodial institution is a long step down from earlier expectations.

Overlying the special influence of *ressentiment* on instruction in the separate fields of knowledge and reinforcing its effects is the "philanthropic" ideology of the school. Students, by definition, are subordinate in status to their schoolmasters; they are in a partially dependent position, and the function of the school is to nurture them. It is appropriate that the school devote itself to their needs and attend to and utilize their interests. Its primary purpose is to serve them.

But an institution designed to nurture the relatively weak and dependent presumably does so because it cherishes their potential strength and autonomy. There would be good reason for it to value most highly those youngsters who show most intellectual vigor and originality in the disciplined handling of ideas; as, in some cultures, a father will love his strongest and most virile sons even though he fears them a little. The *ressentient*, identifying with impotence and resentful of strength, respond very differently. The school, strongly influenced by *ressentiment*, is rather inclined to cherish the weakness of the weak.

Thus one notion that even very poor students of educational sociology grasp eagerly is that schools are generally biased against lower-class students. They certainly are, and this is an important truth. But when the proposition is explored, what it seems to mean in the professional curriculum of education is that middle-class students "have advantages" which they ought to be forced to share more generously. The remedy is to insure that the lower-status students get their share of good grades, scholarships, opportunity for social leadership, and so on.

But these are still conceived almost wholly in middle-class terms. There is no corresponding respect for the lower-status child's own experience of life, his language, and the forms of social organization he spontaneously adopts. It is true enough that the school faces a difficult dilemma; lower-class behavior creates real difficulties in running a formal social organization like a school, quite apart from any question of bias; yet the bias is real and harmful. But professional education both in its curriculum and in its practice tends to respond to the bias as if the chief objection to it was that it gave the privileged too many privileges, rather than with a real, imaginative concern for the quality of life of lower-status youngsters.

This is a major reason why the bias is hard to eliminate. Its most important consequences do not occur in the schools, but in the long run.

Giving the children of Southern Negro migrants more high grades even if they don't read or do arithmetic very well is not really going to help them much in getting into medical school. What is needed is something like the original conception of progressive education, which combined an extremely flexible conception of both educational content and instructional technique with a rather rigid adherence to standards of achievement. This is *genuine* acceptance of the meaning of underprivileged life, and real help in mobilizing the youngster's real strengths to either pull himself out of it or learn to live it more richly, at his own choice. Pushed to extremes, this might mean letting the younger brother of the leader of a "retreatist" gang use the backyard marijuana plot as his project in arithmetic and biology, thus utilizing his need for status in the peer group. But what is far more important, it also means giving him an "A" if—and only if—he solves his problems of cultivation, processing, and marketing in such a way as to show high competence in arithmetic and biology—and an "F" if he lets his marijuana go to pot.

So tough-minded a philosophy has, in fact, rather less chance than marijuana itself of taking root in the emotional climate of the American public school. "Philanthropically" inverted, the "emergent" attenuation of progressive education abandons the controversial undertaking of dealing realistically with the experiences of lower-class life. Then to make up for not taking these children seriously, the school tries to equalize their position by expecting less of them. Simultaneously, it prevents them from learning what they are missing by inflating its credentials and subtly derogating the quest for distinction.

Higher-status children also are discriminated against in the public school, if they attempt to live in school as they do at home and in their social life. They do not share the lower-status youngster's difficulty in earning high grades and scholarships; and they are usually adept enough socially to dominate the extracurriculum despite the attempts of the school to democratize it, especially if such attempts are enfeebled by the school administration's fear of parents' possible political influence. So the discrimination higher-status youngsters encounter is not comparable in kind to that experienced by the lower-status pupils. But as indications of *ressentiment,* the forms it takes are significant, and are especially likely to stultify creativity. Any mode of expression that is highly individualized, extravagant, or overtly sensual is forbidden or discouraged. It is assumed that it is better for the school dance to be one that everyone can afford than one with an especially good band and refreshments; that boys and girls whom nature has provided, for the time being, with especially splendid bodies ought not to be allowed to dress in such a way as to derive any special advantage from them; that the illumination of the school grounds, if there are any, be such as to discourage courtship rather than to suggest the exquisite delights to which nature may be encouraged.

Adolescence is a time when highly individualized, extravagant, and overtly sensual modes of behavior do crop out, despite the position the school takes toward them. But by its disparagement, the school abandons its opportunity to help youngsters create a style suited to their romantic age. The essential first step in encouraging creativity in secondary school youngsters is surely to link their new sexual energy and their occasionally flamboyant quest for identity to meaningful larger aspects of present and past culture, which is what taste means and disciplined self-expression requires. If the baroque manifestations of adolescence instead elicit an attitude of sulky oppression, the adolescents are thrown back onto resources they have not yet developed. The twist may then be as far as they can get by themselves in the face of official disapproval. Moreover, the ideology of the school grudgingly supports the numerous *ressentient*, lower-middle-class youth against the more creative within the youth-culture itself. The school thereby tips the balance in favor of the "teen-age" solution to the problem of adolescence, quietly maintaining support for the unassuming, undiscriminating boy or girl who sees things the way other sensible people do and with other "teen-agers" builds a conventional social group, accepting conventional discipline for occasional stereotyped "teen-age" misbehavior within it. The youngster who is most handicapped by this situation is not the delinquent or the rebel, for both of these are conventional adolescent roles in their own way which society endorses by punishment. It is the innovator who sees things freshly and differently. One does not punish this youngster formally; for to do this would be to admit that he was there and that what he had said was intelligible. Instead, one isolates him by denying him the customary sources of status—that is, recognition for his work and point of view. Then one helps him—helps him to become assimilated within the "teen-age" group. In a little while, it is as if he had never been.

The "philanthropic" refusal to allow excellence to get above itself is not limited to areas, like the fine arts, toward which lower-middle-class American culture is generally hostile or suspicious. Within the school even those forms of distinction that are commonly supported within this culture are treated ambiguously. I suspect *ressentiment* is one factor in the continued, and now apparently rising, complaint about overemphasis on athletics in the school. There is a substantial basis for the complaint in many schools, for athletics is sometimes the only activity that is taken seriously at all. But conversely, athletics is sometimes the only activity that is at all serious, and in which any distinction of style or achievement is permitted or recognized. The clue to whether *ressentiment* is at the root of the complaint lies in the terms in which it is couched. Complaints that the emphasis on the preoccupation with athletics interferes with specific aspects of the academic program are serious and legitimate. What are highly suspect, however, are complaints that the emphasis on athletics allows the athletes to become an elite group and gain favor and eminence unavailable to their less glamorous colleagues. Before considering such protests, one would like to be certain that the history teacher encourages a brilliant and resourceful analysis of American foreign policy with as much joy — and technical assistance — as the basketball coach does brilliant and resourceful play-making and back-court work (for these are not inherently glamorous). It is possible that students respect an elite of athletes because good athletes are encouraged to be proud of themselves for being as good as they can, and that these are the only people left on campus with anything in particular to be proud of.

Among the most important educational consequences of *ressentiment,* then, are failure to recognize the gifted, or to nurture their gifts when discovered; differential drop-out rates among students from different social classes; and fundamental difficulties in curriculum construction that vitiate earnest and costly efforts to adapt the curriculum to the needs of divergent individuals or social groups. *Ressentiment* also influences the total experience of education in ways that are so general that they can hardly even be recognized as problems: the flavor of education itself; whether students will come to think of it as opening their understanding to a wider and deeper range of experiences or as constricting and limiting their range of possible emotional and intellectual response; whether, in the long run, the school tends more to liberate than to alienate. The total social function of education is intimately involved with *ressentiment;* for the secondary school has both a cautionary and a mithridatic function. It is here that one learns to avoid the expression of noble or heroic aspirations in noble or heroic terms, so as not to destroy at the outset the chance that they may be realized. Conversely, it is here that one learns to tolerate without surrender the demands of guilt and humility; to retain, in some measure, the power to continue to enjoy privileges and personal achievements without being disconcerted by the envy they arouse. Now that the differences are neither clearly indicated nor morally defended, many Americans devote their lives to an effort to steal into the first-class compartment without awakening the tourist passengers; and the school is where one first learns how numerous and vigilant they are. The school is where you learn to be an American; and an important part of Americanism is to learn the prevailing norms and limits of achievement and self-assertion and how to maintain them against the encroachments of a mass society that the moral support of a strong egalitarian tradition has made extremely aggressive.

REFERENCES

[1]Max Scheler's *Ressentiment* (Lewis A. Coser, Ed., Free Press, 1961) is the authoritative statement and exegesis of the meaning of *ressentiment*.

[2]The shift from "traditional" to "emergent" values in the schools discussed by George P. Spindler in his classic paper, "Education in a Transforming American Culture" (*Harvard Educational Review*, Summer 1955) might be expressed with equal validity as a shift from the dominance of authoritarian to "philanthropic" modes of *ressentiment*.

[3]See Myron Lieberman, *Education as a Profession* (Prentice-Hall, 1956), especially chapters 9 and 10. A teachers' union, of course, is again very much in controversy.

[4]New York, Random House, 1963.

[5]See Martin Mayer, *The Schools* (Harper, 1961) for an excellent treatment of observations dealing with this point.

[6]Not, to be sure, that college and university people, in the social sciences at least, behaved particularly heroically under pressure. See Paul Lazarsfeld and W. Thielens, *The Academic Mind* (Free Press, 1958) for a canny account of the extent of accommodation, from widespread self-censorship to occasional outright betrayal of colleagues, that occurred during McCarthy's dreadful reign.

Students'
Rights

IF SECONDARY SCHOOL STUDENTS ARE TO BECOME CITIZENS TRAINED IN
the democratic process, they must be given every opportunity to participate in the school and in the community with rights broadly analogous
to those of adult citizens. In this basic sense, students are entitled to
freedom of expression, of assembly, of petition, and of conscience, and
to due process and equal treatment under the law. The American Civil
Liberties Union has already described how such freedoms appertain to
college students in its pamphlet on "Academic Freedom and Civil
Liberties for Students in Colleges and Universities." But the difference
in the age range between secondary school and college students suggests
the need for a greater degree of advice, counsel, and supervision by the
faculty in the high schools than is appropriate for the colleges or universities. From the standpoint of academic freedom and civil liberties, an
essential problem in the secondary schools is how best to maintain and
encourage freedom of expression and assembly while simultaneously
inculcating a sense of responsibility and good citizenship with awareness
of the excesses into which the immaturity of the students might lead.

It is the responsibility of faculty and administration to decide when a
situation requires a limit on freedom for the purpose of protecting the

American Civil Liberties Union. *Academic Freedom in the Secondary Schools*,
2nd ed. New York: American Civil Liberties Union, 1971, 9–20. Reprinted by
permission.

students and the school from harsh consequences. In exercising that responsibility, certain fundamental principles should be accepted in order to prevent the use of administrative discretion to eliminate legitimate controversy and legitimate freedom. The principles are:

(1) A recognition that freedom implies the right to make mistakes and that students must therefore sometimes be permitted to act in ways which are predictably unwise so long as the consequences of their acts are not dangerous to life and property, and do not seriously disrupt the academic process.

(2) A recognition that students in their schools should have the right to live under the principle of "rule by law" as opposed to "rule by personality." To protect this right, rules and regulations should be in writing. Students have the right to know the extent and limits of the faculty's authority and, therefore, the powers that are reserved for the students and the responsibilities that they should accept. Their rights should not be compromised by faculty members who while ostensibly acting as consultants or counsellors are, in fact, exercising authority to censor student expression and inquiry.

(3) A recognition that deviation from the opinions and standards deemed desirable by the faculty is not *ipso facto* a danger to the educational process.

FREEDOM OF EXPRESSION
AND COMMUNICATION

Primary liberties in a student's life have to do with the processes of inquiry and of learning, of acquiring and imparting knowledge, of exchanging ideas. There must be no interference in the school with his access to, or expression of, controversial points of view. No student should suffer any hurt or penalty for any idea he expresses in the course of participation in class or school activities.

The right of every student to have access to varied points of view, to confront and study controversial issues, to be treated without prejudice or penalty for what he reads or writes, and to have facilities for learning available in the school library and the classroom may not be derogated or denied.

1. Learning Materials

Toward these ends policies should be adopted in writing establishing solely educational criteria for the selection and purchase of class and library materials including books, magazines, pamphlets, films, records, tapes and other media. These policies should provide principles and procedures for the selection of materials and for the handling of complaints and grievances about these materials.

The removal from the school library or the banning of material alleged to be improper imposes a grave responsibility. It should be exercised, if at all, with the utmost of circumspection and only in accordance with carefully established and publicly promulgated procedures.

2. Forums

Generally speaking, students have the right to express publicly and to hear any opinion on any subject which they believe is worthy of consideration. Assemblies and extra-curricular organizations are the more obvious, appropriate forums for the oral exchange of ideas and offer the opportunity for students to hear views on topics of relatively specialized interest. Whatever the forum, the faculty should defend the right of students to hear and participate in discussions of controversial issues. Restrictions may be tolerated only when they are employed to forestall events which would clearly endanger the health or safety of members of the school community or clearly and imminently disrupt the educational process. Education, it may be noted, should enable individuals to react to ideas, however distasteful, in rational and constructive ways.

The education of young people to participate in public presentations of opinions and to choose wisely among those that are offered suggests that they help plan assembly programs. The students should have the responsibility for planning other forums, especially those offered by extracurricular organizations: for selecting the topics, choosing the speakers, and determining the method of presentation.

Students may choose speakers from their own ranks, from the faculty, and from outside the school. The community at large may provide speakers who have knowledge and insights that might not otherwise be available to students; it may introduce to the school persons whose presence enriches the educational experience. Controversies that are sometimes involved in inviting outside speakers should not deter faculty advisors from encouraging their presence at school.

Every student has the right to state freely his own views when he participates in a discussion program. Faculty members may advise the students on such matters as the style, appropriateness to the occasion, and the length of their presentations and on the avoidance of slander, but they must not censor the expression of ideas. To foster the free expression of opinions, students participating on panels should have wide latitude to state the differences in their views. For the same reason, questions from members of student audiences are ordinarily desirable and should be encouraged by arranging question periods of reasonable length at the end of talks.

3. Student Publications

The preparation and publication of newspapers and magazines is an exercise in freedom of the press. Generally speaking, students should be permitted and encouraged to join together to produce such publications as they wish. Faculty advisors should serve as consultants on style, grammar, format and suitability of the materials. Neither the faculty advisors nor the principal should prohibit the publication or distribution of material except when such publication or distribution would clearly endanger the health or safety of the students, or clearly and imminently threaten to disrupt the educational process, or might be of a libelous nature. Such judgment, however, should never be exercised because of disapproval or disagreement with the article in question.

The school administration and faculty should ensure that students and faculty may have their views represented in the columns of the school newspaper. Where feasible, they should permit the publication of multiple and competing periodicals. These might be produced by the student government, by various clubs, by a class or group of classes, or by individuals banded together for this specific purpose. The material and equipment for publication such as duplicating machines, paper and ink should be available to students in such quantity as budget may permit.

The freedom to express one's opinion goes hand in hand with the responsibility for the published statement. The onus of decision as to the content of a publication should be placed clearly on the student editorial board of the particular publication. The editors should be encouraged through practice, to learn to judge literary value, newsworthiness, and propriety.

The right to offer copies of their work to fellow students should be accorded equally to those who have received school aid, and to those whose publications have relied on their own resources.

The student press should be considered a learning device. Its pages should not be looked upon as an official image of the school, always required to present a polished appearance to the extramural world. Learning effectively proceeds through trial and error, and as much or more may sometimes be gained from reactions to a poor article or a tasteless publication as from the traditional pieces, groomed carefully for external inspection.

4. School Communications

Guarantees of free expression should be extended also to other media of communication: the public address system, closed-circuit television, bulletin boards, handbills, personal contact. Reasonable access should be afforded to student groups for announcements and statements to the school community. This should include the provision of space, both indoor and outdoor, for meetings and rallies.

The school community, i.e., the administration, faculty and the student organization, has the right to make reasonable regulations as to manner, place and time of using these communication media.

The electronic media are monopolistic by nature, and their audiences are captive. When these are used as vehicles for the presentation of opinions, the guarantees and procedures applied to school assemblies should similarly be invoked with respect to choice of topics, balance of participants and freedom of expression.

5. Restrictions on Political Thought

Not only should the student be guaranteed freedom to inquire and to express his thoughts while in the school; he should also be assured that he will be free from coercion or improper disclosure which may have ill effects on his career.

a. Loyalty oaths. Loyalty oaths are, by their inherent nature, a denial of the basic premises of American democracy. Whether imposed by the school itself, or by an external political authority, oaths required as a condition for enrollment, promotion, graduation, or for financial aid, violate the basic freedoms guaranteed to every individual by the Bill of Rights.

b. Inquiries by outside agencies. The solicitation by prospective private, governmental or other outside agencies or persons of information about students is a practice in which there are inherent dangers to academic freedom. To answer questions on a student's character, reliability, conduct, and academic performance is part of the school's responsibility. But questions about a student's values and opinions may be deemed invasions of educational privacy and impingements on academic freedom. A teacher's ability to resist such invasions of privacy will be strengthened if the school proscribes the recording of student opinions and adopts policies on responding to outsiders' questions that safeguard academic freedom.

Even in schools that have adopted policies to prevent the recording and disclosure of individuals' beliefs, there will be times when the teacher has to rely on his own judgment in deciding to reply or not to reply to questions about students. Both educational and personal liberty considerations should help guide the faculty member faced with inquiries that may invite the disclosure of religious, political, social, and other opinions and beliefs. Education often calls for probing, hypothesizing, and thinking out loud. Reports to persons outside the school on students' opinions therefore threaten the learning process. Moreover, an atmosphere conducive to an understanding of freedom and of the need for an interplay of ideas in a free society will hardly prevail if teachers report to outsiders on opinions expressed by their students.

The opinions and beliefs of secondary school students, although often stated with great enthusiasm, are highly subject to change. Many youths have great eagerness, exuberance, idealism, and propensity for adventure, but limited experience. The community, its laws, its parents, and the schools themselves therefore recognize that students are not as accountable for their actions as adults. Consistent with this attitude, schools should understand this difference and refrain from answering questions about students' beliefs.

6. Freedom of Religion and Conscience

All students are entitled to the First Amendment guarantees of the right to practice their own religion or no religion. Under the terms of the amendment, as repeatedly interpreted by the Supreme Court, any federal, state, or local law or practice is unconstitutional if it has the effect of extending to religion the mantle of public sponsorship, either through declaration of public policy or use of public funds or facilities.

Students' rights in this area are protected by judicial decisions which have found the following practices unconstitutional:

a. The recitation of any form of prayer as a group exercise,
b. The reading of the Bible as a form of worship; mandatory Bible instruction; use of schools for Bible distribution,
c. Sectarian holiday observances,
d. The showing of religious movies in class or assembly exercises,
e. The use of public school facilities for religious instruction, either within school hours or for after-school classes, whether by church or lay groups.

The teaching of religion should be distinguished from teaching factually about religion as, for example, an aspect of world history or of social sciences. Even in teaching about religion, the younger the child, the more wary the teacher must be of indoctrination. Certainly, public schools may explain the meaning of a religious holiday, as viewed by adherents of the religion of which it is a part, but may not seek to foster a religious view in the classroom or otherwise.

Although a salute to the flag and oath of allegiance are commonly accepted practices in school assembly exercises, exemptions should be granted to a student whose religious scruples or other principled convictions lead him to refuse to participate in such exercises. The Supreme Court has held that the protection of freedom of religion under the First Amendment encompasses such exemption on grounds of religious belief. There should be no distinction in this respect between student objection based on religious conviction and that based on non-religious grounds of conscience.

FREEDOM OF ASSOCIATION

The right to individual free expression implies in a democracy the right to associate for the exchange of opinion or the statement of ideas held in common.

1. Extracurricular Activities

Students should be free to organize associations within the school for political, social, athletic, and other proper and lawful purposes, provided that no such group denies membership to any student because of race, religion or nationality, or for any reasons other than those related to the purpose of the organization (i.e., a French club requirement for competence in French). The fact of affiliation with any extramural association should not in itself bar a group from recognition, but disclosure of such fact may be required. Any group which plans political action or discussion, of whatever purpose or complexion and whether or not affiliated with a particular legal party, should be allowed to organize and be recognized in any educational institution. The administration should not discriminate against a student because of membership in any such organization.

Student organizations are entitled to faculty advisors of their own selection. If no volunteer is available, a faculty member should be assigned to provide the required supervision, in order that the organization may exercise its right to function in the school.

The use of rooms and other facilities should be made available, as far as their primary use for instructional purposes permits, to recognized student organizations. Bulletin boards and access to school-wide communications systems should be provided for the use of student organizations, and they should be permitted to circulate notices and leaflets. The legitimate power of school authorities to safeguard school property should not be misused to suppress a poster or piece of literature by reason of objections to its content.

The nature and type of programs, projects and procedures of any student organization should be within the province of student decision, subject only to emergency ban by student government or principal in the event that a proposed activity clearly threatens the health and safety of the students, or clearly and immediately threatens to disrupt the educational process. Such a ban should not become permanent unless its justification is established through open hearings and argument.

A student organization should be permitted to use the name of the school as part of its own name, and to use this name in all activities consistent with its constitution. The school may adopt such regulations as will prevent any student organization from representing overtly or by inference that its views are sanctioned by the school. Restrictions may fairly be placed on the use of the school name in extramural activities (such as participation in public demonstrations or parades), but any such restrictions should be without discrimination in respect to all student organizations.

The administration and the faculty should not discriminate against any student because of his membership or participation in the activities of any extracurricular student association.

2. Out-of-School Activities

The school has no jurisdiction over its students' non-school activities, their conduct, their movements, their dress and the expression of their ideas. No disciplinary action should be taken by the school against a student for participation in such out-of-school activities as political parties and campaigns, picketing and public demonstrations, circulation of leaflets and petitions, provided the student does not claim without authorization to speak or act as a representative of the school or one of its organizations. When a student chooses to participate in out-of-school activities that result in police action, it is an infringement of his liberty for the school to punish such activity, or to enter it on school records or report it to prospective employers or other agencies, unless authorized or requested by the student. A student who violates any law risks the legal penalties prescribed by civil authorities. He should not be placed in jeopardy at school for an offense which is not concerned with the educational institution.

FREEDOM OF ASSEMBLY AND
THE RIGHT TO PETITION

The right "peaceably to assemble" is constitutionally bracketed with the right to "petition the government for a redress of grievances." Accordingly, individual students and student organizations should be permitted to hold meetings in school rooms or auditoriums, or at outdoor locations on school grounds, at which they should be free to discuss, pass resolutions, and take other lawful action respecting any matter which directly or indirectly concerns or affects them, whether it relates to school or to the extramural world. Nor should such assemblages be limited to the form of audience meetings; any variety of demonstration, whether it be a picketline, a "walk," or any other *peaceful* type, should be permissible. The school administration is justified in requiring that demonstrations or meetings be held at times that will not disrupt classes or other school activities and in places where there will be no hazards to persons or property; it also may require advance notice when necessary to avoid conflicts and to arrange for proper protection by faculty or police.

The right to distribute printed material, whether produced within or outside the school, should always be recognized, subject only to limitations designed to prevent littering, except when such distribution would clearly endanger the health or safety of the students, or clearly and imminently threaten to disrupt the educational process, or might be of a libelous nature. But the administration may require that the distributor be a student enrolled in the school.

In general, subject only to reasonable restrictions of time and place, students should be free also to collect signatures on petitions concerning either school or out-of-school issues. Neither the administration nor the faculty should have the right to screen either the contents or the wording of the petitions; they should receive them when presented and give their fullest consideration to the proposals therein.

Similarly, the wearing of buttons or badges, armbands or insignia bearing slogans or admonitions of any sort should generally be permitted as another form of expression.[1] No teacher or administrator should attempt to interfere with this practice on the grounds that the message may be unpopular with any students or faculty, or even with the majority of either group. The exercise of one or another of these techniques of expression may, under certain circumstances, clearly and imminently constitute a danger to peace or clearly and imminently threaten to disrupt the educational process. Such a situation might require staying action by the administration, similar to a temporary injunction, and subject to revocation if and when a hearing determines that the facts no longer warrant it.

Interference in this way with the exercise of student rights should seldom occur, and should be undertaken with the greatest reluctance and only when accompanied by careful explanation.

STUDENT GOVERNMENT

The functions and powers of student government organizations, and the manner of selection of their officers, as well as the qualifications for office, are matters to be determined as the respective school communities think desirable, but certain rights should be guaranteed within the structure of any student government, if it is to fulfill its role as an educational device for living in a democracy.

1. The organization, operation and scope of the student government should be specified in a written constitution, formulated with effective student participation.

2. The government should function with scrupulous regard for all constitutional provisions, which should be changed only by a prescribed process of amendment in which there should be effective student participation.

3. No constitutional provision, by-law or practice should permit decisions, including expenditures of student organization funds, to be made exclusively by the faculty or administration.

4. All students should have the right to vote and to hold office.

5. The statements, votes, decisions or actions of a student incident to his role in student government should be judged solely within the sphere of the school civic life, through the medium of electoral action by his peers, or through preestablished constitutional process. Full and free participation in student government should be encouraged by an understanding that neither marks, course credits, graduation, college recommendations, nor other aspects of scholastic life will ever be adversely affected as a consequence of a stand or action with which faculty or administration may disagree. Nor should such penalties ever be invoked for failure to make financial contribution in support of any school activity.

6. In respect to the selection of officers of the student organization:

    a. All students who meet the qualifications fixed by the school constitution should be permitted to be candidates. However, disqualification for a specified period from participation in extracurricular activities, including student government, might in appropriate cases be imposed as a penalty for serious or repeated infractions of school rules.

b. Candidates should be free to speak without censorship, subject only to equally enforced rules as to the time and place of their speeches.

c. All candidates should have equal opportunity to publicize their campaigns.

d. Candidates should be permitted to group into slates or parties, if they so desire.

e. Voting and vote-counting procedures should make provision for scrutiny by representatives of all candidates.

f. The candidate chosen by vote of the students should be declared elected, with no faculty veto.

g. Any electoral rules which may be adopted should apply equally without discrimination, to all candidates.

STUDENT DISCIPLINE

The regulations concerning appropriate student behavior in the school at large should preferably be formulated by a student-faculty committee. Regulations governing the school as a whole should be fully and clearly formulated, published, and made available to all members of the school community. They should be reasonable. Specific definitions are preferable to such general criteria as "conduct unbecoming a student" and "against the best interests of the school," which allow for a wide latitude of interpretation.

1. The Right of Due Process

To maintain the orderly administration of the school, minor infractions of school discipline may be handled in a summary fashion. In every case a student should be informed of the nature of the infraction with which he is charged. The teacher and/or administrator should bear in mind that an accusation is not the equivalent of guilt, and he should therefore be satisfied of the guilt of the accused student prior to subjecting such student to disciplinary action.

A student's locker should not be opened without his consent except in conformity with the spirit of the Fourth Amendment which requires that a warrant first be obtained on a showing of probable cause, supported by oath or affirmation, and particularly describing the things to be seized. An exception may be made in cases involving a clear danger to health or safety.

The penalties meted out for breaches of school regulations should be commensurate with the offense. They should never take the form of corporal punishment. Punishment for infractions of the code of behavior should bear no relation to courses, credits, marks, graduation or similar academic areas, except in cases where they relate to academic dishonesty.

Those infractions which may lead to more serious penalties, such as suspension or expulsion from school, or a notation on the record, require the utilization of a comprehensive and formal procedure in order to prevent a miscarriage of justice that could have serious effects on the student and his future. Such hearings should therefore be approached not in terms of meting out punishment but rather as an attempt to find the best solution for the student's needs consistent with the maintenance of order in the school.

The procedure should include a formal hearing and the right of appeal. Regulations and proceedings governing the operation of the hearing panel and the appeal procedure should be predetermined in consultation with the students, published and disseminated or otherwise made available to the student body. Responsibility for the decision reached as a result of the hearing rests solely with the administration. It may seek the opinions and participation of teachers and students in reaching its conclusion.

Prior to the hearing, the student (and his parent or guardian) should be:

a. Advised in writing of the charges against him, including a summary of the evidence upon which the charges are based.

b. Advised that he is entitled to be represented and/or advised at all times during the course of the proceedings by a person of his choosing who may or may not be connected with the faculty or administration of the school and may include a member of the student body.

c. Advised of the procedure to be followed at the hearing.

d. Given a reasonable time to prepare his defense.

At the hearing, the student (his parent, guardian or other representative) and the administrator should have the right to examine and cross-examine witnesses and to present documentary and other evidence in support of their respective contentions. The student should be advised of his privilege to remain silent, and should not be disciplined for claiming this privilege. The administration should make available to the student such authority as it may possess to require the presence of witnesses at the hearing. A full record should be taken at the hearing and it should be made available in identical form to the hearing panel, the administration and the student. The cost thereof should be met by the school.

In those instances where the student is being exposed to a serious penalty because of an accumulation of minor infractions which had been handled in summary fashion, or any instance where evidence of prior infractions so handled is presented at the hearing by the administration, the student (his parent, guardian, or other representative) should be permitted to reopen those charges and present evidence in support of the contention that he was wrongfully accused and/or convicted of the minor infraction.

After the hearing is closed, the panel should adjudicate the matter before it with reasonable promptness and make its findings and conclusions in writing, and make copies thereof available in identical form and at the same time, to the administration and the student. The cost thereof should be met by the school. Punishments should so far as possible avoid public humiliation or embarrassment. Group punishment should be used only if every member of the group is guilty of the infraction. Cruel and unusual punishment should never be imposed.

2. The Role of the Police in the Secondary Schools

Where disciplinary problems involving breaches of law are rampant, schools cannot be considered sacrosanct against policemen and the proper function of law officers cannot be impeded in crime detection. Whenever the police are involved in the schools, their activities should not consist of harassment or intimidation. If a student is to be questioned by the police, it is the responsibility of the school administration to see that the interrogation takes place privately in the office of a school official, in the presence of the principal or his representative. Every effort should be made to give a parent the opportunity to be present. All procedural safeguards prescribed by law must be strictly observed. When the interrogation takes place in school, as elsewhere, the student is entitled to be advised of his rights, which should include the right to counsel and the right to remain silent.

PERSONAL APPEARANCE

The matter of acceptable dress and grooming is a frequent issue in schools. Education is too important to be granted or denied on the basis of standards of personal appearance. As long as a student's appearance does not, *in fact*, disrupt the educational process, or constitute a threat to safety, it should be no concern of the school.

Dress and personal adornment are forms of self-expression; the freedom of personal preference should be guaranteed along with other liberties. The reconciliation of the rights of the individual with the needs of the group was well expressed in the decision by California Superior

Court Judge W. G. Watson in the case of Myers v. Arcata Union High
School District. (1966)[2]

> The limits within which regulations can be made by the school are
> that there be some reasonable connection to school matters, deportment,
> discipline, etc., or to the health and safety of the students. . . . The Court
> has too high a regard for the school system . . . to think that they are
> aiming at uniformity or blind conformity as a means of achieving their
> stated goal in educating for responsible citizenship. . . . [If there are to
> be some regulations, they] must reasonably pertain to the health and
> safety of the students or to the orderly conduct of school business. In
> this regard, consideration should be given to what is really health and
> safety . . . and what is merely personal preference. Certainly, the school
> would be the first to concede that in a society as advanced as that in
> which we live there is room for many personal preferences and great
> care should be exercised insuring that what are mere personal prefer-
> ences of one are not forced upon another for mere convenience since
> absolute uniformity among our citizens should be our last desire.

FREEDOM FROM DISCRIMINATION

No student should be granted any preference nor denied any privilege or
right in any aspect of school life because of race, religion, color, national
origin, or any other reason not related to his individual capabilities. It is
the duty of the administration to prevent discrimination and to avoid
situations which may lead to discrimination or the appearance thereof, in
all aspects of school life, including the classroom, the lunchroom, the
assembly, honors, disciplinary systems, athletics, clubs and social
activities.

THE RIGHTS OF MARRIED AND/OR
PREGNANT STUDENTS

The right to an education provided for all students by law should not be
abrogated for a particular student because of marriage or pregnancy
unless there is compelling evidence that his or her presence in the classroom or school does, in fact, disrupt or impair the educational process
for other students. This includes the right to participate in all the activities
of the school. If temporary or permanent separation from the school
should be warranted, the education provided elsewhere should be qualitatively and quantitatively equivalent to that of the regular school, so far
as is practicable.

ACADEMIC FREEDOM AND EDUCATION

The academic freedoms set forth in [this chapter] must be looked upon as more than a line of defense; they are positive elements in the educational process of a democracy. The spirit of these freedoms should permeate the school and their expression should be actively encouraged by faculty and administration. A school which does not respect civil liberties has failed the community, its students and itself.

In 1943, the Supreme Court, in the case of *West Virginia Board of Education* v. *Barnette,*[3] affirmed the basic concept that no agent of a school board can compel a student to surrender his constitutional rights as a privilege of attending school. The majority opinion stated:

> The Fourteenth Amendment, as now applied to the States, protects the citizen against the State itself and all of its creatures — the Board of Education not excepted. These have of course, important, delicate and highly discretionary functions, but none that they may not perform within the limits of the Bill of Rights. That they are educating the young for citizenship is reason for scrupulous protection of Constitutional freedoms of the individual, if we are not to strangle the free mind at its source and teach youth to discount important principles of our government as mere platitudes.

In 1967, the Supreme Court held, in an 8-1 decision, *In re Gault,*[4] that: ". . . Neither the Fourteenth Amendment nor the Bill of Rights is for adults alone."

---

[1]In 1966, a U.S. Court of Appeals upheld the right of Mississippi high school students to wear "freedom buttons" in school "as a means of silently communicating an idea" and therefore legally protected by the First Amendment. (*Burnside* v. *Byars* 363 F.2d 744 1966).

[2]Superior Court of California, Humboldt County (unreported)

[3]*West Virginia Board of Education* v. *Barnette,* 319 U.S. 624 (1943)

[4]*In re Gault,* 87 S. Ct. 1428 (1967)

PART VI

Curriculum Foundations

When we refer to curriculum, we should consider three basic elements: (1) *society*, its institutions, and its present and long-term development; (2) the *student* (individual) and his needs, problems, and learning potential; and (3) the *knowledge* we wish to teach. All three are interrelated, involve curriculum change, and beset those who determine curriculum. For example, the schools must organize and teach a relevant body of *knowledge* that will enable *students* to deal with the perplexities and problems of contemporary *society*.

In referring to society, we should take note that it is constantly and rapidly changing. Indeed, the times are angry, violent, and despairing. War, racism, riots, assassinations, strikes, inflation, technology, bureaucracy, poverty, urbanization, pollution, student unrest, and drugs haunt

America today in various degrees and collectively threaten the foundations of our society. American unity seems to be weakening; patriotism seems to be declining; and the black-white, youth-adult gaps seem to be increasing. In general, the American Dream is being replaced by American cynicism. Admittedly this picture of American society is negative, but the factors listed seem to comprise a significant part of the American scene, to which those involved in curriculum planning must be sensitive.

In the first article, Ralph W. Tyler examines the purposes of schools in relation to the needs of the individual and society. These purposes are to help the individual achieve his full potential, develop a literate citizenry, enhance social mobility, prepare the individual for the world of work, help him chose nonmaterial services, and teach him how to learn. Two additional and related purposes take on special importance today: reaching the disadvantaged, and making the school more effective for a larger portion of the populace. Tyler also points out that in the past the purposes of the schools have been modified, and in each historical period the purposes require reinterpretation.

When we consider the individual, it is important to understand the socio-psychological factors related to his development. Today, a close connection between psychology, teaching and learning is recognized. For example, a successful teacher evaluates the student's self-concept, motivation, and other individual differences related to developmental growth. The art of teaching lies in part in understanding the learner, in knowing his individual psychological and cognitive strengths and weaknesses. Those involved in teaching and planning the curriculum must consider how the child learns, and must offer new and improved ways in which he can fulfill his human potential and become a productive member of society.

With regard to the individual, Charles V. Hamilton examines the issue of black studies as a demand by black students to make the curriculum more meaningful to them as black people. These demands are in part political (and therefore affect society and the way blacks relate to society), in the sense that blacks envision not only the curriculum in need of modification but the entire structure of the (school and) college — the way these institutions recruit black students and teachers and the way they relate to the black community. Hamilton argues that a viable black studies program will prepare the black student to engage society, not withdraw from it.

The third aspect of the curriculum involves learning theories and the knowledge we teach. In general, there has been a recent shift from the learning of separate subjects to the integration of knowledge, from the learning of facts to the learning of concepts. Instead of merely accumulating knowledge, there is a growing trend toward teaching the structure of a subject — its body of concepts and principles that define and delimit its subject matter, as well as its methods of inquiry and research that lead to hypothesis and theories. There is also a demand for relevancy to the real world which will help the learner deal with the problems that confront him outside the classroom.

Jerome S. Bruner discusses the body of knowledge that the schools teach. He reports on the structure of the subject, not something that one "knows about" but that one "knows how to," learning the principles of a subject area and how to solve the problems in the area. He then goes on to examine the nature of a relevant curriculum — the fact that the content should have social relevance (related to the issues and ideas of the world) and personal relevance (related to the individual's needs and goals).

As we look ahead into the future, we can identify a number of changes in curriculum. We should witness a number of conceptual models for analyzing curriculum. Also, there should be greater attention to national goals; focus on over-all designs, rather than piecemeal approaches; centers for studying curriculum changes and diffusing curriculum innovations; greater diversity in teaching approaches and methods of organizing schools; and continued interest in the structure of knowledge and the various theories of learning. Big business, which has recently become interested in the schools, should increase its investments in the educational field. Also, there should be greater emphasis on the affective domain of learning, especially as student alienation and psychological problems become more evident.

In connection with the future, John I. Goodlad examines additional trends. The field of curriculum and instruction will involve greater use of educational hardware, *e.g.*, microfiche, computers as teachers, television, programmed instruction, and various audio-visual devices. The learning sequence will be extended in both directions for all nursery children and for all adults who desire it. The most controversial issue, according to Goodlad, will be related to the introduction of drugs and possibly even electric currents to modify human behavior and enhance the learning process. He concludes his discussion with an essential question which should guide our thinking in the present and future and which is pertinent to the entire section on curriculum, to the entire book, as well as to the entire field of education: "What kind of human beings do we wish to produce?"

RALPH W. TYLER

Purposes of
our Schools

FROM THEIR BEGINNING THE SCHOOLS OF OUR COUNTRY HAVE BEEN
sensitive to the needs and opportunities of our changing society. In the
debates that took place in the early days of our nation over the establishment of free public education, two primary purposes were emphasized.
For the individual child, education was to provide the opportunity to
realize his potential and to become a constructive and happy person in
the station of life which he would occupy because of his birth and ability.
For the nation, the education of each child was essential to provide a
literate citizenry. Since the new nation was ruled by its people, ignorance
among the people would threaten the survival of the country.

INDIVIDUAL SELF-REALIZATION

Today, these remain two of the educational functions of our schools,
recognized by the public generally and firmly imbedded in our thinking
in the light of changed social conditions, new knowledge, and prevailing
attitudes of the times. The goal of individual self-realization is even more
necessary for the schools to stress in our mass society where economic,

Ralph W. Tyler, "Purposes of our Schools." *Bulletin of National Association of
Secondary School Principals*, 52, 1968, 1–12. Reprinted by permission of the author
and publisher.

political, and social demands are frequently heard more distinctly than demands of the individual for education that will enable him to use the rich resources of an industrial society for his own fuller life. Kenneth Boulding, speaking in June, 1966, at the Eight-State Conference on "Prospective Changes in Society by 1980," eloquently expressed the contemporary problem in achieving this purpose.

> The final problem is subtle and hard to put one's finger on; nevertheless, it may be the most important problem of all. This is the problem of the role of the educational system in creating what might be called a moral identity. The obsolescence of older moral identities in the face of enormous technological changes is a problem which underlies almost all others in the social system. . . . In its solution, the educational system would play an absolutely crucial role. It would be precisely indeed in the things which our conservatives despise as "frills" that the development of satisfying human identities may have to be found. It must never be forgotten that the ultimate thing which any society is producing is people. . . . If this principle is stamped firmly in the minds of those who guide and operate our educational system, we can afford to make a great many mistakes, we can afford to be surprised by the future, we can afford to make some bad educational investments, because we will be protected against the ultimate mistake, which would be to make the educational system a means, not an end, serving purposes other than man himself.

One test of our success in educating the individual for self-realization is whether at the end of each year of education he has a wider range of realistic choices in life available to him. If he is being narrowly specialized to fit into a niche in life with a real possibility of very limited choices, he has been miseducated. Each year should open new doors for him and develop new abilities to enable him to go through these doors as he chooses.

LITERATE CITIZENS

The reinterpretation of the development of literate citizens is profoundly important today when both the political problems and the functioning of the political system have increased enormously in scope and complexity. When the activities of government were largely restricted to maintaining law and order, providing schools, roads, and postal services, and protecting property from fire, the issues were easily grasped, and the agents and officers of government were generally known to a majority of the community. Now, the preservation of the nation, the health of the economy, the welfare of those in need, as well as education, have become mammoth operations with national and international implications. The agents and officers of government are known personally to only a small fraction of the people. Moreover, effective citizenship requires participation in a much more complex social system. A few years of schooling are not sufficient to prepare an intelligent and effective citizen, nor are the simple myths, which pass for American history in many places, adequate background for reasoned understanding. Educating a literate citizenry is in itself a major educational task.

SOCIAL MOBILITY

A third purpose of our schools has been recognized ever since the immigrating tide from Europe reached massive proportions in the latter part of the last century. As the children of recent immigrants became a considerable proportion of the school population in several of the states, many of the new citizens began to perceive the American schools as a means by which their children could have a chance through education to get better jobs and enjoy the benefits of American life which they had been unable to do. Hence, in addition to providing opportunities for individual self-realization and educating for intelligent citizenship, the American schools have become a major avenue for social mobility — the means by which the American dream has been made a reality by many thousands of families and by which new streams of vigorous leadership have been injected into our maturing society.

But educating for social mobility has also required new interpretations with each generation. In the '90's, the prevailing notion among educators was that there were a few children among the many immigrant families whose moral character and native intelligence were equal to those of pupils from the middle class, old-American stock. They could make superior records in school if certain handicaps were eliminated. The handicaps recognized then were: limited knowledge of English, little time for study because of the need for their wages or help at home, and lack of supporting encouragement. Equality of educational opportunity meant, in that day, to furnish special help in acquiring the English language, raising money to reduce the time the child had to work, and for teacher and principal to give him friendly encouragement.

Now, we have learned that most children have capabilities in one or more areas and that, in place of estimating educational potential by a single scale of scholastic aptitude, we need to use various means of finding the strengths of each child on which further educational development can be based. Not only do we now expect to find many more children with potential social mobility than did our predecessors, but we have also learned about a broader range of handicaps that we need to eliminate in order that children and youth may move ahead. These include limited experience with standard English, limited access to the influence of educated people, nutritional and other health problems, lack of experience in successful learning, lack of disciplined work experience, and lack of confidence in ability to learn. The particular learning objectives and the kinds of educational programs that can enhance social mobility, we now know, must be designed in terms of the particular strength and limitations of the pupils concerned.

PREPARATION FOR THE WORLD OF WORK

The expectation that the public elementary and secondary schools would prepare the workers needed in our expanding economy was not commonly held until the close of World War I. Farm laborers, construction workers for railroads and highways, domestic servants, and unskilled "helpers" comprised the majority of the labor force. Skilled tradesmen came from Europe or were trained through apprenticeship in this country. But the rapid rate of industrialization and business development after 1910 required many workers with higher levels of skills and understanding such as mechanics, stenographers, clerks, and salespeople. The level of education required came to be expressed increasingly in terms of a high school diploma. Furthermore, specific vocational education was introduced in many high schools with grants-in-aid provided by the federal government. By 1925, the public generally, and the schools as well, were including as one of the purposes of American education the preparation of young people for the world of work.

Since 1925, and particularly since World War II, the rapid rate of technological development in agriculture, industry, commerce, defense, and the health services has so changed the occupational distribution of the total labor force that the chance for a youth or young adult without high school education to obtain employment is less and less. Farmers and farm laborers, who made up 38 percent of the labor force at the turn of the century, now comprise only 7 percent. Similarly, opportunities for employment in unskilled occupations have almost disappeared. Last year, only 5 percent of the labor force was unskilled. The proportion employed in skilled trades is not likely to increase. But there are large increases in the percentage of people employed in engineering, science, the recreational fields, accounting, and administration. Now, not only is high school education essential for most employment, but the percentage of jobs requiring college education is increasing at a rapid rate. Education as preparation for employment is more important than ever before.

But this function also requires continuing reinterpretation. Recent reports, such as the one by President Kennedy's Commission on Vocational Education, chaired by Benjamin Willis, and that of the National Association of Secondary School Principals, have documented the failures of our schools to maintain continuing contact with the needs, problems, and opportunities in educating youth for the world of work.

Mention was made earlier of the sharp shifts taking place in the composition of the labor force. In 1960, only 45 percent of the U. S. labor force was engaged in the production and distribution of material goods, while 55 percent was employed in providing non-material services in areas like the health services, education, recreation, social services, science and engineering, accounting, and administration. In 1967, it was estimated that only 40 percent of our labor force was required to produce and distribute material goods, and this is predicted to shrink to 25 percent by 1980. In spite of these great changes, high school vocational programs are still predominantly focused on production jobs, including farming, although only 7 percent of the labor force is engaged in agriculture.

The shift in demand to persons who provide non-material services poses a particular problem for males. A majority of boys from working-class homes have a self-image of being strong and manually dexterous. This is their notion of a "real man." But the opportunities for employment where physical strength and manual dexterity are important are becoming more and more limited. Instead, the new jobs that are increasingly available require primarily intellectual competence and social skills. Education that helps boys to prepare for employment really begins in the early grades, aiding them to develop a more realistic picture of the world of work and to perceive more clearly what characteristics are required for employment. In these early years, children can develop habits of responsibility, of thoroughness in work, of punctuality, as well as intellectual and social skills. In the junior high school period, career exploration and planning are important phases of the program. One of the most significant changes in occupational education is based on the recognition that every child needs to learn things that will prepare him for the world of work, that what is to be learned is much more than certain specific vocational skills, and that appropriate educational experiences will need to extend throughout the school years. Furthermore, the continuing transformation taking place in the nature and distribution of jobs requires not only the use of current projections of employment demands but also emphasis upon the development of generally useful abilities and skills, rather than confining the training to skills limited to specific jobs. This shift of emphasis will insure that re-education and training, when needed, will be more easily accomplished.

WISE CHOICES OF NON-MATERIAL SERVICES

To maintain and to increase the productivity of the American economy requires not only an ample supply of workers at higher levels of competence but also consumers who want and are willing to pay for the wide range of consumer goods and services which the economy can produce. If the American people wanted only food, clothing, and shelter, a major fraction would be unemployed because these goods can be produced by a small part of our labor force. The desire and the willingness to pay for health, education, recreation, including art, music, literature, sports, and the like create the demand which enables the economy to shift its patterns of production to take advantage of the greater efficiency of technology, without stagnation. This sets a fifth major function of American education, namely, to develop in students understanding and appreciation of the wide range of experiences, services, and goods which can contribute much to their health and satisfaction. Only through education can people learn to make wise economic choices as well as wise choices in the personal, social, and political fields.

The consumer education courses which were constructed in the '20's and '30's emphasized the development of the abilities required to make choices among material products, using information about the serviceable qualities and relative costs of these goods. The chief consumer problem of that period was believed to be to obtain useful products at lowest prices commensurate with necessary quality. Few of these courses dealt with the problems involved in making wise choices of goods and services that furnish non-material values, like the aesthetic values in music, art, and drama; the recreational values of sports; the personal and social values in various educational opportunities; the health values in different forms of health and medical programs. Frequently, English courses sought to develop an appreciation for literature that could afford continuing meaning and satisfaction to the reader, and a small number of courses were devoted to motion picture appreciation aimed to help students make wise choices of the movies they viewed.

Now that a majority of the labor force is engaged in the production of non-material services, the range of possible choices for the consumer is increasing greatly. Hence, the reinterpretation of this purpose in our age opens up a whole new area of consumer education and requires the development of relevant objectives and learning experiences. The wise choice of these services is profoundly important, in the development both of individuals and of our culture. Choices of literature, art, music, recreation, leisure time, educational opportunities, health services, and contributing social services have more to do with the quality of life than most of our material choices.

However, the relatively simple calculations involved in comparing the value of steak at one price with that of chicken at another is not the kind of decision process involved in choosing among non-material alternatives. The educational program will need to extend the opportunities for students seriously to explore experiences and services in ways that help them to perceive values, to find meaning in them, to discover how far they afford satisfaction. Furthermore, to help in making rational decisions, students will need opportunities to review their experiences, to reflect on their impact, to assess the probable future consequences, and to develop the habit of appraising the values of non-material experiences. This is a new area for many schools.

LEARNING TO LEARN

Teaching students how to learn has, in the last ten years, been accepted as another function of our schools. With the rapid acquisition of new knowledge, it is no longer possible to give the student in school an adequate command of the facts in each major subject which will serve him throughout the balance of his life. The school can only start him on a life-long career of continued learning. Hence, an important educational aim today is to teach students to learn and to develop in them a strong interest in continued study together with the skills required to keep on with their learning after graduation.

At educational gatherings, the comment can be heard that this has always been a major purpose of our schools. It has certainly been stated as a desirable aim by educational leaders for centuries; but not only have the particular sources of learning and procedures for study changed with the times but for generations the pattern of school performance has been in sharp contrast to what is involved in learning outside of the formal school situation. In life outside the school, one encounters problems that are not clearly formulated, and he must analyze the situation sufficiently to identify particular problems or to see what questions are involved. He needs to know where he can get relevant information; he needs to be able to attack the particular problems appropriately in terms of the fields in which they can be placed — that is, science, literature, economics, politics, and the like. He needs to be able to verify or validate the procedures he follows and/or the answers or solutions he proposes.

These abilities can be acquired through experience which requires their use. But most schools do not provide much opportunity for this. Typically, the teacher poses the problems or questions rather than the student finding them as he works. The textbook or the teacher is most likely to furnish the answers rather than to require the student to work them out or to find dependable sources. If this new purpose is to be attained, the contrast between traditional study in school and the procedures of life-long learning must be eliminated through making the school experiences examples of continued learning. This requires teachers and students to take on new roles.

The increase in the number of functions which the American schools are expected to serve is the natural result of the changes in our whole society. In the nearly 200 years since this country was founded, society has increased enormously in complexity. Yet, today, the human individual at birth does not differ appreciably from the babies born at the time of the American Revolution. All of the knowledge, skills, and attitudes required to live in modern society must be acquired by each individual after birth. Since society is continuing to increase in complexity and scope, the development of youth for effective modern life increases in difficulty and in magnitude with each generation.

CRITICAL NEW TASKS

The aforementioned six still remain the major functions of American schools, but from time to time special tasks take on immediate urgency. Two of them are stressed today.

We have seen that with the increasing use of technology the demand for unskilled labor has diminished to about 5 percent of the labor force. Yet, in the United States and in other advanced nations, between 15 percent and 20 percent of the population have not acquired sufficient skill and general literacy to qualify for skilled or higher levels of employment. The fact that more than 80 percent of our children have achieved an educational level above the minimum requirements for modern literacy and employment is a tribute to the determination of our people and the efforts of our schools. But this is not enough. Today, 19 out of every 20 of our children can and must be effectively reached by education. We know how to stimulate and guide the learning of children who come from homes where education is valued and where the basis for it has been laid in the home experiences. However, we do not have widely accepted means for reaching children whose backgrounds have given them little or no basis for school work. To reach all or nearly all of these children is a critical task of the present period.

A second urgent task of today is also partly a result of modern technology. As automation has sharply reduced the demand for unskilled labor, the occupations in which there are increasing demands, as noted earlier, are those requiring a fairly high level of education. However, to provide employment opportunities for all our people and to keep our economy fully productive requires a much larger proportion of our youth to complete high school — many more than in the past — to gain professional, semi-professional, or technical competence. To provide these educational opportunities and to insure effective learning for youth from varied backgrounds of training, experience, and outlook is another new and important educational task which we now face. Neither the U. S. nor any other country has previously attempted it.

Mention is made of these two new tasks that the schools are being urgently asked to undertake, not because they involve additions to the basic functions or purposes of the schools but because they should be viewed as important tasks with purposes of their own.

Both of them — reaching the disadvantaged and making the high school effective for a large proportion of the population — must be undertaken with the six basic purposes in mind: to help each individual achieve his highest potential, to develop a broader base of intelligent and active citizens, to make possible social mobility, to prepare each person for the world of work, to help him choose non-material services that will furnish the greatest meaning and satisfaction, and to become a life-long learner.

In making education effective for a larger number of students, consideration must be given to the criticism made by students themselves of the high school program.

The most common complaint they make is its "irrelevance." In many cases, what is being taught could be highly relevant to the activities, interests, and problems of the students, and they fail to perceive the connection. Much of this is due to the separation of the school from the rest of life. For example, the separation of the school from the world of work and the world of community service results in several unfortunate consequences. Many students see the school as something apart from the adult world into which they will be going. This is one of the factors in dropping out of school; and for many students who do not drop out, the apparent lack of connection between the school work and their future lives results in low interest and effort in their studies. From the standpoint of the society, the separation of the school makes more difficult the transition from school to work and from school to constructive community membership. What is needed is the development of bridges to the rest of the community and greater openness in the school to outside persons and activities. We need to be providing cooperative education (work-study programs), community service programs, and other means by which school youth can be actively involved in work experiences, in community services, in joint civic participation with adults, and the like. Students are not likely to use what they learn unless they have practice in identifying problems and difficulties. Dealing with these requires learning — and practice in using what is learned — in situations outside of school.

RESPONSE OF THE SCHOOLS TO CHANGE

Although the American schools, when compared to those of Western Europe, have not rigidly adhered to obsolete programs but have been responsive to the changing needs and opportunities of the times, these educational changes have lagged some years behind the initiating forces, and the adaptation or transformations required in the schools have not always been largely effective. The lag appears to have been due both to the lack of continuing attention within the school to developments in the society and to the common failure of school leaders to translate needed changes into educational purposes and operations that guide the actual conduct of school work.

It has become modern business practice for the corporation to make continuing projections of environmental factors, such as population shifts, new technologies becoming available, and changing patterns of consumer preferences, that importantly affect its work. From these assessments and reassessments of changing conditions, the corporation commonly plans its production and distribution programs, adjusting the future plans each year in the light of facts of the past year. In this way, the company is able to respond quickly to changing conditions and frequently anticipates the changes before they actually take place. Educational systems and organizations could benefit from similar practices. A rationale for such planning procedures exists, and modifications to fit a particular system can be worked out. With such studies and with the attitude that change is the natural characteristic of our society and its institutions, our schools in the future can anticipate new educational needs as well as respond to present conditions more promptly.

Our failure to translate changing needs into guiding purposes and operational plans seems to be largely due to our following the pattern of leadership characteristic of a slowly changing society. Under conditions of very gradual shift, the operational modifications in the system are commonly made by the operators before they are recognized by the leaders. Then, the role of leadership is to explain these changes in terms of accepted principles so that the new practices now in operation are legitimized. Many statements of educational policy have been justifications of changes already under way rather than pointing the direction for new efforts.

Because our society is changing more rapidly with each decade, we must develop educational procedures that can reduce the lag between changing needs and educational programs that meet the needs. The American schools have shown their flexibility in responding to needs in the past. By developing procedures to scan the social horizon, we can anticipate impending changes and understand their probable impact. By employing task forces of scholars, scientists, curriculum makers, and teachers to translate needs into educational objectives and operational plans, we can expect to respond more promptly and more effectively in the future than we have in the past. Over the years, the purposes for our schools have been expanding, and in each generation older purposes require reinterpretation. This is necessary for schools to serve adequately the individual and the society of the times.

CHARLES V. HAMILTON

The Question of
Black Studies

SEVERAL YEARS FROM NOW, WHEN HISTORIANS STUDYING RACE AND
politics in the United States look back on the 1960's, they will see a
decade of innumerable phrases and labels. They will see such terms as
*integration, busing, nonviolence, violence, freedom now, law and order,
black power, community control, white racism, institutional racism, separatism, black nationalism, revolution, black studies.* Hopefully, those
historians will realize the intense political environment out of which
these terms came. These terms were abbreviated ways — and therefore
dangerous because of the great possibility of oversimplification — of
explaining or projecting complicated phenomena. Arising out of an
emotional, intense political struggle, these terms became less the subject for penetrating, in-depth analyses and more the basis on which a
polemical, momentarily dramatic debate was engaged.

The black studies issue is one example of this sort of treatment. The
term rose out of the protest demands of black students on college
campuses in the late 1960's. The demands generally were summed up
in another phrase: "a relevant education." The black students wanted
their exposure to higher education to be "relevant" to them as black
people. They were dissatisfied with the nature of the college curriculum
as it existed in most places around the country — and they were specific

---

Charles V. Hamilton, "The Question of Black Studies." *Phi Delta Kappan*, 51,
1970, 362–64. Reprinted by permission of the author and publisher.

in their criticisms, with particular emphasis on the humanities, history, and the social sciences. They pointed out major substantive gaps in American academia, and many of them concluded that these gaps were as much a function of a value system that deliberately chose the kinds of subjects to include in the curriculum as they were simply the result of scholarship yet to be done. In other words, the failure to depict the true role of black people in American history, or the exclusion of black writers from the reading lists of courses in American literature, for example, was a clear reflection of the values of American academia. Law schools and other professional schools were vehemently criticized for offering a course of study which did not "relate" to the developmental needs of a depressed black community.[1]

Thus the students began to demand black studies as an academic mechanism to overcome these normative and substantive problems. One has to understand that these demands were *political* precisely because they reflected — explicitly and implicitly — a feeling among the students that the colleges and universities were not "legitimate." That is, the students were demanding that the institutions change in many ways: in how they recruited black students, in what they did with the black students once they were on campus, in how the schools related to black communities, in the recruitment of black professors, in the kinds of courses offered. Therefore, as *political* demands for *academic* innovation, the demands were subject to negotiation and compromise. At all times, the demands were focal points of a political struggle. The struggle was political in the sense that the right of the college and university to rule unchallenged in the traditional ways was being questioned. *This was the central question: the question of legitimacy.*

Most schools readily admitted that changes (in curriculum, recruitment, community relations) had to be made. But then ensued an unfortunate period when many of the specific alternatives — which had to be understood as products of a political struggle — were taken as absolute academic ends. And before there was time to examine perceptively the kinds of *academic* changes that could be made, many people began to join the polemical debate. Black studies were called "soul courses"; they were seen as places where a cadre of revolutionaries would be trained; respected scholars admonished that black students needed "higher education" in order to compete, not something called black studies.

If one examined closely some of the black studies proposals, there is no question that he would find many of them being concerned with issues of ideology and what might be called subjective matters. This is so precisely because the proposals were trying to — and in many instances did — articulate a new system of legitimacy. The proposals were rejecting, for example, traditional and widely accepted political science literature that argued in favor of the virtual inviolability of a two-party system. The proposals in that field called for courses that attempted to explore new ways to approach socio-political change in modern America — at least from the vantage point of black Americans. Perhaps those courses were aimed at "getting ourselves together" and at developing political power among black people. Why are these "soul courses" — in the catharsis-serving and demeaning sense of that phrase? Have not some political science courses traditionally been dealing with how groups operated "effectively" in the society? Have not many of the economics courses not only dealt with mere descriptions of the existing economic order but also with ways to strengthen and make that order more viable? Are we unaware of the mass of research carried on on the college campuses by scholars under contract with the government in the natural, physical, and policy sciences? Indeed, virtually all of American education (and surely this would apply to any educational system) has served as a socializing process.

The black students — perceiving blatant weaknesses in that process vis-à-vis their own lives and experiences — were calling for a substantive alternative. They no longer believed in the myth that higher education was value-free, objective, above the social turmoil. Traditional American scholarship has been geared to maintenance of the status quo. The black studies proposals were out to alter that orientation. Professors Seymour Martin Lipset and Philip G. Altbach — who cannot be accused of being generally and unequivocably sympathetic to the black student demands — made an interesting observation on the nature of the university:

> In the developing countries, there is an intrinsic conflict between the university and the society, thereby creating a fertile ground for student political awareness and participation. The university, as one of the primary modernizing elements in largely traditional societies, necessarily finds itself opposed to other elements in its society, and must often fight to protect its values and orientation. Students are often involved in these conflicts and are key protectors of the modern orientation of the university. . . . In the developed nations, on the other hand, no such conflict exists. The university is a carrier of the traditions of the society, as well as a training agency for necessary technical skills. It is a participant in a continuing modernizing development, rather than in the vanguard of such development. University students are not called upon to protect the values of their institutions against societal encroachments. In most cases, they are merely asked to gain the qualifications necessary for a useful role in a technological society.[2]

This is an interesting observation because the black students *are* asking their universities to be in the vanguard of development.

The black students and the black studies demands have a valid *political* point. If this is generally accepted, as very many thoughtful people have conceded, it would appear that the next step would be to begin to work out the kinds of *academic* changes those demands call for. Clearly, the students who have served as the catalyst for this should not be expected to come up with the final answers. Those people who style themselves scholars have the burden of proceeding to try to develop new knowledge consistent with a new orientation.

Much of the empirical work has yet to be done, because the questions have never been asked. What is the feasibility of massive economic cooperative ventures in rural and urban black communities? What is the nature of and significance of the black culture vis-à-vis new forms and styles of political action in the black community? Is it possible to talk about a peculiar "black experience" that has relevance to the way black Americans organize themselves and conduct their lives? What is the impact of the oral tradition on social, economic, and political phenomena? Black Americans have a heritage, a black experience of abrupt cultural transformation to traumatized conditions of slavery in a distant, alien land with a different language and different life styles; to legal freedom from legal slavery in the same place and economic position; to an urban, atomized, technological environment from a rural, intimate, agrarian environment. What is the meaning of this heritage and experience in terms of new adaptive cultural characteristics, characteristics that can sustain black Americans as a viable people? What are the implications of all this for enlightened public policy? What does it mean for the kinds of effort made to bridge tradition and modernity in the black community? What is meant by the "crisis-oriented" nature of the black political experience? What is meant by "political traumatization" (as opposed to "political apathy") that makes this distinction relevant to one trying to understand and deal with the problems of black community development?

These are some of the kinds of questions that their proponents want black studies to deal with. Are these "soul courses"? Are they "separatist," "violent advocacy of revolution," "catharsis-serving" courses? Do they take one *out* of "higher education"?

I believe that, *if these courses are carefully thought out, they will be the epitome of higher education.* They will prepare the student to engage the total society, not to withdraw from it. One is not going to know much about how to proceed with black economic development or with black educational development or with black political development without knowing a great deal about the total economic, educational, and political systems. And if one listens carefully to the major thrust of the student arguments — rather than focusing on particular polemical sentences here and there — this point will come through clearly.

One must understand that the demands made in a particular environment — political, suspicious, hostile — have many functions: They serve to wrench an entrenched, closed system into a new awareness; they serve to state specifically a rejection of old values and to state generally a framework for new values. The new directions *cannot* be very specific; they are new programs for experimental times. All answers are not known. There is a tendency on the part of some people to require certainty of results and consequences before they are willing to innovate. In social dynamics, this is hardly reasonable. Of course, there is the possibility of unanticipated consequences. But if those who led the fight in the American colonies to break with England in the 1770's had waited until they knew the precise consequences, they probably would not have moved. Or, to take a less "ruptured" case, those who began to implement New Deal measures in the crises of the 1930's could not wait until they had definitive answers about results. They were faced with crises, and, hopefully bringing the best judgment to bear, they had to act.

American higher education faces a serious series of crises. The demands for black studies simply point up one area of intense concern. It is unfortunate, but understandable (if one agrees with Lipset and Altbach) that some *so-called* culturally disadvantaged black students had to take the lead in pointing out serious educational weaknesses. And precisely because *they* had to assume the role of innovator in an area traditionally felt to be in the province of "experts," it is quite possible that many people in power positions have forfeited their claim to authenticity. Many of them have been lax and unimaginative and listless for so long that many black students now view them as anachronisms.

If all the colleges and universities now rushing to set up some sort of black studies department are sincere in agreeing to the validity of their moves, then why — the black students ask — did they not recognize the need before now? Why did they have to be prodded and poked and seized? (If they are acting now simply to avoid another sit-in or disruption, then they should be exposed as spineless hypocrites!) The point is that the credibility of many of the schools in the eyes of many black students is so low — the students, indeed, in some instances, question their integrity — that the students do not trust the traditional administrators and faculty to set up and implement a viable program. And this is the crux of the control problem. *The students do not want control because they want to insure easy grades, but because they want to insure a quality program.* They ask: How can the people who have been so negligent and value-oriented in harmful ways now be *trusted* to administer this exciting, vibrant new educational innovation? These are important questions. In a sense, it is the *pride* of established academia that is hurt. And frequently their vanity requires its representatives to call for assurances that "high standards" be maintained — in evaluation of class work, recruitment of professors, etc. It is rather strange to hear such calls issue from a group that has admitted its own failure and ineptness. How could a scholar in American intellectual history, for example, not recognize the genius of W. E. B. DuBois? What sort of standards must have prevailed that permitted such a scholar to assume a position of authority?

Let us consider proposals for black studies submitted by black students. Do the black students have the answers? Obviously not; they are still in the early stages of their formal education. But they have enough insights gleaned from their black experience (a term which some people have come to see as delightfully mystic or just quaint) to know that much of what has been taught is inconsistent with — indeed, irrelevant to — the lives they lead as black Americans. *And it is this recognition that accounts for a great part of the thrust for black studies.* Many of the proposals may sound, and in fact are, extreme and farcical. But one should not be too quick to dismiss the entire "movement."[3]

A Harvard University faculty committee on African and Afro-American studies made the following statement:

> We are dealing with 25 million of our own people with a special history, culture, and range of problems. It can hardly be doubted that the study of black men in America is a legitimate and urgent academic endeavor.[4]

Is American academia seriously prepared to embark on such an important intellectual pursuit? Or will there continue to be nit-picking and polemics and energy-wasting efforts over momentarily glamorous and dramatic issues (kicking white students out of black studies classes, separatism, etc.)? The black students have performed an invaluable educational service by raising in a political context the hard academic questions — a political context, incidentally, which many students perceived to be absolutely necessary, given the arrogance, smugness, and entrenched nature of many sources of power. The question now becomes whether higher education can be perceptive and intelligent enough to deliver the empirical goods.

American professors and deans are not unfamiliar with political struggles on their campuses. Campus politics has a long history in this country: interdepartmental rivalries; personality clashes; competition for promotion and tenure; faculty-wife gossip and clashes; at times, in some places, vindictive vetoing of each others' Ph.D. candidates; bitter maneuvering for fewer and smaller classes (and larger office space) at choice (i.e., not 8 A.M.) hours of the day and week.

But the demands and the criticisms leveled by many black students today will make those perennial squabbles seem like tea parties — or perhaps one should say panty raids. The demands of the black students are not nearly so frivolous. The black students are raising serious politico-academic questions that cut to the core, to the very nature of the university and college systems. The black students are political modernizers vis-à-vis higher education in a way never before experienced on American campuses. And traditional American academia may well flunk the test (a metaphor not entirely unintended) if it does not do its homework (hard, empirical, relevant research and teaching).

---

[1] See mimeographed newsletter issued by Harvard Black Law Students Association, Spring, 1968.

[2] Seymour Martin Lipset and Philip G. Altbach, "Student Politics and Higher Education in the United States," in *Student Politics*, Seymour Martin Lipset (ed.). New York: Basic Books, Inc., 1967, p. 242.

[3] One writer made the following observation: "To recruit thousands of young blacks into hitherto restricted American universities and to fill their heads full of something called black studies is to prepare them for nothing." Arnold Beichman, "As the Campus Civil War Goes On, Will Teacher Be the New Dropout?" *The New York Times Magazine*, December 7, 1969, p. 48.

[4] Report of the Faculty Committee on African and Afro-American Studies, Harvard University, January 20, 1969, p. 14.

JEROME S. BRUNER

The Skill of Relevance or the Relevance of Skills

ABOUT A DECADE AGO I BECAME ACTIVELY INVOLVED IN WHAT WAS TO become known as the "curriculum-reform movement" in American education. The initial objectives of this movement were simple yet moving in their aspiration. The teaching of science (and that was the founding concern soon to be generalized to other subjects) must be made to represent what science was about so that modern man might have some better sense of the forces that shaped his world. The underlying conception was a rationalistic one: By knowing nature and being adept in the ways of thinking of science and mathematics, man would not only appreciate nature, but would feel less helpless before it, and would achieve the intellectual dignity inherent in "being his own scientist."

Looked at as merely an effort to improve the teaching of science and the other disciplines, the reform movement seems admirable in retrospect, though parochial, and from the broader point of view of "man's striving to control the world," somewhat old-fashioned, even a tiny bit absurd. But there were two inadvertent and powerful side effects that were generated that still perturb our educational establishment, and that still go on producing changes in the practice of instruction. One of them is administrative in the broadest sense; the other is psychological.

Jerome S. Bruner, "The Skill of Relevance or the Relevance of Skills." *Saturday Review*, April 18, 1970, 66–68, 78–79. Copyright © 1970 by *Saturday Review*, Inc.

The administrative effect of the curriculum revolution was to redefine the way in which a curriculum was made. The moment one says that physics should be taught not to spectators but to participants, that we should teach physics rather than *about* physics, then the physicist must be brought into the process of curriculum maker, along with the teacher. For the basic assumption is that physics is not so much the *topic* as it is the mode of thought, an apparatus for processing knowledge about nature rather than a collection of facts that can be got out of a handbook. And so, in very rapid succession, some of America's most distinguished scientists and mathematicians became involved with teachers, school superintendents, ministers of education — the lot. First it was physics and mathematics, but within the decade chemists, biologists, anthropologists, economists, and even historians were involved in making curricula of their own. It was a poor project indeed that could not boast a Nobel laureate or a Bancroft Prize winner in its list of consultants. There was stress and strain when working scientists came face to face with the realities of the working teacher or the working school budget. And there were moments of despair when some of my less patient scientific colleagues talked about making their particular curriculum "teacher-proof." It was a little like making love people-proof. But even the complaints about the teacher as spoiler grew out of respect for the basic task of equipping the student with the competency inherent in the subject matter. Nothing must interfere, not even the teacher. In the end, what have emerged from the collaboration of scientists, scholars, and teachers are nationally distributed curriculum materials, embodying points of view about learning to which I shall turn shortly, curricula that represent an extraordinary achievement in academic quality and in the respect they show for the nature of human thought processes. Quietly we have achieved a revolution in the way we make curriculum, and it has now become world-wide, in the developing as in the developed world.

What is meant when we say that physics (or mathematics or a language or some other subject) is not something that one "knows about" but is, rather, something one "knows how to"? Plainly, one is neither quite committing something to memory to be tested by the usual means, nor is one learning to perform on cue like a trained seal or one of Professor Skinner's pigeons. Rather, when one learns physics, one is learning ways of dealing with givens, connecting things, processing unrelated things so as to give them a decent order. It is a way of connecting what one observes and encounters so as to highlight its redundancy, and therefore to make it as obvious as possible. To use what has now become a familiar phrase, it is an approach to learning that emphasizes ways of getting from the surface of the observed to its underlying structure of regularity. In this sense, it is a constant exercise in problem-formulating and problem-solving.

Good "problems," it turns out on closer inspection, are the chief vehicle for good curricula whether one is in an ordinary classroom or alone in a cubicle with a teaching machine. In the main, formulated problems are of two kinds. One has to do more with the formal or analytic structure of the operation — the syntax of the subject. Being able to express acceleration for a set of velocities in an equation, or showing wherein Snell's law for the pressure of light must or must not be a necessary corollary of the conservation theorems — these are examples of exercises principally with the syntactic structure of a body of knowledge. They are problems that relate to logical implication, identity, equivalence, and transformational rules. They are mastered by considering the language and the notational system, and not by looking at rocks and trees.

There is a second set of problems that have to do principally with the semantic aspect of a science. How high is some particular building, or what temperature is needed to desalinate a certain volume of sea water, or what is the perturbation around a foil passing through a given medium, given such and such Reynolds number? There is involved here some form of determination of a value, a way of getting access cannily to a physical phenomenon. Looking at rocks and trees is very much at the heart of it, but looking at them with a highly assisted eye turns out to be central. A good field is one where one doesn't have to go about making such empirical determinations very often, and we know that things are getting better when we can reconstruct how something should be from what is already known rather than being a brave and naked empiricist.

We came to treasure problems of both types: the former are "think" problems, the latter are laboratory exercises. Both are formulated by the instructor, the text, or the manual, and both are important in any science, art, or practical sphere.

But neither is much like problem-finding. When Hahn and Strassman made their fundamental discovery about the transmutation of uranium under certain conditions of bombardment, they wrote that they were unsure how to cope with the surprise of an element changing its atomic weight, which is possible only in alchemy. It was the implausibility rather that the improbability that shook them — as with bridge hands, all of which are equally improbable, but one in a single suit is implausible while a Yarborough of the same probability escapes attention altogether as extraordinary. One has no doubt whatsoever that the hare can overtake the tortoise. Problem finding comes when one senses that there remain some dark problems about whether a divisibility rule may not be consistent with another rule about minimal invariant units in ordinary algebra. Nor is it plain that the invention of the calculus resolves Zeno's paradox once for all. All of these are matters involving the raising of problems, rather than their solution. They require many of the same skills and the same knowledge of underlying regularity of problem-solving. But they basically require the location of incompleteness, anomaly, trouble, inequity, and contradiction.

In none of what we have described thus far is there anything like memorization or performing a particular repertory. Conventional learning theories have little to do with the matter, and it seems inconceivable that there stands between you and understanding a missing word of praise or a chocolate bar. Rather, what seems to be at work in a good problem-solving "performance" is some underlying competence in using the operations of physics or whatever, and the performance that emerges from this competence may never be the same on any two occasions. What is learned is competence, not particular performances. Any particular performance, moreover, may become "stuck" or overdetermined by virtue of having been reinforced. It is like the wicked schoolboy trick of smiling when the teacher utters a particular word, and before long the teacher is using it more often. But to confuse that phenomenon with language is as much of a mistake as confusing the trained seal piping "Yankee Doodle" with the improvisation of a variation on the piano.

You may by now have recognized the parallel between what I am suggesting and what we have come to know about language comprehension and production, and their acquisition. Learning to be skillful with a body of knowledge is much like learning a language, its rules for forming and transforming sentences, its vocabulary, its sematic markers, etc. As with language, there is also the interesting feature in all such learning that what is learned is initially "outside" the learner — as a discipline of learning, as a subject matter, as a notational system. This we shall examine later.

Now, it has been the long-established fashion among traditionally antimentalist psychologists to dodge the issue of skill and competence by asserting that, while common sense may see it this way, the "real" explanation of learning is to be found at the molecular level of discrete stimuli and responses and their connections and reinforcements and generalization. What goes on at the common-sense level, as ordinary learning would be called, is simply a matter of engineering, a case of figuring out how to put the elements together in the right way by the correct contingencies of reinforcement or the management of contiguities. I believe this to be a wildly mistaken model of learning based on some very erroneous ideas that have stood up very poorly to the test of the laboratory or of the classroom.

Let me outline briefly what is meant when we say that human beings learn skills. The simplest form of skill is sensorimotor (tool using, car driving, etc.), and its form of acquisition has been described with increasing precision over the past quarter-century by Sir Frederic Bartlett and his students — Craik, Broadbent, Welford, and others. In broad outline, skilled action requires recognizing the features of a task, its goal, and means appropriate to its attainment; a means of converting this information into appropriate action; and a means of getting feedback that compares the objective sought with present state attained. This model is very much akin to the way in which computerized problem-solving is done, and to the way in which voluntary activity is controlled in the nervous system. The view derives from the premise that responses are not "acquired" but are constructed or generated in consonance with an intention or objective and a set of specifications about ways of progressing toward such an objective in such a situation. In this sense, when we learn something like a skill, it is in the very nature of the case that we master a wide variety of possible ways for attaining an objective — many ways to skin the cat. For we learn ways of constructing a myriad of responses that fit our grasp of what is appropriate to an objective.

One is able to operate not only upon the world of physical objects by the use of sensorimotor skills, but also operate in a parallel fashion upon that world as it is encoded in language and other more specialized symbol systems. For such symbol systems "represent" the world and the relations that hold between its different aspects. Indeed, this is what is so extraordinary about the power to symbolize — precisely that it has this representative function (a matter that surely vexes philosophers, in spite of the boon it bestows on ordinary men). This is what makes the "external" forms of systems like natural language or mathematics or a scientific discipline such powerful tools of culture. By making them part of our own symbolic skill, we are able to use them internally as instruments of our own thought. Physics becomes now an operation of the human mind, and physics thinking becomes a psychological topic. It is an instrument of thought or a skill rather than a "topic."

It was basically this set of convictions that led those of us who were in the midst of curriculum reform to propose that *doing* physics is what physics instruction should be about — even if the instruction had very limited coverage. And we proposed that doing it from the start was necessary, even if at the outset the student had only the vaguest intuition to fall back upon. The basic objective was to make the subject your own, to make it part of your own thinking — whether physics, history, ways of looking at paintings, or what not. There follow from this view of competence as the objective of education some rather firm conclusions about educational practice. To begin with, a proper curriculum in any subject (or in the total curriculum of the school) requires some statement of objectives, some statement of what kinds of skill we are trying to create and by what kinds of performances we shall know it. The essence of such behavioral objectives is the specification of a test of skill — testing the ability to get to an objective in situations and with materials not yet encountered.

Does it sound familiar? Is it not what was initially intended? How did we get so far off the track in setting up our educational practices? Why was this rather simple notion not followed up? I suspect that part of the difficulty was introduced by wrongly focused theories of learning that lost sight of the forest of skilled competence for the trees of perfected performances. But that is only part of it. There is a very crucial matter about acquiring a skill — be it chess, political savvy, biology, or skiing. The goal must be plain; one must have a sense of where one is trying to get to in any given instance of activity. For the exercise of skill is governed by an intention and feedback on the relation between what one has intended and what one has achieved thus far — "knowledge of results." Without it, the generativeness of skilled operations is lost. What this means in the formal educational setting is far more emphasis on making clear the purpose of every exercise, every lesson plan, every unit, every term, every education. If this is to be achieved, then plainly there will have to be much more participatory democracy in the formulation of lessons, curricula, courses of study, and the rest. For surely the participation of the learner in setting goals is one of the few ways of making clear where the learner is trying to get to.

This brings us directly to the problem of relevance, that thumb-worn symbol in the modern debate about the relation of education to man and society. The word has two senses. The first is that what is taught should have some bearing on the grievous problems facing the world, the solution of which may affect our survival as a species. This is social relevance. Then there is personal relevance: What is taught should be self-rewarding, or "real," or "exciting," or "meaningful." The two kinds of relevance are not necessarily the same, alas.

I attended a meeting in Stockholm in the summer of 1969, convened by the Nobel Foundation with the object of bringing scholars and scientists together to discuss the burning issues of the day. We had in attendance as well a panel of university students to voice their own concerns. I recall one session at which two molecular biologists, Joshua Lederberg of Stanford and Jacques Monod of Paris, were discussing the socially risky and morally compelling problems involved in improving man's genetic makeup with the aid of modern molecular biology. When the discussion was nearing its end, several students expressed disappointment in our avoidance of "relevant issues." Why had we not engaged ourselves with the crucial issues of the day: with the developing world, with the population explosion, with the scourge of war?

Jacques Monod replied with Gide's favorite proverb, "Good intentions make bad literature." I would change it to "Good intentions alone. . . ." For it is precisely, again, a question of skill and understanding that is at issue. I am with those who criticize the university for having too often ignored the great issues of life in our time. But I do not believe that the cure in the classroom is to be endlessly concerned with the immediacy of such issues — sacrificing social relevance to personal excitement. Relevance, in either of its senses, depends upon what you know that permits you to move toward goals you care about. It is this kind of "means-ends" knowledge that brings into a single focus the two kinds of relevance, personal and social. It is then that we bring knowledge and conviction together, and it is this requirement that faces us in the revolution in education through which we are going.

I have suggested that the human, species-typical way in which we increase our powers comes through converting external bodies of knowledge embodied in the culture into generative rules for thinking about the world and about ourselves. It is by this means that we are finally able to have convictions that have some consequences for the broader good. Yet, I am convinced, as are so many others, that the way in which our ordinary educational activities are carried out will not equip men with effective convictions. I would like to propose, in the light of what I have said about skill and intentionality, and to honor what I believe about the two faces of relevance, that there be a very basic change in pedagogical practice along the following lines:

First, education must no longer strike an exclusive posture of neutrality and objectivity. Knowledge, we know now as never before, is power. This does not mean that there are not canons of truth or that the idea of proof is not a precious one. Rather, let knowledge as it appears in our schooling be put into the context of action and commitment. The lawyer's brief, a parliamentary strategy, or a town planner's subtle balancings are as humanly important a way of knowing as a physicist's theorem. Gathering together the data for the indictment of a society that tolerates, in the United States, the ninth rank in infant mortality when it ranks first in gross national product — this is not an exercise in radical invective but in the mobilizing of knowledge in the interest of conviction that change is imperative. Let the skills of problem solving be given a chance to develop on problems that have an inherent passion — whether racism, crimes in the street, pollution, war and aggression, or marriage and the family.

Second, education must concentrate more on the unknown and the speculative, using the known and established as a basis for extrapolation.

This will create two problems immediately. One is that the shift in emphasis will shake the traditional role of the teacher as the one who knows, contrasting with the student who does not. The other is that, in any body of men who use their minds at all, one usually gets a sharp division between what my friend Joseph Agassis calls "knowers" and "seekers." Knowers are valuers of firm declarative statements about the state of things. Seekers regard such statements as invitations to speculation and doubt. The two groups often deplore each other. Just as surely as authority will not easily be given up by teachers, so too will knowers resist the threatening speculations of seekers. Revolution does have difficulties.

With respect to encouraging speculative extrapolation, I would particularly want to concentrate on "subjects" or "disciplines" that have a plainly visible growing edge, particularly the life sciences and the human sciences: human and behavioral biology, politics, economics, sociology, and psychology organized around problems, solutions to which are not clearly known. The reward for working one's way through the known is to find a new question on the other side, formulated in a new way. Let it be plain that inquiry of this kind can be made not just through "the social sciences" but equally via the arts, literature, and philosophy, as well as by the syntactical sciences of logic and mathematical analysis.

Third, share the process of education with the learner. There are few things so exciting as sensing where one is trying to go, what one is trying to get hold of, and then making progress toward it. The reward of mastering something is the mastery, not the assurance that some day you will make more money or have more prestige. There must be a system of counseling that assures better than now that the learner knows what he is up to and that he has some hand in choosing the goal. This may be raising the specter of totally individualized instruction. But learning *is* individual, no matter how many pupils there are per teacher. I am only urging that in the organization of curricula, units, and lessons there be option provided as to how a student sets his goal for learning.

Fourth and finally, I would like to propose that as a transition we divide the curriculum into a Monday-Wednesday-Friday section that continues during the transition to work with what has been best in our school curricula up to this point, and a Tuesday-Thursday curriculum that is as experimental as we care to make it — seminars, political analyses, the development of position papers on school problems, "problem-finding" in the local community, you name it. Let it be as controversial as needs be. We are lacking diversity in experiment, and can afford controversy in order to get it. Tuesday and Thursday need be no respecter of conventional teaching qualification. Indeed, it might provide the proper occasion for bringing outsiders into the school and "hooking" them with its challenge. I would also want to bring to the school (or to its pupils on visit) other than the conventional media of learning — film, political debate, and the carrying out of plans of action, all to be subject to scrutiny, discussion, and criticism.

I am no innocent to matters of schooling and the conduct of instructional enterprises. What I am proposing involves a vast change in our thinking about schools, about growth, about the assumption of responsibility in the technological world as we know it. I have wanted to highlight the role of intention and goal-directedness in learning and the acquisition of knowledge, the conversion of skill into the management of one's own enterprises. The objective is to produce skill in our citizens, skill in the achieving of goals of personal significance, and of assuring a society in which personal significance can still be possible.

JOHN I. GOODLAD

Learning and Teaching
in the Future

As a member of the teaching profession, each of us is convinced that education is a powerful force for the improvement of man and mankind. But to assume that the school, as it now exists, carries the central thrust in changing human behavior is to be misled.

First, what the school does in educating the young appears to be less or, at best, no more effective than other factors in determining what the child learns and becomes.

Second, the incidence of nonpromotion, dropouts, alienation, and minimal learning in school suggests that today's schools are obsolescent. They were designed for a different culture, a different conception of learners and learning, and a different clientele.

Third, success in school, as measured by grades, appears to bear little relationship to good citizenship, good work habits, compassion, happiness, or other significant human values which our civilization prizes.

Fourth, a relatively new medium, television, has entered into the business of transmitting to children a large segment of our culture. If the years before a child begins school are taken into account, television occupies more of his hours than schooling from his birth to the time he graduates from high school.

John I. Goodlad, "Learning and Teaching in the Future." *Today's Education: NEA Journal*, 57, 1968, 49–51. Reprinted by permission of the author and publisher.

Our immediate goal as educators should be to increase the intensity of the school so that it can again play a major role in educating the young. We must look to the possibilities of the future in order to provide responsible leadership in planning the kind of education that is to come.

We live in a time when one era of instruction is in full bloom, another is well begun, and a third is embryonic. Let us take a look at all three.

The era that is in full bloom and is about to fade is human-to-human instruction. The prime exhibit of this era is the human-based school — a school almost without machines. Here, we like to believe, children and youth are inducted into the culture, their individual potentialities are discovered and developed, they take on a sense of identity and ultimately transcend themselves, and they are inculcated in those values that make for the ideal adult. Increasingly, however, we have become aware that school is not accomplishing these things with a large segment of our population. Indeed, present-day education appears to increase the gap between the haves and the have-nots.

Nonetheless, we are in an inventive period, and old ways of doing things are tumbling before our drive to increase the effectiveness of the school. We have not yet eliminated track systems, with their self-fulfilling prophecies, nor have we broken down the grade barriers, with their nefarious adjustment mechanism of nonpromotion, nor have we learned to teach inductively, with the child learning for himself the skill of inquiry. But we have caught the spirit of these things.

The challenge now is much less one of inventing than of implementing the several powerful and viable innovations that have appeared during recent years. Human-based instruction in the schools will undergo no revolution during the next 15 years, nor has it undergone one during the past 15. It *will* see an accelerating evolution in curriculum, school organization, and instructional practices, while nonhuman-based instruction will loom ever larger on the horizon.

The era of instruction that will supersede the era of human-based instruction is to be one of man-machine interaction — and the machine is the computer. Although we have lived in the shadow of the computer for a long while, we have used it so little in teaching that we may be inclined to believe its future and our own to be things apart. Nothing could be further from the truth. Computers are already demonstrating their usefulness in teaching spelling, mathematics, reading, and a host of other cognitive skills. Tapes, screens, records, and other audiovisual devices, coupled with the computer, make possible a unique instructional system of sight, sound, and touch.

The computer will continue to march relentlessly into our instructional lives, and there is no reason to believe that it will not come right into the school building. To put a computer terminal into every elementary school classroom in the United States would cost, at current prices, about $1 billion; however, if we were to decide to do such a thing, competition within the industry would undoubtedly cut this figure in half. There are problems involved, especially in hooking up terminals to the computer-instructional system at some remote point, but this can be solved by improving communications connections or by having small computers closer to the schools they serve.

Providing programed sequences by way of computers offers us an efficient means of communicating educational lore. What the teaching profession must do is to *legitimatize* the computer as instructor in those basic areas that can be carefully programed. Then we must explore the question of how computers and people are to live together productively in education.

An important goal for the teaching profession now is to humanize the means of instruction. By this I mean emphasing our very best human values in the substance of the curriculum, and showing concern for both the individual and mankind in the teaching-learning environment. I believe these tasks to be at once so formidable and so important that I welcome the computer and charge it with teaching some of those basic skills and concepts that are only the beginning of educating the compassionate, rational man.

I do not see the computer as the teacher's competitor. Not at all! I see it rather as replacing the teacher for certain instructional tasks that I believe it can and will do better than any human teacher can perform them.

The research challenge is to catalogue those aspects of instruction that are most appropriate for the machine and for the teacher. We must *not* make the teacher a supervisor or coordinator of the computer, or he will become its servant. The teacher may very well contribute to programing, but the interaction should be between student and machine.

For us to take our traditional conservative position with respect to this electronic teacher is to delay progress in education and in the long run to endanger the highly relevant role of the human teacher. The significant task for educators, one that may very well be accomplished better if we turn over some of the other tasks to the untiring machine, is to discover how human beings and machines are to live together productively in tomorrow's learning-teaching environment.

A third era, only dimly visible at this point, is much more hazy in its outlines, and we can only speculate on its characteristics, assets, and liabilities.

When we try to envision the school of tomorrow, we must not be limited by our concept of the school of today. Education is not a static process, and the school of today cannot be considered a sacred or unchangeable institution. After all, every decision governing schools was at one time or another made by man. At the time the decisions governing today's schools were made, fewer data were available.

The men who made those decisions were no brighter than schoolmen today, and they were less well-educated. Therefore, it behooves us to reexamine every decision about schooling: size of building and whether we want one at all, numbers of teachers and whether we need a fully certificated teacher for every 28.5 children, whether the library is to be one that houses real books or computerized microfiche. (A fully automated library with no books but only microfiche is now out of the realm of science fiction into the actuality of college and university planning in the United States.)

We must not continue to assume that tomorrow's school will have X number of qualified teachers for Y number of children or that we will construct a school building large enough for all of the children to be housed. There is no reason at all why we could not employ half the usual quota of fully qualified teachers, using the balance of our money for part-time specialists and a host of instructional aids. And there is no reason at all why we could not plan an educational program that requires a school building only half the usual size, with the balance of the money going for trips, special projects, and individualized activities supervised by the staff or even programed by a computer.

A school is not necessary to teaching and learning. We do not need a school to guide children and youth in grasping their culture. And, certainly, we do not need a school to teach the fundamentals of reading, writing, and arithmetic. But we do need a formal process of instruction with the most able members of our society giving their time to it in planning and programing instructional materials, in computerizing varied programs for learning, and in interacting with other humans in the delightful business of learning from one another.

The computer, which we must legitimatize for learning and teaching in an imminent era, probably will contribute significantly in a still later era to the demise of what we now call school. We shall regard this as undesirable only if we lack faith in the ability of man to fashion a better world.

In viewing learning and teaching for the year 2000 and beyond, it is easier to predict what will *not* be than what will be. A prescribed age for starting school will be meaningless. The computer console with an array of devices for stimuli and feedback will be as natural for the child of the twenty-first century as television is for today's two-year-old. Teaching and learning will not be marked by a standard 9 to 3 day, or a standard September to June year, or a year for a grade of carefully packaged material. The child's age will not be a criterion for determining what he is to learn.

Will learning be any less because there will be no periods, no Carnegie units, no bells, no jostling of pupils from class to class? I think not. The student will be free to concentrate exclusively on a given field for weeks or months or to divide his time among several fields. The variability and comprehensiveness of programed learning sequences will be such that the student, unaided by human teachers, will control a significant portion of his curriculum.

Clearly, the role of teachers will change markedly. Hundreds of hours of their time will go into what will occupy each student for an hour or two. But because thousands or even millions of students might eventually select this hour, the teachers' preparation time will be well spent. And the quality of education will be vastly improved.

School as we now know it— whether egg crate or flexible space — will have been replaced by a diversified learning environment including homes, parks, public buildings, museums, and guidance centers. It is quite conceivable that each community will have a learning center and that homes will contain electronic consoles connected to it. This learning center will provide not only a computer-controlled videotape, microfiche, and record library, but also access to state and national educational television networks. It is even possible that advanced technology will return the family to center stage as the basic learning unit.

The most controversial issues of the twenty-first century will pertain to the ends and means of modifying human behavior and who shall determine them. The first educational question will not be "What knowledge is of most worth?" but "What kinds of human beings do we wish to produce?" The possibilities defy our imagination.

The nerve cells of the brain, far more than muscles or any other organs, are highly sensitive to small electric currents, to a variety of chemicals, and to changes in blood supply. Sedatives, barbiturates, tranquilizers, and various psychedelics provide powerful ways of controlling behavior by direct action on the brain. Similarly, we can manipulate behavior by applying electric currents to regions of the brain. Experiments are now under way with drugs and brain extracts designed to enhance learning or memory.

Aldous Huxley long ago introduced us to the possibilities of genetic selectivity through the availability of sperm and ovum banks. The means of drastically altering the course of human development through artificial insemination, chemical treatment, and electric manipulation are with us. We are already tampering with human evolution. The possibilities for further doing so will be enormously enhanced and refined as we move into the twenty-first century.

We of the teaching profession have tended to get bogged down in the narrow details of our calling, in details pertaining primarily to means: buildings, classrooms, textbooks, and so on. We have seldom gone beyond these trivialities to recognition of the fact that education and teaching are much bigger than schools. Schools are only a convenient means to more important ends, means that may no longer be relevant several decades from now.

As individual leaders, we must assert by our very competence that we know how to manage the means. Our constituencies lose faith in our competence when we hesitate, falter, and in desperation turn to the community for guidance in technique. But the charge to the organized profession is a much larger one. We must raise the level of the dialogue to the truly significant questions of educational ends, and we must be as diligent as our lay citizens in laying bare instructional deficiencies in the pursuit of these ends.

As to ends, let me put them as questions to ask about the educational enterprise:

1. To what extent are our young people coming into possession of their culture?
2. To what extent is each child being provided with unique opportunities to develop his potentialities to the maximum?
3. To what extent is each child developing a deep sense of personal worth, the sense of selfhood that is a prerequisite for self-transcendence?
4. To what extent are our people developing universal values, values that transcend all men in all times and in all places?

A fifth question is the most important, challenging, and frightening of all, now that men possess such manipulative powers: *What kinds of human beings do we wish to produce?* As a citizen and an educator, I cherish the right to participate in the dialogue about it.